THE HONEY AND THE HEMLOCK

THE HONEY
AND THE
HEMLOCK

Democracy and Paranoia

in Ancient Athens and Modern America

ELI SAGAN

BasicBooks
A Division of HarperCollins*Publishers*

Library of Congress Catalog-in-Publication Data
Sagan, Eli.
    The honey and the hemlock : democracy and paranoia in
ancient Athens and modern America / Eli Sagan.
        p.   cm.
    Includes bibliographical references and index.
    ISBN 0-465-03058-0
    1.   Athens—Politics   and   government.   2.   Democracy.
3. Paranoia.   I. Title.
JC79.A8S24   1991
321.8—dc20   91-17682
                                                              CIP

This book is dedicated to
BOB BELLAH:
colleague, teacher, ideal reader,
my indispensable friend
for over forty years.

Contents

PART II
Deep Inside Plato's Cave

PART III
Problematics Within Ancient and
Modern Democratic Society

Acknowledgments

I remain fortunate in my three extraordinary readers: Burton Raffel, who tries his best not to permit me one grammatical mistake, or one stylistic lapse of judgment; Frimi Sagan, who does not permit any self-indulgent or vulgar use of language; and Bob Bellah, who prohibits any exaggerated critique of Plato.

I have found the community of historians of the ancient world remarkably welcoming to a scholar outside its particular academic *polis*. There seems to be an uncommon absence of "stranger anxiety" within that commonwealth. Stanley Burstein has been particularly helpful and encouraging. He took my project seriously from the beginning and has aided me greatly in the area of bibliography. Jennifer Tolbert Roberts, Ronald Stroud, and David Whitehead have all helped along the way.

Lynn Friendly has proved a superb typist and a pleasure to work with.

Steven Fraser is a powerful and exciting editor. He has an amazing capacity to tighten and improve a manuscript. Working with him has been an exhilarating experience.

1

Introduction:
The Great Paradoxical Society:
Ancient Athens

This book is about ancient Athens, and democracy both ancient and modern. Though a great many city-states in the Greek world were democratic in form at some time in their history—Argos and Syracuse, as two foremost examples—none exhibited the stability or the longevity of Athenian democracy. Far from being typical of the Greek *polis*, Athens was the great exception—as was Sparta in its profoundly conservative course—to the valid generalization that can be made of almost all ancient city-states: that they were remarkably unstable in their political life. Democracy in Athens, on the contrary, enjoyed a flourishing two centuries from the time of its founding by Cleisthenes in 508 until its temporary dissolution near the end of the fourth century, a demise caused by the military dominance of Macedonia. And despite the military subservience to Macedonia for the two hundred years that followed, the democracy remained vigorous whenever Macedonian pressure was lifted, and it was not until 102 that democratic society was abolished as a result of exclusively *internal* politics.[1]

Athens becomes the subject of any discussion of ancient democracy because our data for non-Athenian democratic societies are so paltry. If we gather all the information we have for all the other democracies in the ancient world, it would not, in total, come to one-tenth of what we know of Athens.

The study of Athens is so exhilarating and so frightening because it was the most contradictory, the most paradoxical society imaginable. From the moral and human points of view, if one contemplates what it could and could not do, it is almost unimaginable that one human society could successfully contain and reconcile such ambiguities, producing, as Plutarch remarked, men of such excellence and men so notoriously bad, just "as the country produces the most delicious honey and the most deadly hemlock."[2]

The thoughtful reader may immediately object to the word "frightening" in the previous paragraph. Can a rumination on the glorious history of ancient Greece be frightening? But how else can we respond when we read the famous Melian dialogue of Thucydides wherein the *Athenian* delegates announce that they are willing to talk only of interests and power, and not of justice, "since you know as well as we do that right, as the world goes, is only in question between equals in power, while the strong do what they can and the weak suffer what they must."[3]

We know that this tiger and victim dialogue is a pitiful prelude to the Athenian genocide of the Melians. We also know that Thucydides' self-appointed task was the delineation of a universal human nature that would be in existence for all time. This tragic inscription could be written across all the catastrophic histories of *this* century: The Strong Do What They Can and the Weak . . .

On the one hand, quite aside from tragedy, philosophy, psychology, the study of politics, and science, Athens (not our other ancient ancestor, Rome) has given us the greatest gift imaginable: the ideal and the reality of a democratic polity based on a complex and moral conception of citizenship. On the other hand, with the hand that held the sword, Athens bequeathed a cruel and imperial domination of other Greek cities, the slaughter and enslavement of its wartime opponents, the occasional genocide of another *polis*, not to mention the ownership of tens of thousands of domestic and industrial slaves and the almost total exclusion of women from cultural and political life. It is of crucial importance to try to understand what gross immoralities are still compatible with the forms of democratic society. Athens provides us with one of the sharpest examples, if not the sharpest, of this awesome human contradiction.

This book attempts to give a full, three-dimensional picture of Athenian political society, sparing neither praise nor critique. Its method is illustrated by the titles of the first two parts: "The Bright, Clear Air of Democratic Society" and "Deep Inside Plato's Cave." Both are discussions of Athenian democratic society. Greek democracy represents the first appearance on the earth of the most moral, most just, most mature, most humane form of complex society ever invented. We cannot understand it, however, unless we also deal with what E. R. Dodds called the "disagreeable primitive things poking up their heads through the cracks of Periclean rationalism."[4] We must read Greek history keeping in mind Marx's profound comment on modernism: "In our days everything seems pregnant with its contrary."[5] We must make room in our thoughts for both the honey and the hemlock.

The whole enterprise has had for me a peculiarly eerie modern cast. All historians of ancient Greek society have projected onto it the problems and contradictions of their own world. It is natural that those of us who are immersed in the theoretical problems of "modernism" should be struck by the amazing similarities between ancient and modern democracy. It is almost uncanny to go through a recent presidential election (1988) and then read Aristotle, who tells us there are five crucial subjects on which political men deliberate and about which "orators harangue": budget, war and peace, the country's defense, imports and exports, and legislation.[6] Even deeper than this, certain basic contradictions, ambiguities, ambivalences, and problematics haunted Athenian democracy in the exact same manner as they haunt modern societies. Various sections of this book will deal, to a greater or lesser degree, with the problems—to mention only a few of the most important—of narcissism and the corruption of individualism; "fascist" terror; the boundaries of justice; money as a corrupter of democratic equality; ambivalence about leadership and leaders; and the fickleness, arbitrariness, and irrationality of the people. Democratic society is the true subject of this work, though it is ostensibly about Athens.

Aristotle, in his *Nicomachaean Ethics* (8.10 1-6) and in the *Politics* (III, Chapter VII), describes three basic forms of constitution: monarchy, aristocracy, and polity (a limited, or "merit-determined" democracy). For each form there is a corrupted version: tyranny, oligarchy, and democracy. The Greek words for the concept of a corrupted form have been variously translated by modern authors. Eric Havelock uses "their aberrant counterparts"[7]; Ernest Barker, whose translation of the *Politics*

I principally use, employs the word "perversion"[8]: Tyranny is the perversion of monarchy, oligarchy the perversion of aristocracy, democracy the perversion of polity. It is a usage that a psychoanalytically oriented person like myself finds useful. This book, in fact, was originally intended as the first volume of a multivolumed work on the history of democracy and its perversions until I realized that, only if I lived as long as the great Sophocles (a full ninety years) and continued to be as productive as he, would I come close to completing the projected seven volumes, which were to deal with ancient Israel, twelfth-century Europe, the era of Liberalism, and so forth. Forswearing omnipotence, I now intend to skip to the last volume and spend as much time as possible trying to understand the modern world. The world of ancient Athens proves a remarkably good place to start such a project.

One preliminary title for this book was "Democracy in Ancient Athens: Reflections on *Polis*, Power, and Paranoia." The two separate parts of that title deliberately reflected the attempt to combine two basic theoretical approaches to understanding society. The first part was an intended echo of de Tocqueville's *Democracy in America*. The second announced that the hidden, irrational underside of political life—the perversion of reason—is a fundamental subject of this work. Combining both these approaches, I contend, gives us a much more powerful theoretical tool than only one would be.

De Tocqueville's analysis of democracy in America relies heavily on the delineation of the *mores* of society, the norms or the values. The recognition of the existence in *every society* of a system of values has become a fundamental building block of sociological analysis. This system of values is the ultimate determinate of the manner in which people live their lives, both their private and their communal lives. Great changes occur over time in this value system. Slavery is given up; male dominance is challenged—earth-shaking historical movements that do not occur without a fundamental change in the *mores* of society. Slavery is never abandoned until the system of values pronounces it an evil. Democracy is never invented until liberty, equality, and freedom are seen as virtues. It is the great historical–sociological task to try to understand what has produced these fundamental changes.

The brilliance of de Tocqueville's analysis of the value system is that he finds it in contradiction to itself. He calls attention to certain fun-

damental values that are in direct opposition to other equally fundamental values. Radical individualism or absolute freedom in opposition
to the tyranny of the majority. It is a theory of conflict, a conflict of
values resulting in certain inherent contradictions that are pregnant
with the possibilities of tyranny. The future health of democratic society, de Tocqueville tells us, will depend upon its capacity to resolve or
reconcile these contradictions.

One cannot, in my view, talk about values or norms or *mores* without, at the same time, talking of psychology. To understand the values
of human society, one must understand the psychology of the humans
who make society. Psychology alone, however, cannot comprehend society, because psychological needs and conflicts are manifest on a social
plane through the institution of the value system. Understanding the
system of values—especially in its most contradictory aspects—is a
great aid to understanding human psychology (what humans can and
cannot do); understanding the psyche is essential to comprehending the
great contradictions in the *mores*. Just as Rousseau announced that the
person who would talk of politics without talking of morals would
never learn anything about either subject, just so to talk of values
without talking of the psyche is to learn nothing of either form. The
theoretical stance of this work, therefore, is to combine the de Toc-
quevillian emphasis on values with a psychoanalytic analysis of deep,
irrational human needs and contradictions. The complexity and paradoxical nature of Athenian society, it seems to me, requires at the least
this kind of multifaceted analysis.

The concepts of paranoia and the paranoid position—and the relationship of both to the possibility of democracy—loom large in this
work. It seemed wise, therefore, to begin with a theoretical foreword
in which certain concepts are set down in a precise, even slightly dogmatic, manner. The remainder of the book thus becomes the "proof"
of these propositions. It is hoped that certain ideas and concepts that
may seem strange at first meeting will become more and more intelli-
gible as the book continues on its way. Ideally, one should read the
theoretical foreword, as set forth in chapter 2, both before and after
reading the full text of the book. The theory of the paranoid position
and the reality of the democratic society are in constant dialogue with
each other.

No pretense is made here that the great problematics in Athenian society have been even close to fully understood. It will be enough if the inevitable contradictions in *all* democratic societies are sharply perceived for what they are: as large, as complex, as full of ambiguities as human life itself. It is not the intention of this book to replace one simplistic dogmatic theoretical statement with another simplistic dogmatic analysis. Athens and democracy deserve better of us than that.

Seven Stages in the History of Athenian Democratic Citizenship

A brief historical outline of Athenian political history might be helpful as a background to the theoretical argument which follows. The phrase "Athenian democratic citizenship" is preferable to "Athenian democracy" because the two earliest periods—the time of Solon and his reforms, and the tyranny of Pisistratus—both made substantial contributions to the eventual establishment of a democratic society, though the state of neither of those times can be accurately called a democracy.

The question of what constitutes the essential attributes of a democratic society, of course, is of great significance. It must be emphasized right at the start that Athenian democracy, even in its most complete or radical manifestation in the late fifth and fourth centuries, did not include women, slaves, and resident aliens. Substantially less than half the adults resident in the *polis* participated, in any form, in political life. Freeborn adult males constituted the polity.

If, because of these exclusions from sovereignty, we would deny the name "democracy" to such a society, then we must be consistent and do the same to the state established in North America in 1789, whose two-hundredth year we recently celebrated. That democracy also excluded women, slaves, and indentured servants, and in most states, property qualifications for office or voting left the poor outside the boundary of sovereignty. It will be argued in this work that Athens from the time of Cleisthenes (508) onward, and the United States of 1789, are both accurately designated "moderate democratic societies." A radical democracy includes the free male members of the lowest economic classes (that is, the poor), a position reached in Athens in the middle of the fifth century and in America around the time of

Andrew Jackson. The Athenian history of democratic citizenship appears to fall into seven distinct time periods.

Solon and His Reform of Society, c. 600 to 561

At the beginning of the sixth century, Athens endured a monumental social crisis. In a society composed primarily of independent farmers, a great number of these citizens were losing their holdings to creditors, a goodly number actually being enslaved as a result of debt-bondage, and many even sold abroad. Far from passively accepting this catastrophe, the lower orders of society began to manifest various forms of social and political unrest. Violence reached the streets of the city. In addition, the rich nonnoble peasants, who were obviously becoming economically more and more potent, were no longer content to have a few noble families retain a monopoly of political power. They were ready to use violence to gain a share. The situation was pregnant with the possibilities of a long period of social-economic conflict or intense political repression, the establishment of a tyrannical monarchy or even civil war.

None of these morally or politically catastrophic events occurred. Instead, Solon was elected Archon (head of state) in 594 with a specific directive to reform the laws. A brilliant political and economic compromise was engineered by Solon, so crucial for Athenian, and democratic, history that two chapters in this work are devoted to it. We know of no other archaic society that came even close to this sense of commonwealth. Though Solon's compromise did not endure for long, it nevertheless had a profound effect on the spirit and the *mores* of society and unquestionably made the future democratic state possible.

The Tyranny of the Pisistratidae, 561–510

The word "tyrant" in archaic Greek society does not signify an oppressive, authoritarian, possibly sadistic monarch. The closest historical parallel may be the "benevolent despots" of eighteenth-century Europe. In one of those ironic modes in which history expresses itself, some of these Greek tyrants definitely moved society in a nonaristocratic, and therefore democratic, direction. Pisistratus of Athens, and his son and successor Hippias, were definitely that order of tyrant.

For reasons that are hidden from us, the Solonian compromise did not hold. Social and political unrest continued. In 561 Pisistratus succeeded in making himself tyrant of Athens. After five years, he was expelled, only to be brought back later. Again resisted, he withdrew to Macedonia, to return once more in 546, remaining in power until his death in 527. His son Hippias retained the tyranny until his expulsion in 510.

The time of the tyranny of the Pisistratidae was an exuberant one for Athens, involving vast public building activity and the institution of the great festivals of Athena and Dionysus, wherein the canonical recitation of Homer became established and Athenian tragedy had its beginnings. A veritable explosion in commerce occurred, as a result of which Attic black-figured pottery became preeminent in the Greek world and Attic currency attained a commanding position in Greek commerce. In the latter part of the tyranny, we begin to hear the names that would become so important in Athens during the classical period: Cimon, Miltiades, Cleisthenes.

Cleisthenes and the Establishment of the Moderate Democracy, 510–c. 462

Hippias was driven from power in 510 by a combination of the political forces opposed to tyranny and a Spartan armed force. Two years of political conflict followed, the factions of Isagoras contending with those of Cleisthenes. The latter, after forming an alliance with the *demos* (the people), was triumphant and proceeded to reorganize totally the political institutions of Athens. The full scope of this reformation is not visible to us, but the final result was unquestionably a democratic society. Two crucial transformations wrought by Cleisthenes were the substitution of local, residential political identity and performance for the previous kinship mode of activity and the establishment of a new democratic Council of Four Hundred to compete with, and ultimately triumph over, the old aristocratic Council of the Areopagus. We know from the more detailed comparative history of Rome that an hereditary council composed primarily of nobles—in Rome, the Senate—was capable of preserving aristocratic hegemony in a society that otherwise preserved other institutions—an assembly open to all citizens—that indicated a democratic polity. Cleisthenes' trumping of the Areopagus by the formation of a new, democratic Council effectively assured that, in the future, Athens would no longer be subject to aristocratic domination by a patrician senate.

As a result of these and other reforms, the first half of the fifth century at Athens presented a picture familiar to us from England and America in the nineteenth century. Once a free-male moderate democratic polity was established, the society moved more and more in the direction of radical democracy. This fifty-year period also witnessed the great triumph over the forces of the Persian Empire attempting to dominate the Greek world. At the battles of Marathon (490), Salamis (480), and Plataea (479), the Persians were thoroughly defeated and Athens erected in its own mind its great historical "heroic age." After the defeat of Persia, Athenian naval dominance of the Greek world and the Athenian Empire evolved. Themistocles, a radical imperialist, and Aristides "the Just," a moderate one, were two important—and typical—figures of this era.

The Age of Pericles: Radical Democracy, Radical Imperialism, the Efflorescence of Culture, c. 462–431

Ephialtes, a political figure about whom, unfortunately, we know very little, was significant in the creation of the radical democracy. In 462, he succeeded in passing measures that effectively put an end to the Areopagus as a political force. He was assassinated within a year of these crucial reforms. Ephialtes was the mentor of the young Pericles, ultimately the most dominant politician Athens was ever to see. Pericles succeeded in 443 in ostracizing his main political opponent, Thucydides the son of Melisias (not the historian), and was subsequently elected a general (a crucial political post) every year until his death in 429. Among other measures, Pericles introduced the first pay for public service (in this case, jury duty) ever recorded. His name is intimately associated with the full radical democracy at Athens.

He was also, as we shall discuss at great length, unambivalently committed to Athenian hegemony over the Greek world. Freedom at home and domination abroad were his two passionate concerns. He had no scruples in using the revenue from the empire, originally intended to defend against Persia, to erect several huge and beautiful building complexes in Athens. It was an explosive era of Athenian talent and genius: the age of Anaxagoras, Sophocles, Euripides, and Phidias.

Athens in Crisis: Oligarchic Counterrevolution, Catastrophic Military Defeat, 431–403

We know more about this time of Athenian history than of any other. Not only do we possess answers to the question "What happened?" but we also have a rare sense of how it felt to be alive at this period. All this we owe to Thucydides whose extraordinary *History of the Peloponnesian War* is unquestionably one of the greatest works of history ever written. From it, and other historians, we can closely observe a remarkable cast of characters:

Nicias. A moderate democrat. A moderate imperialist. A man of caution. Moderate in everything but his wealth. He was said to own a thousand slaves who worked the silver mines he leased, making him one of the richest men in Athens.

Cleon. The first of the "demagogues," supposed to have corrupted the *demos* and the democratic life of Athens by turning the meetings of the Assembly into a dramatic performance, and by appealing to the baser instincts of the citizens.

Alcibiades. The great hero and antihero of Athenian life. Extraordinarily talented in politics, almost to the point of genius, his amorality and grandiose ambition helped bring Athens to its ruin.

Critias. A brilliant hater of the democracy, exceptionally able, and remarkably savage in his capacity to use any means to dominate society for ideological and egoistic purposes. The first person of truly "fascist" mentality to appear in history.

Theramenes. A moral and political "waffler," caught in a catastrophic time, trapped between an enormous ambition and a not-yet-dead moral sense.

Thrasybulus. A staunch champion of democracy, profound foe of oligarchy. More than ready to risk his life in the defense of freedom. Preserver and restorer of the democratic life during and after the oligarchic coups of 411 and 404.

The great war with Sparta, whose "inevitability" we will critically look at, lasted from 431 to 404 and ended with the total defeat of Athens. In the latter part of the war, in the years 411 and 404, two oligarchic counterrevolutions sought to destroy the radical democracy. Both were very short-lived. The restored democracy, with and without an empire, suffered no new oligarchic threat for almost a hundred years subsequent to these events.

The Golden Age of the Radical Democracy, 403–322

It was an amazingly stable time. Though intense competition for power and honor marked political life—as in all democracies—the Athenians had learned how to combat each other without violence. No class or social brutality, from either oligarchs or lower-class economic radicals, broke the civil peace. Many modern historians, with Periclean stars in their eyes, have downgraded the fourth century as if it were a time of moral mediocrity compared to the glorious fifth century. Such superficial political analysis does not hold. It was a remarkably vibrant democratic era. It was also the greatest age of philosophy ever, giving us Plato and Aristotle, and, therefore, the basis of 2,500 years of Western thought.

Almost all the preserved speeches of Athenian orators date from this century, including those of Lysias, though a resident alien and therefore not a citizen, still a man of profound democratic understanding and passion; Isocrates, a sometimes brilliant, sometimes mediocre and contradictory thinker who lived to be almost a hundred, and from whom we can learn a great deal about life in the first democracy; Demosthenes, the Jefferson-Madison-Lincoln of Athens all rolled into one, though never quite attaining the moral depth of any of these citizens; Aeschines, the great opponent of Demosthenes, especially in matters of foreign policy and the question of how to respond to the increasingly threatening power of Philip of Macedon. Aeschines and Demosthenes were engaged in a democratic, peaceful debate about what was best for the *polis*, and it was for the *demos* to exercise its ultimate sovereignty and decide.

Alternative Periods of Independence with Macedonian and Roman Domination, 322–102

When Alexander of Macedon died in 323, many Greek states, including Athens, thought the time had come to throw off Macedonian dominance of the Greek world, which had been exercised, primarily in the areas of foreign policy and military activity, since 338–335. Totally defeated in this war of independence, Athens was required to admit a Macedonian garrison into the city in 322, and from then on, one or another of the generals who succeeded to Alexander's power controlled the political life of the city. For the next two hundred years, though politics was not dead in Athens, conquerors (including, eventually, Rome) played a crucial role in the internal affairs of the state. For all practical purposes, the classical age of the democratic *polis* was over, even though democratic ideals stayed very much alive, and refused to die until the first century. What the history of democratic politics would have been like if Athens had been able to retain its independence, we will never know.

2

Introduction: Democracy and the Paranoid Position

The human condition is treacherous. No life, even one untouched by tragedy or catastrophe, can accurately be described as tranquil and untroubled. Although philosophers, historians, and psychologists would undoubtedly disagree intensely with each other as to the ultimate *cause* of human discontent, it is a reasonable assumption that almost all would agree about the contingent nature of human existence. In this century, psychology has deepened our understanding of the origins of unhappiness. Even Freud, who invented psychotherapy, that great boon to freedom, remained resignedly pessimistic, in his reflective moods, when he described his view of life as tragic and stated that the aim of psychoanalytic therapy was to bring the patient from neurotic suffering to normal unhappiness.

One great insight of psychoanalytic theory is the developmental view that the psyche, from infancy to adulthood, progresses in highly differentiated stages, that the course of a healthy, "normal" development is to pass successfully from one stage to another. Freud's great insight was that the so-called sexual perversions in an adult are manifestations of a psyche arrested, or fixated, in a particular preadult stage of sexual evolution. We were all "perverts" once; we were all, at one point in development, committed to the "anal-sadistic" view of reality. The true

13

pervert, however, cannot advance beyond his or her particular state of fixation.

The stages in the development of the psyche are not only sexual, however. What one makes of reality, how one perceives the world, also change profoundly from infancy onward. There is a time in childhood, Freud postulated, when the psyche maintains an essentially magical view of the universe, that thinking can operate on the world and the people in it, a time of "the omnipotence of thought." The healthy psyche develops and passes beyond that state, although remnants remain in every adult psyche. The psychotic, on the other hand, never advances beyond the almost total commitment to omnipotence.

This developmental view of the psyche thus teaches us about the causes of human unhappiness, that the road to becoming an adult is an enormously complicated one, full of some unbelievably difficult tasks. All failures to overcome these hurdles result in an increase of anxiety or depression, the two great manifestations of human distress. And no one, it appears, does more than reasonably accomplish this journey.

Essential to the theoretical ground of this book is the concept that—as far as the relationship of the psyche and the world is concerned—there exists a crucial developmental sequence: (1) paranoia, (2) the paranoid position, and (3) overcoming the paranoid position. Clearly the sequence represents an advance in psychic maturity and health. As in all developmental psychological theory, the *telos* of development is a psyche reasonably free of pathology. The essential problematic, nonetheless, is that paranoia and the paranoid position represent stages in the viewing of reality that *every psyche* goes through. Though as adults we no longer suffer from paranoia, it was once, for all of us, the normal expectable condition. We have grown out of it, but it remains accurate to say, in a metaphorical manner, that we are all born paranoid. It is the mission of "good enough" nurturing, aided by those constitutional aspects of the psyche that are able to strive toward health, to help us overcome the paranoid position. All nonpsychotic adults have succeeded, more or less, in going beyond the paranoid position. The question of the *degree* to which this psychic work has been successfully accomplished is crucial.

"Every normal person," Freud writes, "is only normal on the average. His ego approximates to that of the psychotic in some part or other and to a greater or lesser extent."[1]

All adults remain paranoid to some degree or other. Even the most efficacious nurturing, combined with the most fortunate temperament, will leave some significant residue of the paranoid position in the adult psyche.

One could construct a scale from one to ten or from one to a hundred on which every human being could be graded as to the degree to which paranoid response and action determine existence. More pertinent to the concerns of this essay, one could do the same for every human society, past or present. Every society is paranoid, and has succeeded to a greater or lesser degree in overcoming the paranoid position. Furthermore, the degree of the paranoid position can differ profoundly within a society from one decade to the next, even from one year to the next. One could easily chart, for instance, the degree to which paranoid positions have determined the foreign policy of the United States from 1945 to the present. The result would be as dramatic and as significant as the charts of the economy or the stock market.

The degree of paranoid world views determining the value system of society is of crucial importance for any valid theory of social evolution. Social evolution, progressing through various stages in society, can be conceived of as a diminution of paranoid response and action. If the movement from Archaic civilization (Sumer, Egypt) to Classical civilization (Greece, Israel) can be described as a step forward in social evolution, and not merely as a change from one kind of society to another, it should be possible to demonstrate that Classical civilizations were significantly less paranoid than those of the Archaic. So, too, with the development from authoritarian society to democratic society. It will be argued here that democratic society, even the imperfect democracy we simultaneously enjoy and deplore, represents the least paranoid of any form of society yet seen.

I am deliberately using the word "paranoid" rather than "paranoia." Psychosis does not interest us here, except as it sheds light on the behavior of nonpsychotic people. Very few, if any, societies have been psychotic. The "normal psychopathology" of human existence, the "psychotic-like" actions of those who rule society, the extent to which deep irrationalities govern the behavior of nations—all resonate significantly with the concept of "paranoid."

"It is the use of paranoid modes of expression by more or less normal people," Richard Hofstader writes, "that makes the phenomenon significant."[2]

To return to the view that we are all born paranoid, I am cognizant of the fact that exactly the opposite may be argued, that we are fundamentally sane at birth, the paranoid position resulting from some inevitable—and at the moment, inexplicable—dislocations in the developmental process. Nurturing and temperament may make a difference in the resultant degree of the paranoid position, but its absolute necessity is unavoidable. Though this is a crucial question for the theory of child development, it matters not for the aims of this chapter, the assumptions of which remain demonstrable: all persons and all societies are, *to one degree or another*, paranoid, and in the history of the world nothing is of more importance than the differences of degree.

It would be fitting, at this point, to give an elegant definition of the paranoid position, paying particular attention to its causes, but such a task is beyond my capacities. Nor does a review of the psychological literature reveal that any one has yet been able to give us the kind of definition we would like. We find ourselves in the position of Supreme Court Justice Potter Stewart who stated that he was incapable of defining pornography, but he knew it when he saw it. So for the manifestations of the paranoid position. They are immediately recognizable and one senses how various expressions of the condition reflect a fundamental attitude toward the world. Hofstader, whose essay on the paranoid style and American politics is of fundamental importance, also could do no more in trying to define the phenomenon than identify it by its various manifestations. "I call it the paranoid style simply because no other word adequately evokes the qualities of heated aggression, suspiciousness, and conspiratorial fantasy that I have in mind."[3]

The quintessential overriding concern of the paranoid position is the question of control: Who is controlling whom. Are they controlling me or am I controlling them? The aim of all paranoid thought and action is to get a firm grip on that which controls the world. The anxiety that one does not have such a hold is enormous and therefore all activity, mental and actual, is directed toward obtaining a certain kind of controlling power. All manifestations of the radical paranoid position are either shrill laments that we have lost, or are losing, controlling power or fantastical attempts to regain it.

The fundamental paranoid view is that the world, and those who people it, are untrustworthy. Erik Erikson regards the task of the first period of a child's life as acquiring the quality of basic trust. The paranoid learns the exact opposite lesson: Basic distrust is the ground of his or her being. Conspirators and traitors are everywhere. There is no loyal opposition. Those of contrary political positions are not, as the democratic view would have it, entitled to their opinions, since their opinions are traitorous. Former President Richard Nixon's various "enemies lists" were just one comparatively recent manifestation of a problem that has plagued democracy since its birth. The paranoid cry of "treachery" and "subversion" has always posed a basic threat to the democratic order. Aristophanes' trenchant wit, giving the problem a culinary twist, may help us appreciate the oral origin of paranoid anxiety.

"Tyranny" and "Subversive"—that covers every case you judge, large or small. Everything you do, in fact: the universe in two nouns. It's the same all over town. I hadn't heard the word "Tyrant" for fifty years in Athens, and suddenly it's cheaper than smelt. It clutters up the marketplace, chokes the shops—you trip on it. Example. You don't want sardines for supper; what you want is a nice, fat, juicy sea bass. And the man next door,—who incidentally, just happens to sell sardines—starts up: "Sea-bass, huh? That's real rich food—expensive too. Too expensive for a real Athenian democrat. Hey, Mac—why the bass? You want to bring THE TYRANNY back?" Or say you're having herring for lunch, and you want an onion, a pretty, round onion, to keep it company. Have you ever tried to buy that onion? You do, and the woman next door—you know, the one who sells scallions—takes a squint, and: "that Athens pays taxes so you can have fancy food? Hey, Mac—why the onion? You want to bring THE TYRANNY back?"[4]

The mirror image of the conspirators and traitors within society is the picture of the cunning, near-omnipotent enemies without, who have to be constantly defended against. "The manifestation vis-à-vis the external world of the paranoid person's continuous, rigidly maintained directedness of himself is a continuous and preoccupying concern with the defense of his autonomy against external assault."[5] There is a consistent attempt to magnify the power and the cunning of the outside enemy, the "evil empire" of former President Ronald Reagan's fairly recent paranoid parry. Hofstader quotes Senator Barry Goldwater, our most formidable defender against the communist menace in the early

1960s, who advised, "I would suggest that we analyze and copy the strategy of the enemy: theirs has worked and ours has not."[6]

The panic concern with the malignancy of external, hostile powers and the feeling of helplessness because we cannot stop their intrusions into our bodies produce an acute concern with poisoning. In the Middle Ages, the Jews were periodically accused of poisoning the wells. (One could, in fact, produce an accurate description of the paranoid position by merely listing all the accusations made against the Jews over the last eight hundred years.) Several people die of poisoned Tylenol tablets in Chicago, sending the country into a poison panic. More money and time are expended on producing "tamperproof" containers than on the safety of the highways, where hundreds die every week. The speed limit is raised to sixty-five miles per hour with hardly an objection, an action that will kill a thousand times more people than poisoned Tylenol. But poisoning really sounds the paranoid alarm bell. The phenomenal political success of the environmental movement in the 1970s resulted when the idea got across that we were poisoning the planet.

The paranoid is acutely concerned with what goes in and what comes out of the body. Pollution is a constant concern. It becomes necessary, therefore, periodically to purge the body politic of those elements which pollute it. Periodic purges were a necessary activity of the awesome totalitarian movements of the twentieth century. When the most violent oligarchic counterrevolution struck Athens at the end of the Peloponnesian War, the first victims of the terror, in a conscious effort to "cleanse" the *polis*, were the "riffraff" who were corrupting society, sycophants, hangers-on, purveyors of political gossip, and such. External vigilance is required at the entrances to and exits from the body. Paranoid governments are always fanatically interested in, and controlling of, those who enter and leave the country.

The paranoid never believes that even the most extreme measures taken against real and fantasied enemies are sufficient. Catastrophe is always imminent. "Paranoid people," David Shapiro writes, "live in readiness for an emergency. They seem to live in a more or less continuous state of total mobilization."[7] This is a logical condition considering the two fundamental principles of the paranoid view: that the world is basically untrustworthy and hostile and that the only defense is to get into one's power the few basic instruments that control the universe. This leads logically to one of the paranoid's essential modes of action: offense as the best defense. We are acquainted with the psychopathic person suffering from paranoia who attacks someone on the street because that someone was about to attack him; that is a problem for the police and psychiatric social workers. But the mode of political behavior wherein the brilliant Alcibiades convinces the people of Athens to embark on the glorious suicidal invasion of Sicily— in part, because if they did not do so, the Syracusans would ultimately join with Sparta in attacking Athens—such a mode of political action remains a fundamental problem even in the "modern" democratic world we inhabit.

The world frightening and untrustworthy; one's political opponents all conspirators and traitors who would sell the country out to the enemy; one's opponents not a loyal opposition, but the incarnation of treachery and evil—all this being so, assassination becomes the instrument of political policy. Not the wild, psychotic assassination of a President by some deranged soul, but the deliberate, planned, violent elimination of the political opposition ordered by nonpsychotic paranoid people in power. One of the first signs that a fragile democracy is about to go under is the increased use of assassination as a political weapon.

The one psychological mode of action that almost everyone recognizes as intrinsic to the paranoid position (and, in its most exaggerated form, intrinsic to paranoia) is projection: ". . . the attribution to external figures of motivations, drives, or other tensions that are repudiated and intolerable in oneself."[8] If we want to conquer the world, we announce that "they" are the ones who are so intent. If we cannot abide the tolerance that democratic society demands, we discover conspiracies whereby "they" are intent on overthrowing the democracy. Hofstader points out how the Ku Klux Klan, violently anti-Catholic, imitated the Catholic Church by wearing priestly robes, erecting elaborate ritual structures, and creating a complex hierarchy.[9] What the paranoid personality cannot do is to create a significant psychological distance between him- or herself and others. To a degree, there are no others, only friends (a part of me) and enemies (the projection of the bad, repudiated parts of me). Lacking an integrated, internal sense of self, the paranoid cannot conceive of an independent, possibly different, even indifferent, other. Democratic society, on the other hand, rests on the fundamental assumption of the independence and integrity of other people, that they be allowed wishes and desires and lives independent of what others may require of them. The paranoid cannot abide tolerance. People who do not believe in God *must* allow prayer in the schools; people who do not believe their identity is dependent on a piece of cloth, *must* recite the Pledge of Allegiance; women who get pregnant by mistake, *must* have the child. Every democratic society has its frontier on which paranoid forces struggle with those of tolerance.

Democracy and the Paranoid Position

Not only is the paranoid position the single most important threat to any existing democratic society but also overcoming the paranoid position is an essential—if not the essential—circumstance for the *establishment* of a democracy. Going beyond the paranoid position must be accomplished on both the personal, psychological level and on the social level. Individually, there must exist a sufficient number of people among the elites—historically, it was the elite who created democratic societies, responding in part, but certainly not wholly, to demands for equality from nonelite lower classes—who are willing and able to live without a primary reliance on the psychological mechanisms of defense that the paranoid position represents. Conditions must also be favorable socially. Historically, this involves questions of the willingness of the aristocracy to compromise, the question of how united the aristocracy and/or monarchy are in their opposition to democratic movements, the willingness of members of the middle or lower aristocracy to lead democratic parties, and so forth.

Crucial to the argument being made here is the concept that the paranoid position is not only a set of psychopathological symptoms but is, at the same time, a system of successful defenses against a more severe psychopathology, paranoia itself. The neurosis of the paranoid position successfully defends against the psychosis of paranoia. In terms of psychological development, therefore, the paranoid position both works and does not work: works by preventing paranoia; fails to work by making it impossible to transcend itself and move on to a more mature position. What makes it so difficult for people to give up paranoid mechanisms of defense is the unconscious anxiety that, should these mechanisms disappear, one would not march forward into the bright democratic future, but regress precipitously into paranoia itself. Racism and anti-Semitism are two important manifestations of the paranoid position. They serve profound psychological needs for those who hold to them and are difficult to abandon because they are defenses against the extreme panic of paranoia. The paranoid position can never be transcended until paranoia itself is no longer an immediate threat.

In order to understand our present moment in history I am postulating, from the sociological viewpoint and from the perspective of historical development, three distinct stages (that is, ideal types) of historical society. The first we may call the traditional, authoritarian, classically paranoid society wherein sovereignty is exercised either by a monarch (Louis XIV, Frederick the Great) or by an aristocracy of a small group of noble families (the ancient Roman Republic, Venice in modern times). The second stage, democratic society, always arises out of this authoritarian stage, and is made possible only by overcoming the paranoid position sufficiently that the most extreme defenses against paranoia itself are no longer necessary. In this liberal, democratic stage of society, democracy is possible and actual, but many manifestations of the paranoid position (imperialism, racism, and so forth) persist. Our present liberal, bourgeois, capitalist democracy is such a society and the relationship of the freedom of democratic society to the psychological bondage of certain persistent modes of paranoid defense is a fundamental subject of this book.

The third stage of society postulated in this argument lies only in the future, if at all. Its coming will depend on the degree to which paranoid mechanisms of defense can be overcome, allowing such a fundamental transformation of liberal, capitalist society that aggressive warfare and the permanent destruction of the planet, for instance, are no longer real possibilities. That question, of necessity, intrudes itself into this work, but obviously no firm answer is possible at this time.

If we now look at our first stage, predemocratic societies, either those transformed into democracies or those that never undertook that development, we can observe the mechanisms of the paranoid position in their fundamental form. Three basic institutionalized modes simultaneously and effectively defended against paranoia and presented the greatest hindrance to the development of democracy: (1) authoritarian politics (monarchy and aristocracy), (2) militarism (which includes a pathological nationalism), and (3) dogmatic fundamentalist religion. All regressions from democratic society, all situations in which a viable democracy is overthrown, resort to these same institutions. We see this easily in the twentieth-century totalitarian and fascist regimes wherein dictatorship serves the monarchical mode and paranoid ideology (the thousand-year Reich, the world communist revolution) serves the fundamentalist religious necessity. All regressions from democracy involve the reassertion of the fundamental paranoid position. No democracy is possible unless a large group of people in society have the capacity to live without the defenses of authoritarianism, militarism, and dogmatic ideology.

Paranoia is the problem. The paranoid position is the defense. Democracy is a miracle, considering human psychological disabilities.

I recall the evening in November 1980 when Jimmy Carter lost the presidency to Ronald Reagan, the first instance in forty-eight years of an incumbent, previously elected President being defeated in an election. "The people have spoken," announced a somber Carter on television, and then there was a long, pregnant pause. One wondered what the pause meant, what primitive agenda Carter might be dealing with in the deep recesses of his mind. One possible scenario suggests itself: I am not going to call out the army; I am not going to declare the election invalid; I am not going to have my opponent assassinated. Instead, I am voluntarily and peacefully going to give up the greatest power a person can hold in this country and place myself in the hands of my enemy, trusting that he will deal responsibly and legally with me.

Not that the sane and civilized Jimmy Carter was even aware, consciously, of any such struggle. Nor am I saying that there was any possibility that Carter would have resorted to extreme measures. It is the position of this chapter, however, that a responsible, democratic polity can only be achieved by an heroic struggle against paranoia and the paranoid position. (Carter's struggle probably lasted only a moment.) Why else did it take humankind tens of thousands of years to reach the place where responsible democratic societies were possible and that, with the exception of a few ancient Greek democracies, only within the last 250 years? Lacey Smith writes of the "diffuse apprehension" that made it nearly impossible for Tudor society to "put its faith in the motives of others."[10] In no society previous to democratic polities have a large number of people been able to put their faith in the motives of others. That position has only been achieved by a continuing struggle against irrational forces of enormous power. It seems miraculous that human beings could triumph over those forces, no matter how incomplete that victory may be.

Trusting in the motives of others allows for the formation of a conception in political life that does not exist in nondemocratic societies, the idea of a loyal opposition. The paranoid position regards all opposition as disloyal and traitorous to the truth. It peoples the world with conspirators and betrayers. It orders the assassination of political opponents because they are evil, intent on destroying society; any measure taken against them is justified and moral. We who live in a democratic society and take that democracy for granted do not recognize what a great triumph of the capacity for psychic health is the belief that those who differ from one politically can still be considered loyal to the society.

Democratic society achieves that remarkable position by going beyond the personal to the abstract. The paranoid position is intensely personal. All evil wears a specific human face. The individual suffering from paranoia may believe in malicious cosmic forces disrupting and poisoning the world, but the paranoid sees a person or persons behind all life's evils. The Jews are involved in an international conspiracy to bring down the economy; the Russians are sending drugs to the United States to corrupt capitalist society. The examples are manifold. When John Kennedy was killed in 1963, some sophisticated people I knew who came from a nondemocratic society "knew" that the assassination had been ordered by Lyndon Johnson, because who else had so much to gain by it?

Loyalty for the paranoid is always primarily loyalty to a person, the czar, the dictator, or the religious leader, not to an abstract image of freedom or tolerance or, most especially, law. In a democracy it matters not whether you like or dislike your neighbors, or whether you believe that their motives are honorable. What matters is that they are entitled to the protection of the law, just as you are. The law is impersonal, beyond persons, universal. True paranoids are incapable of this imaginative leap. They are only able to live in a society with people whom they like or who think in the same way. When the paranoid position

severely regresses to paranoia itself, the extermination of those in society who are different becomes a necessity. Differences among people
can be tolerated only by achieving an abstract conception of person-
hood. One must respond to the abstract, generalized human quality of
those who superficially differ from one. Paranoids cannot do this. They
suffer from a xenophobia directed internally into society; security and
comfort reside only in a completely homogeneous world.

Psychologically and historically, the fundamental forms for overcoming the paranoid position and establishing a democratic world view
have been law and education. There can be respect for law in nondemocratic societies (for example, ancient Rome) and education for aristocracy is an ancient human mode. The presence of these two cultural
phenomena, therefore, does not in itself indicate a democracy. When
the democratic process begins, however, a highly abstract view of law
and an intense education for democracy—which can arise within the
political process itself—are essential for its success.

Democracy being the least paranoid of any human society thus far
and the process of overcoming the paranoid position (sublimation,
repression, education) always being far from complete, the question
arises, what do democratic societies do with their paranoid inclinations
to keep them from disrupting society? It should be recognized, first,
that all democratic societies differ in the degree to which paranoid
manifestations are present in the polity. It is my view, for instance,
that the United States is close to being as paranoid a country as it is
possible to be and still allow a democracy to exist. I sometimes feel I
am overstating the importance of the paranoid mode, but this chapter
is being written during the height of the presidential campaign of 1988.
When one picks up the daily newspaper, one discovers that an election
that will have a profound effect on the peace of the world and the
welfare of our citizens may be decided on the issues of which candidate
has shown the proper paranoid respect for the Pledge of Allegiance to
the flag and whether or not one of the candidates is a "card-carrying
member of the American Civil Liberties Union," that is, a communist
betrayer of the country. And this in one of the world's great democracies. It makes one wonder if one can give too much emphasis to the
paranoid position. One of the things, then, that a democratic society
does with its paranoid inclinations is to give expression to them.

There is a limit, however, to the degree to which paranoid impulses can be unleashed internally and still preserve the democratic nature of society. One method for maintaining both democracy and the paranoid position is splitting. Certain groups are excluded from the democratic process, denying them the name and function of "citizen." In ancient Athens, women, slaves, and foreign-born residents were all excluded. Poor people and women are always excluded at the beginnings of democratic society. This was true of Solon's Athens and Jefferson's America. Only with the advent of "radical democracy"—Pericles and Andrew Jackson—do poor people attain any measure of sovereignty. And black people, of course, have until only recently been denied democratic citizenship in the United States. Those who are beyond the pale of democratic sovereignty become the objects of aggression through economic and tyrannical exploitation, thus satisfying the paranoid need to sacrifice someone to the jealousy and anger of the gods.

Democratic society, therefore, though a psychological and sociological miracle is no proof against the most barbaric kind of human behavior: imperialism, slavery, genocide, insane warfare, and abject poverty within society. Why this should be so, I cannot say. I cannot explain why Athens, whose democracy was in many ways amazingly responsible, stable, and mature, was in its foreign policy not one ounce more moral than the most paranoid of Greek cities. When it came to genocide and/or the enslavement of captured cities, Athens' behavior matched any of the barbarisms of twentieth-century totalitarian states.

One possible clue to this enigma is that paranoid impulses, though repressed within the boundaries of democratic action, do not simply go away; they seek satisfaction outside the society. Imperialism and democracy have been associates in Athens, in nineteenth-century England, and in twentieth-century America. Warfare as an instrument of national policy has been forsaken only by a handful of states. The trade-off between internal and external manifestations of aggression was perceptively understood by the elder Cato of Rome who, in the second century B.C., asked "What was to become of Rome, when she should no longer have any state to fear?"[11] The answer came in the next century. She would tear herself apart through senseless civil war and destroy the republic. When the paranoid position regresses in the direction of paranoia itself, the impulses of self-destruction become stronger and stronger. Warfare somehow brings things to a crisis; it becomes a terrible temptation. Directing our paranoid aggression outward, we cleanse ourselves and can resume loving each other as we march off gaily to our destruction.

There are, then, severe moral limitations within any form of democratic society yet seen. It is ironic and saddening to think about emerging democratic societies such as Argentina or the Philippines. After great triumphs over authoritarian, dictatorial rule, an heroic struggle results in the formation of a fragile democracy. And should those democracies endure, the societies then become heir to all the great moral contradictions of liberal, bourgeois, capitalist democracies, contradictions that exist, in good part, because the paranoid defenses against paranoia continue to exert such strong influence. The paranoidia of domination, the paranoidia of greed, the paranoidia of self-destruction, all, unfortunately, remain only too compatible with the forms of democratic society.

The Paranoid Position as a System of Defenses

It is important to recognize that what we observe as paranoid feelings or actions are not the disease, but symptoms of the disease. Even those modes of psychic activity that characterize paranoia itself are not the disease but symptoms of the disease. The disease, in the case of paranoia, is a panic-anxiety that one's selfhood could be destroyed. It results from a sense of self so fragile, from a system of adequate defenses so brittle, that the slightest challenge results in a kind of psychic fibrilation, wherein the possibilities of extinction remain ever present. What we observe as mechanisms of paranoia (cosmic forces threatening, grandiosity of an extreme nature, projection of overwhelming aggressive feelings outward, and so on) are a system of defenses erected against this threatened destruction of the self. Paranoid mechanisms operate in essentially the same way, but they address an anxiety about the extinction of the self that is *much less severe* than that exhibited in paranoia. All paranoid mechanisms, nevertheless, are implemented to obtain control over some force or some person who threatens psychic existence. One becomes a paranoid when anxiety-panic is no longer so overwhelming as for the person suffering from paranoia; one can give up paranoid mechanisms only when there is a further and significant reduction or change in the quantity and quality of anxiety.

Both the paranoid and the sufferer from paranoia seek control over the forces that dominate the world. One manner in which to pursue control is to retreat from the world into a magical state, where the omnipotence of thought, or feelings, or words, or movement give one the illusion of safety. The other mode of seeking control is to set out to conquer the world. Those who adopt this manner have made much of the world's history. What they do, in essence, is to project on to society the irreconcilable conflicts within themselves and then they act on society in the attempt to resolve those conflicts.

"The clinical paranoid," Hofstader writes, "sees the hostile and conspiratorial world in which he feels himself to be living as directed specifically *against him*; whereas the spokesman of the paranoid style finds it directed against a nation, a culture, a way of life whose fate affects not himself alone but millions of others."[12]

Those who seek domination over the real world are, essentially, of two orders. The most extreme are on the border between paranoia and the paranoid position and may, like Hitler, oscillate between the two modes, sometimes acting truly psychotically and sometimes shrewdly paranoid. Hofstader has left us a brilliant portrait of this extreme group.

> They regard a "vast" or "gigantic" conspiracy as *the motive force* in historical events. History *is* a conspiracy, set in motion by demonic forces of almost transcendent power, and what is felt to be needed to defeat it is not the usual methods of political give-and-take, but an all-out crusade. The paranoid spokesman sees the fate of this conspiracy in apocalyptic terms—he traffics in the birth and death of whole worlds, whole political orders, whole systems of human values. He is always manning the barricades of civilization.[13]

Even in a stable democracy there are always many more people with this view of the world than we like to admit. In the 1960s the Republican minority whip of the Senate stated that 10 percent of the sixty thousand letters his office received each month were about "the latest PLOT!! to OVERTHROW America!!!"[14] In 1969 when newly elected Vice President Spiro Agnew began his crusading, extremist speeches about what was wrong with America, even though he never mentioned the Jews by name—he attacked Hollywood and the New York press in general—the amount of anti-Semitic mail received in Senate offices skyrocketed.[15]

In contradistinction to this extreme attitude, the more prevalent paranoid mode of seeking domination of the world reflects the normal psychopathology that has made so much of the world's history and brought the world so much grief: that of empire builders, conquistadors, robber barons, builders of states, makers of revolutions, giants of imperialism, and the common, everyday variety of jingo patriot, racist, cold-warrior, including senators, congressmen, governors, and so forth, and so on. The paranoidia of domination is an attempt to defend against fear of the loss of the self by successfully oppressing others. That anxiety underlay the *libido dominandi* was understood by Thucydides. He notes the Athenian appeal to the Sicilians at the beginning of that expedition so catastrophic for Athens: " 'Now, as we have said, fear makes us hold our empire in Hellas, and fear makes us now come, with the help of our friends, to order safely matters in Sicily, and not to enslave any but rather to prevent any from being enslaved.' "[16]

From the committed paranoids of the nonextreme type, domination is a necessity because its alternative is not peace and equality but suffering domination. In their world there are only masters and slaves, no citizens.

" 'We cannot fix the exact point at which our empire shall stop;' " Alcibiades stated in the Athenian Assembly, " 'we have reached a position in which we must not be content with retaining but must scheme to extend it, for *if we cease to rule others, we are in danger of being ruled ourselves.*' "[17] And near the end of the speech to the Sicilians, the Athenians sum up their *weltanschauung*: " 'We assert that we are rulers in Hellas in order not to be subjects, liberators in Sicily that we may not be harmed by the Sicilians.' "[18]

The ancient Greeks, living at a time before Hebrew/Christian morality had made people ambivalent about oppressing others, had a tendency to equate the concept of freedom with the capacity to domineer over other people. "Thucydides (III, 45) makes a speaker use the phrase 'freedom, or the rule over others,' and similar uses can be found in Greek authors from Herodotus (I. 210) to Polybius (V. 106)."[19] "The association of the ideas of love of liberty and love of domination over others is essentially Greek."[20] To lose one's freedom is to lose the most precious sense of self. If one panics at the possibility and if one is an assertive and not a passive person, one is on the road to a petty or a grand tyranny.

There are some, Aristotle writes, who are "filled with a passion for inequality."[21] For the paranoid seeker after domination, equality—the necessity to recognize the true existence of others—is anathema; it stands between him or her and the medicine needed to assuage anxiety. The paranoid who uses domination as a primary defense has an absolute need for a victim, a need as intense as the alcoholic's for drink. If everyone in the adult world must be treated as an equal, there will be no victims. What then will we do with our anxiety-panic? This helps explain the fury with which many people greet the attempts of victimized sections of society to assert their rights to some sort of equality. So much of American national politics today is still driven by the so-called white backlash: "What do they mean that they refuse to be victims?"

If paranoid defenses are fundamentally concerned with control, defenses against the more extreme case, paranoia, are centered on absolute control. The person suffering from paranoia can imagine both total annihilation and total domination of the forces directing the cosmos. This may help us understand totalitarian societies, which exist on the boundary between the paranoid position and paranoia. The ultimate ideal of extreme totalitarian societies in seeking governance over every aspect of personal and political life is exactly analogous to the efforts of the victim of paranoia who wants to control every minute of the day, or every fraction of body movement, or every ounce of solid or liquid that goes into or out of the body. The great antiutopias of this century—*1984, Brave New World*—are caricatures of totalitarian societies and portrayals of a paranoid's paradise.

Related to, but distinct from, dominance is one mechanism of defense against paranoia, what might be called the paranoidia of greed, the attempt to eat up the whole world. This sense that the only way to be secure and to reduce anxiety is to have "more" can be observed throughout the social spectrum from Wall Street billionaires to ordinary people maneuvering to shift the tax burden on to *other* sections of society. Here, as in the paranoidia of dominance, there is a great deal of real-world truth to the paranoid proposition: The more wealth one has the more one is protected from potential catastrophes like ill health, false arrest, the concentration camp. What I am after, however, is not the banal real-world wisdom that announces it is better to be rich than poor but an understanding of the deep irrationalities that underlie accumulation for accumulation's sake. What drives a man who is worth $100 million to take risks that might send him to jail in order to make an additional $400 million? (And get caught, as we have recently seen.) Something very deeply irrational is driving the greed process. It may have more to do with driving our society than we consciously know.

The deep problematic within the paranoidia of dominance and greed is that they require a fantastical belief in omnipotence. They are insatiable and they ultimately prove self-destructive.

Hobbes placed as central to his argument the fact that human beings are driven by a greed for power: "So that in the first place, I put a generall inclination of all mankind, a perpetuall and restlesse desire of Power after power, that ceaseth only in Death."[22] Plato before him saw insatiable greed as a fundamental factor in the destruction of civic virtue: "Every individual, because of his insatiable greed for gold and silver, is willing to toil at every art and device, noble or ignoble, if he is likely to get rich by it—willing too, to perform actions both holy and unholy, nay, utterly shameful—without a scruple, provided only that he is able to sate himself to repletion, like a beast, with all manner of foods and drinks and wenchings. . . . [There are] utterly unfortunate men who are compelled to go through life with hunger always in their souls . . . [It is a] lifelong insatiable pursuit which wholly engrosses each man."[23]

This is a deeply pessimistic statement, implying that we will never have a truly virtuous polity until this universal human drive is overcome. As important as his antidemocratic thrust is Plato's pessimism. In neither *The Republic* nor in the "more realistic" society prescribed in *The Laws* do we get any real sense of how we are to get, historically, from the paranoidia of greed to civic virtue. Plato brilliantly perceives what stands between us and a virtuous society, but he cannot prescribe any reasonable route that history might take to that heavenly kingdom. To say that it will be reached only when philosophers become kings or kings philosophers is a fanciful way of saying "never." We face the exact same problem when we sharpen our psychological insight and see the paranoid position as the great obstacle to the advancement of civic virtue. That tells us nothing about how to overcome it.

The insatiability of greed and dominance requires an extreme magical belief in one's omnipotence, faith that power to control the world will grow larger and larger, that every success only proves that one is unstoppable. The point is quickly reached where a rational assessment of the chances of success or failure becomes impossible. Isocrates, the Athenian orator of the fourth century, having learned the tragic lesson of the catastrophic results of the Peloponnesian War, was a severe critic, at times, of the insatiable greed for power, perceiving the ultimate self-destructiveness of such a course. "He accepts the recognized law of Greek ethics, that power begets folly, folly begets insolence, and insolence begets ruin."[24]

Hobbes, despite his authoritarian inclinations and conclusions, held a strong commitment to reason. He even explains the "restless desire of Power . . . that ceaseth only in Death" as a perfectly *rational* procedure. "And the cause of this, is not always that a man hopes for a more intensive delight, than he has already attained to; or that he cannot be content with a moderate power: but because he cannot assure the power and means to live well, which he hath present, without the acquisition of more."[25]

The history of Athens, as told by Thucydides and Xenophon, was available to Hobbes, who translated Thucydides into English. It disproved his plea for the reasonableness of the drive for power. Before engaging in the pursuit of empire and its sometimes brutal defense after it was established, Athens was one of a handful of large Greek states who engaged in the perpetual warfare common to the *polis*, warfare in which land was occasionally won or lost and soldiers killed to a moderate degree, but which never really threatened the basic existence of the state. When Athens finally lost the Peloponnesian War in 404 B.C., the Spartans and their allies held a meeting to determine what should be done with Athens. The Thebans and Corinthians, two of the most important states allied with Sparta, proposed that Athens should be annihilated, just as she had destroyed other cities: all her men slaughtered, all women and children enslaved. Athens came within an inch of suffering genocide, saved only by the morality or self-interest—we cannot know which—of Sparta. So much for the rationality of piling power upon power, which can be accumulated only by tyrannizing over others. Had Athens been rational it would have stayed content with Hobbes' "moderate power" instead of being led to ruin by the paranoidia of dominance.

Fifty years after that near-holocaust, its memory still resounded in

Isocrates' speech *On the Peace*. "But it is in the nature of things that those who attempt a despot's course must encounter the disasters which befall a despotic power and be afflicted by the very things which they inflict upon others. . . . If, therefore, anyone were to ask us whether we should choose to see Athens in such distress as the price of having ruled so long a time, who could answer yes, except some utterly abandoned wretch who cared not for sacred matters nor for parents nor for children nor for any other thing save for the term of his own existence?"[26]

In the grand irony of history, good fortune for humankind can sometimes result from the self-destructive drive in the paranoid position and in paranoia. In World War II Hitler's invasion of Russia, when England was still unconquered, was the most self-destructive move he ever made. At one point in that invasion, as winter approached, the general of one of his armies called him to advise a strategic retreat until spring when a new offensive could be launched. "No retreats," the Führer ordered. The army involved was almost completely annihilated.[27]

Athens was sufficiently capable of overcoming the paranoid position to make a responsible mature democracy possible among twenty-five to thirty thousand nonslave men, but it was powerless to free itself from the self-destructive *libido dominandi*. Our own democratic society demonstrates remarkable strengths compared with other possible and existing human societies, yet one can never free oneself from the nagging anxiety that we too are capable of an annihilating self-destruction, that a government of reasonable people, sufficiently unequivocally free of the paranoid position, may be as much a fantastical belief as Plato's kings becoming philosophers.

We have reached the great evolutionary question. Having somehow overcome the extreme anxiety-panic of paranoia; having somehow succeeded in sufficiently ameliorating the paranoid position to make liberal, capitalist, bourgeois democracy a reality in many parts of the world, can these democratic societies be transformed into some more humane form of society. And if so, what will it take? Needless to say, I cannot answer those questions. I feel certain of one thing, however. Being reasonable, acting rationally, will be the *results* of this transformation, not its *cause*. Society will not undertake a moral revolution because it is urged to be rational any more than a patient in psychotherapy may be cured by being told to cut out the nonsense.

The question where-can-we-go? can only be answered by fully answering the questions from-whence-have-we-come? and how? It is doubtful that social and economic forces alone were responsible for revolutionizing the world to our present situation from, let us say, 1600, when no stable democratic society existed anywhere on the earth. A profound and almost unbelievable transformation in the psyche was necessary. What weight we should give to philosophy, to religion, to child rearing in accomplishing that miracle remains a fundamental theoretical question. And what profound changes in thought, religion, and child rearing in the years ahead might enable society to overcome the paranoid position to the point where, for instance, abject poverty or the permanent destruction of the environment would be as unthinkable as cannibalism or slavery is today?

One significant fact is cause for a very cautious optimism. There exists in every current democratic society a group of citizens, not a handful of moral geniuses but a sizable group, who have succeeded in their political lives, and in good part in their personal lives, in truly overcoming the paranoid position. They are willing to live without the defenses of aggressive warfare, racism and anti-Semitism, and the extreme competitive atmosphere that pervades every aspect of our social life. I am not postulating a group of saints, but if we are asking society to give up basic paranoid defenses, it is necessary first to know if such a transformation is possible in a reasonable number of individuals. How many such people there may be in any particular society we do not know. Whether they constitute a larger percentage in Scandinavian societies than in the United States, which is committed to ruling the world, it is difficult to say. They are not invisible, nor politically unimportant, but they rule nowhere. Those who represent the moderate, paranoid democratic position rule.

For this "new psycho-class,"[28] we might take a figure, for argument's sake, of 10 or 20 percent. How did they achieve this position of psychological maturity? What manner of religion, culture, education, or child rearing has rendered them possible? And why does the other 80 or 90 percent of the culture remain dependent on the traditional democratic, paranoid modes of defense?

It is amazing how large a part of our politics revolves around the question of how much or how little the paranoid position should determine social policy. Whether it is a matter of Vietnam and Nicaragua, racism and the welfare system, Russia and the defense budget, education and crime in the streets, abortion and the Pledge of Allegiance—over and over again the same underlying, resounding question arises. How paranoid shall this society be? The intensity of the struggle indicates that those representing the nonparanoid, or at least the less paranoid, position, are not impotent. The paranoids, in fact, get elected by claiming that "those others" should not be given the power to threaten the security of the nation. An enormous ambivalence about the paranoid position is evident.

Cautious optimism suggests that if 10 or 20 percent of the people in a culture can become nonparanoid, the transformation cannot be beyond human capacity. Could the majority of a society ever achieve this state? Wisdom requires us to remain agnostic about such a momentous question, no matter how great our hopes may be. Evidence of moral or psychological revolutions in the past does nothing to indicate that such revolutions *must* happen in the future. We may have come to the end of social evolution. Were that the case, human existence is, indeed, threatened, because we may lack the psychological capacity to control the bomb and the destruction of the atmosphere. But why give in to the temptation to close this chapter on the paranoid position with a paranoid apocalyptic vision? There is as much cause for hope as for despair. One may with reason hold to either position. The answer is yet to come.

Athens did not have the capacity to destroy the cosmos with bombs or greenhouse effects. Its rages of *self*-destruction could reach only as far as its own *polis*. The Athenians seemed at times driven by urges that, if expressed, could only bring destruction down on their own heads. At other times, they demonstrated a remarkable capacity for recovery and survival. Athens' history can be read as vindication either of our pessimism or of our optimism. In its greatness and its inadequacies it was, truly, the "school of Hellas"—and of ourselves.

PART I

THE BRIGHT, CLEAR AIR
OF DEMOCRATIC SOCIETY

3

The Founding Miracle: Crisis and Possibility

Athens was engulfed by an economic and social crisis around the year 600 that had a profound effect on its future as a society. The city-state of Rome, remarkably enough, experienced an almost identical moment of urgency a hundred years later, a little after the year 500. Both these crises were brought about by strikingly similar contradictions in social and political life. Though the causes and circumstances of both critical periods keenly resembled each other, there was an enormous difference in the *responses* to this social and moral challenge. Largely because of what occurred at the beginning of the sixth century, Athens ultimately established a new form of human society never before seen on the face of the earth, a mature, stable democracy that would endure for hundreds of years. Rome, on the other hand, responded with a pervasive ambivalence. In the five-hundred-year history of the Republic, it never successfully solved its social problems, especially those of the lower economic classes, and it never came close to becoming a democratic society, though there were important democratic elements in its political system.

We do not understand, and may never understand, the energies that made these different resolutions possible, since the answer may be buried too deeply within the concept of the spirit of society. We do know, nonetheless, a great deal about the social and economic circumstances

37

of these archaic times, a great deal about what form the two crises took and the manner of their resolutions. The uniqueness of the Athenian achievement, our main concern, is amplified and emphasized by the comparative history of Rome.

In 600 Athens was ruled by an aristocracy with no king. This aristocracy derived its political and economic power from the ownership of land. At one time, there had been "kings" but we have no clear picture of the kinds of "kings" there were in Greece after the collapse of the Mycenaean world in the twelfth century. At the beginning of the sixth century almost all of the hundreds of city-states in mainland Greece, the islands, Asia Minor, southern Italy, and Sicily (henceforth, "the Greek world") were under the dominion of essentially the same kind of aristocratic rule, with no monarchy. Archaic Rome presented the same picture, but here there was a detailed mythopoeic history of former "kings," though it is impossible to learn exactly the kind of economic and political power they possessed. In any event, by the time Rome arrived at a social crisis similar to that of Athens, the "kings" were no more. Only the aristocracy ruled.

All these aristocracies were agricultural societies. Merchants and artisans could have amounted to no more than 5 or 10 percent of the population. Below the landed nobles there existed a whole range of individual proprietors, from marginal peasants who owned only enough land minimally to support a family in good years to large landholders who possessed no noble status and were itching for the political power that was the monopoly of the lords. Society had developed far beyond the kinship system and kinship-system forms of communal ownership. Land was held in fee simple; it could be bought, sold, mortgaged, accumulated, and lost. An unfortunate proprietor could find himself landless; the more fortunate, or more provident, or more corrupt, owner could pile parcel upon parcel.

The Impoverishment and Rebellion of the Small Farmer

All peasant societies of individual proprietors, especially after money exchange replaces the traditional mode of barter (though indications are that Athens was not yet a money-exchange economy), present the continuing phenomenon of land being accumulated in fewer and fewer hands. Poorer, marginal peasants lose their land to rich peasants and aristocratic lords. Agriculture is a notoriously hazardous occupation and two or three famine years in a row are enough to wipe out marginal producers. A bad harvest, no matter its reason, leaves the poorer peasant with no seed for the coming year; seed, or money for seed, has to be borrowed; the peasant has only his land to pledge against the loan (in Athens at the beginning of the sixth century, as we shall see, he could also pledge his own body or the bodies of his children); another catastrophic harvest and the farmer becomes landless. In the year of the French Revolution, some French peasants presented a petition that described the process: "A peasant in hard times is dazzled with the offer of ready cash; difficulties are brought upon him by a cruel generosity in lending to him until he cannot repay what he has borrowed. Then his land is seized and sold at a low price to the advantage of the creditor."[1]

It is remarkable how quickly the process of impoverishment can be completed. In Rome, in the first century, the general Cornelius Sulla, successful in his violent bid for the highest power in the state, rewarded his troops with grants of land in Italy. Twenty years later many of these veterans had drifted into bankruptcy and provided a core of discontented citizens ready to back other violent political conspiracies.[2]

The poorest peasants not only lose their land within the legal process of borrowing-mortgaging-foreclosure but also, in many cases, by illegal means. They are forced by rich peasants or mighty lords to make bad bargains or they suffer outright appropriation. This is especially so when a peasant may be away from home for a length of time for military service.

Solon, the creator of the great compromise that freed Athens at the beginning of the sixth century, criticized the illegal arrogance of the rich and powerful.

"It is the people themselves who in their folly seek to destroy our great city, prompted by desire for wealth and their leaders . . . know not how to check their greed, and to enjoy with order and sobriety the pleasures set before them at the feast. . . . They have wealth through their following of unjust works and ways. . . . Neither the sacred treasure nor that of the state do they spare in any wise, but they steal, each in his own corner, like pillaging men."[3]

This process of accumulative impoverishment being continuous, why, at certain points in history, does it reach the moment of social crisis as it did in Athens c. 600 and in Rome c. 500? Much fanciful and not so fanciful speculation has been offered in answer to this question, but the economic data necessary to answer it for the ancient world are completely lacking. One thing we do know. The crises were caused not by the economic degradation of the farmers but by the refusal of the lower classes to remain passive in the face of their impoverishment. That revolutionary initiative brought to both Rome and Athens civil strife that demanded a response from the holders of economic and political power. In Athens, in 594, Solon was elected Archon, with extraordinary powers to revise the laws. It was essential that he address certain fundamental and dangerous sources of social conflict.

There was first the urgent question of the impoverishment and enslavement of the poorest sections of society. Debt slavery was rampant. Aristotle comments that "The whole land was in the hands of a few; and if they did not pay their rents they could be sold into slavery, themselves and their children. And all borrowing was on the security of personal liberty till Solon's time."[4] We may doubt whether *all* borrowing was on the security of persons; some must have been on the security of land as well. It is clear, however, from everything that Solon and Aristotle write, that many men suffered slavery of themselves and their families as the cost of being unable to pay their debts. Many were sold abroad, suffering thereby a double catastrophe.

Archaic Rome presents a comparable picture. The first great flourishing of civil strife there, in 495–494, was fueled by the problems of debt slavery.[5] Unlike Athens, however, where Solon put an end to the practice in one stroke, debt bondage was not abolished in Rome until 326 or 313, more than 150 years after the uprising.[6]

In Athens there was the additional oppression of those known as *hektemoroi*, or sixth-parters, who were required to pay a sixth of their harvest to a landlord or a local noble. We don't know how they got into this situation, whether from default on a loan or as a sharecropping agreement. It is possible that it was an inherited low-status condition. We know from ancient Hawaii, which in some ways resembled archaic Greece, that some peasants were required to work the lord's land without compensation every fifth day, on what were known as "fifth day patches."[7] In any event, Aristotle lists this *hektemor* status as a major ground of dissatisfaction. He also mentions another category of persons, called *pelatai*, about whom we know nothing.[8]

Many of those who managed to live free of servile status still suffered from a crushing burden of debt.[9] Much of the land was heavily mortgaged.[10] And a large class of nonslave but landless citizens became a potential source of civil strife. The cry for a redistribution of the land would resound intermittently in the Greek and Roman worlds for hundreds of years.

We have no lengthy description that illuminates these general conditions in Solon's time but we do have material from Rome. It is true that we cannot know how fictitious is Livy's description of the uprising of 495, but the force of the narrative leads us to believe that, if this particular incident did not happen, the social situation is accurately presented.

When they asked the reason of his condition and his squalor, he replied, while the crowd gathered about him much as though it were an assembly, that during his service in the Sabine war not only had the enemy's depredations deprived him of his crops, but his cottage had been burnt, all his belongings plundered, and his flocks driven off. Then the taxes had been levied, in an untoward moment for him, and he had contracted debts. When these had been swelled by usury, they had first stripped him of his farm which had been his father's and his grandfather's, then of the remnants of his property, and finally like an infection they attacked his person, and he had been carried off by his creditor, not to slavery, but to the prison and the torture chamber.[11]

From the biblical book of *Nehemiah* (5.3) we get this description of the same kind of tyrannical situation about the middle of the fifth century: "Some also there were that said, We have mortgaged our lands, vineyards, and houses, that we might buy corn, because of the dearth. There were also those that said, We have borrowed money for the king's tribute, and that upon our lands and vineyards . . . and, lo, we bring into bondage our sons and our daughters to be servants, and some of our daughters are brought unto bondage already: neither is it in our power to redeem them; for other men have our lands and our vineyards."[12] *Nehemiah* presents a powerful picture of, and pity for, human misery. Despite these conditions, however, we do not have one recorded instance of social strife or revolt from ancient Israel. The passive acceptance of penury and evil was not the mode, however, of the peasant-citizen of Athens and Rome.

No established monarchy or entrenched aristocracy gives up its power, or a significant part of it, unless the political situation accelerates to the point of violence, or the serious threat of violence. It is impossible to determine from our Athenian sources the degree of civil violence that prevailed before Solon's appointment, but it is clear that the threat of serious disorder was palpable. Solon himself wrote "They take no heed of the holy foundations of Justice, who in silence marks what happens and what has been, and who in course of time comes without fail to exact the penalty. Behold, there is coming now upon the whole state an injury that cannot be avoided; she has fallen swiftly into the evil of servitude, which awakens civil strife and war from their sleep—war that destroys many men in the bloom of their youth. By the work of the disaffected, swiftly our lovely city is being worn away, in those gatherings which are dear to unjust men."[13]

Aristotle, in describing the situation, emphasizes the threat of violence and the possible overthrow of the prevailing powers. "This being the political order and the many being serfs of the few, the common people rose against the upper class. When the civil discord had become violent and the two opposing parties had been set against each other for a long time, they chose, by mutual agreement, Solon as their mediator and Archon and entrusted the state to him."[14]

Plutarch adds that some were actually talking revolution, advising the people to choose a leader to set free those in debt, to redistribute the land, and to "make an entire change in the form of government."[15] Clearly, things could not remain as they were without some kind of explosion.

Because of Livy's narrative, our anecdotal material relating to civil violence is many times greater for Rome than for Athens. It can give us some sense of what things may have been like in Athens immediately before Solon's appointment. Continuing the narrative previously quoted about the debtor seized and tortured, Livy writes:

> He then showed them his back, disfigured with the wales of recent scourging. The sight of these things and the man's recital produced a mighty uproar. The disturbance was no longer confined to the forum but spread in all directions through the entire city. Those who had been bound over, whether in chains or not, broke out into the streets from every side, and implored the Quirites to protect them. At no point was

there any lack of volunteers to join the rising; everywhere crowds were streaming through the different streets and shouting as they hurried to the forum. Great was the peril of those senators who happened to be in the forum and fell in with the mob, which would not indeed have stopped short of violence had not the consuls . . . hurriedly intervened to put down the insurrection. But the crowd turned on them and displayed their chains and other hideous tokens. These, they cried, were the rewards they had earned, and they bitterly rehearsed the campaigns they had each served in various places. They demanded, in a manner much more threatening than suppliant, that the consuls should convene the senate; and they surrounded the Curia, that they might themselves witness and control the deliberations of the state.[16]

We cannot find the true *cause* of this kind of civil strife only in the economic and political degradation of the lower classes, because, in many other societies at many different times in history, such deprivations have been passively endured. What is remarkable about Athens and Rome is that the deprived classes, faced with economic ruin, rebelled and demanded an amelioration of their condition. Such a response is not predictable. The passivity of the proletariat, has for instance, plagued the leaders of revolutionary socialism since the beginnings of the nineteenth century. Many women remain passive today in the face of inequality and discrimination.

"Reform, amelioration, abolition came in Greece and Rome," writes M. I. Finley, "as a direct consequence of struggle from below, at times reaching genuinely revolutionary proportions; elsewhere the initiative came from above, from the rulers, in response to grumbling and dissatisfaction, no doubt, but on the whole with little effect, and *none at long range on the social system itself.*"[17] Solon not only relieved the burdens of the poor peasants but also fundamentally reformed the whole of society. In Rome, a different resolution, or irresolution, prevailed, as we shall see.

We find the flavor of this kind of rebellion, if not the actual facts, once again in Livy. In the year 494 "Aulus Verginius and Titus Vetusius then entered upon the consulship. Whereat the plebs, uncertain what sort of consuls they would prove to be, held nightly gatherings, some on the Esquiline and others on the Aventine. . . . This seemed to the consuls, as indeed it was, a mischievous practice." The consuls resorted to the senate for advice, and the latter advised the sternest resistance to these illegal actions.

> When the consuls, thus upbraided, asked the fathers what then they desired them to do, and promised that their conduct of the matter should be no whit less strenuous and stern than the senate wished, it was resolved that they should hold a levy with the utmost severity: it was idleness that made the plebeians lawless. Having adjourned the senate, the consuls mounted the tribunal and cited the young men by name. When no one answered to his name, the crowd, which surrounded the speaker as in a public meeting, declared that it was impossible to deceive the commons any longer; the consuls would never have a single soldier unless a public guarantee were given: liberty must first be restored to every man before arms were given him, that he might fight for his country and his fellow-citizens, not for a master.[18]

How and why such spirit entered the breasts of those impoverished visionaries, who imagined they could ameliorate the basic tyrannical nature of society by political action (violent, if necessary), is one of the great unanswered historical questions. We are the beneficiaries of their remarkable refusal to be passive victims.

Thus did rebellious activity raise the revolutionary cry for redistribution of the land and cancellation of debts that was to haunt the social struggles throughout the whole of ancient history until the collapse of the Roman republic. From Aristotle we have the first recorded instance of this demand. Of Solon, he says, "The common people had expected him to redivide all property."[19] That there was also an insistence on the cancellation of debts, we may assume from the fact that that is exactly what Solon ordered once he had the power.[20]

This call for redistribution and cancellation recurred insistently in Greek history. In 364, Clearchus became tyrant of the city of Heraclea Pontica after receiving the support of the people who "strove for the Redistribution of Land and Abolition of Debts."[21] After Philip of Macedon succeeded in totally dominating the Greek mainland in 338, he called a conference wherein the Greek states were forced into a league under Macedonian hegemony. Under the provisions of the league's articles, though each city-state was to preserve its autonomy, there was to be no cancellation of debts, no confiscation of property, and no redistribution of the land.[22] About sixty years later, when Macedonia became the scene of revolutionary action, Apollodoros became tyrant of Cassandreia and proceeded to confiscate the property of the rich and distribute it to the poor.[23]

Nothing illustrates more sharply the distinction between Athens and Rome than the aftermath of these crises in regard to the land policy for the small citizen-farmer. After the compromise settlement achieved by Solon, who did not redistribute the land, the cry was never again raised in Athens. Perhaps the problem of the individual peasant was permanently solved, or commercial and industrial interests and the needs of the large naval force ultimately provided urban jobs for displaced peasants, or the radical democracy gave the lower classes a sense of political empowerment and, therefore, the capacity to pursue economic goals through political means—about the true cause we can only speculate. In Rome, on the other hand, problems of land-poor citizens continued to plague its history. As late as the end of the second century, more than 350 years after the archaic crisis, Tiberius and Gaius Gracchus came close to revolutionizing the political structure of the state, citing the crying need for a more compassionate land policy for displaced citizens.

Democratic politics, though it many times seeks to avoid the issue, must always address the problem "What shall we do about the poor?" The remarkable fact of the archaic crises in Athens and Rome is that they raised this question with extraordinary urgency.

The Aspirations of the Nonnoble Rich

On the question of the existence in ancient society of economic classes— groups of people who act in concert on the political level because of the commonality of their perceived *economic* interests—it will be argued in a later chapter that postulating such classes, and political conflict between them, is a most reasonable theoretical stance, even for these precapitalist societies. It is a mistake to imagine, however, that the socioeconomic conflict between classes in ancient society took place only between the rich and the poor. The nonnoble rich, thirsting for political power and social status, were a significant force for social change during the archaic period.

At one time, under the influence of Marxist thought and the history of the rise of the bourgeoisie in Europe, historians of the ancient world surmised that these nonnoble rich represented a rising merchant class. We now know this to be untrue for Greece c. 600 and for Rome c. 500. We need no such hypothesis since the comparative study of peasant-agricultural societies in an aristocratic setting always reveals the significant presence of nonnoble wealthy peasants.

In Russia today one may visit an outdoor museum of old wooden structures showing the small hovel of the poor peasant and the complex residence of a rich peasant. True, the latter is no manor house, but it is worlds apart from the houses of the poor, and one can imagine many silver and gold coins buried beneath its floors. That such peasants were even capable of lending money to the great lords we know from actual historical information. In England, this class played a significant part in the political development which, though we cannot call it the rise of democracy, was certainly the beginning of political power for "the commons."

"The first representatives of those classes . . . of the well-to-do but non-noble and non-clerical portion of the population, to enter upon a political career were in England not the townsmen but the rural middle-class landholders. . . . More than once in the first half of the thirteenth century the king summoned 'discreet men,' 'knights' chosen by the sheriffs or elected in the county courts to attend consultations and give their advice."[24]

The limited evidence we have from Athens leaves no question of the existence of such a class in Solon's time. Solon's "creation of a new wealth-based upper-class [in opposition to a birth-based aristocracy] . . . indicates that prominent among his supporters were, as elsewhere, a small but influential group of non-noble rich who aspired to a role in Athenian society hitherto denied them."[25]

The comparative evidence from archaic Rome is again much more extensive, completely confirming the importance of the struggle of this class against the entrenched aristocracy. To be a plebeian and not a patrician did not signify that one was a landless person or an economically marginal peasant. There was a definite and significant plebeian elite that managed to achieve a near-equality to the patricians in matters of political power during the "conflict of the orders" that occupied the fifth and fourth centuries. The law of the Twelve Tables, in the middle of the fifth century, prohibited marriage between patricians and plebeians.[26] Obviously, no such law would be necessary unless there were plebeians that patricians would be tempted to marry. The law was ultimately repealed as the plebeian elite rose to social and political power.

Since both the plebeian elite and the economically disadvantaged peasants had complaints against the aristocracy, a natural, though complex and uneasy, alliance developed between them, both in Rome and Athens. The elite got most of what they wanted; the lower classes managed to obtain significant concessions, though they always remained extremely vulnerable to economic distress.

In Rome in the fourth century, "[T]he patrician monopoly of political and religious power and leadership was openly challenged for the first time by a plebeian upper class whose members had all the necessary qualifications to compete for the consulship except patrician status. Also in this phase ... some of the old economic grievances of the plebeian lower classes for the first time found at least partial redress."[27]

In Solon's Athens, as we shall see, a very similar social revolution that brought empowerment to the nonnoble rich did not take more than a century as in Rome, but was accomplished in one fell swoop, with permanent effect. The rich were never again denied their share of political power. In the process of enfranchising the economically powerful, the aristocratic powers-that-be were also forced to listen, to some significant degree, to the social-economic demands of the economically disadvantaged.

Going Beyond the Crises

Five possible outcomes suggest themselves in this situation of radical social-economic crisis: (1) successful revolt, (2) one-man rule, or tyranny, (3) intense and effective political repression, (4) an ambivalent alternation between repression and concession, continuing unresolution, (5) a deep and meaningful compromise.

Successful revolt. All the historical information we possess indicates that an effective revolution against the reigning aristocracy, either by the plebeian elite or the poor, or some combination of the two classes, was not a real possibility in the archaic world. The aristocracy had clearly rebelled successfully against the monarchy and taken full sovereignty unto itself. No society before the modern era even came close to eliminating the nobility as a potent political force.

Tyranny. The situation before Solon was chosen Archon was ripe for tyranny. This exact state of social strife produced many tyrants in the history of the Greek city-states: a politically stymied ambitious plebeian elite and an inflexible aristocracy.* So prevalent was this condition that Aristotle generalized it as a politically typical situation.

"Now at that time the disparity between the poor and the rich," Plutarch writes, "had reached what one may call its pitch, so that the state was altogether a-totter, and it seemed as though the only way in which it could be established and dissension stayed was if a tyranny should come into being."[29] Aristotle insists on the same inclination towards tyranny being present and adds that Solon frequently mentions the possibility of tyranny in his poems.[30] He writes that the people had expected Solon to redivide all property and that the wealthy had expected only the most minimum of compromise. Solon disappointed them both. He could have become a tyrant by choosing one side over the other, but he "preferred to be hated by both while saving his country and giving it the best constitution possible."[31]

Solon wrote

> Had someone else not like myself taken the reins, some ill-advised or greedy person, he would not have held the people in. Had I agreed to what pleased their adversaries [the nobles] at that time, or what they themselves planned to do against their enemies, our city would have been widowed of her men. Therefore, I put myself on guard at every side, and turned among them like a wolf inside a pack of dogs.[32]

When tyranny did arrive in Athens, with Pisistratus, nearly fifty years after Solon's Archonship, almost all Solon's political and economic reforms remained in place. The tyranny subsequently proved a remarkably benevolent one.

---

*In Syracuse, at the end of the fourth century, Agathocles overthrew the ruling oligarchy and established himself as tyrant by promising the *demos* to abolish indebtedness and redistribute the land. We are not told to what degree these promises were carried out, but judging by similar situations, we may assume something was done though hardly all the people had hoped for.[28]

Intense political repression and an ambivalent continuing unresolution. These possible modes of response are discussed together because they describe the two-hundred-year social history of Rome after the crisis of 495. Repression, like everything else, is a matter of degree. The reigning aristocracy may attempt to suppress all forms of political and economic demand, either from the plebeian elite or from the lowest economic classes. It may also make concessions to the nonnoble rich and join this group in repressing all other economic classes. Several variations are possible. The Roman republic witnessed *some* political and economic concessions to the lower classes (the establishment of the office of Tribune of the people; the abolition, eventually, of debt bondage) and *major* concessions to the very rich plebeians, who could now marry patricians and hold high political office. The degree of compromise and its complementary degree of repression are the crucial factors in determining whether a democratic society becomes possible.

It took almost two hundred years for Rome to work out its nondemocratic, slightly modified aristocratic solution to social conflict. At the time of the severe crisis of 495, it appeared that the society might go in one of several directions. In that year, after a particularly ugly incident in which the people threatened senators with violence, the Senate met to consider what should be done. The question, again, was how to respond to the demands for debt amelioration. Not surprisingly, there were moderate, radical, and severely repressive responses. Publius Verginius advised a moderate compromise: no general amnesty on debts, but relief for those who had served in certain recent wars. Titus Largius argued the radical position: "the whole commons was submerged in debt," and therefore there should be some kind of general lifting of the debt burden. Appius Claudius, the most repressive leader at this time, exhibited what can almost be called a fascist mentality: no compromise whatsoever. "It was not misery but license that had stirred up so great a hubbub." He concluded, "Come, let us appoint a dictator, from whom there is no appeal. At once this frenzy which has now set everything ablaze will be settled. Let anybody strike a lictor then, knowing that the right to scourge and behead him rests with one man whose majesty he has violated."

Appius Claudius' view prevailed and the dictator was appointed, but the Senate was wise enough to seek some compromise, especially as the Volsci, the Aequi, and the Sabines were all threatening Rome and the plebeians would be needed to fight. Appius sought the dictatorship himself, but was refused, and Manius Valerius, much respected by the plebs, was appointed instead. Thus, hope remained that the situation could still be stabilized.[33]

Despite certain disagreements among themselves, the Roman aristocracy was able over the years to present a much more united front in the face of lower-class demands than the aristocratic-oligarchic rulers of Greek city-states. "They could not do without the plebians, but they rarely gave them a chance to exhibit internal dissension, and they never made more than the absolute minimum of concessions."[34] No factor is more important in explaining why democracy never became a reality in Roman society.

Deep and meaningful compromise. If it were not for the history of Athens, we would be forced to declare this last "possibility" as impossible as the first one on our list (successful revolt). Solon and Athens, however, accomplished something that no other archaic society ever succeeded in doing. It is instructive to examine in detail this remarkable achievement.

Conditions Necessary for Compromise

An essential condition for producing the kind of social compromise effectuated by Solon is that the empowered aristocracy be ambivalent and disunited on the question of how severely the rebellion should be crushed. "A harmonious oligarchy," Aristotle wrote, "does not easily cause its own destruction"[35]—an idea echoed in the twentieth century by Lenin and Mao Tse-tung.[36]

In Greece and Rome the rebellious challenge from below was met by a complex response from those in power. A significant proportion of the aristocracy agreed that some compromise with the demands of the poor should be made. Solon was himself an aristocrat of moderate wealth and power. From the sparse evidence from Athens and Rome we cannot determine whether the sympathetic response arose from moral recognition of validity in the demands of the poor or from a pure utilitarian conception that the health of society demanded a compromise that would result in peace between the classes. Knowing the complexity of human beings, the response was probably an intricate combination of both factors. A comparative study of nineteenth-century England and Russia in the early twentieth century would probably reveal much more about aristocratic and oligarchic responses to demands for democratization.

In Athens, the significant piece of evidence that the ruling powers were willing to compromise is the fact that Solon did not seize power, like a tyrant, but was appointed, *with almost general consent*.[37] The philosopher Democritus reflected in the fifth century on what made the choice of Solon as arbitrator for Athens possible: "He finds the only possible answer to lie in some ethics of consent on the part of the privileged classes of that period . . . discord in Solonian Athens did not come to the breaking point; it proved negotiable."[38]

At this point I can only raise, but not even try to answer, some questions of enormous import. What made the Roman aristocracy capable of accommodation within rather narrow limits? What made the Athenian aristocracy capable of making concessions of an order never seen before in the history of the world? What made other aristocratic-oligarchic societies, such as Sparta, totally incapable of compromise? Does the answer lie in the amount of pressure exerted from below? Were Athenian *Thetes* (the lowest class) capable of a sustained rebellious mood the impoverished Roman plebeians could not match? Or does the answer lie in the complex and subtle dynamics of relationships between the three economic classes: aristocracy, rich peasants, and the poor? Could it be that something in the spirit of Athenian aristocracy recognized a limit below which a citizen should not be pushed, that even the poorest citizen had the right to remain a citizen and not a slave? One cannot read the poetry of Solon without recognizing that something remarkably human existed in that culture, a sense of the reality of the existence of others, no matter how poor they might be, something the Romans (and certainly the Spartans) would never come to understand.

> *Into this sacred land, our Athens, I brought back*
> *a throng of those who had been sold, some by due law,*
> *though others wrongly; some by hardship pressed to escape*
> *the debts they owed; and some of these no longer spoke*
> *Attic, since they had drifted wide around the world,*
> *while those in the country had the shame of slavery*

upon them, and they served their masters' moods in fear.
These I set free; and I did this by strength of hand,
welding right law with violence to a single whole.[39]

What we find throughout ancient history is that not only does the aristocracy—in some cases—have the capacity to compromise but also that members of the aristocracy become leaders of the democratic movement. Solon, though of moderate wealth, was by birth a member of the high aristocracy; his father was said to be descended from Codrus, an early king of Athens. The fact that he was chosen Archon, an office open only to those of noble birth, confirms his aristocratic origin.[40] In the fifth century, after the death of his political mentor Ephialtes, Pericles became the leader of the forces that instituted the radical democracy in Athens. He was of the highest aristocratic birth. And in Rome, when the last great attempt at truly revolutionary change was instigated in the late second century, the leaders of the rebellion, Tiberius and Gaius Gracchus, came from the highest social order. Their father had been a censor; their mother was the daughter of the great Scipio Africanus who had defeated Hannibal; Tiberius' father-in-law was Appius Claudius, a powerful patrician; Gaius was son-in-law to Publius Crassus, the wealthiest man in Rome. Both Appius and Crassus supported Tiberius' reforms.[41]

So important is this phenomenon that it has led the historian de Ste. Croix to state "no democratic revolution had much chance of success, or of leading to a stable democracy, unless the impoverished masses received leadership from some members of the governing class."[42] This was certainly true in the ancient world. If individual members of the aristocracy could go so far as to become leaders of the *demos*, they must have been capable of sympathy with the demands of the underprivileged. This being so, it is reasonable to postulate that this sympathy also pervaded other members of the noble class, with no desire to become political leaders in opposition to the aristocracy but representing a powerful force ready to compromise on matters of social policy, as in the case of Tiberius Gracchus. We should not underestimate this capacity of the most powerful in society to identify with the aims of economic and political democracy. It—or its almost total absence— may well be one of the most important factors determining the outcome of social struggle.

Since there are always *some* members of the ruling class inclined toward concessions and even ready to lead the *demos* toward its aspirations, and always *some* members eager to meet any rebellion with total repression, the final outcome becomes dependent on the numbers of aristocrats holding each position, and their relative power. An important factor is how much rivalry the ruling forces exhibit *amongst themselves*, and how this rivalry expresses itself in differential positions toward the demands of the *demos*. In the Greek world it often happened that intense rivalry between members of the aristocracy opened the door to economic and political remedy. In the city of Heraclea Pontica an attack by Athens in 424 was followed by a revolution that overthrew the established oligarchy. Though there was a preexisting potential for a popular rebellion, the immediate occasion of the revolt was a conflict amongst oligarchs. A certain Eurytion, a member of the oligarchy, was prosecuted by his enemies on a charge of adultery and forced to suffer the humiliation of being placed in the stocks in the agora. Seeking revenge, he engineered a political coup with the aid of his friends, and probably with the tacit support of the *demos*. After seizing power, he broke the aristocratic monopoly on office holding, instituted pay for military service and possibly for political service as well, and substantially increased the power of the popular assembly. Like Solon, however, he stopped at certain measures and did not redistribute the land and even left unchanged the high property qualification for membership in the Council.[43]

This inclination and capacity of certain members of the aristocracy to assume leadership of the *demos*, and the willingness—perhaps even necessity, since it lacks leaders of its own—of the *demos* to accept such leadership, produces in some circumstances a particular form of corruption: an upper-class "demagogue" using the people for his own egoistic purposes in a struggle for power against rival oligarchs. The *demos* usually gets very little and finds its trust betrayed. The history of the Greek city-states provides us with many such examples, and, in Rome, Livy tells us, in the year 385 Marcus Manlius Capitolinus became "the first of all the patricians to turn demagogue and to cast in his lot with the plebeian magistrates. He abused the nobles, he courted the favor of the plebs; and swept along by the breath of popularity and not by good counsel chose rather to be reputed great than virtuous. Moreover, not content with agrarian proposals, which had ever served the tribunes to stir up sedition, he began an attack on credit; for he held that debt was a sharper goad, since it not only threatened poverty and shame, but terrified the freeman with the thought of shackles and imprisonment."[44] The permanent benefit for the people of all this political turmoil was almost nil. The Roman lower classes never learned how to take power for themselves, over and over again putting their hopes and trust in leaders they assumed would take good care of them, and participating in a degraded vicarious sense of power. "You boast that you are Lords of the World," Tiberius Gracchus exhorted them, "but you do not possess a foot of land which you can call your own."[45] During the first century, in the civil wars that destroyed the Republic, some leaders such as Marius or Caesar were known as *populares*, meaning they were supposed to represent the interests of the plebs. They did institute certain measures that satisfied economic demands, but they never had any intention of giving the people real political power.

Thoughtful historians have puzzled over this fundamental difference between the city-states in Greece that succeeded in establishing democratic constitutions and Rome. "Instead of working towards thorough-going constitutional reforms," de Ste. Croix writes, "the Roman lower classes tended to look for, and put all their trust in, leaders whom they believed to be . . . 'on their side.' " He offers an interpretation of the difference: "One explanation . . . was the existence at Rome, of a whole series of insidious forms, of the institution of patronage and clientship, from which most of the Greek cities (Athens especially) seem to have been largely free."[46]

This explanation however, merely pushes the basic questions one step deeper. Why, we may ask, did Roman culture institutionalize dependency, patronage, and clientship while some Greek city-states did not? Why were the lower classes in Rome so easily corrupted by the promise of protection? Clientage and patronage are symptoms of a basic passivity in the Roman people, not its cause. Maybe, at this point in our historical understanding, we can do no more than assert that the lower classes in Greece had a certain spiritedness that was absent in Rome. That spirit may have made all the difference.

Solon: Overcoming the Paranoid Position

To return to the central situation we are trying to understand—the complex value system in Athens at the time of Solon—we can reflect again on the fact that the crisis was resolved by compromise, and compromise meant exactly that: no one class got all it wanted; the human inclination for absolute tyranny, on the one hand, and for true equality, on the other, were both denied. The crisis was resolved neither by a successful rebellion of lower classes nor by a regimen of total repressive terror by the aristocracy. Crucial for the future of Athens, the poorer elements in society received enough economic amelioration and juridical power to maintain their dignity as citizens. Solon, the great spokesman for this resolution, reflected something very powerful in the society that allowed for mature, sane behavior. "To the common people I have given such a measure of privilege as sufficeth them, neither robbing them of the rights they had, nor holding out the hope of greater ones; and I have taken equal thought for those who were possessed of power and who were looked up to because of their wealth, careful that they, too, should suffer no indignity. I have taken a stand which enables me to hold a stout shield over both groups, and I have allowed neither to triumph unjustly over the other."[47]

All societies are held together either by virtue or by naked force, in most cases, by a complex combination of both. Force includes tyranny, terror, torture, and economic dependency. Virtue includes citizenship, civic virtue, respect for the law, the eros of sharing common goals and values. Solon helped transform Athens at this time of social crisis by insisting that virtue, rather than force, would have the most prominent part in social cohesion. In almost biblical language, he gives us this paean to law and justice:

These are the lessons which my heart bids me teach the Athenians, how that lawlessness brings innumerable ills to the state, but obedience to the law shows forth all things in order and harmony and at the same time sets shackles on the unjust. It smooths what is rough, checks greed, dims arrogance, withers the opening blooms of ruinous folly, makes straight the crooked judgement, tames the deeds of insolence, puts a stop to the works of civil dissension, and ends the wrath of bitter strife. Under its rule all things among mankind are sane and wise.[48]

In Rome, no one with political power ever had that kind of vision of justice. In Israel, no one with this vision ever held political power. In Athens, miraculously, the vision and the power came together in one remarkable moment.

4

The Founding Miracle:
Compromise, Reconciliation,
and Continuing Strife

When Solon was elected Archon, chief executive officer of the Athenian state, in 594, it was no ordinary appointment. He was to be Archon with extraordinary powers to decree legislation and to revise the entire structure of government.[1] His fundamental task was to heal the rift between rich and poor and restore Athens, if possible, to a sense of social cohesiveness, to reaffirm the feeling of one united polity. Solon was a perfect choice: "He was chosen archon to succeed Philombrotus, and made mediator and legislator for the crisis, the rich accepting him readily because he was well-to-do, and the poor because he was honest."[2] Acceptable to both sides, he possessed a remarkable vision of what could and could not be done within that society.

Though Aristotle states that Solon was "the first champion of the people,"[3] all indications are that he championed neither the rich nor the poor. The one class that got most, if not all, of what it wanted was the class in the middle, the rich peasants, the plebeian elite. Solon's intent was to give to the poor what he felt they were entitled to and no more: "To the demos I have given such a measure of privilege as is sufficient, neither robbing them of their former rights nor holding out the hope of greater."[4] As a result of his compromise, the *demos* neither ruled nor reigned, though its economic distress was greatly ameliorated and the people had more political and judicial rights than they had previously possessed. It is clear that Solon mistrusted the capacity of the common people to rule; he said "The *demos* will best follow its leaders when it is neither driven by violence nor given too free a rein."[5]

It is really not anachronistic to describe Solon as a liberal. He rejected both the radical rich and the radical poor, holding to the ideal of a limited sovereignty, a polity ruled by elites who maintained sufficient compassion for the disadvantaged. Plutarch remarks, "In this he pleased neither party, for the rich were angry for their money and the poor that the land was not divided."[6] None of our sources, however, including Aristotle who was dedicated to the idea that a "middle-class" society was the most stable and most just, mentions that the nonnoble rich, as we shall see, had very little to complain of.

Though committed to an ideal of justice, Solon was no ideologue, recognizing that the inadequacies of human nature place a severe limit on what can be accomplished in one generation. When asked if he had given the Athenians the best laws possible, he answered "The best they would receive."[7]

Before examining in detail how Solon went about his work, it can be profitable to try to imagine the ideal of society he carried in his mind. No great political leader does his work without some ideal conception of what society should look like. It is not anachronistic, I believe, to imagine that Solon's ideal was close to our own: liberal, bourgeois, democratic. Bourgeois, in that the monopoly of political power held by the aristocracy was seriously curbed and in that private property and the power of money-wealth became sacred. Money was now to rule society; no poor aristocrat, no matter how high his birth, could exert political power unless he had wealth or very close connections with wealth. Democratic, in that even the poor would have some say in government and, most especially, in the courts. Liberal, to the degree that a limit was set on how much degradation a citizen could be subject to. And, finally, liberal and bourgeois in that the way was opened for social mobility but the society continued to be ruled by elites. To the elites of birth were added those of wealth. Room was even made within the elite for people with intellectual, political, or military talent. I am fully cognizant of the danger of projecting back into ancient society our own problems and ideals, but I wonder how different the ideals of the limited, precapitalist, slave democracy established by our Founding Fathers were from the vision of Solon.

For the poor, Solon abolished the institution of debt slavery. He abrogated the status of the *hektemoroi*, those required to give up one-sixth of their harvest. He brought back from foreign slavery as many former Athenian citizens as he could find.[8] He even went so far as to cancel all existing debts.

"When he had taken power," Aristotle writes, "Solon freed the people both then and for the future by making loans on the security of a person's freedom illegal; he passed laws, and instituted a cancellation of debts both private and public which men called *seisachtheia*, for they shook off their burdens."[9] The cancellation of debts also included the revocation of land mortgages:

> *I call to witness at the judgement seat of time*
> *one who is noblest, Mother of Olympian*
> *divinities, and greatest of them all, Black Earth.*
> *I took away the mortgage stones stuck in her breast,*
> *and she, who went a slave before, is now set free.*[10]

Debt slavery and the position of the *hektemoroi* were abolished for all time. Money debts and land mortgages a bourgeois liberal society cannot, of course, live without. It was a one-time attempt to restore the harmony of the *polis*. After that, with the exception of the enslavement of citizens, business returned to normal.

The political empowerment of the rich peasants and the destruction of the political monopoly of the aristocracy were accomplished by one simple, elegant change in the constitution. Most classical historians agree (though some strongly disagree) that before Solon there were three property classes in Athens: *Hippeis*, who, as the name implies, were capable of maintaining a horse and using it in military exercises, the assumption being that only aristocrats belonged to this class; *Zeugitai*, who were able to afford the armor of a hoplite and fought in hoplite ranks; and *Thetes*, the remainder of the citizenry down to the poorest of the poor.

Solon did two revolutionary things. He created a new class at the very top of the structure, the *Pentakosiomedimnoi*, and he set an *economic* definition for each class, based on the amount of harvest a man's property produced each year. To be entitled to *Zeugites* status, one's property had to yield two hundred measures of harvest, either wheat or olives. *Hippeus* status required three hundred measures. *Pentakosiomedimnoi* required five hundred measures, the name meaning "five-hundred-measure men," taking one as far from an aristocratic ideal as one could imagine.[11]

The various state offices, including the very highest of Archon and Treasurer, were now distributed to several classes according to property qualifications.[12] It is generally assumed that only *Pentakosiomedimnoi* could become Treasurers and that the other most important offices went only to the first two classes.[13] Since ex-Archons automatically became members of the highest government body, the Council of the Areopagus, the new constitutional change brought the nonnoble into that body. In essence, this revolutionary change meant that, except for the usual status considerations reflecting birth that always exist, wealth became a fundamental measure of the man in Athens. It was the first "bourgeois revolution."

In the long, 2,600-year struggle to achieve equality within human society, sometimes subsumed under the concept of "rights," a particular pattern develops. The poor—and the poor are the problem—first achieve judicial rights, then political rights. Having secured these two, the struggle begins for economic rights and for gender equality, a struggle we are in the midst of today. When the process begins, the poor are granted and/or achieve equality before the law, at least in the ideal. We know that wealth or its absence still makes true judicial equality impossible. Solon's Athens made an extraordinary advance toward judicial equality though the poor remained almost totally excluded from political power.

Fourth-century Athenian historians, including Aristotle, believed that Solon brought the lowest class, the *Thetes*, into the Assembly for the first time. This is seriously doubted by many present-day historians, who consider it too revolutionary a step, one that the moderate Solon would not have taken.[14] They believe that the lowest class was already represented in the Assembly before Solon's time. There are indications that during the sixth century, the Assembly did contain elements of the poorest class.[15] Lacking definite information, one can only speculate. The historians Hignett and Stavely cannot imagine that the *Thetes* attended the Assembly before Solon,[16] and yet, comparative data from Rome indicate that an Assembly could be open to all and society still be completely controlled by the reigning aristocracy. We do not know when the assemblies of the Greek city-states and of Rome were first established. My own inclination is to regard them as ancient institutions brought to the Mediterranean lands by the very first invasions of the Indo-European peoples. One can imagine them enjoying a certain primitive democracy, analogous to the full meetings of all warriors among the barbarian tribes who overran Europe during and after the collapse of the Roman Empire.

As the conquering Indo-European warriors settled on the land they had overwhelmed, differences in wealth and political power developed to the point where a powerful, small aristocracy ruled and a large mass of poor became political and economic subjects. The Assembly, where all male members of the *polis* gathered together, would still meet. It would be the one institution where the concept of citizenship, which implies a certain moderate, but definite, degree of equality, could originate and be confirmed. As has been stated, there was a unique spirit within the economically oppressed classes in archaic Greece and Rome that refused to remain completely passive when faced with economic catastrope; it would not be surprising to discover that some institutional means nurtured that spirit. It is not unreasonable to surmise that all citizens could attend the Assembly, both before and after Solon, though real power remained with the aristocracy and its Council of the Areopagus, just as real power remained with the Senate in archaic Rome.

Whatever the true circumstances, it is clear that Solon added almost nothing to the political potency of the poor. The chief magistrates were chosen only from the first two classes and the powerful Council of the Areopagus was controlled exclusively by aristocrats and the nonnoble rich.[17] We have definite indications that the Archonship was not opened to the third class until 457, fifty years after the democratic reforms of Cleisthenes.[18] Hignett estimates that in the time of Solon the two top classes represented no more than one-fifteenth of the citizen body.[19] Historians today are in disagreement over whether Solon created a new Council of Four Hundred, one hundred from each of the four tribes, to counter the influence of the Areopagus. If he did set up such a Council, we know absolutely nothing of how it worked and, therefore, have no way of knowing whether or not it was an instrument of democratization. We may also doubt whether that particular political empowerment, if it did exist, reached down into the two bottom classes.

In the matter of judicial rights, however, Solon took revolutionary measures. He provided that in the courts, in Aristotle's words: "Anyone might seek redress on behalf of those who were wronged."[20] There were to be no restrictions on who could appeal to the courts. Living in a society like ours, totally dominated by lawyers in judicial matters, we find it remarkable that throughout its whole history Athens never developed the institution of the bar. Eventually, especially in the fourth century, certain individuals earned handsome incomes by writing speeches for those pleading in the courts, but prosecutions, defenses, and appeals always remained a personal matter, undertaken by the individuals involved. Athens never developed the office of public prosecutor. All civil and criminal actions had to be brought by individuals. Aristotle emphasizes that the opening of judicial actions to all citizens, regardless of property class, was one of Solon's most important democratic measures.

The reforms went even further. Previous to Solon, the Council of the Areopagus had clearly acted as a court to try cases, certainly criminal cases. Solon established new courts, open to all the people, to which appeal could be made against the verdict of a magistrate.[21] Aristotle writes: "The feature which is said to have contributed most to the strength of the democracy [was] the right of appeal to the *dikasterion* [jury court], for when the people have the right to vote in the courts they control the constitution."[22]

We may be skeptical about how much the *demos* was able to control the constitution under the prevailing circumstances, but the right to sit on juries was a crucial one. Such activity becomes a school for democracy wherein the capacity for citizenship develops apace. If a person's judgment may be accepted in a jury trial, it becomes no tremendous step to assert that his judgment may be equally valid in the politics of the state. Since courts and the judicial process are supposed to promote justice—and often do—whereas the state remains concerned with who dominates whom, it may be by reason of this contrast, that the great human impulse toward equality first shows itself in the judicial process.*

Was it a democracy, a proto-democracy, on-the-road-to democracy,

---

*Later in this book, I discuss the importance of law in overcoming the paranoid position. Since the paranoid position includes the necessity of domination, law, by overcoming the paranoid position, necessarily allies itself with equality.

or a thing in itself? Democracy almost defies definition, for if we mean by "democracy" true equality between all adult members of society, excluding neither women, nor minorities, nor the poor, then there never has been a democratic society. All societies we call "democratic" would be, by this definition, only imperfect representations of democracy. By what right do we call Athenian society of the latter part of the fifth century a "radical democracy," when it excluded women, slaves, and foreign residents? Is it sufficient that all adult males shared some kind of equality and shared in political decision making? Where does one draw the line of exclusion? If nine thousand Spartan citizens, known as "equals," tyrannically oppress a much larger society, and yet share, amongst themselves, a strict equality, is that a democracy? And what of the five hundred or so nobles who ruled the Republic of Venice, sharing the autocratic rule equally with each other? Obviously, there is no mathematical formula that can be applied to this question.

I believe that there are, and have been, societies it is proper to designate as "democratic," even though they have excluded from sovereignty more people than they have included. Athens in the fifth and fourth centuries and the United States at its founding, when it excluded women, slaves, and most of the poor, were both democracies. We have to go beyond mathematics to something more ambiguous. The Greeks themselves provide us with one powerful insight. By the end of the fifth century, most political discussion contrasted two fundamentally different kinds of constitutions: democratic and oligarchic.[23] An oligarchy is government by the few; democracy means government by the people, the word *demos* meaning "the people" or what we might call "the common people." Many English scholars translate the term as "the commons." The contrast between oligarchy and democracy became, in political thought, a contrast between the few and the many.

"Our constitution," Thucydides has Pericles say in the famous funeral oration, "does not copy the laws of neighboring states; we are rather a pattern to others than imitators ourselves. *Its administration favours the many instead of the few; that is why it is called a democracy.*"[24] Aristotle defines all constitutions as giving sovereignty either to One, or Few, or Many; each category is represented by two typical forms of society. *One*: monarchy and tyranny. *Few*: aristocracy and oligarchy. *Many*: polity (a limited or mixed democracy) and democracy.[25]

The concept that democracy is government by the many has great value. It goes beyond numbers to conceive of democracy as a *process*. To sympathetically describe a polity as one in which many are sovereign implies a value judgment that rule by many is *better* than rule by a few. Further, if *many* is better than *few*, then *most* is better than *many*, and *all* may be the ultimate goal. A truly democratic society, deep within the system of values, implies that politics is not static but somehow aims toward a goal, a *telos*. That is why nine thousand Spartan "equals" or five hundred Venetian high nobles represent nothing of democracy; their equality is merely amongst each other. Their only accomplishment is to make of these societies governments of the few, rather than of the one. Oligarchies, precisely. They aim toward no *telos*; they are perfect as they are, closed societies with no intention of changing, with no important ambivalence about the exclusion of most from political power.

Democratic societies, in contrast, almost invariably give utterance to ideals of equality far beyond the reality found in these polities. The *future* is included in the democratic ideal. Jefferson's pronouncement that all men are created equal is a familiar one. Pericles, in the funeral oration just quoted, goes on to say: "If we look at the laws, they afford equal justice to all in their private differences; if to social standing, advancement in public life falls to reputation for capacity, class considerations not being allowed to interfere with merit; nor again does poverty bar the way, if a man is able to serve the state, he is not hindered by the obscurity of his condition. The freedom which we enjoy in our government extends also to our ordinary life."[26] One need know nothing of Greek history to know that such pronouncements describe an *ideal* state; no such equality has existed in any historical human society. These ideals of equality are nevertheless necessary to a democratic society. When such a society begins to lose touch with, or care little for, not only the reality but also the *ideal of equality*, the democracy may be in danger of passing over to some other form of society.

It may be helpful, for theoretical insight, to consider this splitting between ideal and reality, a condition we too easily take for granted since it pervades totally our political and personal lives. It is made possible only by a particular psychological operation. We would like to know what is going on in the psyche when a person passionately, and with great sincerity, states that all-men-are-created-equal and yet has no intention of seeing women, black slaves, and the poor as "men," at least for now. What relationship, if any, has this particular psychological mode to the concept of the paranoid position being elaborated here? Unfortunately, we cannot even come close to answering that question. To answer it, we need to know more than we know at present about the workings of the psychological mechanism of splitting.

First elaborated by Melanie Klein, it represents a very primitive (that is, developmentally early) mode of psychic defense. The psychoanalyst Otto Kernberg, who has done fundamental work on the pathology of borderline psychotics, has asserted that splitting is the primary mechanism for people with borderline pathologies, whereas repression is the primary mode of defense for neurotics. The recourse to splitting represents a greater degree of psychopathology.

We have learned that an individual may advance far into adult life and function extremely well in a complex modern world, and yet carry with him or her, almost completely untransformed, some very primitive views of reality and modes of defense. The same may well be true of societies. It is not only that Pericles and Jefferson were personally deeply conflicted and split but also that the value systems of the societies for which they were the most extraordinary spokesmen carried the same kind of deep, almost borderline psychological splitting. A passionate commitment to the ideal of equality, combined with an equally powerful capacity to exclude most people from grace, is a signal that symptoms of borderline pathology can be active even within a democratic polity. It may be asked how much this could eventually help us understand the deep motives for warfare, imperialism, and slavery.

The average democratic society thus represents a culture in moral conflict between ideal and reality. A good portion of its history consists of how it does, or does not, resolve that conflict. If the extension of democratic equality to all people involves the closing of the fissure produced by splitting, then it is not inappropriate to remark that the process of full democratization is one by which a society attains health.

If a democratic society, though it be an imperfect reality, is moving toward a perfect equality; if it contains within its system of values a *telos*, a goal toward which it is striving; if the ideal has importance equal to the reality—if all this is so, there is a way in which all democratic societies are related to all others, a way in which each participates in some grand, ideal historical evolution. I observe two fundamental patterns of political and moral evolution in regard to democracy, moral because that which evolves toward equality is, by definition, moral.[27] This connection between equality, morality, and justice was made, according to J. Walter Jones, by St. Thomas Aquinas who "saw more deeply into the true meaning of justice when he wrote that it is the function of justice to lead unequals to equality, and that only when this equality has been achieved is the task of justice performed."[28]

The first evolutionary pattern of democratic societies concerns rights. Equality before the law is the first stage; equality in the political realm (one person, one vote) is the second stage. These achieved, gender equality and economic equality are immediately placed on the democratic agenda. (Racism debilitates democratic evolution in those societies wherein it is a fundamental problem.) Since we are currently deep into the struggle to establish gender and economic rights, and since the ambivalence about granting such rights is at fever pitch in most democratic societies, it is difficult to know how long the struggle will go on, how many way stations there may be on the road to equality, how many regressions and repressions we will suffer. It is equally difficult to know what economic equality might mean in this post-Gorbachev, post-Mitterand world where communism is a dead letter and nobody knows what socialism is. Economic equality may turn out to mean only that no one is allowed to suffer economic catastrophe or debilitation.

In ancient Athens, the most advanced democracy of the classical world, only the first two stages of judicial and political equality were reached. Even the ideal of Athenian democracy never included women or freeing slaves. The sense that democracy is a process toward equality explains why many historians of ancient society write about Athens as though it reached its political acme in the fifth century B.C. and as though the fourth century was, somehow, a political and moral anticlimax, suffering from some kind of moral entropy. The truth is that fourth-century Athens was a vigorous, stable, healthy democratic state. No oligarchic counterrevolution threatened its democratic status; participation by the lower classes in political life was as vigorous as ever.[29] But Athenian democracy had fulfilled its ideal; there was no more promise, only everyday reality. Gender equality, the end of slavery, the achievement of some sort of economic equality were not on the agenda.

Within the terms and ideals of that society, further moral political progress was impossible. It is the unconscious perception of these facts that makes some historians speak of the fifth century as the great age of Athenian democracy, because in the fifth century, with the achievement of the radical democracy, Athens fulfilled the extent of its promise. In the fourth century, no matter how remarkable the polity, little, if any, revolutionary fervor remained. Once again, charismatic politics had given way to bureaucracy, though a bureaucracy of an amazingly high order.

The second evolutionary pattern that I observe in the overarching world history of democracy and political equality has three stages. The first stage is the great-refusal-to-become-a-victim. This involves no universal statements about the rights of man and very little concern with whether or not justice is done to others. It celebrates the triumph of activity over passivity. The politically and economically oppressed use their greater numbers as a power instrument to take citizens' rights unto themselves. Once that goal is achieved, there is little or no concern for others who may lack rights. The political activity of the rising bourgeoisie in the cities of early modern Europe illustrates this stage, as does the bread-and-butter unionism of the American Federation of Labor in the first fifty years of its existence, when it consciously resisted attempts to universalize the struggle of labor against capital, pursuing only immediate (and attainable) economic interests.

The second stage in this developmental series occurs when the struggle for political or economic rights becomes generalized and universalized. This happens for the first time only with the rise of Liberalism: Locke's life, liberty, and property and Jefferson's pursuit of happiness being two of the most succinct statements of this universal justice. Liberal, bourgeois, capitalist democracy is the great product of this struggle for an ideal universality of rights. We are well aware how many people may be excluded from sovereignty under this kind of constitution, but the ideal is crucial and must be kept alive if the struggle to include more and more groups within the sovereignty is to succeed.

The third stage in this evolutionary series is reached when the society is capable of demonstrating real sympathy with the disadvantaged living within the polity. Our present democratic society demonstrates a profound ambivalence about taking, or not taking, the steps necessary to advance into that third stage. Economic rights, whatever exactly they might be, are crucial to this effort.

It seems fair and accurate to say, regarding these developmental stages, that Athenian democracy had successfully entered only the first stage. Not until democracy was born again, in modern Europe, was the second stage reached. Athenian democracy was, essentially, egotistical, though no democratic society can live without some ideals. In Athens, however, there were no statements about the universal rights of man, no important ambivalence about the oppression of women or of slaves. It was utilitarian and it worked for those who were members of the club. It worked amazingly well. Other Greek states, such as Argos and Syracuse, tried democratic systems at various times in their history. None of them demonstrated the stability and democratic responsibility of Athens. One may criticize Athens for not having accomplished more but has one's own society accomplished as much?

Considering the argument that democracy is not a static reality but a process toward an ideal goal of equality, we should not regard the notion of stages too strictly. No clear lines are drawn and there is much overlapping. Once the democratic ideal is set in motion, its full potentiality may become visible at certain times or to certain individuals. We should not be surprised to find Demosthenes in the latter part of the fourth century expressing these rather "advanced" sentiments: "He who claims your indulgence as having acted for the good of the commonwealth must be shown to possess the spirit of the commonwealth. That spirit is a spirit of compassion for the helpless, and of resistance to the intimidation of the strong and powerful; it does not inspire brutal treatment of the populace, and subservience to the potentates of the day."[30] The "spirit of the commonwealth" projects, always, an ideal nature, a kind of idealization unusual in Athens. Athenian democrats fought gloriously for their own interests, but would have understood no political pronouncement that began "All men."

To return, then, to the question raised some distance back as to what kind of society Solon left Athens. Whether or not it can be labeled a "democracy," it was a society squarely on the road toward democracy. No guarantees could be made that the polity would reach the goals set for it, but neither could there be any question as to its direction. The lower classes, threatening civil violence, had refused to remain victims. The powers that be had responded by granting judicial rights to all male citizens and full political rights to the nonnoble rich. No one could imagine how far the society might travel. With hindsight, we can see that an enormous potential had been unleashed.

Crucial to the reality and the potential was the fact that the Solonian compromise had been made possible only by a commitment to trust. Aggravated civil strife and civil war had been avoided because the potentially warring classes decided they might trust each other. Both rich and poor put their faith first in Solon and second in the social and economic program he decreed. Solon did not leave Athens in any near-utopian situation—in the short run, in fact, the compromise almost completely broke down—but a remarkable assertion had been made within the value system of the polity. Having achieved a basic level of trust, people might deal rationally with the problems of society. More of virtue and less of violence was to hold society together.

The founding miracle proved alas, to be only a man-made miracle, not God-decreed. No gates of paradise opened up; made by men, it could easily be rescinded by these same men. Solon, himself, was profoundly pessimistic as to whether his compromise would provide permanent political stability. He left the country, hoping the Athenians could work together under his laws without his presence.

"Now when these laws were enacted, and some came to Solon every day, to commend or dispraise them, and to advise, if possible, to leave out or put in something, and many criticised, and desired him to explain, and tell the meaning of such and such a passage, he, knowing that to do it was useless, and not to do it would get him ill-will, and desirous to bring himself out of all straits, and to escape all displeasure and exceptions, it being a hard thing as he himself says,

In great affairs to satisfy all sides,

as an excuse for travelling, bought a trading vessel, and, having leave for ten years' absence, departed, hoping that by that time his laws would have become familiar."[31]

Aristotle tells us that for four years things were peaceful in Athens, "but in the fifth year after his Archonship they did not appoint an Archon because of the dissension, and four years later the same thing happened again for the same reason."[32] Renewed civil strife brought the imminent possibility of tyranny. After another four years, a certain aristocrat named Damasias was elected Archon and in an obvious attempt at establishing a tyranny, remained in office for two years and two months until he was "forcibly removed."[33] We cannot know whether the aristocrat Damasias represented the interests of his class or whether he allied himself with the nonnoble rich and/or the poor to continue the antiaristocratic thrust of Solon's revolution.[34]

Once again, to put an end to "the civil strife," the Athenians decided to try to compromise. Ten Archons were chosen, five from the nobles, and five from the nonnobles (three "men of the country and two from the artisans"[35]—whatever these expressions may mean). I will deal at length later with the concept that all city-states have been plagued with an inordinate amount of violent class conflict. It is remarkable to observe how similar situations of civil strife may produce almost exactly the same institutions to deal with it. We read this narrative of class conflict and compromise about 1,800 years after the post-Solonian period:

> In the 1190s the "simple citizens" of Milan were the main source of communal revenues, yet they were entitled to only one-fifth of the places in the consulate. In 1198 the fully organized *popolo* suddenly broke in upon the Milanese scene, as the commune passed fitfully over to podestaral rule, and for the next fourteen years Milan had alternating periods of civil war and deeply divided government. With the intervention of the Emperor Otto IV, a major settlement was agreed upon in 1212; and from this time on, half of all offices of the commune were to go to the *popolo*, the other half to the nobility.[36]

Many Italian cities of this period had recourse to the same mathematical attempt to resolve social conflict. Milan and almost all the other city-states of northern Italy, after intense periods of civil strife, ended up as monarchies of one form or another.

Athens, remarkably enough, although it tried tyranny for almost forty years, subsequently embarked on the enduring road to a true democracy. Despite the temporary failure of his compromise, Solon bequeathed to Athens a remarkably precious gift: the ideal conception and the sometime reality that the state could be one polity, one community wherein people rationally and peacefully settle their conflicts. Far different was the conception of Plato, who, deliberately ignoring the whole history of Athens, commented on the situation of all city-states in the fourth century: "For each of them is very many cities but not a city. . . . There are two, in any case, warring with each other, one of the poor, the other of the rich."[37] This might be true of almost all, if not all, other Greek cities, but Athens was the great exception. Democracy and only democracy made it whole.

Tyranny

Despite the heroic efforts of Solon, Athens was not spared the particular Greek experience of the "tyrant." The Solonian compromise between class interests was clearly not working or a would-be tyrant would have gained few supporters. In 561, thirty-three years after Solon's Archonship, Pisistratus made himself tyrant with the help of a bodyguard voted him by the Assembly. Twice he was expelled and twice he returned to power, the last time in 546, permanently. He and his sons ruled until 510.

The Greek word "tyrant" does not describe a cruel, harsh, dictatorial, possibly sadistic, leader. A tyrant was an autocrat. Tyranny represented, in Aristotle's analysis, rule by the one, but the rule of a tyrant was no more ferocious or inhumane than that of a king. A tyrant was essentially a king who had seized power illegitimately, a usurper. Within a kingdom, the sovereignty of the king is legitimate and a legitimate succession to the kingship is established, usually by a son of the monarch. A Greek tyrant always carried with him an air of illegitimacy, the taint of usurper never left him, even though the tyranny might last for three generations, with sons or brothers succeeding to power. The overthrow of a tyrant always had the emotional resonance of restoring legitimate order to the *polis*. Politically, he was a king; emotionally, he remained a usurper.

All Greek tyrants seized power within aristocratic societies, not within kingdoms, and therefore expropriated the sovereignty of the ruling aristocracy. To accomplish this coup, the tyrant obviously needed allies, who could come either from disaffected members of the nobility or from the nonnoble rich and the *demos*. An antiaristocratic thrust was an essential element in all situations of Greek tyranny.

It was a transitional phenomenon. "Tyranny in Greece . . . seldom endured to the third generation."[38] Like all such transitional phenomena, it seemed to serve a primarily negative purpose. It broke the back of the traditional society. Recourse to one-man rule in such times of social evolution and crisis is a circumstance that can be observed in several revolutionary periods of history.

In the ancient Greek world, there were two distinct periods of tyrannical rule. The first, the rule of what I like to call "tyrants proper" occurred in the seventh, sixth, and the very beginning of the fifth centuries, sometimes referred to as "the age of tyranny." Miletus, Ephesus, Mitylene, Samos, Corinth, Sicyon, Megara, Epidarus, Naxos, Athens, and Syracuse all produced tyrannies which lasted from one to three generations. Gelon of Sicily, who assumed the tyranny in Syracuse in 485, was the last representative of these tyrants proper.

The second period of so-called tyrants begins with Dionysius of Syracuse (405) and includes Clearchus of Heraclea Pontica (364) and Agathocles of Sicily (317), to mention only a few. In my view, these "tyrants" were different from those of the age of tyranny, and should rather be called "proto-monarchs." They are the result, not of the evolution of the city-state, but of its breakdown. I will discuss later the tendency of all city-states to proceed toward monarchy as an attempt to resolve the otherwise irreconcilable social conflicts tearing the polity apart. This last group of Greek "tyrants" was really preparing the way for a monarchical solution, which had definitely not been true of the tyrants of the Archaic age.

In the fourth century, unlike the earlier time, the word "tyrant" has a definite pejorative meaning, as when Aristotle states that tyranny is a perversion of monarchy.[39] Aristotle's famous comment on tyrants spans both the earlier and later periods with most relevance for the political struggles of the fourth century. "Tyrants . . . are drawn from the populace and the masses, to serve as their protectors against the notables, and in order to prevent them from suffering any injustice from that class. The record of history attests the fact; and it may safely be said that most tyrants have begun their careers as demagogues, who won the popular confidence by calumnating the notables."[40]

In the days of Periander of Corinth (c. 625) and Pisistratus of Athens (546) the concept of tyranny carried no such negative implications, but Aristotle is correct that a fundamental thrust of the tyrannical mode was to curb and weaken the political power of the aristocracy, thereby increasing social mobility within society, giving people of lower social class an opportunity to move upward.

It is no longer fashionable—and was never correct—to talk of capitalism or the bourgeosie in ancient Greece, but it is remarkable how
closely tyranny in the Archaic age is associated with sea trade and the
more urban city-states.[41] "From the coasts of Asia Minor bordering on
wealthy Lydia to the banks of the Euripus, the Saronic Gulf and the
Gulf of Corinth, the list of tyrants coincides as it were with a map of
great ports . . . the connection [between tyranny and the exportation
of pottery] is obvious—ceramics, the clue to international commerce,
shows us Miletus as mistress of the markets in the time of Thrasybulus,
then Corinth under Cypselus and Periander, and finally Athens under
the Pisistratidae."[42] There is no need to postulate a large industrial or
commercial class in these city-states. Even Athens was, by later standards, a very small place. Fifty wealthy, sophisticated, politically ambitious merchants, combining with the nonnoble agricultural rich, could
make an enormous difference in the politics of the state. A city that
lacked such a leavening (like Sparta) would be a very different place.

We have no actual evidence that tyrannical governments were supported by such a combination of nonaristocratic landholders and commercial interests in the cities, but we do have some confirming data
for the notion that the tyrants assisted those of nonaristocratic status
and countered the power of the aristocracy. Pisistratus of Athens established a revolving loan fund for peasants, which allowed the lower-
and middle-class landholders to continue in possession of their property. He also established a board of thirty "deme-judges" [deme was
the local political unit in Athens, of which there were about 140], who
went on circuit. These "national" judges preempted the judicial power
of local potentates, who came from the landowning aristocracy.[43]

We cannot compare what occurred in Athens in the sixth century
with the experience of Argentina in the twentieth century A.D., but
Juan Peron showed a remarkable resemblance to the Greek tyrants of
the Archaic age. He was an autocrat, but by no means the sadistic
totalitarian of European experience. And he came to power with the
backing of "the people." "Peronism featured mass antagonism toward
the oligarchy [which, in Argentina, definitely included the landed ar-
istocracy]."[44]

In Greece tyranny, though short-lived, accomplished a veritable revolution in the structure of society, comparable to that upheaval, lost in
the mists of history, when kingship gave way to aristocratic rule. In
those states that experienced a tyrannical reign, the almost-monopolistic

hold on political power by the landed aristocracy was *permanently* abolished. "When the rule of the Greek tyrants ended, as it usually did after quite a short period, of a generation or two, hereditary aristocratic dominance had disappeared, except in a few places, and had been succeeded by a much more 'open' society: political power no longer rested on descent, on blue blood, but was mainly dependent upon the possession of property (this now became the standard form of Greek oligarchy), and in many cities, such as Athens, it was later extended in theory to all citizens, in a democracy."[45] Thus, ironically, an autocratic rule paved the way, in some cases, for a democratic society.

After the rule of the tyrant, Greek city-states became either narrow oligarchic societies where a combination of money power and old landed wealth excluded all others from sovereignty or they undertook the amazing transition to democracy. Corinth, Sicyon, Megara, and Epidaurus illustrate the oligarchic resolution.[46] The list of democracies includes Naxos, c. 500, after the fall of the tyrant Lygdamis who ruled from c. 545–524;[47] Athens, where the democratic revolution led by Cleisthenes followed the fall of the Pisistratidae in 510; and Syracuse in Sicily following the death in 466 of the tyrant Hieron. Of the Greek democracies besides Athens, we know the most about Syracuse, whose democratic institutions resembled those of Athens in many ways. Its democracy failed of stability, however, and suffered irreparable damage by the latter-day "tyrants" (really proto-monarchs) Dionysius and Agathocles.

In Athens, the time of the tyranny was one of expanding economic prosperity. Attic black-figured pottery became the foremost vessels in the Greek world; Athenian coinage gained enormous respect. Pisistratus adorned the city with buildings and spent large sums on the city-wide festivals of the Panathenaea and the Dionysia. Athens seemed on its way to becoming, culturally and politically, the foremost city in the Greek world.[48]

For two years after the expulsion of the Pisistratidae in 510 B.C. political conflict, complicated by the presence of a Spartan military force, prevailed in Athens. Finally, the liberal aristocrat Cleisthenes triumphed over his rival Isagoras by allying himself with the *demos*. The democratic future of Athens was assured. Solon's ideal promise of a class society that would not be wracked by political violence would become a reality.

5

The Spirit of Society: Citizenship, Freedom, and Responsibility

The greatest invention of ancient Greek society, the benefits of which have been bequeathed to us, was the concept and practice of citizenship. In a society where there are no citizens, there are only rulers and subjects. Sovereignty in these societies may reside in a few, as in an aristocracy or oligarchy, or in one, as in a monarchy. In either case, there is no equality between rulers and subjects. Citizenship is the great gift and the great prerequisite of democracy, for a citizen, in Aristotle's brilliant definition, is a person capable of both ruling and being ruled. Some few have to rule, but it need not always be the same few. He remarks: "[T]he fact remains that the good citizen must possess the knowledge and the capacity requisite for ruling as well as for being ruled, and the excellence of a citizen may be defined as consisting in 'a knowledge of rule over free men from both points of view' [i.e., that of the ruler as well as that of the ruled]."[1]

The remarkableness of this view of the world becomes apparent when we look at the relationship of democracy to the paranoid position and observe that democracy is only made possible by overcoming the paranoid mind-set. In the latter view, the only two alternatives offered by life are to rule or be ruled. Remaining in the paranoid position makes the alternation of rule—the basis of citizenship—impossible.

Once one understands "the knowledge of rule . . . from both points of view," once the ruler recognizes that he will be a subject tomorrow, the harshness and arbitrariness of rule must soften. For Machiavelli it was incumbent on the citizen "neither arrogantly to dominate nor humbly to serve."[2] Rule by citizens is an entirely different experience from rule by oligarchs or monarchs.

Though we take our citizenship for granted, as a God-given right, it is remarkable how young a child it is on the face of the earth. For one not so brief moment it existed in Greece and, to a certain extent, in the Roman Republic. In the approximately 1,200 years between the establishment of the Roman Empire and the beginnings of communes in the Italian city-states in the twelfth century A.D., there was no citizenship anywhere on the earth—only rulers and subjects. The Italian early modern experience with citizenship endured for only a short period of time. Only with the rise of liberalism and democracy in the seventeenth and eighteenth centuries did citizenship achieve what we hope will be a permanent existence.

Once the ancient world had passed on, the rising dominance of Christian thought and ideals over the West, from about 400 A.D., kindled a certain ambivalence about tyrannical rule and a desire to ameliorate its worst aspects. The beneficent hierarchy, however, allowed for no alternation in rulership.

"The *respublica christiana*," writes William Bouwsma, "was necessarily organized as a hierarchical system in which lower ends were subordinate to higher, and inferior powers to superior; authority in the entire structure descended from above. . . . Self-determination, in this view, could only appear . . . as a violation of the very structure of reality, and political duty appeared to consist only in patient submission and obedience. Man, in this system, was always and necessarily a subject; he could not be a citizen."[3] When we consider that, outside of Europe, there have been, at most, only a very few places that have independently created the concept of citizenship (some would argue that there have been no other such societies) we begin to see how remarkable a political creation it was, how difficult to maintain, and how fragile a democratic society necessarily is. With what pathos we read of the affair of Vladimir Dremlyuga, a railway electrician from Leningrad, arrested in August 1968 in Red Square for protesting the Soviet invasion of Czechoslovakia by Russian tanks. "All my conscious life I have wanted to be a citizen—that is, a person who proudly and calmly speaks his mind. For ten minutes I was a citizen, during the demonstration."[4]

A great many inherent human psychological disabilities must be overcome before a viable citizenship is possible. Ancient Greek society, and particularly Athens which we know most about, had grave difficulties overcoming the paranoid position and remained, in many respects, profoundly ambivalent about citizenship. For a good number of people, Aristotle's notion of citizenship represented only an ideal situation; the concept of freedom denoted, not the capacity to rule and to be ruled, but the capability of domineering over others. I have already noted that the equation of freedom and ruling over others can be found in Thucydides, Herodotus, and Polybius.[5] To make a commitment to citizenship, one must forswear the lust to dominate. This is a very difficult psychological maneuver, however, especially for those whose proclivity is to seek power within society.

Since it is eros which binds society together, and since eros must have an object, the transformation process from hierarchy to citizenship involves a transfer of love from the ruler or rulers (fear as well, of course) to one's country. Love of country has been an essential element in the creation of democratic society, but it contains several dangers. First, it was especially true of Athens that many prominent political actors came to feel their love was not reciprocated, that they had been betrayed by its object. "Love of country [philopoli]," Thucydides has Alcibiades say, "I do not feel when I am wronged but I felt it when secure in my rights as a citizen."[6]

The second danger is that, under the banner of the eros of patriotism, other states will be oppressed. Nothing in the nature of citizen-democracy makes catastrophic warfare or imperialism impossible. Third, the love of country may degenerate into a paranoid stance in relationship to the state. Totalitarianism becomes a possibility. The abstract notion of the state begins to carry all the authoritarianism previously exercised by the monarch. Symbolically, people may begin to bow down before the power of the state. Hobbes, torn between a love of freedom and a dismay at citizenship, had to assert that the free man is the individual who is subservient only to the state.[7] No alternation of ruling and being ruled for him, only an imaginary fantasy state, wherein there was freedom but no citizenship. Citizenship—ruling and being ruled—cannot be divorced from ideas of freedom, equality, and justice. Democratic society inevitably requires all these ideals.

Democracy, Freedom, Equality, Justice

No matter how much present-day political theorists may disagree about the fine shades of differences of meaning of "democracy," "freedom," "equality," and "justice," no matter what disagreements classical scholars may entertain about the precise meanings for the ancients of *demokratia, eleutheria* (freedom), *isonomia* (equality), *dike* (justice), and *parrhesia* (free speech)—the fact remains that for most caring people living in a democratic society, these great human conceptions of political reality cannot exist without each other. Over and over again, Athenian orators and philosophers brought into close conjunction two or three of these essential ideals. Demosthenes contends that citizens are public spirited because "in a democracy each man considers that he himself has a share in equality and justice."[8] Isocrates says: "[I]t is for the protection of the person that we have established laws, that we fight for freedom, that we have our hearts set on the democratic form of government, and that all the activities of our lives are directed to this end."[9]

The critics of democracy based their opinions on the fact that it produces an *excess* of freedom and equality, an excess of justice being impossible. From this negative point of view, nevertheless, the assumption is made that democracy and freedom and equality go together. The eighth book of Plato's *Republic* records this interchange:

> "And does the greediness for what democracy defines as good also dissolve it?"
> "What do you say defines that good to be?"
> "Freedom," I said. "For surely in a city under a democracy you would hear that this is the finest thing it has, and that for this reason it is the only regime worth living in for anyone who is by nature free."[10]

Aristotle, unlike Plato, can see the good in democratic society but is profoundly skeptical of its capacity to prevail over the possibilities of injustice in such a polity. For him, as for the others, freedom and equality are the natural concomitants of democracy. "The underlying idea of the democratic type of constitution is liberty. . . . Liberty has more than one form. One of its forms consists in the interchange of ruling and being ruled. . . . The other form consists in 'living as you like.' Such a life, the democrats argue, is the function of the free man, just as the function of slaves is *not* to live as they like. This is the second aim of democracy. Its issue is, ideally, freedom from any interference of government, and, failing that, such freedom as comes from the interchange of ruling and being ruled. It contributes, in this way, to a general system of liberty based on equality."[11]

We thus perceive that any democratic society, no matter how it may restrict sovereignty, gives birth to ideals of freedom, equality, and justice. It thereby imagines, if only faintly, a society it hasn't yet seen, one in which all people are truly equal and truly free. I realize that these remarks modify to some degree my previous statement that Athenian democracy was essentially egocentric and contained no universal ideals of rights. Compared to the ideals of Liberalism, Athenian democracy *was* woefully narrow, even in its ideal existence, but no society exists without ideals, and Athenian society, wherein only a limited minority of adults held political sovereignty, still necessarily adopted the goals of freedom, equality, and justice.

Equality

In a passage, previously noted, in the funeral oration of Pericles/ Thucydides, there occurs a wonderfully idealized view of the kind of equality supposed to exist in Athenian society: total equality before the law, complete merit-based considerations for those who seek political office or power. It is clearly an ideal statement. Reality, in both Athenian society and our own democratic polity, did not and does not live up to this exemplary condition. In both societies, however, there is enough reality-truth in the pronouncement to preclude the accusation of hypocrisy. As an ideal it is remarkable, one that only democratic society could advance.

In extraordinary circumstances, when human possibilities for moral perception and action are being raised as never before, one or two remarkable individuals may perceive the full moral implications of the ideals elaborated within the value system of society and express ideas of equality enormously far in advance of anything the society is really capable of considering. The value-laden distinction between Greeks, who stood for the civilized world, and barbarians, who were outside the pale of full humanity, was supported by almost everyone in Greek society, including the great moralists Plato and Aristotle. Yet the sophist Antiphon—about whom we know almost nothing—wrote a treatise *On Truth* in the fifth century wherein he asserts

> [Those who are born of a great house] we revere and venerate: those who are born of a humble house we neither revere nor venerate. On this point we are [not civilized, but] barbarized in our behavior to one another. Our natural endowment is the same for us all, on all points, whether we are Greeks or barbarians. We may observe the characteristics of any of the powers which by nature are necessary to all men. . . . None of us is set apart [by any peculiarity of such natural powers] either as a Greek or as a barbarian. We can all breathe air through our mouth and nostrils.[12]

This may remind us of nothing so much as Shylock's plaintive cry: "If you prick us do we not bleed?"[13] And it probably did as much to change fifth-century attitudes toward barbarians as did Shylock's speech to ameliorate Elizabethan anti-Semitism. Yet such a statement could originate only within a society that had raised high the banner of "equality."

Justice

Even though judicial rights are the very first rights to be obtained by nonempowered classes, under a democratic society these prerogatives are enormously expanded. Equality under the law becomes equality of protection from the state and from an arbitrary or oppressive judicial process. The Athenian citizen, writes J. Walter Jones, "is not to be condemned unheard, as under the tyrants and oligarchs; not to be put on trial a second time for the same offence; not to be singled out for punishment by retrospective enactment unless at least 6,000 of the people vote for the proposal; not to be subjected to corporal punishment except as a last resort."[14] There is something profound in the nature of democratic society that constantly seeks to expand the concept of "human." It may not always triumph, and there were those in Athens, some of them with great power, who were repelled by the notion of an open society, but it is always present. And there is something in the nature of rights that somehow seeks a further and further limit.

Freedom of Private Life

Democratic polities arise only in posttraditional or "modern" societies, those in which ties of kinship are no longer the primary forms holding society together. The power of the kinship system must be overcome and transformed before any democratic society is possible. Thus, the tremendous importance of individualism and the individual in democratic polities. The relationship of the individual to the state becomes a fundamental problem in all postkinship, posttraditional societies, not only in the public life of the society, but in private affairs as well. Reading the cultural history of the most "advanced" countries in the nineteenth and twentieth centuries, and seeing how difficult it has been to get the state out of people's beds—that is, to arrive at the point where whatever goes on between consenting adults is their business only—observing this, we can reflect on how remarkable is the democratic ideal that one's private life, assuming it does not trespass on the rights of others, is one's own business. This was a fundamental concern in Athens. "The freedom which we enjoy in our government," Pericles says in Thucydides' history, "extends also to our ordinary life. There, far from exercising a jealous surveillance over each other, we do not feel called upon to be angry with our neighbour for doing what he likes, or even to indulge in those injurious looks which cannot fail to be offensive, although they inflict no positive penalty. But all this ease in our private relations does not make us lawless citizens. Against this fear is our chief safeguard, teaching us to obey the magistrates and the laws."[15]

Every great cultural advance has its own particular worm that eats the goodness from its core. Every new virtue develops a characteristic vice. Narcissism and egotistical individualism present themselves simultaneously with the rise of individual freedom. The critics of democracy saw only the excesses of individualism, not its virtues. Aristotle comments:

> The democrat starts by assuming that justice consists in equality: he proceeds to identify equality with the sovereignty of the will of the masses; he ends with the view that 'liberty and equality' consist in 'doing what one likes'. The result of such a view is that, in these extreme democracies, each man lives as he likes—or, as Euripides says, 'for any end he chances to desire.'[16]

One should not, as critics do, confuse the thing with its excess. Freedom of private life is one of the great gifts of democratic society. The struggle to make that ideal a reality seems, however, never ending. The recent successful attempts to decriminalize the private acts of adults and the inflammatory debate over abortion indicate that people do not easily abandon the impulse to pass criminal judgment on what goes on in other people's sexual lives.

Freedom of Speech

The Greeks had a word that meant "free speech"—*parrhesia*. Demosthenes emphasizes the extent of that freedom when he contends that in Sparta one is not allowed to praise the constitution of Athens or any other state, whereas in Athens one can make any claim one wishes on that score.[17] It is remarkable how much praise of Sparta was allowed in Athens, even during the height of the Peloponnesian War. Aristophanes' play *Lysistrata*, an antiwar drama produced during the latter part of the great war, ends with a chorus of Spartans singing the praises of Sparta and Athens. One cannot imagine a French play in 1917 ending with a chorus praising Germany, without imagining as well the arrest of the author and the trial for treason.

Athens experimented for a few years with censorship of free speech in matters concerning the state's imperial foreign policy. In 440 B.C. the island of Samos revolted against the Athenian Empire, declaring its independence. After Athens had succeeded in putting down the revolt, it branded some of the Samnian prisoners as punishment for defying the hegemony of Athens. In that same year an Athenian decree restricted some of the freedom of expression in the theater, probably to forestall adverse comment by the tragic and comic poets on this act of barbarism. Three years later, when the crisis passed, the decree was withdrawn.[18]

The incident was not forgotten, however, and when Aristophanes wrote the *Babylonians* in 426, "the cruelty of Athens towards her subjects was compared to the cruelty of Darius towards the Babylonians, and the Chorus represented the Allied states treading a mill as slaves and among them Samos 'branded with letters. . . .' For this cruelty Aristophanes attacked the magistrates and above all Cleon, the advocate of the massacre of Mitylene [in response to a revolt by that city against the Athenian Empire in 427], who responded by prosecuting him *unsuccessfully* on a charge of treasonable action."[19]

The comic poets were allowed the same freedom of critique we allow our political cartoonists, and, like ourselves, the citizens many times laughed at the critique and then proceeded to award the victim more political honors. Aristophanes again vehemently attacked Cleon in 424 in *Knights*. The play was awarded a first prize. Cleon was elected the next year as one of the generals (*strategos*), one of the most important offices in the state.

An extraordinary human drama was played out in the theater of Dionysus in Athens in the spring of 415, though only a few who witnessed it could fully appreciate its tragic nature. It was sixteen years since the outbreak of the Peloponnesian War. Neither Sparta nor Athens had been able to prevail; neither side was capable of enforcing a lasting and stable peace. Furious at their inability to defeat Sparta, the Athenians became more and more reckless, more and more savage. The previous winter they had tried to force the neutral island of Melos to join the Athenian alliance. Melos refused. Athens conquered the island and proceeded to commit genocide, killing all the adult males and enslaving the females and male children. In the same winter of 416/415, the Athenian Assembly voted to mount a huge expedition to conquer the island of Sicily, none of whose city-states was involved in the war. Desperate to defeat the Spartans, which they could not do, Athens determined to vent its rage on Syracuse—a grossly paranoid act pregnant with the agitated self-destruction that accompanies many paranoid actions. If Athens had succeeded in conquering Sicily, it is difficult to see how that would have led to winning the war. Domination of Sicily would not have overcome the fundamental obstacle to victory, Athens' inability to defeat Sparta on land. The risks were enormous. If Athens suffered defeat in the Sicilian campaign, it might never recover sufficiently to continue the war against Sparta. The actual result—which no one could have known in advance, though a thoughtful person would have feared it might happen—was a catastrophe for Athens, with perhaps ten thousand men and many hundreds of ships lost. It broke the back of Athens' military strength, preparing the way for the ultimate defeat of Athena's city.

In that spring of 415, before the brilliant and splendid fleet embarked, Euripides presented his play *The Trojan Women* at the annual festival of Dionysus. The savagery of the slaughter of Melos is echoed over and over again. The play is more a recitation of the horrors that human beings visit on each other than a drama—as if one were to write an oratorio on Hiroshima. The possible future destruction of Athens is also foreseen in a manner that could only produce a shudder in those sensitive enough to hear. All warfare is insane, Euripides was announcing. Let the makers of war ruminate on their own annihilation. "Lost shall be the name on the land, all gone, perished. Troy, city of sorrow, is there no longer." The play closes with a vision of Athens, "Mourn for the ruined city, then go away to the ships."[20] Euripides was not imprisoned, not even brought to trial. He was awarded the second prize.

"Aelian [third century A.D.] seems outraged," writes the translator Richmond Lattimore, "that Euripides came second to Xenocles; I can hardly understand how the Athenians let him present this play at all."[21] An almost unbelievable contradiction obtains. Athens, paranoid to the point of self-destruction in regard to warfare and the domination of other city-states, remains remarkably sane within the confines of the *polis*.

Not surprisingly, the critics of democracy found exactly in these freedoms and equalities the grounds for their dislike. For Plato and Aristotle, democracy, and especially the radical democracy of Athens, yielded an excess of freedom and equality. For Plato democracy was a topsy-turvy world wherein those who should be ruled are the rulers. "That a father . . . habituates himself to be like his child and fears his sons, and a son habituates himself to be like his father and to have no shame before or fear of his parents—that's so he may be free; and metic [resident alien in the city who is not a citizen] is on an equal level with townsman and townsman with metic. . . . As the teacher in such a situation is frightened of the pupils and fawns on them, so the students make light of their teachers, as well as of their attendants. . . . And the ultimate in the freedom of the multitude . . . occurs in such a city when the purchased slaves, male and female, are no less free than those who have bought them. . . . A man who didn't have the experience couldn't be persuaded of the extent to which beasts subject to human beings are freer here than in another city. . . . there come to be horses and asses who have gotten the habit of making their way quite freely and solemnly, bumping into whomever they happen to meet on the roads, if he doesn't stand aside, and all else is similarly full of freedom."[22]

Plato, of course, is assuming that all freedom must necessarily lead to excess, and, therefore, ultimately to a lack of freedom. An excess of liberty makes people not free, but servile. The debate has gone on for centuries. Somewhere around 100 A.D. Tacitus remarked that fools "identified *licentia* and *libertas*."[23] One has only to read the current discussions concerning narcissism and radical individualism in our society[24] to perceive that whenever society decides to enshrine freedom as a norm within the value system, the symptomatic behavior of egotism and self-indulgence cannot be far behind.

The crucial question is, does the egotism of freedom drive people to disregard the law and, therefore, the rights of others. When Aristotle writes, as quoted above, that in "extreme democracies each man lives as he likes," he immediately goes on to say: "This is a mean conception of liberty. To live by the rule of the constitution ought not to be regarded as slavery, but rather as salvation."[25] This point had already been addressed by Pericles/Thucydides who followed praise of the great freedom of private life with the specific statement that this does not make the Athenian citizen contemptuous of the laws and the magistrates.[26] Thucydides clearly disapproved of lawless egoism quite as strongly as did Aristotle.

Another critique of the ideals of democratic society concerns the concept of equality. All men are not alike, so runs the argument, either intellectually or morally. A society runs best—and is most just—

when benefits are distributed according to the contribution a citizen makes to society, either by his capacities or by his moral insight. In a democracy, however, this argument insists, all share equally in the benefits of society regardless of their unequal contributions to its health. Plato and Aristotle argue this critique in almost identical words. Plato: "The democracy . . . would be . . . a sweet regime . . . dispensing a certain equality to equals and unequals alike."[27] Aristotle: "The oligarchs think that superiority on one point—in their case wealth—means superiority in all; the democrats believe that equality in one respect—for instance, that of free birth—means equality all round."[28] The argument is specious. In a democracy, even an extreme democracy, the people may reign (that is, may hold the ultimate sovereignty), but they do not rule. Elites rule even the most radical democracy. Nor can it be blithely assumed that justice requires that uneven contributions to society be rewarded with unequal benefits. One may argue, with the same validity, that those blessed with greater capacities have an even greater obligation to contribute their superior skills. It is a question of a first principle—on what grounds one takes one's stand—whether one feels the world suffers more from too much equality or from too much hierarchy.

The Spirit of Society

One great, permanent insight left to us by Greek culture is the perception that societies differ profoundly in the spirit that sustains and drives them, much as individuals living in the same culture may differ enormously in their personalities and characters. Athens and Sparta present the perfect case study. No examination of democracy, especially one that questions why one society was transformed into a democratic polity while another became a garrison state or a repressive oligarchy, should fail to consider the spirit of society a significant factor. By the time they appear on the historical horizon, Athens and Sparta—and Rome—all have crucial differences of spirit. What accounts for these differences, when and where and why the character and personality of the society became fixed, will undoubtedly be debated by historians for years to come. It is certain, however, that when we first observe Athens, at the time of Solon, the democratic genius is already in the air—if not the democratic genius, at least the nonparanoid spirit—and by the fifth century it is the primary characteristic of the society's spirit.

The contrast with Sparta struck all thoughtful Athenians, especially Thucydides who gives us an extraordinary descriptive passage of the differences. William Arrowsmith comments on the passage, giving his own translation: On the one side is Spartan *apragmosyne*—a traditional conservatism, distrustful of all innovation, governed by an austere military discipline of restraint; a quietism of policy which verges, it seems, on apathy, but based upon the old Greek sense of a natural *dike* of boundaries and behavior against which it was *hybris*, or *polypragmosyne* to trespass. On the other side is Athenian *polypragmosyne*[29] . . . the very pith and spirit of Athenian enterprise, its dynamic of *pleonexia*, the expansive *hybris* of energy and power in a spirited people; an *eros* or libido, a *libido dominandi*.[30] The Corinthians address the Spartans:

> The Athenians are addicted to innovation, and their designs are characterized by swiftness alike in conception and execution; you Spartans have a genius for keeping what you have, accompanied by a total want of innovation, and when forced to act you never go far enough. But the Athenians are adventurous beyond their power, and daring beyond their judgement, and in danger they are confident. . . . Moreover, there is a swiftness on their side as against procrastination on yours; they are never at home, you are never far from it; for they hope by their absence to extend their acquisitions; you fear . . . to endanger what you have left behind. They are swift to follow up a success, and slow to recoil from a reverse. . . . A scheme unexecuted is with them a positive loss, a successful enterprise a comparative failure. The failure created by the miscarriage of an enterprise is soon filled by fresh hopes, for they alone are able to call a thing hoped for a thing got, by the speed with which they act on their resolutions. . . . To describe their character in one word, one might truly say that they were born into the world to take no rest themselves and give none to others.[31]

Though this illumination of the Athenian spirit says nothing about the spirit of democracy, it is somehow present. The *libido dominandi* is the great problematic within this explosion of human energy—not that Sparta ever declined the opportunity to oppress others either within or without its *polis*. I will treat later the problem of democracy and domination: it is too great a question to be addressed at this point. One may say of Athens that it suffered from an *excess* of spirit, one that knew no bounds.

All democratic societies ultimately depend on the democratic mores of the society for the preservation of democracy. No set of laws, no institutions, no complex bureaucracy, no intricate mechanisms of checks and balances is sufficient to preserve a democracy and maintain its health if the democratic spirit takes leave of the hearts of the people. Institutions help, making a democracy possible, but they are lifeless without the democratic genius. An historical analysis attempting to demonstrate, only on the basis of an analysis of institutions, why, or why not, a certain state achieved democratic status is doomed to fail. Democratic institutions, though essential to the preservation of democracy, are never the ultimate cause. Madison, at the beginning of the American republic, saw this with great clarity: "If it be asked what is to restrain the House of Representatives from making legal discrimination in favor of themselves and a particular class of society? I answer, the genius of the whole system, the nature of just and constitutional laws, and *above all* the vigilant and manly spirit which actuates the people of America, a spirit which nourishes freedom, and in return is nourished by it."[32]

Ancient Greek thought not surprisingly, perceived exactly this overriding importance of the spirit. Aristotle writes: "There is no profit of the best laws, even if they have been sanctioned by every citizen of the State, unless men have been trained by habit and formed by education in the spirit of their society."[33] Justice Learned Hand echoed this insight in the twentieth century. "Liberty lies in the hearts of men and women; when it dies there, no constitution, no law, no court can save it."[34] Our tragic century has provided many examples of the failure of brilliant constitutions to save unfree societies.

Optimism about human nature is essential to the democratic spirit. By overcoming the paranoid position of basic mistrust, democracy substitutes a basic trust of one's neighbor, of the citizen one does not know, of one's political opponent. Democracy is impossible unless many people trust each other, reflecting an optimistic view of what a large number of humans are capable of. Second, and this is what principally disturbed the critics of democracy, if the governing of society is to be put into the hands of the many, rather than the few, the assumption is that the many are capable of governing. Plato's fundamental criticism of democracy centers on this: only the few have, or will ever have, he insists, the capacity to govern properly. As governance is put in more and more hands, the quality of political life declines precipitously. The democratic view takes the opposite position. It mistrusts governance by the few, fearing tyranny. The leaders of society are to be checked at all points, their term in office subject to careful review, their leadership terminated when it violates the wishes of the *demos*. In its ideal form, democracy may even, as Thucydides/ Pericles tells us in the famous panegyric to a democratic society, create a new man. " 'In short, I say that as a city we are the school of Hellas; while I doubt if the world can produce a man, who where he has only himself to depend upon, is equal to so many emergencies and graced by so happy a versatility as the Athenian.' "[35]

Pessimism about human possibilities always underlies antidemocratic thought. How responsible, mature, and stable was Athenian society? Was it the moral chaos described by Plato? Did it, as Thucydides tells us, descend after the death of Pericles on a degraded path led by crude and unstable demagogues? The answers to these questions are surprisingly simple and unambiguous, when one lets the data speak for themselves, leaving behind the prejudices of the hierarchically inclined.

Responsible Democracy

Nothing is truer than the cliché that announces that eternal vigilance is the price of freedom. A people unable or unwilling to fight for democracy, to risk life for its preservation, is destined to lose its liberty. The militant defense of democracy must be continuous because, as Aristotle tells us, there are some who are "filled with a passion for inequality."[36] Men filled with such a passion successfully engineered two oligarchic counterrevolutions in Athens, one during the latter part of the great war in 411, and one at its very end in 404. It is remarkable how quickly, how militantly and responsibly the democracy responded. Neither coup lasted more than eighteen months before democracy was restored in the city. In 411, with the war still in progress, the bulk of the Athenian fleet and fighting forces were stationed at the island of Samos, where distorted reports of the coup at Athens presently arrived.

News of the situation in Athens reached Samos through unfriendly channels coloured by fear and exaggeration for political effect. The troops, driven to fury by the misrepresentation that the Four Hundred [the oligarchs in Athens] were abusing their wives and children and holding them as hostages for their good behaviour, were only prevented from stoning the adherents of oligarchy in their midst by the proximity of the enemy's fleet and the influence of Thrasybulus and Thrasyllus, who bound them all, oligarchs and democrats, Athenians and Samians, by solemn oaths to stand together, uphold democracy, fight the Peloponnesians vigorously, treat the Four Hundred as enemies, and have no traffic with them. Setting themselves up as the People of Athens, they deposed their generals and replaced them with others, among them Thrasybulus and Thrasyllus. They took the view that Athens had seceded; that with Samos to fall back upon they could conduct the war with virtually undiminished resources; that, if worst came to worst, they could settle down elsewhere than at Athens and found a new state. In the conduct of the 'sailor rabble' throughout this terrible crisis—their ready response to prudent and patriotic leadership, capacity for self-reorganization, determination to live up to their most heroic traditions—Athenian democracy was commended by its works.[37]

The response was equally vigorous in 404, though Athens was exhausted from losing the war and the coup was supported by the Spartan conquerors. Democratic exiles gathered in Thebes and then reentered Attica, establishing themselves at a strong point in Phyle, which they used as a base ultimately to win the city back from the oligarchs. Ironically, one of the most important supporters of this militant defense of the democracy was the orator Lysias who was not even an Athenian citizen, but a resident alien in the city. He and his brother were scheduled for execution by the oligarchs in order that their property might be confiscated. The brother was killed and most of the property lost, but Lysias escaped and proceeded to Phyle where he supplied two thousand drachmas and two hundred shields for the cause before going off to hire three hundred mercenaries. Though denied citizenship after the restoration through a technicality of the law, Lysias lived out the rest of his life in Athens, writing speeches for citizens to deliver in court and orations on public issues.[38] He was the very image of a responsible, committed, nondemagogic citizen, without whose presence no democratic society is possible.

After the earlier coup in 411, the justifiably frightened *demos* of Athens had enacted a law designed to outlaw any activity that contravened the democracy. It also required all citizens to take an oath "over an unblemished sacrifice before the next festival of Dionysus."

I shall kill by word and by deed, by vote and with my own hand, if I can, anyone who subverts the democracy of Athens, whoever holds public office after its suppression, and whoever tries to become a tyrant or helps to install one. And if anyone else kills such a person I will regard him as blameless before the gods and demons as having killed an enemy of the Athenian people. And I will sell all the property of the man who has been killed and give half to the man who has killed him and hold nothing back. And if anyone dies while killing such a person or attempting to kill him I shall treat him and his children well just as if they were Harmodius and Aristogeiton [the tyrannicides of the late sixth century who had become canonized by Athenian public opinion] and their children. I dissolve and reject all oaths for the overthrow of the Athenian democracy whether in Athens, or in the camp of the army, or anywhere else.[39]

Oaths, however, were no proof against the passion for inequality, and when oligarchy returned in 404 it established the worst political terror Athens had ever experienced. In thirteen months more than 1,500 people were exterminated either as political opponents or to appropriate their wealth. The oath of 410 had promised death to anyone holding office after the overthrow of democracy; the terror of 404-403 undoubtedly raised the passion for revenge. The history of the Greek city-states was replete with incidents of democrats or oligarchs returning to power after a bloody civil-class war and slaughtering hundreds or even thousands of political opponents.

Despite this, the Athenian *demos* acted with almost unbelievable generosity when it regained state power. It declared a full and general amnesty for all who had engaged in the oligarchic adventure, except for the Thirty Tyrants (who were the leaders of the coup) and twenty-one of their closest associates and executioners (Aristotle says thirty-one, but most textual criticism today believes there is a duplication of one figure of ten).[40] All others, no matter what they had done, were to be free from the burden of criminal suit being brought against them and free to enjoy full rights as citizens. Those who led the restored democracy, especially Archinus, one of the principal stalwarts at Phyle, meant to preserve that amnesty at all costs.[41] "When one of those who had participated in the return," Aristotle tells us, "began to take up complaints in violation of the amnesty, Archinus took him before the Council and persuaded the Councilmen to have him executed without trial. He achieved this by telling them that now was the moment when they must show whether they were willing to save the democracy and to live up to their oaths. For if they were going to let this man off, they would encourage others to act as he did; but if they executed him, they would set a warning example. This was actually the result. For when he had him executed, nobody ever dared to violate the amnesty again."[42] Ironically enough, an illegal act ("without trial") brought health to the *polis* in time of crisis.

Archinus followed up this prosecution by having a law passed authorizing any defendant who claimed he was protected against a proposed suit by the amnesty to bring his own action into the courts to have the case dismissed. The court must first decide this question before any prosecution could begin.[43] The result of this intense maneuvering was exactly what the democracy required. The terrible wound in the *polis* was healed. In the fourth century those who had taken part in the coup served on juries, attended the Assembly, were members of the Council, and were even elected ambassadors and generals.[44] Despite his serious reservations about democracy, especially the radical democracy of Athens, Aristotle, unlike Plato, never let his position blind him to the virtues of Athenian society.

In fact, it appears that their attitude both in private and in public in regard to the past disturbances was the most admirable and the most statesmanlike that any people have ever shown in such circumstances. For, apart from having wiped out all considerations of guilt in regard to the past events, they even refunded at common expense the money which the Thirty had borrowed from the Lacedaemonians for the war [against the democrats]. . . . For they thought that this was the way to start the restoration of concord and harmony, while in other countries the democrats, if they come to power, do not even think of making any contributions out of their own money, but, on the contrary, seize the land for redistribution.[45]

It cannot be emphasized enough that this occurred after humiliating defeat by Sparta in a war that lasted, on and off, for twenty-seven years and brought catastrophic ruin, including the loss of empire and a close encounter with possible annihilation. An amazing spirit of sanity moved within this incredibly contradictory people, who could commit genocide against city-states beyond the state boundaries and yet enforce the most magnanimous concept of justice within their own *polis*.

The subsequent history of Athens fully justified the optimism of this great amnesty. Throughout most of the fourth century, oligarchy was a dead issue. Even Isocrates, who argued for a return to the constitution of "the ancestors" and the dominance of the Council of Areopagus, praised the present constitution. "For if we compare our own government . . . not with the democracy which I have described [that is, that of the ancestors] but with the rule which was instituted by the Thirty, there is no one who would not consider our present democracy a divine creation."[46]

"Oligarchy was so discredited in Athens by the rule of the Thirty," Peter Krentz writes, "that for three generations it was not a respectable alternative. Plato commented that the Thirty made the previous government look like gold by comparison. [*Epist.* 7.324d] Criticism of democracy continued . . . but no group in the first half of the fourth century actively sought to replace the democracy with yet another oligarchy."[47]

In the latter part of the fourth century Athens was again subject to oligarchic, or restricted democratic, rule. The retrogression was the direct result of a failure in foreign affairs. After the death of Alexander, Athens revolted against Macedonian hegemony in Greece. Defeated in that endeavor, in 322 it was forced to modify its constitution in the oligarchic direction. Antipater, the Macedonian general, desired to establish an oligarchy. He imposed a property qualification of two thousand drachmas for voting and holding office, which substantially took away the civic rights of most of the citizens.[48] For more than two hundred years thereafter the constitution varied between full democracy, on the one hand, and narrow oligarchy on the other. It is significant, however, that throughout that period every regression from democracy was forced upon Athens by external powers, and not until 103/102 B.C. did an oligarchic counterrevolution arise totally from within Athens, temporarily destroying the democracy.[49]

So enduring was the democratic spirit that the class war between the oligarchs and the *demos* continued into the first century. Less than fifteen years after the oligarchic coup of 103/102, one Ariston returned to Athens after sojourning with Mithridates, singing the praises of the Pontic king and announcing that great aid was to come to Athens from him. The *demos* rose up, elected Ariston a general, murdered members of the aristocratic party, and confiscated their property, thus violently restoring the democracy.[50] But Athens was not a free agent. The Roman conqueror Sulla restored the oligarchy in 83 B.C., this regime lasting until 48, when Julius Caesar reestablished the democratic government. It lasted less than ten years. A new oligarchy came into existence in 39/38, but this, too, must eventually have given way, for under the Roman Empire, decrees of the *demos* were issued again.[51]

Some writers on ancient society would have us believe that Athenian democracy was like a brilliant comet, illuminating the sky for a brief moment in the fifth century. This is totally false. The democracy was vigorous and healthy throughout the fourth century and had Athens been free of foreign domination, it might have maintained such good health for many centuries more. The near-barbarians were at the gates, however. To blame Athens for the collapse of her democracy makes as much sense as to blame the Czechoslovakian people for the failure of their 1968 uprising.

It is interesting how many have internalized the critiques of Plato and others and can still, in this century, term Athenian democracy "irresponsible," when exactly the opposite was the case. Within the limited boundaries of the male, nonslave population of *one* city-state, the Athenians had a unique and remarkable lesson in justice to teach.

6

The Health of the Democratic *Polis*

Aspecious argument has been raised by some observers about the relationship of political life to leisure, that is, the opportunity to live off other people's labor. To lead a full life as a civic minded citizen, so runs this contention, one must have leisure to contemplate in repose the needs of the state and to serve the political apparatus. The practical result of this form of apology, in reality, is a polity completely controlled by the wealthy—oligarchs and aristocrats. Plato tried to create in his Guardians a leisured class whose task it was to run society, their leisured status determined by intelligence and moral insight, not money. We have yet to see such a society.

To make possible a nonoligarchic, nonaristocratic society, that is, a democracy, the logical solution is to pay citizens for the services they render the state. Since this is obvious, and rather simple, we cannot say that, where such payment did not exist, people had not thought of it. Nonpayment for political service is the perfect means to perpetuate oligarchic values. A healthy, responsible, stable democracy demands money compensation for those who serve the *polis*.

It is of great significance that, as far as our data show, Athens was

95

the only Greek or ancient Italian city providing such compensation.[1]*
Payments began in the time of Pericles in the fifth century: magistrates
and members of the Council received compensation, the former according to the nature of their work; members of juries were compen-
sated at the rate of two obols a day, raised to three obols in 425.
Payment was instituted for attendance at the Assembly in the beginning
of the fourth century, the amount being raised as the century (and
possibly inflation) progressed. Payment for Assembly attendance was
given only to a fixed number of citizens, who, we assume, arrived first
and established a quorum.[2]

An attempt has been made by certain historians to minimize the
credit due Athens for this revolutionary invention by insisting the funds
for payment came from the tribute of the Athenian Empire, making
the radical democracy only a product of the imperialistic domination
of other city-states. Granted that the Athenian state budget was in fine
shape in the fifth century because of tribute from the empire, the fact
remains that in the fourth century, when this source of revenue no
longer existed, not only did all previous payments continue, but payment for attendance at the Assembly was instituted at the beginning of
the century, when Athens had not yet recovered from the catastrophic
results of the great war.[3] Easy as it might have been to start the process
when funds were readily available, Athens clearly learned the lesson of
what was required to maintain a free and open democratic society and
continued the practice through lean years.

Almost all offices of the Athenian state, including membership on
the Council, were of one year's duration. The ten generals, who constituted the most important offices, could be reelected year after year.
Pericles, for instance, maintained his dominance of the political process
by, among other things, having himself elected general annually. Membership on the Council was restricted to one year and one reelection.
Every year five hundred citizens were elected to the Council and perhaps an additional seven hundred served in various administrative
offices.[4] When one considers that the highest estimates of the number
of citizens at the beginning of the Peloponnesian War range from
35,000 to 50,000 and at the end of the war from 15,000 to 25,000,[5] it

*We do have some indication that other democratic city-states also provided such pay-
ment.

becomes apparent that a remarkably large number of citizens had legislative or executive experience in the state. Gomme estimates that "a quarter to a third or more of citizens over thirty at any one time had such political experience as membership of the council gave; the difference, that is, in experience and knowledge, between the average councilor and the average citizen in the assembly at any time was not great."[6] If we add to this participation in central governmental affairs the vigorous local political activity in the 139 to 140 demes of Attica (which we will discuss later) we are forced to conclude that Athens was probably the most participatory democracy that ever existed in a large, complex state.

And a large, complex state it was. The participation required of ordinary citizens in a polity with few professional civil servants is best illustrated by Rhodes' description of the activities of the Council (*boule*). The Council of Five Hundred was chosen annually, fifty from each of the ten tribes, in a procedure combining election and sortition. No citizen could serve more than twice. With the board of ten generals, the Council served the executive needs of the Athenian state. The Assembly (*ekklesia*) of all citizens provided the legislative function, though the analogy with our legislative and executive branches is not quite accurate. Each year, therefore, five hundred "raw" Athenian citizens managed the essential functioning of the state.

"In this way by the late fifth century the boule had come to play a vital part in the running of the state. It retained, of course, its original probouleutic function, in consequence of which it received foreign envoys, heard reports from Athenians holding regular or extraordinary appointments, and discussed every matter which might be the subject of a decree of the assembly. It had come to be regarded as generally responsible for the financial well-being of Athens. . . . involved in assessing and collecting the tribute paid by the members of the Delian League [the Athenian Empire]; we have seen it interested in the sacred treasuries which were so important to Athens in the Peloponnesian War. The boule supervised the poletae, which placed state contracts of all kinds, the apodectae . . . who received state revenue, and the colacretae, who . . . made payments on behalf of the state. The part which it played in finance was typical: routine work was handled by a number of separate committees, each active in a limited field, while the boule supervised them all . . . and so was able to piece together the whole picture, and to advise the assembly if a new tax was needed, or if the money was not available for a new undertaking. For the army the boule's responsibility was slight . . . but it played an important part in Athens' naval organization. . . . The great public buildings of the Periclean period were supervised by the boards of popularly elected epistatae, but the boule was involved in the approval of plans (though the assembly sometimes claimed the right to decide even points of detail). The administration of festivals was shared between the priests and boards of hieropoei, and some at any rate of the hieropoei were appointed from the boule, while the boule as a whole was involved in the Eleusian Mysteries and the Dionysia."[7]

Obviously, this kind of complex administrative machinery could not run efficiently with almost five hundred new councilors chosen each year without a year-to-year continuity provided by professional civil servants (either free men or slaves) who could teach the new councilors the state's business. Unfortunately, we have almost no evidence of their existence, but they must be assumed. The ultimate decisions, however, were made by the Council. It was a unique and unprecedented education in democracy.

Jones has pointed out that, although Athenian democracy was optimistic about human nature in contrast to its philosopher critics, in one regard it was thoroughly distrustful. It exercised an almost absolute control over its elected leaders, subjecting them to constant review in order to minimize arrogance and prevent tyranny.[8] First, almost all offices were limited to one year's duration. Second, all magistrates were subject to scrutiny after being elected or appointed to office to determine if they were fit to serve. On completion of service, every official underwent a complex review process called *euthyna*. Within thirty days of leaving office, the magistrate had to present his records for financial audit. If he survived this scrutiny successfully, then a board of ten state examiners chosen by lot sat for three days to hear all charges of misconduct against the official, which could be brought by any citizen. Only when this review had been successfully completed was the official allowed to travel out of the country, to transfer his property, or even to make an offering to a god.[9] Third, magistrates, including those on the board of generals, could at any time be prosecuted under a process of *eisangelia* for such offenses as attempts to overthrow the democracy, the taking of bribes, and treason.[10] Hundreds of magistrates and generals were prosecuted under this process in the fourth century, with many of them executed for their alleged misconduct.

The positive result of these processes was that political control, for good or evil, really rested with the *demos* in Athens. "And what civil discord might not erupt in Athens," writes Jennifer Tolbert Roberts, "when it had no public offices higher than the men who led its armies? A century of bloodshed in Rome was to show what could happen when the same men served as political leaders and military heroes: at Athens it was the vigorous use of the machinery of control which prevented the military character of the [board of generals] from posing a threat to the democratic constitution."[11]

And not only Rome. One need only look around the world today to observe how enormously important the military remains in the politics of many states and how it almost always represents an antidemocratic presence. Failure to control the military has been the primary obstacle to the establishment of democratic society in many countries in the twentieth century. After the democracy was established, Athens, though it was subjected to oligarchic counterrevolution, never suffered from a military coup.

This remarkably responsible political behavior came about because Zeus had imparted to all men "the qualities of respect for others and a sense of justice." It was the antidemocratic Plato who put into the mouth of Socrates' adversary, Protagoras, the great moral and psychological argument for the possibility of a responsible democratic society. Resorting to myth to make his point, Protagoras relates that when people were first created by the gods and given their qualities by Epimetheus and Prometheus, they were inadequately structured. Weaker than the beasts, people were being destroyed by them. They lived only in scattered groups, incapable of the art of politics, which includes banding together for warfare. When they did come together in fortified cities, they so lacked the capacity to live with one another in peace that they warred continually with each other until they abandoned the *poleis* they had erected. Fearing the total destruction of the race, Zeus sent Hermes to implant in people the qualities of respect and justice. When Hermes asked whether only a select few were to be the recipients, as with other talents such as doctoring, Zeus imperiously replied: "To all. . . . Let all have their share. There could never be cities if only a few shared in those virtues, as in the arts."

Protagoras then proceeds to answer an argument that Plato/Socrates would raise many times in his critique of democracy: that only a few can achieve expertise in the *techne* of politics and it is therefore a profound mistake to assume that all people should participate in the making of political decisions. "Thus it is, Socrates, and from this cause, that in a debate involving skill in building, or in any other craft, the Athenians, like other men, believe that few are capable of giving advice, and if someone outside those few volunteers to advise them, then as you say, they do not tolerate it—rightly so, in my submission. But when the subject of their counsel involves political wisdom, which must always follow the path of justice and moderation, they listen to every man's opinion for they think that *everyone must share in this kind of virtue; otherwise the state could not exist. . . . for a man cannot be without some share in justice, or he would not be human.*"[12]

Only a myth? Someone once said a myth is a story that never was true and always will be. All democratic societies rest on the mythic foundation that Zeus gave to *every* person the capacity for "justice and moderation and holiness of life."[13] Democracy is only possible if that myth is true—at least in part. The Athenians were extravagant and impassioned enough to believe it.

The Waxing of Democracy

From the beginnings of truly democratic society with the reforms of Cleisthenes in 508 until the middle of the fourth century, Athenian politics presents the picture of an ever-increasing and ever-widening democracy. People of the lower economic classes increasingly had the capacity to make political decisions and to attain political office. Except for the very brief oligarchic counterrevolutions in 411 and 404, the graph of democratic participation moved constantly upward. By the middle of the fourth century, Athenian democracy was as "radical" or as "equal" as it had the energy and capacity to be. At that point, unless reforms were made in the direction of women, slaves, and foreign-born residents, or unless the cause of significant redistribution of economic resources was undertaken—all of which seemed impossible within the value system of the culture—the morally expansive nature of society had nowhere else to go, having fulfilled its promise.

We do not have voluminous evidence of the expansive nature of the democracy, but all we have supports the contention that the radical democracy of the fourth century was the *telos* toward which the society was evolving. Three distinct periods can be observed in this process: (1) from Cleisthenes (508) to the death of Pericles in 429; (2) from the age of the "demagogues" to the fourth century; (3) the fourth century itself.

From Cleisthenes to Pericles

Cleisthenes' reforms left Athens, in addition to the Assembly which had existed since the beginning of time, with two councils, the Council of the Areopagus, also of ancient origin, and the new Council of Five Hundred, created by Cleisthenes. The Areopagus Council was the instrument of the old aristocracy, its membership consisting of those previously elected Archon (nine in each year), an office restricted to the two highest property classes. The new Council of Five Hundred was made up yearly of fifty members from each of the "tribes" created by Cleisthenes. These tribes did not represent the old kinship system; they were merely an artificial creation of Cleisthenes, the purpose of which was to substitute political and local loyalties for ancient kinship ties. This Council clearly represented the increasing democratic impulses in the society. We don't know how the duties and the power were divided between the two councils, but the assumption is that Cleisthenes' Council prepared the business that was to come before the Assembly and the Areopagus exercised primarily judicial, and possibly some executive, functions.

The Areopagus suffered a significant diminution of powers in the fifty years after Cleisthenes, finally exercising a minimal function within the state. From 487, the Archons, instead of being directly elected, were chosen by lot from a group of five hundred candidates selected by the local demes. The prestige of the office plummeted, in turn lowering the prestige of the Areopagus, its ranks now being filled by relative nobodies instead of by people of the highest status.[14] In 462 the democratic party led by Ephialtes (who was Pericles' mentor and who was assassinated some months later; we don't know the motive for the assault) stripped the Areopagus of most of its powers, turning them over to the other Council, the Assembly, and the popular courts. We know almost nothing of the specifics of these transfers, but they surely represent a strengthening of the democratic against aristocratic elements.[15]

During the same period, property qualifications for holding office were gradually lowered; for some magistrates they were completely eliminated.[16] We know, for example, that the office of Treasurer of Athena was originally restricted to members of the two highest property classes and that in 457 it was opened up to members of the third class.[17] As the century went on, many historical property requirements were simply ignored. Making political office available to those without wealth made payment for service in office essential. We don't know exactly when compensation for serving on the Council and in the courts was established, but believe that it commenced before Pericles' death in 429.[18]

The institution of law courts (*dikasterion*) in which decisions were rendered by large juries was a powerful instrument of democratization. Many of the judicial powers taken from the Areopagus and the magistrates during the course of the fifth century were invested in these jury-law courts. At the beginning of each year a list of six thousand jurors was drawn up from volunteers. In actual cases juries usually numbered several hundred. There was no institution of elected or appointed judges to decide important cases as is the circumstance with us. A magistrate presided over a trial, but the jury rendered the verdict and decided on the punishment. Many of these trials had significant political implications. Every important magistrate at the termination of his office was subject to a review of his official conduct. Any dispute resulting from this process was referred to a jury court for decision. Even crimes against the state were so decided except for a few cases that were given to the full Assembly for decision.[19] When we consider the power of these courts and of the Council of Five Hundred and the scope of an Assembly open to all citizens who cared to, and were able to, attend—we observe how supreme was the sovereignty of the *demos* of Athens.

Politics during this period, not surprisingly, split along class lines: people of aristocratic and oligarchic tendencies versus the people. Each faction had its leader but sometimes the signals were mixed. Aristotle writes: "The first leader of the people was Solon, and he was followed by Peisistratus, both of them aristocrats of good family. After the fall of the tyranny there were Cleisthenes, an Alcmeonid [a high aristocratic family], and he had no opponent after the expulsion of Isagoras and his supporters. Then Xanthippus was the leader of the people and Miltiades leader of the aristocrats; then came Themistocles and Aristides. After them, Ephialtes led the people and Cimon the wealthier classes; then Pericles led the people while Thucydides [not the historian], a relative by marriage of Cimon, led the other group. After the death of Pericles, Nicias . . . was the leader of the upper classes, while Cleon . . . led the people.''[20]

In contrast to almost every other city-state in Greece, this class competition for political power did not, at first erupt. Only in 411, when pressure from the war was enormous, did violent class warfare break out. Ephialtes was assassinated and Themistocles and Aristides were ostracized for the legal period of ten years (Aristides was recalled before the decade was up). Over all, however, Athenian political struggles were as legal and peaceful as those of any stable democracy in the twentieth century. Though the Athenians knew that politics is a game of who gets what, when, and how, they stopped short of killing as an instrument of political policy.

Despite the trend toward full democracy, the aristocracy maintained a high degree of political control in one area, at the highest level, the board of generals (*strategoi*). Ten *strategoi* were elected each year, usually one from each of the ten tribes; most significantly, they could be re-elected year after year without limit. The *strategoi* were not only military commanders, each leading the units from his tribe, but the office soon developed into a political power base as well, with some members of the board of generals becoming politically dominant. Themistocles, Cimon, Nicias, Alcibiades, and Cleon all served as generals, and Pericles' almost total dominance of political life from 443 until his death in 429 was institutionalized by his election as a *strategos* in almost every one of those years. A society undergoing transition from aristocratic to democratic rule will tend to entrust military matters to members of the aristocracy, who have traditionally been involved with hunting, riding, and fighting. The aristocratic charisma may prevail in wartime, as a normal regression to a more primitive mode of psychological support. Warfare was incessant in Athenian society—as in almost all Greek city-states. This allowed the aristocracy a continued hold on political life.

The capacity of the aristocratic elements, Cleisthenes to Pericles, not only to accommodate themselves to the democratic process but also to become leaders of the *demos* was extraordinary. Pericles, of the highest aristocratic birth, led the *demos* and increasingly extended the boundaries of the democracy. Though he faced the inevitable problem that develops when a great and efficient charismatic leader succeeds in capturing the loyalty of the people, he did not set himself up as tyrant. The *demos* virtually abdicated its rule and deposited its sovereignty into the hands of Pericles. He did not betray that trust, but such blind acceptance has plagued democratic society ever since. Every leader for whom the *demos* renounces its sovereignty does not have the integrity of a Pericles.

With Pericles and Athens it worked, but the sharp eye of Thucydides recognized that democracy had been compromised. "Pericles indeed, by his rank, ability, and known integrity, was enabled to exercise an independent control over the multitude—in short, to lead them instead of being led by them; for as he never sought power by improper means, he was never compelled to flatter them, but, on the contrary, enjoyed so high an estimation that he could afford to anger them by contradiction. Whenever he saw them unreasonably and insolently elated, he would with a word reduce them to alarm; on the other hand, if they fell victims to a panic, he could restore them to confidence. In short, what was nominally a democracy became in his hands government by the first citizen."[21]

The Age of the "Demagogues"

To the dismay of the conservative critics of democracy, this aristocratic constraint on the reign of the people came apart on the death of Pericles. "As long as Pericles was the leader of the people," Aristotle writes, "the state was still in fairly good condition, but after his death everything became much worse. For then the people first chose a leader who was not in good repute with the better people (*epieikeis*), while, in the earlier period, the political leadership had always been in the hands of the latter."[22] The new leaders, the infamous "demagogues," were not middle class or poor people. Most were wealthy, but they derived their wealth, not from the land, as did the aristocracy, but from commerce or trade.[23] They were a "bourgeois" or "capitalist" element in a precapitalist society. They were, in a word, *nouveau riche* and the Greeks invented the word—*neoploutos*—at just that time in order to describe them.[24]

The rise of these uncouth, irresponsible politicians who, supposedly, appealed to the worst instincts of the *demos* is the inevitable consequence of an ever-widening democracy, which must entail a diminution of the power of the old aristocracy. The pattern has been repeated many times in the last two centuries. Antidemocratic thinkers like Aristotle and Thucydides complained that the leaders no longer led the *demos* but sought only to flatter and please the people.

"After Cleophon," Aristotle deplores, "there was an unbroken series of demagogues whose main aim was to be outrageous and please the people with no thought for anything but the present."[25] This description seems to be almost a direct reference to the remarks of Thucydides: "With [Pericles'] successors it was different. More on a level with one another, and each grasping at supremacy, they ended by committing even the conduct of state affairs to the whims of the multitude. This, as might have been expected in a great and sovereign state, produced a host of blunders."[26]

The philosophers and the comic poets apparently objected most, not to the fact that these officeholders were *nouveau riche* and represented the interests of the poorer classes, but to the style in which they conducted the affairs of the state. They were vulgar. Aristotle comments that Cleon, "appears to have corrupted the people more than anyone else by his violence; he was the first to shout when addressing the people, he used abusive language, and addressed the *Ekklesia* [the Assembly] with his garments tucked up when it was customary to speak properly dressed."[27] One hears the voice of the Boston Brahmins bewailing the rise of the Irish politicians with their shirtsleeves, their whiskey, and their vulgarity. The comic poets had a field day. Syracosius was described "as running around the *bema* yelping like a hound dog." The nicknames accorded this new breed demonstrate how far from aristocratic grace Athens had fallen: "Bleary Eyes," "Smoky," "Hempy" (that is, fit for hanging), and "Quail."[28]

The reputations of these new politicians was so blackened by the critics of democracy that the truth did not emerge until the twentieth century, when a new breed of historians, skeptical of all received dogma and passionately committed to democracy with all its faults, demonstrated that Cleon and Hyperbolus and Cleophon were not merely ranters and ravers but astute, efficient, and even dedicated politicians. As for virtue, they were neither better nor worse than what had gone before—or what was to follow.[29]

The intense antidemocratic critique of the so-called demagogues is remarkably similar to current criticisms of democracy and the supposed loss of civic virtue. The villain today is mass culture or mass society or television. Just as it was not then clear whether the critics of ancient democracy believed the demagogues to be the cause of the people's stupidity or that the people's stupidity gave rise to the demagogues, so today, it is not clear whether the current critics believe the insipid nature of television elections is caused by the stupidity of the people or the people's simplemindedness is engendered by the television. Critics of this ilk seem to agree that there was a time when American politics and American elections were more rational, more mature, and displayed a commensurately greater share of civic virtue than today, when television, mass culture, and mass society have brought out the worst in the electorate (or allowed it to predominate). When was that time of great civic virtue and mature electorates? When Ulysses S. Grant was elected President for two terms—a full eight years? When we all marched triumphantly into the Spanish-American War and Teddy Roosevelt charged up San Juan Hill? Television being lacking, who or what was the corrupter then?

The Fourth Century

Democracy in Athens in the fourth century was a remarkably stable affair. We do not have a shred of evidence of an attempt at an oligarchic coup. Only an onslaught by Macedonian arms brought down the radical democracy. All the tendencies toward a full democracy, implicit since Cleisthenes, came to full flower. The end of the revenues from the empire did not force a cut in payments for political service. On the contrary, payment for attendance at the Assembly was introduced and, in addition, the Theoric Fund was established.[30] This fund provided a small sum to most citizens on each of several holidays such as the Dionysia and the Panathenaea, so they might attend the theater or take the day off from work to enjoy the festivities.[31] The sum was small but the psychological enhancement of the sense of citizenship—the sense that Athens belonged to *all* Athenians—was of great importance. Demacles, an orator and politician of the middle of the century, pronounced it "the glue of democracy."[32]

The board of generals became increasingly open to citizens of middle- and lower-class origin. Cleon had already been elected *strategos* in 425–422 and this tendency toward openness continued in the century that followed. Predictably the aristocracy found it intolerable that common people should become so empowered. The comic poet Eupolis, observing the tendency at the end of the fifth century, lamented: "In previous times, the *strategoi* were taken from the highest families, now they come from the scum of the people."[33]

As Hignett has noted, Aristotle delineated the final shape of fourth-century Athenian democracy in *Politics*, wherein he gives a list of rules conducive to a radical democracy:

First came numerous precautions against the aggrandizement of the various magistracies. Their holders are to be chosen by the people and from the people; if a property qualification is needed for any office it must be kept as low as possible. Appointment must be made by sortition to all offices, or at least to all those not requiring special experience or technical qualifications. The term prescribed for the tenure of office must be brief, and re-election must be forbidden altogether or restricted to a second term for almost all except military offices.

These rules are followed by others calculated to ensure the supremacy of the people in the assembly and the law-courts. All judicial business, or the greater part of it (including the audits of the magistrates, constitutional questions, and all cases of private contracts), is to be decided by all citizens or by a body chosen from all. Sovereignty in all questions is to be reserved for the ekklesia [the Assembly]; all independent authority must be taken from the magistrates or confined within the narrowest limits. In a radical democracy the only body that can be trusted to share power with the ekklesia is the popular council. There must be provisions for state payments for the magistrates, council, law-courts, and if possible the ekklesia as well. No claim to privilege based on superiority of birth, wealth, or culture can be admitted. . . .

In this description Aristotle has done little more than reproduce the characteristic features of Athenian democracy as he knew it from his own experience.[34]

Social Mobility: The Open Society

The political health of an open society—and a radical democracy is the most open of any polity—is intimately and intricately linked with the process and problems of social mobility. Even in the most radical democracy, *the people reign, but they do not rule.* Elites rule. Elites of birth, money, brains, or ability. Supreme sovereignty may lie with the *demos,* who hold the ultimate power to choose those who lead society, but the actual running of the state and the making of crucial decisions lies with a group of elite rulers. In most democracies, the people's main role is to decide which group of elites should rule. The radicalization of democracy encompasses, therefore, not only an ever-widening choice of those who reign, but also an increase in social mobility and commensurate increase in political mobility. People with outstanding abilities, ambition, or the capacity to manipulate others find it easier to enter the ranks of the elite, regardless of low birth and poverty.

Social mobility concerns not only the ambition of individuals but also the great historical movement upward of a whole group of people or class. With the institution of radical democracy people who never before participated in reigning may now do so. The process is never accomplished without the formation of a small group of leaders among the formerly disenfranchised. In a radical democratic society, wherein all men are created equal (even though, as George Orwell quipped, some are more equal than others), those of consuming ambition, born without high connections of wealth, will seek to organize disadvantaged groups of the *demos* as a springboard from which to catapult into the ranks of the elite. Then are played out all those poignant dramas of radical leaders who have attained political power and must now decide how much, or how little, they intend to betray those who put them there. The possibilities range all the way from Eugene Debs, who declared plaintively that he did not wish to rise *from* the working class but *with* the working class, to the near-criminal union leaders so expert in exploiting those they represent.

The healthiest polity—once a society has begun the process of becoming open—offers many peaceful routes by which new members may reach the ranks of the elite from classes usually excluded. This requires of the original members of the elite a tolerance, maturity, and vision not always present. To tolerate the ambition of others and recognize that their desires and one's own may be alike, those with established political power must overcome the paranoid position. Most of the time they cannot accomplish that transformation.

Merit is the one concept that keeps the path up to the elite open; those of the lower classes who have the capacity should be allowed to climb that path. The first elaborate statement of this view occurs in a speech of Thucydides/Pericles we have already discussed, a section of which concludes: "If a man is able to serve the state, he is not hindered by the obscurity of his condition."[35] It may be an unlikely ideal, but the myth of unlimited social mobility, rags to riches, log cabin to White House, can have enormous power within a democratic society, especially those unencumbered by aristocratic baggage as America or Athens in the fourth century. The myth, which has had more potency in America than in Athens, must have a sufficient basis in reality. Aristocratic attitudes are the most injurious to a meritocracy. In Athens the Board of Generals was the last bastion of aristocratic influence and we can see that power crumble during the late fifth century. Cleon was the first political leader to become a general as a *result* of his political power with the *demos*. Previous to this, people attained political power as a consequence of their service as a general. Almost all the prominent politicians up to the death of Pericles were generals. In the fourth century, this process of discrimination had gone a long way: very few prominent political leaders were also generals.[36] Aristocratic influence was at a nadir. High political power and influence were dependent primarily on the exercise of unusual political capacity.

The decline of aristocratic values inevitably produced intense resentment in those still committed to them. The comic poet Eupolis scorns this new breed of pretend-generals in two fragments that have come down to us from about 415. "We old timers didn't use to run things like this. In the first place we had for our city generals from the greatest houses, first men of wealth and breeding. We revered them like gods—they practically were. As a result we met no disaster. But now whatever the situation we make our expeditions with convicted scapegoats in command."[37] And even more bitterly: ". . . and no longer, Lords Miltiades [the hero of Marathon], let swinging teenagers rule us, dragging the generalship around their ankles."[38] The great stability and efficiency of the fourth-century democracy, though not without its problems, being a human society, demonstrated that, despite Eupolis' trenchant wit, the passing of aristocratic dominance need not have been lamented.

Questions of social mobility are intimately connected with considerations of money. Every radical democracy has been a monied society. The possibility of making large amounts of capital in a short time is the finest fuel available for the social-mobility engine. The "demagogues" of the latter part of the fifth century clearly illustrate this point. Cleon's father operated a tannery worked by slaves and was rich enough as far back as 460/459 to underwrite an important performance at the Dionysia festival. Hyperbolus probably made his fortune operating a lamp factory.[39] In the fourth century, such people were fully integrated into the political system; the cry of "demagogue" was raised no longer; merit—and wealth—became the obvious means to political power. The most stable democratic society, though not necessarily the most just, is one in which the people reign, but elites rule, and in which "new men" of unusual wealth or unusual ability, or both, are allowed to rise easily into the rarefied atmosphere of the elite. Fourth-century Athenian democracy was stable because no organized discontented class of people was knocking at the doors of political power, and being refused entry.

This description of an extensively open, and primarily monied, elite fits exactly, of course, our own society of the last fifty years. It is a fascinating experience to go back and read radical tracts of the late 1940s about "America's 100 richest families," or "who owns America?" wherein the Rockefellers, the Morgans, and the Mellons feature so prominently and compare them with *Forbes* magazine's current analysis of the country's five hundred richest people. It is remarkable how many have made their fortunes in the last forty years. It is also remarkable that David Rockefeller does not always make it into the top one hundred. At least at the top, ours is an astonishingly open society.

This has profound implications for the relationship of capitalism to democracy, historically at least, since the future course of both remains obscure. Capitalist enterprise—manufacturing, banking, and commerce—has existed since the formation of Archaic civilizations, thus predating capitalism as a dominant system. It was important in fifth- and fourth-century Athens which cannot be designated a capitalist society.

Capitalist enterprise has proven to be one of the most extraordinary means of social mobility, allowing people born to moderate or few-means to rise into the elite in one lifetime. The problematic is that the elite becomes a monied elite, primarily concerned with money matters. As Aristotle noted, the few continued to rule. The democratic political process can counter this. It gives voice and power to the many and provides to those of rare ability a vehicle of ambition for their own paths into the elite. It remains a very large question whether a democratic, capitalist society is of the few or of the many. In the final analysis, it is probably most accurate to say that it is *both* and therein lies its fundamentally contradictory nature.

Democracy and the Middle Class

We lack any data that would indicate how many Athenian citizens could be thought of as belonging to an upper, middle, or lower class, but Athens in the fourth century had many of the attributes and values of a middle-class society. Though there is great ambiguity and uncertainty in the notion of a "middle class," historically there seems to be a close connection between middle-class society and moderate and radical democracy. Can there be a social parallel between Athens in the fourth century, with both active social mobility and political stability, and nineteenth- and twentieth-century Western societies? In terms of the mobility of whole classes, Marx's nineteenth-century belief was that the proletariat would advance to the highest political power, a social revolution was in the making, and the expropriators would be expropriated. In actuality in this century in advanced capitalist societies, because of trade unionism, the welfare state, continued high employment rates, and an incredible economic prosperity, large sections of the working class, overcoming former attitudes of passivity, have moved into the middle class, thinking of themselves as middle class and enjoying middle-class comforts and middle-class values. The many have become middle-class citizens, at least in their own minds.

Aristotle would argue that this is the healthiest development possible for a polity. His comments, demonstrating a prodigious capacity for political analysis, deserve to be quoted at length:

In all states there may be distinguished three parts, or classes, of the citizen-body—the very rich; the very poor; and the middle class which forms the mean. Now it is admitted, as a general principle, that moderation and the mean are always best. We may therefore conclude that in the ownership of all gifts of fortune a middle condition will be the best. Men who are in this condition are the most ready to listen to reason. Those who belong to either extreme—the over-handsome, the over-strong, the over-noble, the over-wealthy; or at the opposite end the over-poor, the over-weak, the utterly ignoble—find it hard to follow the lead of reason. Men in the first class tend more to violence and serious crime: men in the second tend too much to roguery and petty offences; and most wrongdoing arises either from violence or roguery. It is a further merit of the middle class that its members suffer least from ambition, which both in the military and the civil sphere is dangerous to states. It must also be added that those who enjoy too many advantages—strength, wealth, connexions, and so forth—are both unwilling to obey and ignorant how to obey. This is a defect which appears in them from the first, during childhood and in home-life: nurtured in luxury, they never acquire a habit of discipline, even in matters of lessons. But there are also defects in those who suffer from the opposite extreme of a lack of advantages: they are far too mean and poor-spirited. We have thus, on the one hand, people who are ignorant how to rule and only know how to obey, as if they were so many slaves, and, on the other hand, people who are ignorant how to obey any sort of authority and only know how to rule as if they were masters of slaves. The result is a state not of freemen, but only of slaves and masters: a state of envy on the one side and on the other contempt.[40]

A society of only two classes is unproductive of citizens—people capable of both ruling and being ruled. Those of the middle class, sharing middle-class values of moderation, Aristotle maintains, are the most predisposed to true citizenship.

The adjective "middle-class" can be variously defined. Economically, it means being of moderate wealth or income, neither rich nor poor. Sociologically, it signifies a certain kind of middling status and access to power. Equally important is the notion of middle-class values. When 80 percent of the American public defines itself as "middle class," it not only indicates that people perceive themselves as neither rich nor poor, but also that they aspire to a certain system of values, including comfort, moderation, restraint, lack of flamboyance, and conservatism in life-style, though not necessarily in politics. When Lasch and Bellah[41] criticize American society for its narcissism and radical individualism, implying that somehow these excesses pose a threat to democracy, they are saying that American middle-class citizens have begun in large numbers to ape the aristocracy in life-style. Conspicuous consumption, flamboyance in dress and sexual behavior, and indifference to community ties reflect an aristocratic contempt for solid, bourgeois virtues. Aristotle would have recognized it immediately for what it is: "they never acquire a habit of discipline. . . . people who are ignorant how to obey any sort of authority."

Aristotle, however, was trapped between his acute powers of observation and his theoretical prejudice against a radical democracy. He believed such a democracy would become an oppression of the many over the few and probably lead to tyranny. And yet the middle-class values he praised so highly were exhibited nowhere in greater profusion than in the very Athens his theory of radical democracy condemned. In Aristotelean terms, Athens in the fourth century was the great middle-class society. Social mobility, propelled by merit or money, was at a height. No violent civil strife disturbed the peaceful, democratic discussion of what was to be done within society.

With all its virtues, both ancient and modern middle-class democracy exhibits extraordinary moral contradictions. These democracies have been compatible with the existence of slavery, imperialism, insane warfare, and abject poverty that is destructive of human aspiration. To understand political life in all its dimensions, we turn to the consideration of the dark underside of the democratic *polis*.

PART II

DEEP INSIDE PLATO'S CAVE

7

Moderate Antidemocratic Movements and Oligarchic Death Squads: The Coups of 411 and 404

It all began—as did so much in Athens during those wartime years—with Alcibiades. At the beginning of the disastrous Sicilian expedition in 414, Alcibiades had fled Athenian jurisdiction to avoid prosecution and probably execution for the mutilation of the protective statues of Hermes and for a mock performance of the Eleusian mysteries, both acts of extreme sacrilege. Psychologically incapable of being out of the center of action, Alcibiades retreated, not to some remote, possibly barbarian state, but to Sparta. Having been betrayed, he felt, by his native city (most would argue that he had done the betraying), he was determined to use his intelligence and energy to bring Athens down. He convinced the Spartans permanently to occupy the fort of Decelea in Attica, a strategically impressive move, and urged the Lacedaemonians to construct a large fleet of ships to aid the subject states of the Athenian Empire, many of whom rose up in revolt after the catastrophe in Sicily in 413.

From this point until the end of the war in 404, sea power was the crucial element determining the course of hostilities. The Peloponnesian War had gone on so long—and was probably destined to remain stalemated unless fundamental strategic changes were accomplished—because Sparta remained the great land power while Athens retained overwhelming naval superiority. Unless Athens became a land force to

deal with, or Sparta succeeded in challenging Athenian naval hegemony, no foreseeable end of hostilities was in sight. Athens' naval
recovery after the debacle in Syracuse was remarkable. To heal the
wounds in the state and promote the greatest financial efficiency, a
board of ten Advisors (*probouloi*) was appointed to guide the state
through these critical times. Those on the board represented the most
respected citizens in the *polis*, including the playwright Sophocles. One
hundred and fifty new ships were constructed in twelve months, ships
available to put down the revolts of the subject peoples.

Sparta, meanwhile, had taken Alcibiades' advice and was erecting a
naval force of its own. Money was the problem. Naval forces required
regular pay for rowers and fighters; Sparta was short of this kind of
cash. The need brought a new force onto the stage of the war, one that
would eventually make the crucial difference: the Persian Empire. The
two Persian satraps (governors) in Asia Minor, Tissaphernes and Pharnabazus, began playing in the troubled waters of the collapsing Athenian Empire, hoping to salvage as much as possible for Persia from
the termination of that empire. And the Persians had the cash to fill
the Spartan need. One possibility, clearly, was that Tissaphernes and
Pharnabazus could play Sparta and Athens off against each other to
the point of exhaustion so that the Great King of Persia could ultimately pick up the pieces. In any event, a Spartan fleet sailed to the
islands of Ionia and the cities of Asia Minor, with Alcibiades on board
as chief adviser and Persian cash as an enabling fund.

With Alcibiades, however, nothing remained stable for more than
six months. Serious discontent with his presence arose in Sparta and
the word went out to have him executed. Learning of this, he escaped
to the court of Tissaphernes in November 412 and entered into his
service. Always free with the most sinister advice, Alcibiades urged the
satrap to play the two exhausted antagonists against each other and
then take over the Greek states of Asia Minor. This golden boy of
Athens was capable, however, of playing at least three different games
at once, and he decided to use his supposed influence with Tissaphernes to catapult himself back into the good graces of Athens.

The island of Samos was the main military base of Athenian naval
and land forces. Most of the generals of the army were stationed there,
with ground and naval troops. It was to play a crucial part in all the
events of 411. Alcibiades sent a message to "the leading men" (*duna-*

totatoi) on Samos to spread the word among the "best men" (*beltistoi*)[1] that he was capable of having Tissaphernes abandon the Spartan cause and come to the aid of Athens, provided the Athenians recalled Alcibiades and overthrew the democracy, substituting an oligarchic form of government (government by "the few"). The positive response this remarkable message provoked proved it was not merely the fantasy ravings of a paranoid traitor. Many of the "leading and best men" were more than ready to recall Alcibiades and modify the constitution in the direction of oligarchy, thereby, they thought, enabling the continuation of the desperate war against Sparta. The response was immediate. A small group led by the infamous Peisander, who was to become one of the main leaders of the oligarchic coup, left Samos to meet with Alcibiades to plan this astounding counterrevolution.

We will attempt to understand, in this and the next chapter, the nature of antidemocratic thought and action in Athens, but it may be helpful to suspend the narrative and say a word or two here about the great variety of antidemocratic feeling. In Athens, as in all democracies, criticism of democratic life ran the full gamut. The least violent and least passionate were those of moderate antidemocratic feeling who truly felt that not *everybody* should have a say in the running of the *polis*, certainly not the poorest and the dumbest. They would have been content to restrict political power and sovereignty to those best able to exercise it. "The moderates," William J. McCoy writes, "were patriotic men of conservative bent who supported the democratic government of Athens but who were willing in crucial and difficult situations to impose various checks on the democracy for the good of the state."[2] These moderates, it must be said in their defense, were perfectly willing, without any recourse to violence, to accept the reintroduction of the full, radical democracy after the collapse of each of the two oligarchic coups.

On the far right ranged those fully committed to the violent overthrow of the democracy and the institution of a narrow oligarchy, and willing to resort to any means to achieve this end: assassination, illegal trials and executions, every form of political terror. In the twentieth century, fascist tactics have made us fully acquainted with this form of antidemocratic politics.

Situated between these two poles of opposition to democracy were the antidemocratic "moderates" willing to ally themselves with those capable of using the worst forms of oligarchic terror. Theramenes, one of the most important political leaders of this period, was a protypical representative of this position. Originally a member of the Thirty Tyrants of 404, who perpetrated the worst of the terror, he eventually broke with them as a protest against their excesses, and was executed. In the speech he made before his death, he stated his position succinctly: "I am forever an enemy of those who do not think that a good oligarchy could be established until they should bring the state to the point of being ruled absolutely by a few."[3] Yet his antidemocratic sentiments contain a certain aggression and mean-spiritedness indicating why someone like Theramenes took so long to see where the oligarchic death squads were heading: "But I . . . am forever at war with the men who do not think there could be a good democracy until the slaves and those who would sell the state for lack of a shilling should share in government."[4] The democratic versus antidemocratic controversy always poses the question whether humankind is one species or two.

To return to the chronicle of events: We don't know the details, but it seems clear that Alcibiades' propositions, especially the one bringing Tissaphernes to Athens' side, met with a positive response not only from all sections of antidemocratic sentiment but from loyal democrats as well. After returning to Samos from his meeting with Alcibiades, Peisander journeyed to Athens to convince those still at home to go along with the plan. Desperate to receive aid in the struggle with Sparta, the Athenian Assembly was sympathetic to Peisander's appeal. There was serious opposition, especially from those most concerned with sacred matters (Alcibiades had been condemned for sacrilege), but Peisander was instructed to proceed, with ten ambassadors, to negotiate with Alcibiades and Tissaphernes.

Peisander had much more sinister work to do in Athens, however, and he accomplished it with great aplomb, primarily because his oligarchic allies in Athens were so well organized and so ruthless. During the fifth century, Athenian aristocratic life had become permeated by the phenomenon of *hetairiai*, private, mostly secret, associations of comrades or friends, who met on a regular basis for various purposes. The word most often used to describe them is "clubs." Many ultimately had a political dimension. At their most innocent, they served a social purpose: small groups of men meeting to drink together, recite poetry or speeches, and possibly to engage in sexual indulgence with hired "flute girls." Plato's *Symposium* is a brilliant reconstruction of the atmosphere of such a club meeting, with much talk of sex, but no actual performance.

Members of the clubs rendered aid to each other, in such situations as lawsuits, or in supporting the politically ambitious. The most vicious of these clubs became the center of violent antidemocratic feeling. It was to these that Peisander opened up his heart, expressing his hopes for counterrevolution. "Pisander also went the round of all the clubs already existing in the city for help in lawsuits and elections," Thucydides tells us, "and urged them to draw together and to unite their efforts for the overthrow of the democracy."[5]

It is crucial to realize that there was strong and widespread opposition to the democracy, and that a substantial group of nonpsychotic politicians were willing to use *any means* to abolish it. After Peisander left on the embassy to Alcibiades and Tissaphernes, some of the club members banded together and assassinated Androcles whose crimes were that he was a leader of the *demos* and that he had been largely responsible for Alcibiades' banishment a few years before. "There were also some other obnoxious persons whom they secretly did away with in the same manner."[6] "Obnoxious," that is, to these aristocratic scions of the "best families" in Athens. Nonpsychotic human beings are capable, under the banner of cleansing society, of obliterating an "obnoxious" human being as one would a worm or a grass snake. The mastermind behind these terrorist tactics, after Peisander left Athens, was the orator Antiphon, noted for his aristocratic prejudices and for his extraordinary capacity to compose speeches for people involved in lawsuits to deliver in court, a person enormously capable within the parameters of the society in which he lived. He was, Thucydides asserts, "one of the best men of his day in Athens. A man of superior intellect who could ably express his thoughts in words, he never willingly came forth in the Assembly or competed in any public contest since he was suspected by the people on account of his reputation for cleverness. He was, however, the one man most able to help both in the courts and before the Assembly those who required his advice."[7] Such a man was capable of ordering the execution of Androcles and other "obnoxious" people who were guilty of nothing more than exercising their constitutional rights.

So successful were those death squads that they succeeded in terrorizing the whole city. The ordinary political institutions used by the *demos*, in particular the Assembly and the jury system, were of little value in dealing with a secret conspiracy of powerful citizens. At the start of the coup, the oligarch clubs completely dominated the political scene.

While the terror was being established in Athens, Peisander and his delegation met with Tissaphernes and Alcibiades, his spokesman. Tissaphernes had no real interest in giving aid to Athens; whether Alcibiades knew this from the beginning, we do not know. Tissaphernes made so many unreasonable demands as the price of his assistance that the Athenian ambassadors left in disgust and returned to Samos. Those committed to the oligarchic coup decided to drop Alcibiades and the hope of Persian aid, but continue with the conspiracy, both at Athens and in Samos.

From this point on, we can clearly differentiate two fundamentally different antidemocratic political positions and two fundamentally different prescriptions for the "reform" of the Athenian state. The moderate position endorsed a limited democracy in opposition to the radical democracy dominant in the *polis*. It would restrict the franchise to approximately five thousand citizens, those capable of supplying their own hoplite armor and weapons. All financial subsidies paid by the state to citizens for political service would end. The moderates were committed, nonetheless, to continuing the war against Sparta at all costs. This meant that, if they had to choose between letting the radical democracy continue and betraying the state to Sparta, they would opt for the democratic alternative. Most significantly, they were committed to using constitutional means to achieve their ends and would accept the radical democracy if legal means could not transform it. Many of these moderates unfortunately got sucked into the oligarchic antidemocratic maelstrom and found themselves endorsing policies and committing actions they originally had no intention of undertaking. At such critical and revolutionary times, the flood of history has a way of sweeping mere people before it.

The aims of the oligarchs and their death squads were precise. They wished to establish the tyrannical rule of a small, narrow oligarchy and to put narrow oligarchies into power in the allied cities controlled by Athens. They were determined to destroy both the radical and moderate democratic opposition and were prepared to use any available terror. These oligarchs wished to pursue and triumph in the war against Sparta, but they were prepared, when they perceived their counterrevolution was failing, to betray the city to the Spartan enemy. They preferred defeat and the dominance of Sparta to even a moderate (that is, nonradical) democracy. One could understand a great deal of history of the world if one could perceive clearly the psychic motivation of these haters and betrayers. What inward panic were they fleeing that they were compelled to unleash terror on their own city?

After the failed meeting with Tissaphernes, Peisander met with the oligarchic clubs on Samos, setting a coup in motion on that island, and then returned to Athens. Along the way, he and his colleagues established oligarchic governments in several of the subject states and took with them, from these states, hoplite forces that could be trusted to do Peisander's bidding. They were not needed. The city had been so thoroughly cowed by the oligarchic terror that Peisander and Antiphon could destroy the democracy without official violence. The Assembly agreed to set up a committee of thirty (dominated by the counterrevolutionaries) to revise the constitution and submit its proposals to the *demos*. In a special meeting of the Assembly, held outside the walls of the city to ensure that the oligarchic faction would dominate, a new constitution was proposed and adopted. First, all payments for civil functions were abolished. Second, full franchise was to be restricted to 5,000 (membership in this select group was vague; the list was never published). Third, a new Council of Four Hundred was created to rule the state in the interim.

The conspirators prepared everything with great care. A few days after the Assembly met outside the walls, the new Council of Four Hundred gathered, each councillor with a dagger beneath his cloak. They were backed by 400 or 500 of the hoplites Peisander had brought from the island states and by 120 "young bravos who had terrorized Athens" for the past several months. This formidable force burst into the democratic Council chamber, paid the members of the Council their wages for the remainder of the term, and ordered them to leave or, obviously, lose their lives.[8] The coup was executed without loss of one drop of blood. Terror had so silenced the people that in the four months in which the Four Hundred retained their oligarchic power, very few citizens were executed.

A similar attempt at counterrevolution in Samos was a total failure. Between the two scenes of action, the balance of political power was exactly opposite. The strength of the radical democracy in the Athenian state lay with those who served in the fleet, almost all of whom were of the lowest economic and social class, the *thetes*. The fleet was stationed in Samos, thus denuding Athens of those most inclined to support militantly the democratic constitution. Although the troops on Samos had certain oligarchic clubs, they must have had an ad hoc quality compared to the permanence of the club establishments at Athens. Though oligarchy might succeed at Athens, it had no chance on Samos. The oligarchic death squads on Samos were not impotent, however, and one of their first acts was to assassinate Hyperbolus, who had been a leader of the radical democracy at Athens until he was ostracized in 416. In exile at Samos, he was obviously politically active, since the terrorists conceived of him as a logical first target.

The Athenian terrorists on Samos allied themselves with a group of three hundred Samian oligarchs who wished to overthrow the democratic state. The attempted coup was met by a democratic alliance of Samian patriots, sailors and leaders of the Athenian fleet, and several important generals of the Athenian army. The democrats were immediately victorious; thirty of the oligarchic ringleaders were executed; the coup had failed.

When news of the Four Hundred at Athens reached Samos, the Athenian armed forces were in an uproar and ready to bring civil war to Athens. This would seriously have threatened the situation vis-à-vis Sparta. Two generals, Thrasybolus and Thrasyllus, took over leadership of the democratic forces and bound them together, "oligarchs and democrats, Athenians and Samians, by solemn oaths to stand together, uphold democracy, fight the Peloponnesians vigorously, treat the Four Hundred as enemies, and have no traffic with them."[9] They were determined to preserve the democracy. "They took the view that Athens had seceded; that with Samos to fall back upon they could conduct the war with virtually undiminished resources; that, if worst came to worst, they could settle down elsewhere than at Athens and found a new state."[10]

To prosecute the war more vigorously, the leadership and the *demos* on Samos decided to recall Alcibiades, who was still maintaining, with great energy, the fiction that he could bring substantial aid from Tissaphernes. Not long after Alcibiades' return to Samos, delegates from the Four Hundred arrived to convince the troops of the legitimacy and benign intentions of the new government at Athens. Rumors of civil terror preceded the delegation and the enraged *demos* wanted to sail immediately to overthrow the oligarchs.

"Now it was," Thucydides writes, "that Alcibiades for the first time did the state a service, and one of the most special kind. For when the Athenians at Samos were bent upon sailing against their countrymen, in which case Ionia and the Hellespont would most certainly at once have passed into possession of the enemy, Alcibiades it was who prevented them. At that moment, when no other man would have been able to hold back the multitude, he put a stop to the intended expedition, and rebuked and turned aside . . . resentment . . . against the envoys."[11] For once, the extraordinary charisma of the man was used in the interests of moderation and rationality.

In the city of Athens, the oligarchs remained in power only four months. Without any military action from the troops on Samos, the counterrevolution collapsed from its failure to capture the Athenian citizens' loyalty. The Four Hundred never published a list of the five thousand who were to rule the city under the moderate constitution and it quickly became apparent that they had no intention of sharing the rule with others. Moderate antidemocrats became outspoken enemies of the oligarchic regime. The latter, finding its power slipping away, decided to betray the city to Sparta rather than fall victim to the reinstated democracy.

Of the oligarchs, Thucydides tells us "Their first wish was to have the oligarchy without giving up the empire; failing this to keep their ships and walls and be independent while, if this also were denied them, sooner than be the first victims of the restored democracy, they were resolved to call in the enemy and make peace, give up their walls and ships, and at all costs retain possession of the government, if their lives were only assured to them."[12] When they realized that the oligarchs were going to bring the Spartans into the city, the citizenry turned on them and the coup was over. Most of the leaders of the Four Hundred fled to the Spartans at Decelea. A few, including the brilliant Antiphon, remained in Athens, and were subsequently tried and executed, despite the fact that, according to Thucydides, Antiphon's speech in his own defense was the most powerful ever delivered in an Athenian court.[13] Politics, even in a democratic society, not only answers the questions of who gets what, when, and how, but also, human nature being what it is, easily accelerates toward the more awful question: who dies?

404: The Terror of the Thirty Tyrants

In 405 the Athenian fleet was completely annihilated in the battle of Aegospotami. For all practical purposes, the war was over. Sparta ruled the Greek world. Its principal general, Lysander, established narrow oligarchies, committed to friendship with Sparta, in numerous Greek states. It is not surprising that he should desire to do the same at Athens and considering the history of 411, that a group of oligarchic Athenians should be more than willing to set up an oligarchic state under Lysander's supervision. What was not foreseen, and what remains incredible, was the barbaric depth and extent of the terror instituted by the thirty "tyrants." Nothing in the history of Athens since the democratic reforms of Cleisthenes (with the significant exception of the activities of the death squads in 411) indicated that such totalitarian terror was possible in this great city, the school of Hellas. These thirty were not a group of psychopathic gangsters; most of them came from the finest families in Athens. None gave any indication of psychosis. A very sick worm gnaws at the psyche in many "leaders of society." To understand why human politics is so often a tragic tale, we must try to comprehend the nature of that parasite.

Several months passed between the battle of Aegospotami and the final capitulation of Athens. During this period, without any assistance from Lysander, the oligarchic clubs, strengthened by the return of all political exiles banished by the democratic state, welded themselves into a formidable, united, secret political conspiracy. All clubs were to take orders from a central committee of five, who styled themselves "ephors" (with the two Spartan kings twenty-eight ephors were the political rulers of Sparta). Ten tribal governors, one for each tribe, were appointed, who "directed what measures should be passed by their votes, and who were to be magistrates; and they had authority to do anything else they wished."[14] The democracy produced no equivalent organization, either secret or open. All the oligarchs needed to overthrow the constitution was a little help from Lysander.

Xenophon's narrative of these times (contradicted by Aristotle) names Critias, the son of Callaeschrus, as the leader of the oligarchic conspirators and of the terror which followed.[15] Whether or not he was the foremost oligarch, he played a crucial role in the events of 404. Of an aristocratic family, he was a leading intellectual of his day, an author, an associate of the sophists, of Alcibiades, and of Socrates himself. Even after his vicious role in the terror was known, Plato in the fourth century named a dialogue for him and mentioned him sympathetically in two other dialogues as an associate of Socrates. He was savage, ruthless, and a hater of equality. He was known to have said that "the finest constitution is that of Sparta," and with even more sinister portent, "all changes of constitution involve bloodshed."[16] Tradition has it that in some Greek city a monument was erected to Critias after his death, on which, "A personified Oligarchy was shown setting fire with a torch to Democracy. The epigram read: 'This memorial is for the good men who for a short time restrained the accursed Athenian people from arrogance [hybris].' "[17] This brings to mind the twentieth-century totalitarian metaphor that democracy is a cancer that has to be excised from the body politic. For some, underneath all the capacity for efficient, rational political action there lies a deep, irrational, vicious hatred.

After several months of trying to hold out for better terms, faced with starvation as well as defeat, Athens finally capitulated to Sparta. The oligarchic conspirators, with the Spartan commander Lysander as enforcer, were in complete control of the *polis*. A meeting of the Assembly, observed by Lysander, created a commission of Thirty to draft a new constitution and govern the state meanwhile. Lysander ordered the resolution adopted and so it was. One of the first acts of this new ruling cabal was to bring to trial a group of democratic leaders, including several generals, who had opposed the peace treaty with Sparta and could be counted on to give trouble to the oligarchic junta. The trial was orderly (the verdict has survived in written form). Those accused were duly executed. No violent protest ensued.[18]

The Thirty now took an action apparently approved by most people. A group of sycophants (who made money bringing people to trial or blackmailing them with the threat of trial), takers of bribes, and pilferers of public funds were brought to court, found guilty, and executed. It was a "cleansing" of the city, and though most, if not all, of those charged were undoubtedly guilty of some crime, history has taught us that this kind of political ritual purification is most often a prelude to civil terror. The Thirty declared "that the city must be purged of unjust men."[19] The Thirty, obviously, would delineate who was just and who was not. To consolidate their rule and prepare themselves for any action, the Thirty established a corps of 300 floggers—an organized punishment and death squad—and asked Lysander to establish a Spartan garrison of 700 hoplites who took up their quarters on the Acropolis.

In the eight months they held power, the oligarchs executed about 1,500 citizens and resident aliens and banished an additional 5,000, all this in a *polis* of only about 25,000 free men. Some were executed or banished because of political opposition or supposed opposition or suspected future opposition, but many were executed merely for the sake of appropriating their wealth. A list of 3,000 protected citizens was published. All others could be executed or have their property confiscated on the flimsiest pretext.[20]

One can understand the "rationale" for mass terror against the democratic opposition, to cleanse the *polis* of this disease and build a permanent oligarchic state. The execution and banishment of citizens to seize their wealth, however, was a self-destructive act, revealing deep irrational springs of oligarchic action. The 5,000 or so who were banished did not disappear from the world. They became the backbone of the exiled forces that returned to Athens and overthrew the oligarchy. What did the oligarchs imagine they would do? Did they fantasize that 700 Spartan troops made them invulnerable? How long did they expect to enjoy the wealth they commandeered over the corpses of their fellow citizens? It was a psychopathology bordering on psychosis, occupying the frontier between the paranoid position and paranoia itself, like the worst excesses of the twentieth-century totalitarian states.

One of the first objects of this gangster behavior was the city's population of resident aliens (*metics*), many of whom were quite wealthy: perfect targets. The orator Lysias, himself a victim of this particular terror, tells the story:

> At the meeting of the Thirty, Theognis and Peison made a statement that some of the metics were disaffected, and they saw this as an excellent pretext for action which would be punitive in appearance, but

lucrative in reality. They had no difficulty in persuading their fellows, to whom killing was nothing, while money was of great importance. They therefore decided to arrest ten people, including two of the poorer class, to enable them to claim that their object was not money, but the good of others, as in any respectable enterprise.[21]

Peison and Theognis entered Lysias' house. Theognis went into the factory attached to the house to inventory the stock and the slaves there. Lysias succeeded in bribing Peison, who took him to another house, from which he escaped to the port and thence to the state of Megara. Lysias' brother, Polemarchos, was not so lucky; he was seized, taken to prison, and forced to drink hemlock. Not even the pretense of a trial. The Thirty appropriated the fortunes of the two brothers, including 120 slaves.[22]

The terror, like all terrors, produced many dramatic and pathetic scenes wherein average, sensual human beings courageously attempted to cope with a situation in which they were the helpless victims of human depravity. A court speech written by Lysias reveals a tale of politics and mythic emotion that could have come from the pen of Euripides: an Athenian real-life tragedy.

Now, when sentence of death, gentlemen, had been passed on them, and they had to die, each of them sent for his sister, or his mother, or his wife, or any female relative that he had, to see them in prison, in order that they might take the last farewell of their people before they should end their days. In particular, Dionysodorus sent for my sister— she was his wife—to see him in prison. On receiving the message she came, dressed in a black cloak . . . as was natural in view of the sad fate that had befallen her husband. In the presence of my sister, Dionysodorus, after disposing of his personal property as he thought fit, referred to this man Agoratus as responsible for his death, and charged me and Dionysius his brother here, and all his friends to execute his vengeance upon Agoratus; and he charged his wife, believing her to be with child by him, that if she should bear a son she should tell the child that Agoratus had taken his father's life, and should bid him to execute his father's vengeance on the man for his murder.[23]

The data remaining to us fail to indicate whether Agoratus was brought to trial or if he escaped punishment under the provisions of the amnesty proclaimed by the restored democracy.[24] We cannot know whether the dying Dionysodorus' cry for vengeance was ever satisfied.

All extended political terrors eventually eat up their creators: the French Revolutionary terror and the Bolshevik experiences confirm this. The Athenian oligarchic terror was no exception. The most dramatic and best documented Athenian example was the execution of Theramenes. He had played a crucial role in almost every important political development at Athens between 411 and 404. One of the foremost members of the Four Hundred in 411, he was almost the first to turn on them and played an important part in their overthrow. He was the principal negotiator with Sparta after the defeat at Aegospotami, settling the final terms of Athens' capitulation. When the Thirty Tyrants were appointed, he was included in their number. He was the best of a very bad lot. Commentators continue to disagree as to how much of an oligarch or "moderate democrat" he was. Lysias condemned him for his extraordinary capacity to change sides; Aristotle regarded him as a moderate seeking a mean between oligarchic and radical democratic extremes. In our time, William J. McCoy finds him innocent of oligarchic beliefs, whereas Antony Andrewes blames him for Athens' difficulties in the latter part of the war.[25] It is true that he did turn on both oligarchies when they went to extremes, in betraying the city to the Spartans in 411 and commencing the uncontrolled terror in 404. Yet one wonders what he was doing in bed with these terrorists in the first place? Did not the experience of 411 indicate that he should have declined the opportunity to be among the Thirty? He seems to have been enticed by their intentions and then repelled by their actions. In any event: "Nothing in his life became him like the leaving of it."[26] His sense of the heroic and the dramatic, in the teeth of death, proclaimed him a true Athenian.

First he spoke out against the terror: "But it is not honourable, as it seems to me . . . for people who style themselves the best citizens to commit acts of greater injustice than the infamous used to do. For they allowed those from whom they got money, to live; but shall we, in order to get money, put to death men who are guilty of no wrongdoing?" This kind of provocation put his own life in jeopardy. The Thirty, spreading the word that Theramenes had to go, called a meeting of the Council, making sure that it was attended by a group of young bravos with daggers hidden under their cloaks.[27] Theramenes was immediately brought up on charges and given the opportunity to defend himself. His defense was successful enough to influence many of those present.

We may read the speech as condemning the speaker for staying so long within the den of depravity. "When these Thirty began to arrest men of worth and standing, then I, on my side, began to hold views opposed to theirs."[28] First, Leon the Salaminian was put to death, though guilty of no crime or trespass. The Thirty then arrested Niceratus, the son of the great war hero Nicias, from one of the wealthiest families in all Athens. He also demurred, Theramenes insists, when Antiphon (not the orator), a loyal patriot, was executed. "I objected also, when they said each of us must seize one of the resident aliens." Despite so many objections, Theramenes remained a member in good standing of the Thirty. And this while many sincere democrats had fled the city, organized a resistance in exile, and even succeeded in capturing Phyle in Attica, which was to become their base for recovering the state. Theramenes knew how to get to Phyle. Instead he stayed in Athens, a member of the ruling junta, objecting over and over again as more and more people were executed. If Theramenes was a "moderate" in his antidemocratic position, he was an extremist in the tolerance he seemed able to call on when it came to the extermination of his fellow citizens. If the Thirty had not murdered him, how long would it have been before he voluntarily left that execution ground? In the chapter that follows, an attempt will be made to understand why such civil terror becomes possible in a democratic society—and we will keep Theramenes in mind, as well as Critias.

"Theramenes replied with such spirit that the Councillors openly showed their approval of his words. Critias then moved forward his assassins, struck Theramenes off the list of the Three Thousand, and in the name of the Thirty condemned him to death. Before the eyes of the terrorized Council, Theramenes was torn from the sanctuary of the altar . . . and was dragged across the Agora to drink the deadly cup of hemlock. As he tossed the dregs to the ground, he proposed a mocking toast 'to the fair Critias.' "[29]

Theramenes' objection to the arrest and execution of Leon of Salamis was echoed by a more important person in the history of the world, the great Socrates himself. The psychopathology of the oligarchs detracted very little from their cleverness. Their method was to involve as many ordinary citizens as possible in their illegal acts. An arrest and execution having been decided on, the Thirty would direct some simple citizens to carry out the deed, thereby involving as many as possible in the political holocaust. Socrates, in Plato's dialogue *Apology*, tells the tale.

> When the oligarchy came into power, the Thirty Commissioners in their turn summoned me and four others to the Round Chamber and instructed us to go and fetch Leon of Salamis from his home for execution. This was of course only one of many instances in which they issued such instructions, their object being to implicate as many people as possible in their wickedness. On this occasion, however, I again made it clear not by words but by my actions that death did not matter to me at all—if that is not too strong an expression—but that it mattered all the world to me that I should do nothing wrong or wicked. Powerful as it was, that government did not terrify me into doing any wrong action. When we came out of the Round Chamber, the other four went off to Salamis and arrested Leon, and I went home. I should probably have been put to death for this, if the government had not fallen soon afterward.[30]

It is one of the great tragic ironies of history—and remains, despite numerous attempts to explain it, a mystery—that, had the oligarchic terror executed Socrates, it would have saved the restored democracy the trouble of doing so.

The actions of the terrorists produced more and more exiles dedicated to the overthrow of the junta. They fled primarily to Megara, Argos, and Thebes, states sympathizing with their aims. Using the captured strong place of Phyle as their base, the democratic exiles increased so in number that they could challenge the Thirty in direct combat. A stroke of good fortune aided the democratic cause: political conflicts at Sparta forced Lysander to withdraw, leaving the oligarchs without their primary support. In a pitched battle fought in Piraeus, the democrats prevailed, Critias was killed, and the democracy ultimately restored to the city.

Before their final defeat, the Thirty performed an act of terror so horrifying that it reminds us of nothing so much as the mass deportations and exterminations of the twentieth century. It is almost impossible to comprehend how so-called "civilized" human beings can regard other people's lives as so much trash to be disposed of when it appears convenient to do so. The town of Eleusis was part of the city-state of Attica, possibly second to Athens in importance. Realizing their hold on the government was no longer secure, the Thirty decided to prepare a place of refuge to which they could retreat in case of defeat. They chose Eleusis, near the border of Attica, the closest town to Sparta. Critias and the rest of the Thirty went to Eleusis, accompanied by the Athenian cavalry. They held a review of the townspeople, claiming that they were determining how many additional soldiers were needed to garrison the town. The citizens, they insisted, must register and pass out of the gate of the town. As they did so, they were seized and bound, and turned over to Lysimachus, the commander of the cavalry, to be taken to Athens. The following day they were "tried" in the Odeum, while the Spartan garrison—fully armed—observed the scene. Critias instructed the "jurors" to cast their ballots for execution, with which order they duly complied. We are not told by Xenophon whether these executions actually took place, or whether the Eleusinians were held prisoner, or exiled, but the town of Eleusis had been swept clean of its citizens and made safe as a refuge for terrorists.[31]

The question is not why did the fair city of Athens produce a group of voracious assassins, but rather why were there so many of them and how could they so easily seize power. Every democratic society has people suffering from this form of moral psychosis. The great historical circumstance was not that Hitler sent out the call to the German people, but that so many responded with such alacrity and such vehemence. There are a number of people in the United States today who would be willing to join a death squad, particularly if it resonated with those perennial forms of American maliciousness: racism, anti-Semitism, and homophobia. Whether a democracy lives or dies becomes, therefore, a question of numbers and power: how many troops on each side. The still unsolved profound sociological mystery is what determines these relative strengths, what manner of political development, economic catastrophe, conflicts of values, or ambivalences of child rearing produce historical catastrophes and triumphs. As we expectantly watch the newly liberated countries of Eastern Europe struggle heroically to establish and maintain democratic institutions, we become acutely aware, not only that fundamental attitudes toward the paranoid position and democratic freedom are asserting themselves, but also of how crucially important will be the numbers of people holding to various positions. If the great democracy of the ancient world, one of the most magnificent societies ever seen, was still capable of producing a significant number of citizens suffering from moral psychosis, then we are forced to consider that there are always barbarians, not only at the gates, but also within the walls.

8

Antidemocratic Thought, the Beginnings of Totalitarian Theory, and the Origins of Political Terror

It is important to distinguish between antidemocratic thought and a critique of democracy. It would be absurd to hold that democracy—though possibly the best polity imaginable—is a perfect political system, or that, with certain improvements and adjustments, it can be made so. E. M. Forster's "two cheers for democracy"[1] says it precisely. A critique of democracy, an analysis of the inherent contradictions in its functioning, is still compatible with a strong sympathy with its basic aims.

Antidemocratic thought is a much different thing. No matter that it concentrates its criticisms on the inevitable inefficiencies and absurdities of democratic politics, its underlying postulate consists of an attack on the basic premise of democratic life: the fundamental equality of all human beings. "Equality" is an ambiguous word and the ambiguity surrounding it has been used to criticize the democratic state. Plato upbraids democracy for "dispensing a certain equality to equals and unequals alike."[2] One must immediately ask: equal and unequal in what particular respect? No one claims, not even the wildest, radical democrat, that all people are equal in their intelligence, or in their capacity to make accurate political judgments, or in their concern for justice. The democratic view regards all people as equal, in Jefferson's sense, in their rights to life, liberty, and the pursuit of happiness. Plato and other proponents of antidemocratic thought seem to be criticizing democracy for absurdly giving an equal say in the affairs of the state to people with unequal capacities to make mature judgments. Such is the manifest content of their argument and this is a problematic within democratic society. Underlying these stated opinions, in my view, is a contempt—and a fear—of the very idea of human equality. Many people find something exceedingly frightening in a world in which, as Demosthenes put it, "each man considers that he himself has a share in equality and justice."[3] Some despise the notion that everyone else is an equal, if only in the moral sense. Without understanding the contempt and the fear of equality, we will not be able to comprehend the great war between democratic and authoritarian politics and the millions of lives lost in that conflict.

In Athens, at the end of the fifth century B.C., the oligarchic view was that the democracy should be abolished. Certain "moderate" democrats—whether they should more properly be termed "moderate antidemocrats" is a question—took the position that it was wise "to impose various checks on the democracy for the good of the state."[4] The expedition to Syracuse, which had proved so disastrous, had been voted in the full Assembly, where all citizens had the franchise. The loss of a major war always threatens the legitimacy of the reigning government. As Athens came closer and closer to losing the war, it was natural that the radical democracy should be blamed. Inevitably certain "moderate" elements, with no particular hatred for democracy or equality, concluded that the health of the state required a restriction of the democracy, in order that more responsible elements in the citizenry should have more say in state affairs. So persistent was this manner of thinking that, even after the oligarchic catastrophe of the Thirty, a man named Phormisius introduced a proposal that citizenship be restricted to those owning land, which would have disenfranchised almost five thousand citizens.[5] The proposal was defeated, the radical democracy restored.

Restrictions on full democracy may be imposed in various ways: the right to vote may depend on property qualifications or on the capacity to provide hoplite armor; voting may remain universal, but the right to hold major office may carry property or other restrictions; the political center of power may be transferred from the Assembly to the more restricted membership of the Council.[6] Those who are excluded usually have less money than those who remain; those with less money are considered also to have less education or culture and less judgment, and to be more inclined to pursue their own narrow interests rather than the larger concerns of the *polis* as a whole. For those seeking "moderate" reforms in the democracy, this manner of reasoning was axiomatic and yet there remained the fundamental question: Are the best rulers of society to be found among "the best people"?

The problem with this analysis of the actions of "moderate democrats" is that there exists not one piece of written evidence to confirm McCoy's view that "In the last decade of the Peloponnesian War the moderates were patriotic men of conservative bent who supported the democratic government of Athens but who were willing in crucial and difficult situations to impose various checks on the democracy for the good of the state."[7]

As soon as the critics of radical democracy start speaking, what comes out of their mouths is not a reasoned analysis in favor of a restricted democracy, but rather various forms of prejudiced argument based ultimately on the conception that lower economic classes are lower in every way. Herodotus, himself a supporter of the democratic regime, had already presented this basic antidemocratic position in his history in the middle of the fifth century. A fictionalized debate takes place in sixth-century Persia. Otanes had taken the democratic position and Megabyzus responded to him:

> I agree with Otanes in all that he has said against tyranny, but he does not give the best advice when he recommends giving power to the people, for nothing is *more ignorant and violent* than the foolish mob. It is intolerable for men escaping the arrogance [*hybris*] of a tyrant to subject themselves to the arrogance [*hybris*] of the *uncontrolled demos*. A tyrant at least knows what he is doing, but the people do not. How could they know when *they have never been taught and have no personal experience of anything good?* The people rush headlong into politics without a thought, like a swollen river.[8]

The accuracy of Herodotus' perception of the basic prejudice underlying the antidemocratic position is revealed by a pamphlet, written probably in the 420s, originally collected in the works of Xenophon (who clearly did not write it), and subsequently ascribed to an anonymous "Old Oligarch." He writes "In every country the elite [*to beltiston*] is opposed to democracy. For among the members of the elite there is least wantonness and injustice, and the greatest exactness as regards the things which benefit a gentleman [*ta chresta*], whereas among the people [*demos*] there is most ignorance, disorder and vice [*poneria*]. For more than others they are driven to shameful deeds by poverty, lack of education and ignorance. Some might say that one should not allow all these people to speak on an equal footing . . . but to reserve these rights to the cleverest [*dexiotatoi*] and the best men [*aristoi*]. But the Athenians . . . allow the vulgar people [*poneroi*] to speak. . . . any wretch can get up and find what is good for him and his peers. . . . The Athenians realize that the ignorance, vice and goodwill of such a man is of greater advantage to them than the good man's excellence, wisdom and ill-will. . . . Habits such as these . . . are the best way to preserve the democracy."[9]

These are the rantings, one may say, of some prejudiced intellectual mediocrity, but Plato, and the fictionalized Socrates as his spokesman, cannot be so categorized. Pericles, Plato has Socrates argue, corrupted the Athenian *demos* and the state, which eventually turned on him. "For I am told that Pericles made the Athenians *idle* and *cowardly* and *talkative* and *covetous*, because he was the first to establish pay for service among them."[10] As if the *aristoi* (the best people), of whom Pericles— not to mention Critias—was one, were not capable of being idle and cowardly and talkative and covetous. And in the *Republic* Socrates begins his most virulent attack on democracy with a wild statement clearly contradicted by the history of Athens: "The democracy . . . comes into being when the poor win, killing some of the others and casting out some, and share the regime and the ruling offices with those who are left on an equal basis."[11] Plato knew very well that from the time of Cleisthenes until the writing of these words the only large-scale civil killing that had taken place in Athens had been done by oligarchic mad dogs.

Once democracy has been institutionalized within society, anti-democratic thought is overwhelmingly the product of prejudice against poor people. A small minority may reason their way, unencumbered by irrational prejudice, to an antidemocratic or moderate democratic position, but they are few. The vast majority of people holding antidemocratic views are driven by intolerance. Prejudice may vary enormously in its intensity. Normal, average anti-Semites, for instance, who really don't like Jews and make anti-Semitic jokes on social occasions, are a long way from becoming concentration camp guards or instigators of a pogrom. They suffer from bias rather than hatred. But this form of disease is related to the more virulent, catastrophic forms. Plato was a long way from being Critias, but somehow, in the dark, irrational part of the mind, they could understand each other. Each found the *hybris* of the *demos* intolerable, though they differed profoundly in their choice of means to eradicate it.

All prejudice originates in fear of the stranger. One does not feel biased against, one does not hate, that which is not also feared. Anxiety about the strangeness of others is the beginning of intolerance. The greater the commitment to the paranoid position, the greater the fear of otherness, the more intense will prejudice and hatred become, the more violent and catastrophic the means used to "cleanse" society of the particular pollution. In Athens there were no Jews and no blacks. Poor people, and the radical democracy that represented their aspirations, served the need for a scapegoat.

Plato, it must be said, cannot be so easily dismissed. He clearly recognized that turning political power back to the aristocracy that had possessed it before the establishment of the radical democracy was not the answer to the inadequacies of the *demos*. The aristocracy could be as cowardly and as covetous as the *demos* portrayed in Plato's drama. The tolerance for Critias notwithstanding, the experiences of 411 and especially 404 would convince anyone that the nobly born might also exercise injustice and tyranny.

Plato's solution to the problem of justice within society was remarkable: a new aristocracy was to be created, one that drew its power and position, not from wealth and birth, but from wisdom and education for justice.

"Political power must therefore be given to a select group of wise good men, who would impose a good way of life on the rest by a rigid system of education and control."[12] This nonaristocratic solution still reflects the basic assumption of the antidemocratic position: The vast majority of people cannot be trusted to control their own lives.

Ironically, the events at Athens demonstrated that, if democracy was to be restricted to make it more efficient and more just, the wisest course might be to end the political participation of all those whose wealth was *above* a certain set amount. The "best people" had proven to be the worst people.

"Once upon a time in my youth," Plato writes in the so-called seventh letter, "I cherished . . . the hope of entering upon a political career as soon as I came of age. It fell out, moreover, that political events took the following course. There were many who heaped abuse on the form of government then prevailing, and a revolution occurred. In this revolution . . . thirty came into power as supreme rulers of the whole state. Some of these happened to be relatives and acquaintances of mine, who accordingly invited me forthwith to join them. . . . No wonder that, young as I was, I cherished the belief that they would lead the city from an unjust life . . . to habits of justice . . . so that I was intensely interested to see what would come of it. Of course I saw in a short time that these men made the former government look in comparison like an age of gold."[13]

One problem was—and is—that status considerations played a crucial role in determining the antidemocratic stance. Democracy rose to power within, and in conflict with, aristocratic society, and aristocratic prejudice against lower or low status people has been a fundamental impediment to democratic life. A certain linguistic usage reflecting this prejudice permeated Greek thought. There existed a

> social terminology in which high and low status individuals are regularly characterized as the good (*agathos* ["good"], *aristos* ["best"], etc.) and the bad (*kakos* ["bad"], *poneros* ["burdensome"], etc.) and a properly run society is one in which the "good" rule and the "bad" are ruled.[14]

Our "Old Oligarch" provides us with a prime example. "If you are seeking to establish good government [*eunomia*], you will first of all see the straightest kind of men establishing the laws for their own good. Then the good men [*chrestoi*] will punish the wretches [*poneroi*]; they will determine the policy of the city and prevent madmen [*mainomenoi*] from deliberating, speaking or meeting in assembly."[15] His "natural" aristocratic prejudice is further revealed when he states that "The practice of physical exercises and the pursuit of culture have been brought into disrepute by the common people as being undesirable because they realize that these accomplishments are beyond them."[16] The old virtues, we are being told for one of the first times, but by no means the last, are no longer held in honor.

Some found it intolerable that people with certain occupations were allowed to participate in political decisions. Xenophon has Socrates describe the Athenian Assembly as being composed of "dunces and weaklings," who earn their living as "fullers or cobblers or builders or the smiths or the farmers or the merchants, or the trafficers in the market-place who think of nothing but buying cheap and selling dear."[17] And a fragment tentatively assigned to Andocides prays: "May we never again see the charcoal burners coming from the mountains into the city, nor their sheep, their cattle, their wagons, and their pusillanimous womenfolk, nor old men and working-class people putting on full hoplite armor."[18]

Greek democracy could not escape such criticism even after its demise. Cicero in Rome in the first century B.C. condemns it for establishing a situation in its assemblies where it was a simple thing for demagogues to stir up "artisans and shopkeepers and all that kind of scum."[19]

We may be inclined to dismiss these outbursts as the prejudiced ravings of small-minded bigots until we read the long discussion in Aristotle's *Politics* on the question of whether craftsmen and mechanics (*banausoi*) should be allowed to become citizens or not. One of the greatest minds of the Greek world concludes that "The best form of state will not make the mechanic a citizen. . . . for a man who lives the life of a mechanic or labourer cannot pursue the things which belong to excellence."[20] In those states that do admit laborers to citizenship, Aristotle elaborates, the result is a situation wherein some can achieve excellence as citizens (those who do not labor with their hands) and a whole group of them (the mechanics) cannot—obviously not the best form of state.

In our own society status considerations of money, achievement, occupation, and, sometimes, birth play such an important role in our day-to-day relationships that we ascribe a certain "naturalness" to such concerns and do not see the deep, irrational origins of this manner of reacting and feeling. A strong concern with status relations is a paranoid defense erected to bolster a fragile self-esteem and a fragile self. Why does a higher status make us feel more worthy? And why does feeling "more worthy" make us feel more real? All considerations of status are erected on a foundation of prejudice: that a person of more wealth or more success is somehow more of a person than one with less. The Greek obsession with "the best people" and the denigration of certain occupations was just such a prejudice, finding its origin in the same place as all prejudice. It might have been innocent enough had it not held democracy in the balance. Democracy, and certainly a radical democracy, is possible only when this paranoid view, which ascribes worth to certain externals, is overcome. Consider how enormously difficult it is to believe that all people are created equal, even living in a society that proclaims that message as one of its founding ideals. We begin to appreciate how fragile a thing radical Greek democracy was.

One underlying anxiety—sometimes stated, sometimes not—runs through almost all antidemocratic ruminations: that a radical political democracy will lead to economic democracy; that the *demos* will use its political power to ameliorate its economic condition at the expense of the "best people." We have noted already the continuing fear running through the society about the cancellation of debts and redistribution of land, an anxiety still expressed by Cicero in the middle of the first century B.C.[21] There was a tendency on the part of many people, as with us today, to regard politics as solely a question of interests, with ideals and the good of society as a whole playing no, or very little, role. If such were the case, if the lower classes attained political power, their "interests" would dictate that they take from the rich what they themselves desire. The antidemocrats did not seem to notice that, in the stable radical democracy of fourth-century Athens, nobody was prevented by the *demos* from getting—and remaining—rich. When the second great coming of radical democracy occurred in the nineteenth and twentieth centuries, the anxiety on the part of the "best people" that democracy would mean "socialism" or "communism" played a crucial role in all antidemocratic political activities.

The Beginnings of Totalitarian Theory

In the history of the evolution of Western society, ancient Greece and ancient Israel played a crucial role. In the scheme of social evolution, these two societies, which I call *Classical civilizations*, succeeded to, and went beyond, the Archaic civilizations of Mesopotamia, Egypt, Mycenae, and such states. Talcott Parsons calls Israel and Greece "seedbed" societies, indicating that they accomplished a radical advance in cultural evolution.[22] Israel, as we know, was the progenitor of three religions—Judaism, Christianity, and Islam—that have profoundly influenced the history of the world. What Western civilization owes to ancient Greece needs no elaboration. When the various influences on Western civilization finally came together as one culture in Europe in the twelfth century A.D., four independent cultural influences were joined into one complex civilization: those of ancient Greece and ancient Rome, the Judeo-Christian, and the Germanic (Franks, Anglo-Saxons, and Normans).

Ancient Greece and Israel brought profoundly different elements to this unique cultural phenomenon, but there was one view of the world which they shared and which set them off from the Archaic cultures that had preceded them. In the highest realms of thought and moral perception—represented in Israel by the prophets and in Greece by philosophy and democratic political practice—the concept developed that human nature could be morally transformed through education, culture, and religion. It is not a question of whether or not human nature can be changed, since that is precluded by definition if one defines a thing's nature as that which, in essence, it is. It is a matter of declaring that human nature is such that human beings are capable of moral transformation, of becoming more just than they have been and of being able to create and establish a society manifesting a greater sense of justice than any society that went before. The prophets of Israel declared that God demanded such a transfiguration; Greek philosophy declared that human nature itself called for such a transformation; democratic society declared, in essence, that moral evolution was an historical reality.

"By spiritual means," Ernest Barker writes, "Plato sought to regenerate man and society. . . . This is implied in the fundamental conceptions of the *Republic*. The State is the product of men's minds: to reform the State, we must reform men's minds. . . . true justice can be realized only when the mind acquires its true habit. . . . the possibility of a permanent reform of men's minds depends . . . on the character of social conditions."[23]

What is extraordinary in Plato's conception is the notion that there can be "a permanent reform of men's minds." This incredible conceit did not originate with Plato, however. Democratic political practice, as enunciated by Pericles and Thucydides, had already proclaimed that certain political institutions were capable of creating a new kind of man:

> Our constitution does not copy the laws of neighbouring states; we are rather a pattern to others than imitators ourselves. Its administration favours the many instead of the few; this is why it is called a democracy. If we look to the laws, they afford equal justice to all in their private differences; if to social standing, advancement in public life falls to reputation for capacity, class considerations not being allowed to interfere with merit; nor again does poverty bar the way, if a man is able to serve the state, he is not hindered by the obscurity of his condition. The freedom which we enjoy in our government extends also to our ordinary life. . . .[24]
>
> In short, I say, that as a city we are the school of Hellas; *while I doubt if the world can produce a man*, who where he has only himself to depend upon, is equal to so many emergencies, and graced by so happy a versatility as the Athenian.[25]

Plato, too, wished to produce a new man, though the versatile Athenian was very far from being his model.

There is no important human ideal that is incapable of corruption. By that strange and perverse psychic alchemy wherein great ideas corrupt the world, the marvelous conception that human society is capable of significant reform became perverted into the beginnings of totalitarian thought. Ideology is the perversion of wisdom. No sooner had the ideal of a new man appeared on the scene than the perverted conception of a controlled society quickly followed. *Totalitarianism* is really too modern a word to describe accurately what was being proposed. *Paranoid society engineering* is much closer to the truth. "Paranoid" because total control of the society, impossible in reality, was being postulated and because repression of freedom was a necessary instrument. "Social engineering" because the mass of human beings were to be regulated as things to be moved around at will, to make the world orderly. Society and the human beings who composed it were to be treated like some piece of complex machinery that could be regulated, by proper mechanical technique, to proceed in the direction of "greater justice."

In the seventh book of the *Republic*, Socrates, having expounded at great length on the nature of the new just society, trembles not at the manner in which such a utopia is to be created. "When true philosophers . . . come to power in a city . . . taking what is just as the greatest and the most necessary . . . they will provide for their own city." "How?" asks the convenient Glaucon. "All those in the city who happen to be older than ten they will send out to the country; and taking over their children, they will rear them—far away from those dispositions they now have from their parents—in their own manners and laws that are such as we described before. And . . . the city and the regime . . . will itself be happy and must profit the nation in which it comes to be." And then Glaucon asserts agreement in the portentous voice of the social engineer: "That is by far the quickest and the easiest way."[26]

Had we lived in the nineteenth century, we probably would have dismissed this cast of mind as the unnecessary utopian fantasies of a great genius. The catastrophes of the twentieth century—the mass transportations and deportations (not to mention executions) all in the name of building a new society and creating a new person—give us pause. We have lived to see as many people annihilated in the cause of creating a "just" society as in the interests of naked power. The paranoid dream of a perfect society turns out to be one of the most dangerous weapons ever invented by human beings. No claim is being made here that Plato was even close to being a tyrant capable of horrible acts, but it is important to emphasize the cast of mind that proposes that, in the interests of justice, all those over ten years of age should be transported to the country. We have come to know what human beings, in mass society, are capable of. Plato's *Republic* is a grandiose effort to reconcile two powerful—and opposite—tendencies. One is a profound belief in the primacy of justice, the other an equally powerful paranoid anxiety that freedom inevitably means loss of control. The *Republic* is both a utopia and an anti-utopia, a place of perfect justice and of no freedom.

This kind of utopian thought involving paranoid social engineering did not arise in Rome. Only when there is a real "threat" of democracy and extensive freedom does the totalitarian mind become active. In Rome there never was an actual possibility that radical freedom could triumph and, therefore, there was no need to restore order through total control. The aristocracy never lost domination of the *demos*; no exaggerated fear of freedom ever became palpable; none of the enormous contradictions of a "modern" world ever presented themselves.

At this point, one theoretical speculation may be in order. Speculation, because there are no known sociological facts from the ancient Greek world that would support such a conclusion; the history of the last two centuries, on the contrary, does provide an immense amount of confirmatory data. In an historical circumstance where political freedom and democracy are urgently being fostered within society, an overwhelming anxiety arises from the breakdown of the kinship system that is a necessary concomitant of this historical process. We do have one significant fact for Athens: When Cleisthenes instituted the democracy, he abolished the old tribal system of four kinship tribes and substituted a purely political system of ten "tribes" based on residence, not birth. Any dissolution of kinship forms of social coherence will provoke an anxiety of separation.[27] The total paranoid control promised by all schemes of social engineering and by totalitarian societies are attempts to heal the terrible wounds caused by the destruction of kinship forms of social solidarity. They create, in fantasy or in reality, a solidarity more inflexible, more controlling, more overwhelming than any kinship system ever provided. The catastrophic history of this century demonstrates how frightening a forced entry into the modern world, a world of liberty and democracy and tenuous kinship ties, can be. We may speculate that the rise of the theory of paranoid social engineering, together with the actual existence of a totalitarian state in the Greek world (Sparta, which we will look at presently), was, psychologically considered, a defensive measure erected to counter the increase of anxiety caused by the destruction of the kinship world.

Many will feel that the attribution of paranoid social engineering is palpably unfair to Plato. I am considering a cast of thought, not an actual political program. And when we look at the *Laws* of Plato, a work written late in his life and about which there is general agreement that it was set down as a more realistic counterpart to the *Republic*, we find the same authoritarian cast of mind at work. After describing at length the reformed religious beliefs of his new state, Plato prescribes the mode of dealing with heresy: Those who do not abide by the new forms are to be denounced to the court; the guilty are condemned to five years of solitary confinement, denied contact with any other human being except those subjecting them to intense religious training. Prisoners still not converted after five years are to be put to death.[28] Dodds responds to the incredible modern reverberations of these notions by noting, quite correctly, "In this respect the nearest historical analogue is not the Inquisition, but those trials of 'intellectual deviationists' with which our generation has become so familiar."[29]

The point is neither to condemn nor to absolve Plato but to try to discover the nature of the parasite gnawing at the psyche of one of the greatest men who ever lived. If Plato was tempted, if only in his imagination, to become a Grand Political Inquisitor of the *polis*, what might we expect from Critias and Antiphon, who would not recognize justice if they stumbled on it? Two things, I suggest, were crucial: *a fright of freedom and a contempt and hatred for the concept of equality.* The one mechanism that could allay both these anxieties simultaneously would be a social situation in which a small elite group severely restricts the freedom of the mass of people. If such restriction is undertaken in the interests of "justice," then an enormous psychological and moral ambivalence is reconciled in one stroke. It is the institution of absolute control under the banner of an ideal that makes totalitarian societies so difficult to comprehend. Aristotle's complaint that in democracies "each person lives as he likes"; Isocrates' declaration that the Areopagus, the old Council of the Athenians, should regain its power to control the *private* lives of citizens; Plato's criticism that in a democracy "everyone . . . is allowed to do what he likes"—all are of a piece. In each case, the prescription is the same. The *demos* must give up its freedom and elite rulers must assume pervasive control of all aspects of life, both public and private.[30] Human beings are to be engineered by other human beings into living a more orderly, more just life: a totalitarian utopia.

The socially engineered society performs a strange dialectical movement in regard to family and kinship ties. Urgently sought after originally because of the threatened total collapse of the kinship system, it insists upon breaking all still existing family loyalties and substitutes for them a fierce subordination to the state as the ultimate, the omnipotent, and all-embracing kinship system. Such is the meaning of Socrates' plan to transport all those over ten beyond the borders of the city. The state will become mother and father, uncle and aunt, older brother and sister to the new citizens.

All of which brings us to Sparta. Pausanias was the great Lacedaemonian hero of the war against the Persians, having commanded the allied Greek forces in 479 at the battle of Plataea which drove the Persians back to Asia. Pausanias subsequently became the first Spartan to extend Lacedaemonian influence far beyond the Peloponnese, liberating the Greek cities of the islands and of Asia Minor from Persian hegemony. This personal power ultimately went to Pausanias' head, and he ended up betraying the interests of the Spartan state (c. 470). Having learned that his traitorous behavior had been discovered, he fled for safety and asylum to the temple of Athena of the Brazen House in Sparta. It would have been sacrilege to drag him violently from the altar at which he was a supplicant. The Lacedaemonians were hesitant how to proceed. The mother of Pausanias appeared on the scene, said not a word, picked up one brick, placed it against the door of the temple, and returned home. In no time, the Spartans completely walled in the entrance. Pausanias died of starvation either in the temple (Diodorus, XI, 45. 6–7.) or plucked from the temple a moment before death to prevent pollution of the shrine (Thucydides, I, 134).

In 371 the Spartans were defeated by the Thebans and their allies in the battle of Leuctra, suffering such defeat that their military dominance of Greece was destroyed forever. When it became known which soldiers had been slain and which had survived the cruel battle, the mothers, fathers, friends, and relatives of the slain acted out all manner of rejoicing, celebrating the fact that their sons had died for the state and were thus blessed. The fathers of those who survived hid themselves at home among the women, not daring to show themselves in the public square.[31] Survivor guilt, one may say, of near psychotic dimensions that only a totalitarian state could inspire and exalt.

The attempt to determine the true nature of Spartan society is an historian's frustration. With two of our main sources, Plutarch's *Lycurgus* and Xenophon's *Politea* (Constitution) *of the Spartans*, it is impossible to determine how much is idealized myth and how much actual sociological fact.[32] When Xenophon tells us, for instance, that "in Sparta there is no more physical love between men and boys than there is between parents and children or brother and brother. I am not surprised that some find this difficult to believe. . . . "[33], the question becomes not whether male homosexual activity was practiced in Sparta, but how much we can believe of the *rest* of what Xenophon is telling us when he has calmly presented us with this palpable falsehood.

For the purposes of the argument being made here, it does not matter. For the idealized historical myth states that the lawgiver Lycurgus, in one generation, instituted a radical social revolution in

Sparta, creating, in essence, a totalitarian state. The question for the historian is how much the actual state in Sparta conformed to this totalitarian myth. Was it really such a total state or merely a controlled engineered society? It would be of great interest to know, for instance, whether a certain kind of eugenic engineering was seriously practiced by exposing weak infants at birth, by insisting on the participation of young women in athletics so they would become physically superb mothers, and by having older men lend their wives to younger and more virile ones for the purpose of child rearing. Or whether it was true that young husbands continued to live in their communal, all-male arrangements, sneaking in to cohabit with their wives in the darkness. Young men were not allowed to live openly with their wives until they were thirty.

Myth or not, historical Sparta felt obliged to imitate it as much as possible. All observers of the society agreed on one thing. It was the most completely controlled state of any in the Greek world. The poet Simonides insisted that, as horses are broken when colts, so the Lacedaemonians are " 'the tamer[s] of men' " who "trained the citizens to obedience to the laws, and made them tractable and patient of subjection."[34] Images of the nonfree order of the natural world came readily to mind. Plutarch wrote that "Lycurgus trained the citizens neither to wish nor to be able to live as individuals. Like bees, they were always to be integrated with the state, swarming round their leader, almost beside themselves in their eagerness and rivalry to belong wholly to the state."[35] And Aristotle, whose relationship to freedom was much more complex than Plato's, criticized the educational system of the Spartans for teaching, essentially, only one virtue—courage—which resulted in their becoming "beast-like."[36]

People of antidemocratic, authoritarian temperament have been attracted to, and approving of, the Lacedaemonian state. Even during the Peloponnesian War some Athenian youths of oligarchic inclination wore their hair long in imitation of the Spartan style. Critias, we have observed, was a great enthusiast of the Spartan constitution. The list of Sparta's admirers includes Xenophon, Plato, and several twentieth-century enthusiasts of the totalitarian state.

There is no general agreement today about what truly constitutes the concept of "modernity," what are the basic constituents of the "modern world" or the "modern state." One factor, however, is definitely worth consideration in this context. No modernity, no modern world, is possible without a breakdown and transformation of the kinship system. Such a breakdown will generate great anxiety, which in turn will force people to seek defenses against that anxiety and to seek institutions that restore or preserve the intense bonds of the kinship system. "Totalitarian" thought and institutions are an inevitable reaction to the enormous conflicts that "modernism" generates. The Spartans were one of the first societies to erect totalitarian institutions as a way of saying "No!" to the "modern" world, attempting thereby to ensure that "modernism" would not happen.

The Psychological Origins of Political Terror

This section will try to bring together into one coherent theoretical statement separate insights into the origins of violent antidemocratic feeling and action that end in oligarchic terror. In essence, an answer will be sought to the question: What makes a scion of a wealthy, aristocratic family, assured of economic comfort and of a valid place in society, become a member of an oligarchic death squad?

The issues involved are of enormous importance. No one has yet satisfied our fierce desire to understand these unimaginably complex matters. Does one finish reading *The Authoritarian Personality* by Adorno and others or Arendt's *Eichmann in Jerusalem*[37] saying "Yes, now I understand the catastrophes of the twentieth century"? Trying to comprehend the Greek experience, in regard to which we have some distance, feeling neither guilt nor responsibility, may, it is hoped, contribute something toward that understanding.

Three fundamental psychic experiences are essential to the creation of antidemocratic terror: fear and contempt; a passionate quest for almost total control; and an inordinate amount of unrepressed primitive aggressive impulses. The expression of all three is essential to the creation of a totalitarian state. Two by themselves will not do. The difference between paranoid social engineering, as sometimes formulated by Plato, and the actualities of the Spartan totalitarian society lies in the fact that the social engineering position lacks the raw primitive aggressive energy of the terrorist or totalitarian system. In Plato's case, humanly enough, the demand for justice stands in the place where, in the totalitarian syndrome, aggression resides. Therefore, the sweeping contradictions in his work: fear and contempt, control, *and* justice. Each of the three elements of the terrorist stance—fear-contempt, control, and aggression—are primary manifestations of the paranoid position. Basic distrust of the world underlies, and presides over, each.

Fear and Contempt

Though fear and contempt can generally be clearly differentiated, in their manifestations, they are intimately related. Contempt is a defense against anxiety. Fearing someone perceived as inferior, one defends against the anxiety by saying, in essence: "How can I be afraid of such a lowly person when he is so contemptible?" I would like to suggest, further, that there is always a strong undercurrent of anxiety on the part of any person or any group that dominates over another person or group, especially if the latter shows signs of overthrowing that domination. No matter how secure the slave owner's position may be, there is always a dread that the domination will not hold, that matters will, in fact, become reversed and the slaves become masters. We can clearly observe contempt as a mechanism for handling anxiety and dread of the reversal of domination in the conflict between men and women, wherein masculine contempt for women reflects the primitive fear of what women may do to men.[38] Aristotle, in his discussion of the causes of social revolution (either from democratic or oligarchic inclination), lists fear and contempt as primary causal factors.

"Contempt," he asserts, "we can see . . . in democracies, when the wealthy despise the disorder and anarchy which they see prevalent."[39] Underneath that contempt, can we also observe a dread that such disorder and anarchy will result in an appropriation of property, that the position of economic domination will cease to hold?

Democracy arose in a struggle against aristocracy. Contempt for nonaristocrats, especially those with social pretensions, has always been an essential of the aristocratic position. Here again, an underlying fear that aristocratic dominance will not continue, that the objects of tyranny will become the new rulers, is transformed and expressed as feelings of denigration. Whenever democracy is attacked in its early stages, it is accused of overthrowing aristocratic virtues, though its real crime is the abolition of aristocratic privilege. One of the supposed goals of the terror will be the restoration of aristocratic values. The Thirty, Xenophon tells us, was determined to make Athens a city fit for "gentlemen" (*kaloi k'agathoi*).[40]

A key to understanding lies in Aristotle's pregnant phrase (as translated by Barker) that there are those whose "minds are filled with a passion for inequality." Aristotle is describing a particular circumstance, not making a generalization about humankind. He is addressing a circumstance in which a person conceiving himself as superior to the general run of citizens finds that, because of democratic equality, he gets only an equal share of honor, profit, or power and not the greater share he feels is his due.[41] There is much to be gained by going beyond this circumstance, by generalizing the insight that there are those whose minds are filled with a passion for inequality, *regardless of the particular occasion.* They are born with—or acquire, as a result of inadequate nurturing—a contempt for equality. Over and over again, we can observe, in the oligarchic mind, this attitude of contempt for those who would presume to be equal and a fear of the freedom in society that makes this pretension possible.

We have already noted the monument erected to Critias, praising him for restraining "the accursed Athenian people from arrogance."[42] The *hybris*, obviously, of the *demos* in thinking they were as good as their betters. From the history of archaic Rome, Gnaeus Marcius Coriolanus has become for us, through the works of Plutarch and Shakespeare, the very symbol of aristocratic arrogance and hatred for the commons.

"Why do I see plebian magistrates, why do I, after being sent beneath the yoke and ransomed, as it were, from brigands, behold Sicinius [a tribune of the plebs] in power? Shall I endure these *humiliations* any longer than I must? When I would not brook Tarquinius as king, must I brook Sicinius? Let him secede now and call out the plebs; the way lies open to the Sacred Mount and the other hills."[43]

Much can be learned from this brief outburst of rage. Other people's freedom occasions humiliation (*indignates*) for Coriolanus. He becomes less of a person, his self-esteem is critically lowered because others, whom he considers inferior, regard themselves as equals to, as free as, himself. He, a great military hero who has suffered for his country (under the yoke and ransomed), must now greet Sicinius as an equal.

An outrage, a humiliation. He rages on as if freedom were a scarce commodity in a zero-sum game: the more Sicinius has, the less Marcius has. Sicinius' claim to equality is, for Coriolanus, a threat to his own freedom, to be equated with the tyranny of Tarquinius. We may recall that Thucydides (III, 45) uses the expression "freedom, or the rule over others," the implication being that to give up the rule over others is to give up one's freedom. That is precisely Coriolanus' primitive, paranoid view: the plebs' freedom takes away his, which can only be restored by reducing the plebs to their previous position of inferiority.

And thus the enormous rage, the "ulcerations of anger," in Dryden's rendering of Plutarch.[44] In Coriolanus' distorted paranoid view he is struggling, not to maintain an unjust domination over others, but to win back his liberty from those who have taken it away. Can anyone deny that whatever means undertaken in that struggle is justified? In our own day, another great conservative, who had no intention of using violence against the polity, told us that, "Extremism in the defense of liberty is no vice."[45] Rage, justification, excess—we come close to perceiving the motives of those who would use *any* means to destroy democratic equality.

To close this section on fear and contempt, let me relate an experience I found uncannily revelatory of the unconscious, irrational motives determining political attitudes. It was November 1970 and James Buckley had just been elected U.S. Senator from New York. Buckley was the first of a new breed of politicians, those who openly declared themselves "Conservative" with a capital "C," to be elected to a major office. It was a landmark occasion in America's turning away from the New Deal and Liberalism. Attending a board meeting of a local private school the Wednesday after election day, I walked from the parking lot with a fellow member whose grandfather, I knew, had made millions in the textile business. There were no realistic financial worries in that family. The man was jubilant over the election results; a new era was coming; the country was finally returning to its senses. And then he burst out: "And that will show those welfare mothers!" Their *hybris*, their contention that they had *rights* to live a life without degradation, had obviously been eating away at the debased form of freedom he carried in his soul. Those "welfare mothers," exactly like the tribune Sicinius, had posed a dire threat to his liberty. Now, possibly, he could breathe again.

Absolute Control

All situations of dominance—of men over women, of rich over poor, of politically powerful over politically helpless—have both a utilitarian and a paranoid dimension. The utilitarian is easy to understand. Those with the power get most of the goods of the world, the goods, that is, that can be fought over: money, property, luxury. It seems an obvious fact of human nature that people want those things so badly that they are quite willing to take them away from others. The passionate desire for things, however, never remains in a purely utilitarian state. It immediately gets involved with the paranoidia of greed (discussed later in the book). It is also true, I believe, that greed for things is not a significant motivating factor contributing to oligarchic terror or a totalitarian state. Many totalitarians, like Savanorola and Lenin, have been ascetics.

The paranoid dimension of dominance may be the most consequential for human history, though on the surface the utilitarian may seem most important. This paranoid quality, then, in addition to being about who owns the scarce commodity of freedom, is centrally about control, and ideally about absolute control. All psychological systems of dominance aim, ultimately, at absolute control. First, to be dependent on no one but oneself for one's existence, and second, to recognize no other independent being. "This absoluteness," writes Jessica Benjamin a feminist theoretician, "the sense of being one (my identity is entirely independent and consistent) and alone (*There is nothing outside of me that I do not control*) is the basis for domination—and the master-slave relationship."[46]

Total domination is necessary, first, because of the pervasive anxiety that the roles of master and slave will be reversed. No tyrant really believes, in the most primitive regions of the psyche, in the permanency of his tyranny. A dominance so fragile can only be maintained by constant vigilance and the most consummate control. There is, second, the overwhelming necessity to prove that one has absolutely no need of anyone else. Such a fiction—a psychological impossibility—can be maintained only if those upon whom one is dependent give what is needed immediately, without resistance, without ambivalence. A paranoid vision of an omniproviding mother who responds, like a robot, to one's every wish.

Compared to tyranny, democracy is a messy, inefficient, unpredictable, uncontrolled society. The vote of some ignorant, garlic-smelling, uneducated peasant may affect the whole course of one's life—when the vote is for war, for instance. Could one imagine a situation of greater *dependence* upon others? For the person of oligarchic extremist temperament, this is the most horrifying situation imaginable. The resort to assassination and political terror may seem a small price to pay for the restoration of order. Other people's freedom drives some people insane. Total control pretends to be the only existent antidote to that madness.

This helps us understand the enormous importance of torture and mind control ("brainwashing") in totalitarian societies. It is true that torture has a utilitarian dimension. It is a deterrent to political opposition and it may extract valuable information from the victim. In almost all totalitarian societies, however, the torture regime goes out of control. It is not merely the sadistic impulses of the torturer that are responsible, but also the victim who refuses to talk or confess, who refuses to accept the validity of the regime, who refuses to abandon his or her assumption of the right to freedom. The "examiner" will use any means, including the most primitive, to force a confession or a conversion. This immediately becomes the great metaphor, the amazingly accurate objective correlative, of the struggle for control that goes on in the primitive parts of the torturer's psyche. He operates physically on the victim, but also metaphorically on himself. No relief is possible until the victim is forced to admit: There is no freedom, I abandon the concept of independent existence. For the severely paranoid, torture becomes a ritual exercise that must be performed over and over again.

Absolute control postulates absolute distrust of the world. Democracy, on the contrary, involves taking great risks which can only be taken under an optimistic assumption. For the oligarchic extremist, such risk, such optimism, such trust is intolerable.

Primitive Aggression

When the drive toward total control fails, when the defensive mechanism of contempt no longer works in repressing fear, when the *demos* refuses to remain oppressed—when any of this occurs—primitive rage at the untrustworthiness of the world rises, and such rage always requires an object. To become a member of an oligarchic or fascist death squad, however, requires something additional: an absence of the "normal" mechanisms of repression and sublimation, available to most people in most societies, that inhibit the acting-out of such primitive rages.

Political murder is psychologically different from ordinary criminal murder. Criminal murder requires a psychotic or near-psychotic perpetrator. Political murder is undertaken, or authorized, by seemingly ordinary, respectable members of the community, capable of functioning very well within the complexities of a "modern" society. In one regard, however, they differ profoundly from their social colleagues: They allow that a certain murderous rage is legitimate. In Rome, Appius Claudius, the Younger, c. 471, "hated the plebs with a hatred that surpassed his father's: What? Had he been beaten by them? Was it in his consulship, who had been chosen as pre-eminently fitted to resist the tribunician power, that a law had been passed which former consuls had prevented? . . . His wrath and indignation at this thought drove his fierce spirit to torment the army with a savage exercise of authority. Yet he was unable to subdue them."[47] A perfect candidate, had the time been right, to lead an oligarchic coup and command squads of terrorists.

The frailty of the human psyche being what it is, a certain number of people among the leaders of society will always suffer from the kind of moral psychosis we are delineating and trying to understand. Numbers, then, become crucial. How many? What percentage? Appius Claudius became politically ineffective because *the majority* of the patricians did not support his murderous inclinations and because the plebs refused to remain passive under such pressure.[48] In some societies, however, the use of political terror—assassination, disappearances, torture—on the part of the ruling oligarchy becomes the "normal" condition. Aristotle advises the rulers of oligarchies, if they wish to stay in power, to abandon their extreme aggression toward the *demos*, as exhibited in those states where the oligarchs take an oath that reads: "I will bear ill will to the people, and I will plan against them all the evil I can."[49]

With all the evidence before us, including the voluminous information from twentieth-century death camps, we are still baffled by the question, "How could human beings do such things?" The poet Percy Bysshe Shelley (1792–1822) tried his hand at answering that question. The cannibal in such people, he tells us, never died. In St. Peter's Fields, Manchester, England, in 1819, there was a huge rally of sixty thousand people, including an unusually large group of women and children, to promote the reform of parliament and the extension of the franchise. None of the participants carried arms and they engaged in no provocative or violent behavior. The magistrates seized the speakers and ordered the Hussars and the yeomanry to charge the crowd. Numbers are disputed, but at least six hundred people were killed or wounded. Robert Stewart, second Marquess of Londonderry, known to history as Lord Castlereigh, was the leader of the English government of that time, a man of enormous political gifts and accomplishments. Shelley, hearing the news of the Peterloo massacre, was moved to look into Robert Stewart's black soul.

> As I lay asleep in Italy,
> There came a voice from over the Sea,
> And with great power it forth led me
> To walk in the visions of Poesy.
>
> I met Murder on the way—
> He had a mask like Castlereigh—
> Very smooth he looked, yet grim;
> Seven blood-hounds followed him:
>
> All were fat; and well they might
> Be in admirable plight
> For one by one, and two by two,
> He tossed them human hearts to chew,
> Which from his wide cloak he drew.[50]

Castlereigh becomes, clearly, a symbol for all those who conceive that it is legitimate to murder innocent people in order to retain one's political power.

One thing seems clear. There is a pathological condition of the psyche that hates democracy, equality, and freedom with as much passion as human beings have ever felt about anything. Some people have it to a greater degree, some to a lesser. Some societies exhibit it in moderation, others run mad with it. Only by understanding it will we ever begin to know why oligarchic terror overwhelmed Athens twice within seven years. To call it "paranoid" or "paranoia" is, at the least, to give it a "local habitation and a name."[51]

9

Clubs, Factions, Political Parties, and Mass Action

This deliberation on the necessity of political parties for democratic life may be regarded as an extended footnote to the two previous chapters.

The coups of 411 and 404 would have been impossible without the oligarchic clubs which were the true driving force behind the counterrevolutions. These clubs were not formed for this purpose. They began, possibly in the "Dark Ages" of Greece that preceded the Archaic age, as societies of aristocrats who congregated for social, ritual, or political purposes.

It is probable that from their beginnings in ancient times membership in these societies was secret, a condition that continued into the historical era. Something in the very nature of aristocratic life is conducive to "clubbing." The *demos* in the ancient world, no matter how potent politically, never learned the virtues of, or the power to be attained by, these *hetaireiai*. Even when they were not engaged in violent oligarchic counterrevolution, these societies played a powerful role in Athenian political life. "He who would understand Athenian politics," writes W. R. Connor, "must understand Athenian friendship. He must inform himself not only about the meetings of the assembly and the council, but about the gatherings of families and friends as well."[1] The most important institutionalized form of such gatherings were the secret meetings of the *hetaireiai*.

Their continued existence explains the antidemocratic nature of their thought and action. Those who play a dominating role in society, who tyrannize over others, like to associate with people playing the same role, sharing the pleasures and anxieties of domination. The clubs also became a perfect means by which aristocratic-oligarchic factions could exercise political power. In essence, they evolved into secret political cells. Plato regarded them as a threat to the justice and stability of the *polis*. "The greatest enemy of all to the whole state," he writes in the *Laws*, is the person who, "by introducing a man into office, enslaves the laws and brings the state under the domination of the clubs."[2] Plato has in mind any faction within society, not just the *hetaireiai*, that does not concern itself with the interests of the *polis* as a whole. As was cruelly demonstrated in 411 and 404, secret political parties posed a continuous threat to democratic life if not countered by assertive democratic action.

The *demos* can respond in one of two ways to the formal organization of the oligarchies. It can form factions or political parties of its own, or it may resort to the less formal mode of mass action. The paralysis of the unorganized *demos* in the face of an organized secret conspiracy is brilliantly portrayed by Thucydides, narrating the events of 411. Many modern historians talk of Athens as a "face-to-face" society wherein everyone of importance knew everyone else and what their intentions were. Thucydides demonstrates that this was not quite the case and, further, that the politically unorganized are at an enormous disadvantage against a coherent political faction.

> Fear, and the sight of the numbers of the conspirators, closed the mouths of the rest; or if any ventured to rise in opposition, he was presently put to death in some convenient way, and there was neither search for the murderers nor justice to be had against them if suspected; but the people remained motionless, being so thoroughly cowed that men thought themselves lucky to escape violence, even when they held their tongues. An exaggerated belief in the number of the conspirators also demoralized the people, *rendered helpless by the magnitude of the city, and by their want of intelligence with each other, and being without means of finding out what their numbers really were.* For the same reason it was impossible

for any one to open his grief to a neighbour and to concert measures to defend himself, as he would have had to speak either to one whom he did not know, or whom he knew but did not trust. Indeed all the popular party approached each other with suspicion, each thinking his neighbour concerned in what was going on, the conspirators having in their ranks persons whom no one could ever have believed capable of joining an oligarchy; and these it was who made the many so suspicious and so helped procure immunity for the few, by confirming the commons in their mistrust of one another.[3]

We have no evidence from Athens of any institutions that might be deemed political parties in either the fifth or the fourth centuries. We do have much data about what are most accurately termed "political factions." From the time of Cleisthenes and his struggle with Isagoras at the end of the sixth century, until the end of the Peloponnesian War, we can distinguish a "liberal" or radical democratic and a "conservative" faction within Athens, and for most periods can even name the leader of each. In the late 460s, Ephialtes was the leader of the radical democratic faction and Cimon the head of the conservatives. When Ephialtes was assassinated in 461, Pericles, who had been his right-hand man, assumed control of the democratic faction. After the death of Cimon, the conservatives, "seeing that Pericles was . . . grown to be the greatest and foremost man in all the city," countered his power by appointing Thucydides, the son of Melias, to head their faction. He took up his task with great vigor, engaged Pericles on the hustings, and set about to organize the persons of "worth and distinction" on a more formal basis. Whereas previously they had been scattered all over the state, he somehow brought them together in one body and "their combined weight . . . was able . . . to make a counterpoise to the other party."[4]

Plutarch wrote this description in the second century A.D. and it may be distorted by memories of the history of the Roman Republic and its factional struggles. Unfortunately, we do not know how these factions operated in Athens, how they managed to bring their supporters to the Assembly, to get their followers elected to the Council, or have them chosen for the important offices. Lacking data, we assume most of the politicking was done on a face-to-face, informal, friendship and colleague basis, but we cannot know for sure.

The *demos* can also defend itself against attack by an organized oligarchy by mass action. Mass action may be a permanent part of the political landscape, or it may be exercised only in times of intense political crisis or change. The mass protests against the war in Vietnam and the intense activity for civil rights in the 1960s are examples of crisis activity. Fundamental political change, involving a permanent rearrangement of alliances, may also call forth mass action. In Athens at the end of the fifth century a whole group of "new men" rose to political power, the so-called "demagogues." Some historians claim that they achieved this revolutionary result by "A new pattern of politics . . . in which the allegiance of large numbers of citizens came to be as important, even more important, than alliances with narrow circles of influential men. The new politician worked by 'shaping mass alliances rather than by negotiating with different power groups to obtain a balance.' "[5] We are aware that leaders such as Cleon and Hyperbolus had specific groups of followers, and it might be accurate to talk of Cleon's faction, but of organized political parties we hear nothing.

The oligarchic coup of 411 demonstrates the difference between the people-in-mass expressing political power and the people paralyzed. The most vocal, most assertive, most determined element of the *demos* was in Samos, manning the ships, fighting the war. At home in Athens, the organized oligarchic clubs succeeded in terrorizing the rump of the *demos*. In Samos, however, the mass of the people completely overwhelmed the oligarchs and saved the democracy. Not that mass action does not require leadership—Cleon in Athens in the 420s or Thrasybulus in Samos in 411—but the power of these leaders derives from their ability to arouse large numbers of people to vote or to take direct action; it is not found in organized, narrow parties or clubs.

The historian Josiah Ober asserts that Athenian democracy in the fourth century presented a picture of a political elite (such as Demosthenes or Aeschines) dependent on a power base of mass support. The direct democracy of the Assembly, where 6,000 or more came together, and the mass juries of the law courts, which could number as many as 1,500, provided the institutional setting that made this possible. The people then ruled as well as reigned.[6] If this analysis for Athens is correct, such a situation is possible (or has only been possible), it is clear, with a direct democracy in a very small state. Representative democratic government, to remain stable and ward off oligarchic conspiracy, seems to require political parties, at least it has up to now.

We cannot understand oligarchic clubs or the political parties of modern-day democracies unless we recognize that they stand in intimate relationship to the breakdown of the kinship system. When the kinship system no longer provides a sense of purpose, place, and order, people seek other institutions to supply these universal human needs. Loyalty to the state cannot satisfy them though some people attempt to embrace patriotism as a substitute. A principal function of the Greek *hetaireiai* was to provide these types of kinship supports. A study of the local political clubs in America during the first half of this century, especially in ethnic neighborhoods, will reveal how large a role the solidarities and conflicts of a kinship nature played.

The Nature and Function of Hetaireiai

The limited data on size support about what we expect: One club had a membership of twenty-three; another was about the same size.[7] The psychology of small groups of this kind indicates that forty, or perhaps fifty, would be the maximum. The feeling of solidarity and comradeship—undoubtedly the primary stimulus for these associations—would become diluted if they were larger than this. Not surprisingly, most of the clubs were bound by an oath.[8] Sociability was a prime objective, some of it quite innocent, with a little drunkenness perhaps. Some engaged in literary or intellectual conversation, as portrayed in Plato's *Symposium*. Most clubs, however, did not have a Socrates to set the tone. Entertainment was of the usual frivolous kind one associates with men of no particular aspirations who get together for an evening's pleasure. Plato contrasts the politician with the philosopher. The latter had no interest in "the eagerness for office of the clubs . . . and their parties and dinners and revels with flute-girls."[9]

More sinister were the irreverent and sacrilegious activities of some clubs, some of which seem to have been organized for those purposes. "The 'Tribali' held sacrilegious feasts at which the members devoured the 'feast of Hecate' and the testicles of the pigs slain for sacrifice at the opening of the [Assembly]. The club of Cinesias held feasts on forbidden days, made sport of the gods and the laws of the state, and

crowned these impious actions by the assumption of the name 'Ca-
codaemonistae.' [Making sport of the gods and of Athenian laws.][10]
College boys' pranks, perhaps, but there is something in the nature of
such actions (and in the nature of people who do not outgrow them)
that is uncongenial to the spirit of democratic society. The mutilation
of the *hermae* (statues of Hermes placed in front of houses for protection
and good fortune) on the eve of the departure of the expedition to
Sicily caused a political upheaval in Athens. It ultimately led to the
downfall of Alcibiades, who, in Thucydides' opinion, could have saved
Athens from disaster in Syracuse. It may have been merely a prank
perpetrated by one of the sacrilegious clubs, or it may have been a
disruptive political act. Most people in Athens considered it an attack
on the democracy.[11]

Within the institutional framework of the Athenian city-state, the
clubs served two important, practical purposes. Thucydides describes
them as "associations for the management of lawsuits and elections."[12]
Everyone agrees that the Athenians were one of the most litigious people ever, reflecting the heightened competitive nature of their society.
Whether more committed to this form of social action than the population of the United States is an open question, but two significant
differences between Athens and modern democracies are apparent.
First, in ancient times (and in the Roman Republic)[13] lawsuits were
a crucially important instrument in the struggle among aristocratic
and oligarchic factions for political power. Intense—often violent—
competition between aristocratic and oligarchic families and factions
prevailed in almost all city-states, not only in ancient times but also in
Italian states of the late medieval period. In the law courts one could
conquer one's opponents without resort to violence. The second fundamental difference was the complete absence of lawyers in the ancient
Greek world. All prosecutions and all defenses in court were undertaken personally. We know that in Athens, in the fourth century, the
rich hired experts to write their court speeches, but the speech had to
be delivered personally by the claimant or the defendant. Many of the
extant speeches of Demosthenes, Lysias, and Isaeus are of this nature.

Often engaged in legal action and lacking lawyers, the politically
prominent Athenian depended on the members of his club to support
him. The situation created many complex and interesting modes of
defensive action. One was the "friendly prosecution." Fearing prose-

cution by his opponents for some illegal action, the sophisticated Athenian would induce a friend or a member of his club to bring suit against him on the same charge. This prosecution would be either sloppily pursued or dropped before going to trial. In a second trial brought by a genuine prosecutor, the defendant's speech would conspicuously refer to the failure of the previous suit.[14] A more potent tactic was the countersuit. Expecting to be prosecuted, a citizen would employ a friendly agent to institute an action against the potential prosecutor. The more serious the charge, the better. All manner of personal misdeeds and knaveries committed in the past were looked into. Fearing his own conviction, the prosecutor often abandoned his intended suit. In Xenophon's *Memorabilia*, Crito complains that he is being harried by sycophants bringing suits against him as a form of blackmail, the legal actions being dropped when money changed hands. Socrates, always an advocate of seeking out specialists, advised Crito to engage Archedemus as his defender. Expert in such matters, Archedemus immediately began a counteraction against one of Crito's persecutors, using every tactic available. In no time, the suit against Crito was abandoned.[15]

Club members could be counted on to perform another special function: to commit perjury in the defense of a fellow member. In the prosecution speech Demosthenes wrote for Ariston against Conon, a main tactic was to impeach the testimony of Conon's fellow club members. "But it stands to reason, that these men, who have been partners in his drinking bouts and have shared many deeds of this sort, have given false testimony." Ariston further impugns their veracity by emphasizing the oligarchic sympathies of those who have testified. "I am inclined to think . . . that many of you know Diotimus and Archebiades and Chaeretimus, the grey-headed man yonder, men who by day put on sour looks and pretend to play the Spartan and wear short cloaks and single-soled shoes [in imitation of Spartan austerity], but when they get together and are by themselves leave no form of wickedness or indecency untried." (More than fifty years later, long after the second oligarchic coup of 404, this kind of "playful" antidemocratic activity of imitating Spartan ways was still in fashion, reminding us of nothing so much as the leather boys of today who "play" at swastikas.)

Ariston/Demosthenes delivered the final stroke by invading the minds of the perjurers. "What! Are we not to give testimony for one another?

Isn't that the way of comrades and friends? . . . Do some people say they saw him beaten? We will testify that he wasn't even touched by you. That his cloak was stripped off? We will testify they had done this first to you. That his lip has been sewn up? We will say that your head or something else has been broken."[16]

Plato's *Apology* emphasizes one of the ironies of real world justice and injustice, and their relationship to organized personal contact, when Socrates argues that, "it would have been possible for him to have escaped conviction had he been willing to devote himself to those matters which engage the attention of the majority at Athens—finance, the attainment of office, political parties, and clubs."[17]

Beyond the narratives of 411 and 404, we have surprisingly little—one could say almost no—data about independent clubs combining for political purposes, but it is a reasonable assumption that they may sometimes have done so. We do have the story of one political tactic so complex and so clever as to be worthy of the great Mayor Richard Daley himself. In the year 418/417 the rivalry between the conservative General Nicias and the flamboyant Alcibiades came to a head. The Assembly approved a vote of ostracism in that year, each side hoping that the leader of the other faction would become the chosen victim. Hyperbolus, a political leader, supported the vote for ostracism, hoping to get rid of Alcibiades. The latter was too clever for a mere mortal like Hyperbolus, however, and he "effected a union of parties, and having reached an agreement with Nicias, turned the vote of ostracism against Hyperbolus. But, as some say, it was not Nicias but Phaeax with whom he came to terms, and it was the latter's hetaery whose support he received in driving out Hyperbolus."[18] With Alcibiades and Nicias or Phaeax against him, the unfortunate Hyperbolus had no chance and he was ostracized, taking up residence at Samos, where he was assassinated by the oligarchs in 411. The complexity of these maneuvers indicates that the club factions could join together in common action and that they could deliver the votes in the Assembly. How they did this remains a mystery.

We are left with many unanswered questions. How did the democracy of the fourth century operate so efficiently without the existence of political parties? Was it because the threat of an oligarchic counterrevolt was reduced to almost zero by the events of 411 and 404, and their aftermaths? It is almost certain that permanent parties, commanding permanent loyalties, did not exist. But how powerful were the factions? Was there an organized faction of Demosthenes and one of Aeschines? An anti-Macedonian and a pro-Macedonian faction? Factions, as opposed to parties, would have much less permanence and could shift every year or even every month or so, but they would represent some level of organization and they could manage a polity the size of Athens.

Or was it, as Ober argues, that the mass democracy of Athens made it possible for the *demos* to rule as well as reign, allowing for the existence of a certain number of elite politicians but not of a permanent power elite?[19] Certainly, we must take into account the Assemblies of 6,000 or more citizens; the power of the jury courts recruited from 6,000 chosen by lot each year; the 500 elected to the Council every year; and the 700 other magistrates rotated annually—all in a citizen population of 25,000 to 30,000. This type of participation may epitomize the profound break between the nature of Athenian democracy and modern democratic polities.

10

The Eating of the Gods

The Athenian political year was divided into ten more or less equal parts, each called a prytany. In the sixth prytany of every year the full Assembly of the Athenian people decided on whether or not a vote of ostracism was to be held in that year. No debate on the question was allowed: a simple "yes" or "no" decided the issue by majority vote. If the answer was affirmative, a short time later the *demos* voted to select the person to be ostracized. Every citizen who wished to participate wrote the name of his "candidate" on a pottery shard (*ostrokon*) and deposited it in a roped off part of the Agora under the supervision of the Council and the Archons. A minimum of 6,000 shards had to be cast in order to effectuate the procedure. Plutarch says that the magistrates first determined whether this minimum requirement had been fulfilled before sorting the ballots. About the next step in the procedure, unfortunately, our data fail us. We do not know whether the "winning" candidate needed 6,000 ballots to be exiled, or whether, the minimum of 6,000 votes having been cast, the candidate with the most votes was so punished. The chosen political scapegoat had to leave Attica in ten days and remain in exile for ten years, though he retained control over his property and the income therefrom. After this decade, having cleansed the *polis* by his absence, he was returned to full citizen rights.[1]

• • •

In the deep, irrational strata of the psyche, human beings experience profound ambivalences about political leadership. These are not the familiar oedipal conflicts between father and son, projected onto the relationship between a political leader and his followers, which are much easier to understand than the more primitive preoedipal conflicts where catastrophic rage and all-consuming love struggle endlessly against each other, where it makes ritual sense to eat the god one has adored, expressing the ultimate of love and destruction in one act.

The theorists of ritual and religion who have concerned themselves with the importance of irrationality in human life have been struck by the widespread phenomena of the dying god: the god who is killed and eaten; the god who is eaten, dies, and rises again; the god who himself becomes the human sacrifice. Not even the most skillful reading of the human intellect can discover a *rational* basis for such belief and ritual action. The explanation lies in the hidden irrational needs of the psyche. Familiar to many is the complex Aztec ritual wherein a man is chosen to impersonate the god and for a year enjoys all the comforts of women, fine food, and entertainment. He is then stripped of his godly appurtenances, slaughtered, and eaten.[2] Less well known, but marvelously revelatory of the ambivalence toward rulers, was the ritual exercise in ancient Tahiti where, at the inauguration of a new king, a group of designated celebrants urinated and defecated on him as a mark of ultimate respect and degradation.[3] Known to all is the ritual extensively practiced within our culture of drinking the blood and eating the flesh, in a highly symbolic, sublimated way, of God's son, himself God.

All successful rituals help resolve a basic ambivalence in the psyche. If the ritual deeply reflects irrationality that is because the conflict it addresses is deeply irrational. We never completely resolve our ambivalence about the gods. Even in a highly sophisticated, modern democratic society—especially in times of crisis—the need both to exalt and degrade those who lead us manifests itself.

Some historians have offered quite rational explanations of the two important phenomena in Athens that are the prime concern of this chapter: the practice of ostracism and the oftentimes harsh and punishing treatment of political leaders and generals. In the interest of trying to understand how society really works, and going beyond simplistic explanations of truly complex matters, I suggest that the rational and irrational explanations of certain political phenomena are not incompatible with each other, that using one should not exclude the other. The importance of certain political rituals in a complex democratic society may lie precisely in the fact that they satisfy a rational and an irrational purpose *simultaneously*. Rather than argue that ostracism was a totally rational procedure because it eliminated the threat of tyranny, or that it was completely irrational because it so closely imitated the forms of human sacrifice, perhaps we can find the true explanation in that it simultaneously satisfied both rational and irrational needs. It lessened the threat of tyranny and satisfied the need to eat the god. If we here emphasize the irrational dimensions of political life, it is not because they are considered more important than the rational, but because they have been neglected. We all seek comfort in human rationality.

It is interesting that, even in ancient times, some thinkers clearly perceived the irrational aspects of certain political behavior. Plutarch states more than once that the reasons for the practice of ostracism were not exactly what they were commonly accepted to be. "Moreover," he says in his life of Aristides, "the spirit of the people, now grown high, and confident with their late victory [over the Persians], naturally entertained feelings of dislike to all of more than common fame and reputation. Coming together, therefore, from all parts into the city, they banished Aristides by the ostracism, *giving their jealousy of his reputation the name of the fear of tyranny*."[4] In his life of Themistocles, he goes even further, arguing that the primary purpose of ostracism was to cleanse the rancorous, poisoned psyche of the populace. He perfectly understood paranoia, though he did not know the term. "At length the Athenians banished him, making use of ostracism to humble his eminence and authority, as they ordinarily did with all whom they thought too powerful, or, by their greatness, disproportionable to the equality thought requisite in a popular government. For the ostracism was instituted, not so much to punish the offender, as to mitigate and pacify the violence of the envious, who delighted to humble eminent men, and who, by fixing this disgrace upon them, might vent some part of their rancor."[5]

Plutarch errs, I believe, in placing too much emphasis on envy and rancor. There was a *legitimate* fear of tyranny in Athens less than forty years after the overthrow of the Pisistratid tyrants. The overweening ambition of some men is a realistic threat to democracy. The brilliance of the institution of ostracism lay in its combination of realistic, legitimate political interests with a very primitive mode of psychic release.

There is an even more profound human disability: Some people cannot abide righteousness and turn on the overmoral, those who care more for moral considerations than the common value system of the culture allows. "Some men," writes Isocrates, "have been so brutalized by envy and want and are so hostile that they wage war, not on depravity, but on prosperity; they hate not only the best men but the noblest pursuits; and . . . they take sides with wrong-doers and are in sympathy with them, while they destroy, whenever they have the power, those whom they have cause to envy."[6] Careful observers of American politics have noticed that a certain amount of sleaze—but not too much—is not a disability for some politicians, but makes them more electable. They are perceived as being not too far ahead of the crowd and as not inclined to make moral demands on the *demos* it is unprepared to meet.

The hazards of being overly righteous are beautifully illustrated in Plutarch's cautionary tale of the ostracism of Aristides. True or not, it is an accurate portrayal of a human attitude toward leadership. To vote for the ostracism of a particular person, the citizen was obliged to write the name of the intended victim on a pot shard. Many citizens could not write and therefore required assistance to exercise their democratic prerogative. One fellow on his way to the perverse election, happened to ask Aristides himself to write the name "Aristides" on his shard. Curious, the "candidate" inquired whether Aristides had ever done him any harm. "None at all," the citizen responded, "neither know I the man; but I am tired of hearing him everywhere called the Just." True to his reputation, the statesman wrote his name on the shard. When he left the city after being condemned to ten years in exile, he prayed that Athens might never have occasion to regret the injury they had done him. In contrast, as Plutarch reminds us, Achilles fervently desired that the Achaians should someday mourn the mistreatment of their greatest hero.[7]

Speeches and literature describing political phenomena can teach us a great deal about unconscious and irrational motivation. In the topsy-turvy world of role-reversal that Aristophanes delighted in, he gives us in *Knights* an insightful dialogue between the Chorus and Demos. "Demos," the Chorus begins, "you are our all-powerful sovereign lord; all tremble before you, yet you are led by the nose." Chorus insists that Demos, who should be leading society, is subject to flattery and trickery and led astray by the skill of orators. Things are not what they seem, replies Demos: "It is with a purpose that I play this idiot's role, for I love to drink the lifelong day, and it so pleases me to keep a thief for my minister. When he has thoroughly gorged himself, then I overthrow and crush him." Chorus immediately perceives the brilliance of the maneuver. "Your ministers, then, are your victims, whom you nourish and feed up expressly in the Pnyx, so that, the day your dinner is ready, you may immolate the fattest and eat him."[8]

Aristophanes is not equating human sacrifice and political behavior. His purpose is not only to amuse but also to illumine the irrational, and seemingly unexplainable, activity of the democracy. It is remarkable that he uses a metaphor replicating the Aztec ritual of letting a chosen one play the god for a year before being killed and eaten. In laughing, we immediately acknowledge that there is a truth here. Unlike the Aztecs, Demos let some politicians play god for more than a year before victimizing them and some political hero-gods suffered no extraordinary punishment. Nor, when a former hero of the *polis* is tried, ostracized, or executed—and it is remarkable how many suffered that fate—is a sublimated form of eating the god the *only* factor to consider in trying to understand the complex act. It is, however, a significant factor and we ignore it at the risk of utilizing a less-than-adequate theory of political behavior.

Ostracism

That Athens, after thirty-five years of tyranny, should not allow a tyrant to assume power again, is understandable and requires no explanation. That rational human beings should construct legal and political means to accomplish a rational end agrees with our assumptions about the pragmatic quality in human nature. Knowing the history of Athens up to 508, we could expect the newly constructed democracy of Cleisthenes to create legal and political procedures guarding against the return of tyranny: indictments in the courts, trials before the Assembly or the

Council, laws against correspondence with foreign powers (a favorite mode of tyrants for gaining political power), and so forth. We would not expect the primitive ritualistic nature of the institution ultimately adopted. The law of ostracism and the way in which it functioned project an almost science fiction story of a never-never land where people practice strange rituals of sublimated human sacrifice and purification. Shirley Jackson's uncanny story "The Lottery" about random human sacrifice in a small New England town, with its tension between matter-of-fact, everyday reality and primitive irrationality, comes as close as anything to describing the eerie milieu of Athenian ostracism.

It is important to keep in mind that ostracism was a fifth-century ritual. Once the full radical democracy had come to power and achieved its remarkably stable position, ritual political sacrifice was no longer necessary. Though the law of ostracism was supposed to have arisen with Cleisthenes (c. 508), the first known example is from the year 487. The last victim was Hyperbolus in about 416. There are only ten generally accepted cases of ostracism, though many more have been suggested. More than half of the attested cases occurred in the 480s. It is remarkable how many of the foremost politicians of Athens were ostracized during the forty- to fifty-year period 487–443: Megacles in 486; Xanthippus, the father of Pericles in 484; the just Aristides in 482; Themistocles in the late 470s; and Thucydides, the son of Melesias (the political opponent of Pericles), in 443.[9] Pericles, though convicted of embezzlement and fined soon after the outbreak of the great war, never came close to being exiled, though many must have desired it as a fragment from the comic playwright Kratinos attests: "There goes our squill-headed Zeus, Pericles, with the Odeion [a small theater] for his skull-cap—since the ostrakon missed him!"[10]

We cannot comprehend the psychological necessity of such sublimated human sacrifice and purification without keeping in mind that one of the great developmental tasks of the fifth century in Athens was breaking down and transforming the kinship system, creating a "modern" world. In a kinship-system society no one individual can stand out too much from the full community.

"Although the Kaingang respect power they cannot tolerate any kind of intensification of it; for such intensification is felt by them to be disruptive. Through their insistence on the primary importance of the other person and their failure to reward achievement, Kaingang have suppressed processes that encourage the concentration of power in the hands of outstanding individuals."[11] Athenian society in the fifth century can certainly be characterized as fundamentally ambivalent about the concentration of power in one political individual. Ambivalent, not only from fear of the reestablishment of tyranny—a real consideration—but also because of a basic uncertainty about the advisability of leaving the kinship system behind and allowing individualism to run riot.

The political system instituted by Cleisthenes gave the final death-blow to the kinship system and its penetration into political life. His complex system of demes, trittys, and "tribes," all based on residence, not kinship, gave birth to a "modern" democratic society. Simultaneously with this social revolution, the institution of ostracism was invented. It took almost a hundred years for the transformation to a nonkinship polity to take place. When the memories of kinship political affiliations had grown so dim as to become unimportant, the ritual of ostracism became obsolete. In the fourth century, with the nonkinship political system stabilized and rationalized, this sublimated form of human sacrifice was unnecessary.

There may be a profound connection between human sacrifice and the breakdown of the kinship system. In *At the Dawn of Tyranny*, I offer an hypothesis that the ritual of human sacrifice was characteristic of only one form of human society, the first stage of monarchical–state polity which developed out of the primitive, kinship stage, a form designated "Complex Society." It was further argued that human sacrifice was a psychological defensive measure undertaken to contain the anxiety provoked by the breakdown of kinship forms of social cohesion.[12]

The breakdown and transformation of the kinship system can be a continuing social process that does not end with Complex Society and all advances into "modernism" involve a further stage of that process. Fifth-century Athens, twelfth- through fifteenth-century Europe,[13] and nineteenth- and twentieth-century Western culture exhibited a particularly heightened and intensified process of disintegration of the kinship system, provoking predictable anxieties and the sublimated—or not-so-sublimated—forms of human sacrifice in an attempt to contain those anxieties. (In Europe the almost complete destruction of the Jews made human sacrifice no metaphor.) The psychological brilliance of

Athens allowed it to make the revolutionary transformation, aided only by the institution of ostracism—and by the invention of tragedy, itself a sublimated expression of human sacrifice, with the inevitable destruction of the hero. (But that is a whole subject in itself.) That ten, possibly twenty, at the most fifty, politicians were subjected to ten years of exile, then returning to full citizen rights, was a remarkably small price to pay, considering human psychological disabilities, for such an extraordinary social advance.

Ostracism was also used as a powerful weapon in the game of democratic politics. The story of the exile of Hyperbolus has been told. In addition, the Pericles faction almost certainly maneuvered the ostracism of Thucydides, the son of Melesias, to get rid of its foremost rival. There is good reason to suspect that the exclusions of Cimon and Aristides were of the same order. An interesting archaeological find seems to confirm this hypothesis in the case of Themistocles. In 1937 American excavators discovered, on the north slope of the Acropolis, in a deep well shaft almost forty feet below the surface, 190 pottery shards inscribed with the name of Themistocles. Since only a small number of distinct handwriting styles were represented, the assumption is that the anti-Themistoclean faction had prepared hundreds of these ballots for distribution among those voting and had discarded their surplus to avoid detection of their organized factionalism.[14] We know that they were successful as Themistocles is one of the well-attested victims of ostracism.

It would be exciting to have more data about one tantalizing speculation: the relationship of ostracism to early democracy. We have some evidence that the practice existed, at least for a time, at Argos, Megara, and Miletus, but we know nothing about its relationship to democracy in these states. Of Syracuse we know a bit more. It was introduced there in 454 in clear imitation of Athens when Syracuse was a fledgling democracy. Names of intended victims were written on olive leaves (*petala*), giving rise to the name "petalism."[15] In Syracuse the developing democracy gave way to a new form of tyranny at the end of the fifth century and never developed the full maturity of the Athenian *polis*. Somehow, in some way, it seems that ostracism makes psychological sense in the development from a tyrannical-authoritarian rule to a democratic state. The almost complete lack of comparative data makes it difficult to say why that might be.

Human sacrifice is an aggressive act; ostracism is a sublimated aggressive act. Continuing sublimation of aggression is a human possibility and ostracism was not abandoned without an even more sublimated form taking its place. "What is certain," writes Jennifer Roberts, "is that around the same time as ostracism was either abolished or abandoned, the Athenians began to make use of another device which, like ostracism, could be deployed not only against men in office but against private citizens as well—the [graphe paranomon], or indictment for illegal proposals."[16] Any citizen who made a proposal in the Assembly could be prosecuted by any other citizen on the grounds that the proposal was illegal because it had not been properly submitted to the Assembly or the Council, that it negated a previous law not yet overturned, or that it contravened the "customs" (nomoi) of the Athenians. Pending prosecution of the case, the proposal was held in abeyance. Though a few speeches of Demosthenes demanded death as a punishment, no known conviction imposed anything but a fine.[17]

At almost exactly the same historical time, 420 to 410, we begin to get impeachment trials under the format designated eisangelia. More serious than graphe paranomon, eisangelia indictments resulted from accusations of "treason, subversion of the democracy, . . . taking bribes to make proposals contrary to public interest, and breaking promises to the State."[18] In these cases, death was often the punishment. We will later look more closely at the impact of eisangelia trials in the fourth century, when there were literally hundreds of cases, and attempt to disentangle their rational from their irrational aspects. The point here is that, concerning the apparently necessary ritual of eating the god, there appears to be a direct line from the psychology of human sacrifice to ostracism to treason trials and executions of leaders. Long is the road to the resolution of human ambivalence.

The Execution of the Generals after Arginusae

When the gods are negligent in their primary duty to provide omnipotent support, human rage knows no bounds. Frazer tells us of the people in nineteenth-century Sicily who, during a severe drought, took the statues of the saints from the churches and threw them, face down, into the dry river beds to show them how it felt to eat the dust and vowed not to remove them until the rains returned. Famine, drought, earthquake are most likely to trigger rage against the gods. Human gods—democratic politicians—are most vulnerable when the state suffers a loss in war or a national humiliation (like the failure to recover in short order hostages taken by another country). Many historians contend that the German loss in World War I, and the "humiliating" peace treaty that ended it, contributed greatly to the success of the Nazis with their plans to wipe the shame of that defeat off the face of Germany. In a mature democracy, the killing of the failed god can be accomplished in a highly civilized manner: The President is conspicuously "dumped" in the next election.* Athens, on the contrary, never completely gave up executing those who had failed it.

By the year 406, the great war between Sparta and Athens had become primarily a naval one. The Lacedaemonians had succeeded, with the help of Persian finances, in constructing a formidable fleet capable of contesting Athenian naval supremacy. The conflict clearly would be won by whichever state could destroy the other's fleet. In this year, close to the Arginusae Islands off the coast of Asia Minor, the Athenians won a magnificent victory in "the largest battle ever fought between Greek navies."[19] Though the Athenians lost twenty-five ships, they succeeded in capturing seventy from the Spartans. They also liberated a good part of their fleet, blockaded at Mitylene. It was a resounding victory where defeat would probably have meant the end of the war. The eight generals in charge of the battle, instead of being crowned with laurel were illegally condemned to death in the Assembly; six were executed in Athens; two had gone into exile, refusing to return for trial, knowing the temper of the Athenian people.

Why this incredible outcome?[20] After such a naval battle, amid a sea full of the wreckage of ships, there are injured or shipwrecked sailors to be rescued, and corpses to be collected for proper burial. Ordinarily attending to the survivors and the dead was the fleet commander's first duty when fighting ceased. At Arginusae, two things interfered with this operation. At Mitylene, about twelve miles from

---

*The case of Richard Nixon is worth speculation. Although Watergate was the proximate cause of his political demise, the United States' loss of the war in Vietnam and failure to secure an honorable peace may have made him a scapegoat and triggered his precipitous fall. Ronald Reagan, facing no such disability, survived Iran-Contra unscathed.

the scene of the battle, a Spartan flotilla of fifty ships was blockading ships under the command of the Athenian general Conon. The Spartan commander, hearing of the defeat, would be determined to make his escape. After their victory, the Athenian generals, ignoring the survivors and the corpses, met to confer about their next move. It was wisely decided to send part of the fleet immediately to Mitylene, the balance to remain behind to care for the survivors and the corpses.

Some time had been lost and a huge storm arose before those designated for the task could begin to seek out the quick and the dead. The sailors refused to set out. "The captains were unable to get the men to move before the storm grew so violent as to prevent any attempt to get to sea."[21] Many who could have been rescued were lost; most of those who gave their lives for Athens ended in a watery grave. Instead of being elated at the outcome of the battle, the people of Athens were outraged at the generals. In a mature democratic society, an investigation would clearly be in order. In Athens, a lynching was engineered. The Assembly voted to depose the eight generals and ordered them back to the city for trial. The two who refused to return and went into exile understood the demon *demos* better than the six who trusted in the laws.

The trial of the generals in the Assembly took place on two different days. Full legal protection of the defendants was abrogated by the first day: "Defenders of the generals were interrupted and shouted down, and the generals themselves were not given the full time prescribed by law to defend themselves."[22] Despite these problems, the generals made their point and it began to appear that they would be acquitted, but fate in the form of approaching darkness postponed the vote. The trial was not resumed until several days later, after an interruption to celebrate the festival of Apaturia, the feast of the *phratriai*, or kinship brotherhoods. The gaps in the ranks brought to mind the losses of the men at Arginusae and saddened the celebrants. Opponents of the generals played on the hysteria and paranoia of the people and when the trial was resumed the smell of lynch-law was in the air. The cry of revenge for the neglected dead was evoked when a man spoke out, claiming he had been one of those shipwrecked and had saved himself by clinging to a tub. He heard the drowning men cry out that the people should be told: "The generals had not rescued the men who had shown themselves the best in service to their country."[23]

A certain Callixeinus proposed in the Council that all the generals should be tried in common and that whatever time they had been given the first day should suffice for their whole defense—both motions clearly illegal. The Council nevertheless adopted these measures to govern the second day of trial in the Assembly. In the Assembly, Euryptolemus and others accused Callixeinus of having made an illegal proposal; they evoked the *graphe paranomon*, which should have halted the trial until the legality of the motions was determined. Some approved, but the majority cried out "it was monstrous if the people were to be prevented from doing whatever they wished."[24] In further contempt for the law one Lysiscus proposed that if the motion of *graphe paranomon* was not withdrawn, the proposers of the motion should be tried with the generals. So loud was approval of this totally illegal, unprecedented action that Euryptolemus backed down. The constitution still lived in some men's hearts, however: several of the *prytaneis*, the presiding magistrates at the Assembly, refused to put to vote the question of the generals' guilt on the grounds that it was not legal. Callixeinus, blood-incensed, shouted that these *prytaneis* should themselves be judged. Terrified, all but one agreed to proceed with the trial. That one would himself one day feel the full vengeance of a maddened *demos*. He was Socrates, son of Sophroniscus, who announced that, "in no case would he act except in accordance with the law."[25]

Euryptolemus made one last attempt to save the generals by an appeal to reason, but reason had fled the Assembly that day. First, he agreed that, if found guilty, the generals should be subject to the ultimate penalty, but suggested that they should first be allowed a fair trial conforming to the laws.

"If this is done, the guilty will incur the severest punishment, and the guiltless will be set free by you, men of Athens, and will not be put to death unjustly. As for yourselves, you will be granting a trial in accordance with the law and standing true to religion and your oaths, and you will not be fighting on the side of the Lacedaemonians by putting to death the men who captured seventy ships from them and defeated them—by putting to death these men, I say, without a trial, in violation of the law. What is it, pray, that you fear, that you are in such excessive haste? Do you fear lest you will lose the right to put to death and set free anyone you please if you proceed in accordance with the law, but think that you will retain this right if you proceed in violation of the law, by the method which Callixeinus persuaded the Senate to report to the people, that is, by a single vote? . . . You would do a monstrous thing if, after granting in the past to Aristarchus, the destroyer of the democracy and afterwards the betrayer of Oenoe to your enemies the Thebans, a day in which to defend himself as he pleased, and allowing him all his other rights under the law,—if, I say, you shall now deprive the generals, who have done everything to your satisfaction, and have defeated the enemy, of these same rights."[26]

Very few have ever succeeded by talking sense to a maddened people. After the execution of the six generals who had returned to Athens, a remarkable thing, so pathetically typical of the Athenian *demos*, occurred. Now that there was no recalling the dead, now that the human sacrifice had accomplished its task, "the Athenians repented, and they voted that complaints be brought against any who had deceived the people."[27] Callixeinus and four others were arrested but escaped at a time of civil disturbance. Callixeinus ultimately returned to the city, "was hated by everybody and died of starvation."[28] A little research in the annals of human sacrifice might reveal a ritual wherein the executioner in the sacrificial rite becomes, by some inexorable logic, the next victim.

The extraordinary self-destructive quality of this whole affair is remarkable, occurring as it did at a time when Athens, in the last years of the war, was fighting for its life. We could understand better if the generals had lost the battle, if final defeat was staring the Athenians in the face, and a scapegoat was needed to give the *demos* some solace in its despair. But a magnificent victory had been won. It is almost as if Athens, perceiving a final triumph as a real possibility, decided to throw that chance away in some totally irrational, suicidal act.

"The Athenians paid a high price. The eight generals killed or exiled . . . were not available for service in 405 or 404, which turned out to be the last year of the war. The ill will and suspicion raised by the affair also deprived the Athenians of Theramenes' experienced services. . . . Thrasybulus, likewise, suffered from the same animus and was not . . . elected [a general]. The skill and experience of all these men would be badly missed."[29] If an individual were so recklessly to throw away his life's chances, we would give a clinical name to his behavior. The self-destructive dimension in the paranoid position should never be underestimated.

"No Athenian general," Kagan reminds us, "had ever before been executed."[30] Fined, exiled, ostracized, yes, but this trial was the first to end in judicial killing. One could plead the psychologically debilitating experience of almost thirty years of war. Such a plea loses all validity, however, when we discover that the impeachment and sometimes execution of generals formed a regular part of Athenian political life in the fourth century.

Impeachment and Execution of the Generals

The collapse of the Athenian Empire and the total defeat of Athens in the great war did not bring a period of peace to Athena's city. During the fourth century, Athens and all the major Greek cities were constantly at war somewhere in the Greek world. Generals, elected annually but subject to unlimited reelection, continued to play a major role in Athenian life. The fourth century witnessed a differentiation in the functions of political and military leaders. Whereas in the fifth century almost all the major politicians were also generals (Themistocles, Aristides, Pericles, Nicias, Alcibiades), in the century that followed almost no major political figure served as a *strategos*. Athenian generals led a hazardous existence, beset with danger not only from the ranks of the enemy.

In the winter of 379/378 two generals whose names are not known to us were tried by the court on a charge of *eisangelia*. They had been stationed on the frontier between Attica and Boeotia and when the Thebans rose up and liberated themselves from Spartan occupation, these Athenian generals, without authorization from the home government, assisted the Thebans. The Athenian *demos* was angry, not at the fact that the generals helped the Thebans instead of the Spartans, since all Athenian sympathy was with Thebes, but with the fact that the generals took action without approval from the city. One can understand that, in the interest of civil discipline, the generals, if found guilty, should be deposed. They were, however, sentenced to death.

One, wisely, had fled into exile before the trial. The other was duly executed.[31]

Seventeen years later, the Athenians were busily extending their influence in the area of Thrace and the Chersonese. The operation presented some complex military and diplomatic maneuvers and the Athenians were not successful. The *demos*, in its frustration, vented its anger against the generals in charge. Leosthenes, during the course of the activities, lost five triremes and six hundred Athenians were captured. He was condemned to death and his property confiscated. Kallisthenes made a truce with Perdiccas, the king of Macedonia, which the king subsequently betrayed. For being so gullible, Kallisthenes was executed. (The judicial excuse, in such cases, was usually that the general had been bribed, that he was venal, not incompetent.) Ergophilos, a colleague of Kallisthenes, was acquitted before the same tribunal of the same capital charge but was deposed and fined. Their successors, Autokles, Menon, and Timomachos, had no greater success; all were deposed and Timomachos was fined. Kephisdotos signed a treaty that was rejected by the home city; he was fined a huge sum (five talents) and "barely escaped with his life." Two other generals were subsequently deposed for failure to bring home a diplomatic or military victory.[32]

The American twentieth-century social game of blaming-the-victim was obviously played in fourth-century Athens as blaming-the-generals. Such sacrificial scapegoating was not confined to Athena's city. The Carthaginians crucified their general Hanno when he lost a crucial fort before the First Punic War.[33] Only an extraordinarily mature society can lose a decisive battle or a war and not regress into some primitive ritual of punishment.

The great Athenian general Nicias, leader of the catastrophic expedition to Syracuse, was tragically aware of the irrational anger of the *demos*. By 413 the situation before Syracuse was hopeless; all wise counsel advised the Athenian forces to save whatever could still be salvaged and retreat immediately. But Nicias would not retreat:

> In his public speech on this occasion he refused to lead off the army, saying he was sure the Athenians would never approve of their returning without a vote of theirs. Those who would vote upon their conduct, instead of judging the facts as eye-witnesses like themselves

and not from what they might hear from hostile critics, would simply be guided by the calumnies of the first clever speaker; while many, indeed most, of the soldiers on the spot, who now so loudly proclaimed the danger of their position, when they reached Athens would proclaim just as loudly the opposite, and would say that the generals had been bribed to betray them and return. *For himself, therefore, who knew the Athenian temper, sooner than perish under a dishonourable charge and by an unjust sentence at the hands of the Athenians, he would rather take his chance and die, if die he must, a soldier's death at the hand of the enemy.*[34]

Nicias got his wish. The Syracusans made sure he didn't return to Athens to be tried for treason.

So pervasive was general bashing in fourth-century Athens that Demosthenes declared, possibly with some rhetorical exaggeration, that generals ran a greater risk of being executed by Athenian courts than of dying on the battlefield. "So scandalous is our present system that every general is tried two or three times for his life in your courts, but not one of them dares to risk death in battle against the enemy; no, not once."[35] Mogens H. Hansen finds evidence in the limited data available to us that only three generals were killed in battle during the fourth century, whereas six (possibly eight) were sentenced to death by Athenian courts.[36] Our data are slim, but certainly sufficient to indicate that Demosthenes' critique may not have been an exaggeration.

What do we make of all this? What does it teach us about the nature of the *demos*? Historians have opposing views of this matter of eating the generals. Jennifer Tolbert Roberts and Hansen have studied the problem in most detail. One gives a rational, the other an irrational, explanation of the phenomenon. Roberts argues that the impeachment, conviction, and execution of military leaders assured democratic control in the state, keeping the military from domineering over society: "And what civil discord might not erupt in Athens when it had no public offices higher than the men who led its armies? A century of bloodshed in Rome was to show what could happen when the same men served as political leaders and military heroes [and, we might add, a century of antidemocratic violence and fascist terror in our own century]: at Athens it was the rigorous use of the machinery of control which prevented the military character of the [*strategia*] from posing a threat to the democratic constitution."[37]

There is an important truth here, but was the number of generals convicted and the extreme violence used really necessary to the result praised by Roberts? President Harry S. Truman removed General Douglas MacArthur during the Korean War when the latter took on himself the prerogatives of the executive branch, but no one was executed to make sure it didn't happen again. Even Roberts' statistical study causes us to wonder. She indicates that out of 1,420 generals, only about 50 were impeached, with only two-thirds of those convicted, leaving a conviction rate of "only" 3 percent. This figure does not allow for "a very large number of additional trials for which the evidence has not yet come down."[38] We may assume, perhaps, a conviction rate of 5 percent. Can we imagine five out of one hundred U.S. Senators being convicted for corruption, bribery, or treason without a great outcry from the press and the people about how uncontrollably corrupt our nation has become? Five out of a hundred is a large corruption rate.

Contrary to Roberts, Hansen argues that there was something "sinister" in this whole process:

> It is impossible to decide in which cases the generals convicted were guilty of treason and corruption and in which cases the Athenian jurors were guilty of miscarriage of justice. But the astonishingly high number of trials leaves us with a rather sinister dilemma. *Either* the Athenian people must have elected and appointed a high number of treacherous and corrupt generals *or* the Athenian jurors must have convicted a high number of honest leaders on false accusations. No matter whether the generals deserved the sentences passed on them or not, the numerous *eisangeliai* cast a shadow over the Athenian democracy and indicate that a direct democracy may employ the same judicial methods as a totalitarian state. So the Athenians behaved as *tyrannoi* not only against their allies but also against their own leaders.[39]

I believe that *both* these explanations are true. The process served a profoundly important *rational* purpose. In a state constantly at war, where the generals played an important political role, it maintained the *demos* as the ruler of the state. At the same time, at the moment of execution it satisfied a more sinister, more primitive *irrational* need: to eat the gods, especially when they failed to deliver omnipotent protection. It may be that this particular mode of political behavior was maintained over centuries precisely because it satisfied rational and irrational needs simultaneously. It may be that much of our political life can only be understood by keeping this kind of ambiguity in mind.

11

The *Demos* as Tyrant

The great moral problematic within democratic society arises from the unfortunate circumstance that the momentous development of sovereignty from the one to the few to the many does nothing to guarantee the just nature of society. All sovereignty, no matter by whom exercised, is subject to perversion in the form of tyranny. A king may be a monarch or a tyrant; a ruling clique may be a responsible aristocracy or an oppressive oligarchy; the *demos* may dispense justice or exercise oppression. Given the pervasive moral ambivalence in the human psyche, the chances are that most kings will be both just and unjust, most ruling cliques will be both responsible and morally reprehensible in their actions, and most governments controlled by the *demos* will display a pervasive moral vacillation. The fact that a majority is acting out its wishes—and that is the least definition of a democracy—says nothing about the just nature of those actions. Nothing in the nature of majority democracy prevents the *demos* from playing the tyrant.

One major qualification is necessary. When a minority imposes its will over a majority, injustice is inherent. The white minority in South Africa is exercising a double injustice. Proponents of democracy have rightfully insisted upon the inherent justice of majority rule. The sovereignty of the *demos* eliminates one basic injustice but it hardly eliminates all. It is theoretically possible, in a democratic society, *without violating the basic premises of democratic action* (that is, majority rule), for 88 percent of the American people (white) to decide by an overwhelming margin to put 12 percent of the people (black) into labor camps, just as the representatives of the people ordered 100,000 Japanese-Americans into nontorturing concentration camps. It is intolerable in a democratic society, as the cry in the Assembly had it during the trial of the generals after Arginusae, that the *demos* was "to be prevented from doing whatever [it] wished."[1] The issue of justice depends directly on the question: What do the people wish for?

This problematic, this basic differentiation between majority rule and justice, was clearly recognized in Greek political thought, and was used by the opponents of democracy as an argument against its claim to legitimacy. In one of the few brilliant passages collected under the name of Xenophon (its authorship is uncertain) the possibly-too-brilliant Alcibiades confronts the senior statesman of the Athenian democratic *polis*:

They say that Alcibiades, when he was less than twenty years old, had a conversation about laws with his guardian, Pericles, the leading man of the city.

"Tell me, Pericles," he said: "Can you explain to me what law is?"

"Certainly I can," replied Pericles.

"Then explain to me, do. For whenever I hear people being praised for being law-abiding citizens, I think that no one can really earn that praise who doesn't know what law is."

"There's no particular difficulty about your wanting to know what law is, Alcibiades. Laws are what the mass of the citizens decree, meeting together and taking counsel, and declaring what can be done and what can't."

"Do they think one ought to do good or evil?"

"Good, of course, my boy, not evil."

"But . . . if it's not the masses, but a few, as happens under an oligarchy, who come together and enact what is to be done—what do you call that?"

"Everything the sovereign power in the city decrees to be done, after taking counsel, is called a law."

"Even if . . . a tyrant who rules the city makes decrees for the citizens—is that law too?"

"Yes, whatever a tyrant as ruler enacts, even that is called a law."

"But . . . coercion {bia} and the negation of law—what is that, Pericles? Isn't it when the stronger compels the weaker to do what he wants, not by persuasion, but by force?"

"Yes, I suppose so," said Pericles.

"Then whatever a tyrant compels the citizen to do by decree, without persuading them, is the negation of the law?"

"Yes I agree," said Pericles. "I take back what I said, that everything a tyrant decrees without persuasion is a law." Alcibiades goes on,

"But when the few make decrees, using not persuasion but force— are we to call that coercion or not?"

"I should say," replied Pericles, "that whatever anyone compels anyone else to do, whether by decree or otherwise, without persuasion, is coercion rather than law."

"Then . . . everything the masses decree, not persuading the owners of property but compelling them, would not be law but coercion?"

"Let me tell you, Alcibiades," said Pericles, "when I was your age I too was very clever at this sort of thing; for I used to think and talk about the very things you now seem to be interested in."

"Ah, Pericles," said Alcibiades, "if only I had known you when you were at your very cleverest in such matters!"[2]

Pericles cannot solve the basic dilemma posed by Alcibiades. One cannot answer the problem of what is just within society as against what is unjust by calling one "law" and the other "coercion." One does not solve the problem of potential tyranny by making the majority sovereign. The great question of what makes a society just (exercising only a minimum of coercion, or tyranny) remains unanswered.

Aristotle, with his usual great acumen, compromised slightly by a proaristocratic bias, perceived that the *demos* becomes a collectivized monarch, capable of dispensing justice or exercising tyranny:

In democracies which obey the law there are no demagogues; it is the better class of citizens who preside over affairs. Demagogues arise in states where the laws are not sovereign. The people then becomes an autocrat—a single composite autocrat made up of many members, with the many playing the sovereign, not as individuals, but collectively. . . . However that may be, a democracy of this order, being in the nature of an autocrat and not being governed by law, begins to attempt an autocracy. It grows despotic; flatterers come to be held in honour; it becomes analogous to the tyrannical form of single-person government.

Both share a similar temper; both behave like despots to the better class of citizens; the decrees of one are like the edicts of the other; the popular leader in the one is the same as, or at any rate like, the flatterer in the other; and in either case the influence of the favourites predominates—that of the flatterer in tyrannies, and that of the popular leader in democracies of this variety.[3]

It is probably accurate to say that *all* democracies exhibit a combination of just and tyrannical behavior, that the question of justice or tyranny in a democratic society or any society is always a matter of degree. No democracy is perfectly law-abiding or presents a picture of perfect justice, yet no democracy can exist without a minimum of respect for the law. In a democracy, certainly in a radical democracy, no one is to blame for injustice except the *demos*. (Athens, as shown in this work, seems to conform to this pattern.)

The great moral, political, and human question becomes, what is it that makes a society dispense more or less justice? Aristotle's response, as we have seen, emphasizes respect for the law over arbitrary power. The laws must be sovereign, not the *demos*. But this is an ambiguous answer for the laws are not of supernatural origin. They are made by the *demos*. It is true that in the trial of the generals after Arginusae the laws were trampled on by the temporary madness and arrogance of the people, but Socrates was executed without any violation of the law. And laws can, and do, legitimize tyranny, as the fictionalized Alcibiades so brilliantly demonstrated. Consider the laws of slavery, for instance, and what we today call apartheid. They are essentially tyrannical laws. Respect for the law is enormously important for a just society, but like majority rule, a necessary, but hardly a sufficient condition for justice. If Aristotle is right in his emphasis on respect for law, that pushes the question one step backward: Why do some people revere the law and others treat it with contempt?

Plato was convinced that no group subject to class interest, neither the *demos* nor a narrow oligarchy, could be counted on to dispense justice; exactly the opposite was true. The solution was to take sovereignty away from the people and the narrow interest groups and place it with a small elite, trained for, living for, a moral government. Plato, however, did not really imagine that such a constitution would ever be established.

Many years later, a great political theorist, and, providentially a maker of an actual constitution—James Madison—wrestled with the same theoretical problem. In the tenth Federalist Paper, Madison addresses the question of "faction."

At this point, using Madison's discussion, it seems appropriate to give a serviceable definition of the necessarily overworked word "justice" as used in this chapter. For Madison there were essentially two forms of political action: one undertaken for the good of the commonwealth as a whole, the other serving the interests of only a segment of the commonwealth, contravening the common good and sacrificing "the rights of other citizens."[4] Madison designated the latter "faction." Just political action, therefore, serves the interest of the commonwealth as a whole and does not take away the rights of citizens. If we question, for instance, whether it is just that some people receive greater economic rewards (higher wages, greater wealth) than others within the same community, one can argue that it is so only if the whole commonwealth benefits. Indeed, that argument has been made many times: economic incentives resulting in disparities of wealth ultimately result in greater economic productivity, benefiting the entire society. Not to argue that complex question, the point being made here is that this contention assumes any social action is justified if it serves the common good. The argument for unequal economic rewards is also, therefore, an argument for a just society.

Unjust social action, as discussed here, is analogous to the activities of Madison's "faction." The ultimate extreme of factional activity would be economic or political domination—tyranny.

Madison immediately recognizes that factional activity by a minority interest presents no serious theoretical problems. "Relief is supplied by the republican principle [that is, majority rule], which enables the majority to defeat its [the faction's] sinister views by regular vote." Factional activity can be controlled even when it "masks its violence under the forms of the Constitution." The more serious problem occurs when "a majority is included in a faction."[5] The Athenian experience was in the foreground of Madison's thought. He comes to the remarkable conclusion that in a direct democracy there is *no cure* for the problem of majority factionalism; the *demos* inevitably becomes a tyrant.

A pure Democracy, by which I mean, a Society, consisting of a small number of citizens, who assemble and administer the Government in person, can admit of no cure for the mischiefs of faction. A common passion or interest will, in almost every case, be felt by a majority of the whole; a communication and concert results from *the form of Government* itself; and there is nothing to check the inducements to sacrifice the weaker party, or an obnoxious individual. Hence it is, that such Democracies have ever been spectacles of turbulence and contention; have ever been found incompatible with personal security, or the rights of property; and have in general been as short in their lives, as they have been violent in their deaths.[6]

The solution to this problem, Madison erroneously contends, lies in a change in the form of government. A republic (representative government) is not subject to the same disabilities as a democracy (direct government). First, the elected representatives will behave more morally than the people as a whole and political elites will tend to act more in the interests of the commonwealth than the convened *demos*. Madison does not tell us why this should be so, though we note that he twice uses the word "may": "whose wisdom may best discern the true intent of their country. . . . it may well happen that the public voice pronounced by the representatives of the people, will be more consonant with the public good."[7] Madison might have wondered whether Aristotle was right and the crucial question was not the form of government, but the spirit of society. For Aristotle, the question was, how highly are the laws regarded. Madison may judge correctly that the representatives of the people will seek the common good (though we certainly know of many elected representatives who are more corrupt than the people as a whole). In some representative democracies *something* in the mores of the society inspires those elected by the *demos* to act justly. No amount of complex political theory can successfully get around the necessity of defining that "something."

Madison argues, second, that the republican form of government allows for a much wider polity than a direct democracy, which is limited in territorial extent. The wider the polity, the greater the number of factions and interests, making it less likely that one faction will dominate and, therefore, tyrannize over society as a whole. "A religious sect, may degenerate into a political faction in a part of the Confederacy; but the variety of sects dispersed over the entire face of it, must secure the national Councils against any danger from that source."[8] Madison could not have imagined that the mechanisms of mass society and the frightful prospect of modernism would someday make a duly elected totalitarian state possible.

All kindly political theorists have searched for the something that would guarantee a just order of society. Aristotle found it in a reverence for the laws, though he could not tell us why one society enjoyed it and another did not. Plato sought a just, narrow, moral elite who would rule society, though he never discovered how philosophers were to become kings or kings philosophers, and finally put his highest, most practical trust in the laws. We are still left with the problematic of what leads to the establishment of just laws. Madison hoped that the problem would solve itself through the diversity of representative government and the separation of powers, whereby no one power could become strong enough to overwhelm the others, but history has taught us that no political technique, no complexity of constitution, can save a nation hell-bent on the path of moral self-destruction.

In truth, we are left with the necessity of laying our hopes for a just society on a very fragile reed, the *demos* itself. It is not the most reassuring prospect. The Athenian *demos*, the most morally spirited of any in the ancient world, could behave at times like an arrogant, inconsistent, frightened tyrant. As the comparison of Athens with other states demonstrated, there can be a profound difference between one *demos* and another. Pericles/Thucydides reminds us constantly of the unique nature of the Athenian people. Madison was optimistic, not only because of the rise of representative government but also because he perceived in America a new kind of *demos* capable of overcoming the political disabilities of ancient democracy. The *demos* is, after all, made up only of people. That is the great disability all political theory has attempted to overcome.

Fickle, Subject to Flattery, Faithless

In the year 390 A.D. the people of Thessalonica rebelled against the Roman Empire, murdering with great brutality a captain of the imperial garrison. Maddened by these actions, the Emperor Theodosius ordered his troops into the Greek city. On the emperor's orders, they gathered the citizens in the circus, and began an indiscriminate slaughter. A few days later, Theodosius—the most important *Christian* emperor to rule after Constantine—repented of his murderous orders and sent an embassy to cancel them. It arrived too late; seven thousand people had already been executed.[9] No ancient historian used this story as an exemplary tale demonstrating the essential fickleness of kings, thereby casting aspersions on the legitimacy of the institution of monarchy.

When the *demos* of Athens—a collectivized monarch—behaved in the identical manner, opponents of democracy used this inconsistency of action to illustrate the basic inefficiency and illegitimacy of democratic politics. In 428, the fourth year of the great war between Sparta and Athens, the city-state of Mitylene on the island of Lesbos rebelled against the Athenian Empire, declared its independence, and sought alliance with Sparta. It took Athens almost a year to put down the rebellion and recapture the city, which surrendered at discretion. Several of the leaders of the revolt were sent as captives to Athens, where the fate of Mitylene was argued in the full Assembly of Athenian citizens. It was decided, "in the fury of the moment . . . to put to death not only the prisoners at Athens, but the whole adult male population of Mitylene, and to make slaves of the women and children."[10] As an enraged monarch might, they sent orders to the Athenian general on Mitylene "to lose no time in despatching the Mitylenians." Its anger spent, however, a cruel *demos* could alter its decree. "The morrow brought repentance with it and reflexion on the horrid cruelty of the decree, which condemned a whole city to the fate merited only by the guilty."[11] At a new meeting of the Assembly, called to reconsider the verdict, occurred the brilliant debate over Mitylene either recorded, or composed, by Thucydides. The genocidal position was argued by Cleon, who had proposed the punishment in the first Assembly. Thucydides is careful to note that he was "the most violent man at Athens, and at that time, by far the most powerful with the commons."[12]

After the debate, a new vote narrowly declared life for the Mitylenians. Then commenced a true race against death:

Another galley was at once sent off in haste, for fear that the first might reach Lesbos in the interval, and the city be found destroyed; the first ship having about a day and a night's start. Wine and barley-cakes were provided for the vessel by the Mitylenian ambassadors, and great

promises made if they arrived in time; which caused the men to use
such diligence upon the voyage that they took their meals of barley-
cakes kneaded with oil and wine as they rowed, and only slept by
turns while the others were at the oar. Luckily they met with no contrary wind, and the first ship making no haste upon so horrid an
errand, while the second pressed on in the manner described, the first
arrived so little before them, that Paches had only just had time to read
the decree, and to prepare to execute the sentence, when the second
put into port and prevented the massacre. The danger of Mitylene had
indeed been great.[13]

Our pleasure in the high drama, the miraculous narrow escape, the
Homeric details of barley-cakes and oil, should not prevent us from
pondering the fact that the greatest *demos* in the ancient world had
composed such a horrible drama. It was not necessary to wait until the
twentieth century and the rise of mass culture and politics to discover
what the people, empowered and enraged, are capable of.

It is helpful to think about the *demos* not only as a collectivized
monarch exercising sovereignty, but also as a collectivized person suffering from the same anxieties, ambivalences, and disabilities of any
one human being. The people of Athens are shown to us as believing
in their own omnipotence and becoming enraged when they discover
they do not possess such power. We see them over trusting of their
leaders, then disappointed and infuriated when they feel they have been
misled or betrayed. The normal paranoid mechanism of projecting on
to leaders and/or enemies seems overly active in most democracies
and Athens was no exception. The vengeful behavior of the *demos* after
Arginusae can only be explained by its fury on discovering that Athens
and its generals were not omnipotent, that they could not win the
battle, seize the Spartan ships blockading Conon, win the war, *and* save
all the survivors in the sea. A choice had to be made. The paranoid
commitment to omnipotence knows nothing of priorities; for it, everything is possible. Thucydides notes on many occasions that repeated
success can bring a people, not to a realistic appraisal of its powers,
but to a belief in its own omnipotence. "Because of their current good
fortune," he writes, "did the Athenians expect to be frustrated in nothing, and believed that regardless of the strength of their forces they
would achieve equally what was easy and what was difficult."[14] Thus

Thucydides on the banishment, early in the war, of the generals Pythodorus and Sophocles on their return from Sicily, where they concluded a peace instead of subduing the island. The Athenians contended that the generals must have been bribed, that that was the only possible reason for their moderation, since Athenian arms were powerful enough to prevail anywhere.

The collectivized person is also constantly struggling with the universal human ambivalence about independence and dependence. Like a child, the *demos* longs to put its entire trust in the hands of its leaders, becoming enraged when the leaders, like parents, fail to deliver omnipotence, omniscience, or moral perfection. This disenchantment does not prevent the pattern from being repeated over and over again. (I recall two sophisticated, knowledgeable political operatives telling me in 1978 that they had grown disillusioned with Jimmy Carter; I silently wondered how they could have become illusioned in the first place.) The desire to be illusioned runs very deep in the human psyche. The best defense against it, Demosthenes tells us, is distrust, "for that part of the soul with which we trust is most easily taken captive."[15] Much of Athenian democratic politics can be understood if we keep in mind the powerful impulse wholly to trust a particular leader and the equally powerful ambivalence which uses distrust as a fundamental mechanism of defense. The fining, banishment, and execution of so many generals was the inevitable outcome of such ambivalent, symptomatic behavior.

The *demos* was, and is, acutely responsive to flattery. No one gets elected in a democratic society without flattering the electorate. Candidates who take the moral high road instead of using vulgar demagoguery make sure they celebrate the voters for being the kinds of people who prefer moral to vulgar politics. The Athenians, especially after the rise of the so-called demagogues, were acutely aware of this problematic in democratic life. Aristophanes evoked many a laugh by mocking such susceptibility. "You observe," writes Isocrates, a severe critic of the democracy, "the nature of the multitude, how susceptible they are to flattery; that they like those who cheat them with becoming smiles and brotherly love to those who serve them with dignity and reserve."[16]

It was always necessary to compliment the electorate, even before the days of television and mass communication. We should not blame television for the insipid nature of our politics. The *demos* has never gotten high grades for sophistication or maturity of deliberation. There is, too, something potentially sinister in the game of flattering the people. The *demos* seems to despise the flatterers even as they elect them and demand the flattery. Isocrates observes that, "we employ the kind of advisers whom no one could fail to despise, and we place these very same men in control of all our public interests to whom no one would entrust a single one of his private affairs."[17] Remember the Aristophanes-like poster of Richard Nixon: Many who would never have bought a used car from such a man still voted him President.

Those who despised the democracy for their own reasons inevitably exploited this democratic disability to discredit the entire egalitarian enterprise. Isocrates argues that monarchy is preferable to democracy because kings employ "the most sagacious" people for their advisers, unlike the *demos* who are interested only in those who know how to manipulate the crowd.[18] The argument is specious. How many stories are there, from the days of Plutarch to the seduction of the Romanovs by Rasputin, of monarchs rendered helpless by flatterers, bringing disaster on the people and themselves.

The problems of flattery, fickleness, and faithlessness are inherent in the nature of sovereignty itself, not merely in the nature of the imperfect *demos*. Over and over again the *demos* behaves like an ordinary monarch. How many kings have turned on their advisers for giving disastrous advice? "For even if the masses are deceived, they later usually hate those who have induced them to do things that are not good."[19] How many crowned rulers have treated their most intimate advisers contrarily, despising them and seeking their counsel? There is a fundamental ambivalence toward rulers, leaders, those who give us advice, or those who flatter us. The *demos* was merely the last actor to enter on to the historical stage and manifest this inconsistency. Plutarch, with psychological insight, ascribes part of the problem to "sheer perversity":

> "But . . . do not States put in office men who live licentiously and wantonly?" They do, and pregnant women often long for stones, and seasick persons for salt pickles and the like, which a little later they spew out and detest. So the people of democracies, because of the luxury of their own lives or through sheer perversity . . . make use of those

who happen to turn up, though they loathe and despise them, then take pleasure in hearing things said about them as the comic poet Plato puts into the mouth of the People itself:

> *Take my hand as quickly as you can;*
> *I'm going to choose Agyrrhius general.*[20]

What's wrong with monarchy? Monarchs are the great problem in monarchy. What's wrong with aristocracy? Aristocrats are the great problem in aristocracy. To whom do we ascribe the failures of democracy? People are the great uncertainty in democracy. If we could eliminate people from The People, our problem would be solved. All prescriptive political theory breaks on the rock that, ultimately, people hold the sovereignty in a democratic society. Even Plato's super-moral guardians and the elected representatives in Madison's republic are not *Uber-menschen*, but ordinary people, perhaps more talented than most. The creation of an elite based on merit cannot alter our humanness.

Isocrates' analysis corresponds in significant degree with this thesis. There are, he says, only three forms of polity: oligarchy, democracy, and monarchy; in *each* form (that is, in *every* polity), the answer to the question of justice is the same. If those whom the sovereign places in charge of public affairs are "most competent and . . . will most ably and justly direct the affairs of state," then all three forms will be governed well. Conversely, if those appointed are "most brazen and the most depraved and who take no thought for the things which are advantageous to the commonwealth," the "government will correspond to the depravity of the men at the head of their affairs."[21] It is a simple analysis: good men produce good government and bad men the opposite. It does, however, allow us, or even urge us, to push the question one step further: What makes for good men?

We are back to the ultimate question of justice within society, especially in a democratic society. Isocrates' view, and in the final analysis Thucydides' as well, is that, assuming the existence of democratic governments, some will act wisely and justly and others foolishly and arrogantly. Circumstance (perhaps the winning or losing of a war or a plague), and the spirit or spiritedness of the people are decisive factors. The future holds the prospect of a certain number of democratic polities, some of which will be governed justly and others not. This analysis lacks historical, developmental dimension because the Greek world and especially democracy were so young that no evolutionary analysis of democratic society was possible. *Without such analysis, however, there is no answer to the problem of justice within society.* Therefore Plato and Aristotle could never answer the question.

One may reject the historical evolutionary view, but to do so is necessarily to assume a pessimistic position. If all that the future holds, as Thucydides would have it, is more and more repetition of the past, then human history has no meaning and the problem of justice within society has no answer. If the human psyche lacks an evolutionary, developmental thrust to overcome the paranoid position; if the psyche does not strive toward a democratic polity as a matter of psychic health; if the history of democracy, especially since the rise of liberalism and the creation of the great democratic societies of the nineteenth and twentieth centuries, shows no developmental impulse toward a more and more mature and more and more inclusive society (women, the poorest people), then justice will always remain a matter of mere chance and we will never awaken from the nightmare that is history. The fundamental question is whether it is possible to create a new *demos* capable of more mature and just action than in any polity yet seen.

Commitment to the paranoid position is always a matter of degree, as is allegiance to democratic values. The prophets of ancient Israel and the philosophy of Socrates and Plato postulated the possibility of a fundamental transformation within human nature. Athenian democratic society resulted from such a transformation. So, too, did liberal, democratic, bourgeois society. We may here extract an optimistic conclusion from Thucydides' view of history: If such radical transformations have occurred in the past, one cannot deny their possibility in the future. The only one cure for the *demos* as tyrant is a *demos* capable of renouncing tyranny.

The Demos as Imperialist

In the Greek world, with the exception of Plato and a few others, any considerations of justice stopped at the frontiers of the city-state. Athens was no exception. In its relations with other polities Athens showed not an iota more concern for moral considerations than did the most primitive of Greek societies. Thucydides' unbearable statement that justice is only a question between equals and that, otherwise, "the strong do what they can and the weak suffer what they must"[22] was not meant to apply to affairs *within* the *polis* but to relations between states. The words were spoken not by some Sicilian tyrant, or by the assembly of Spartan "equals," but simply by "the Athenians." Nothing demonstrates more clearly the capacity of the *demos* to play the tyrant than its thorough commitment to the imperialist policy of the Athenian Empire and its willingness to support the most violent measures to build and defend that hegemony. We recall that the first vote in the Assembly in regard to punishment for the Mitylenians was for genocide. The vote was rescinded only when Diodotus convinced a small majority that it would not be the most prudent course. Diodotus deliberately rejected any moral consideration. "The question is not justice, but how to make the Mitylenians useful to Athens."[23] The *demos* had grown accustomed to speaking with a tyrant's voice.

Beyond such normal considerations as that all power corrupts, that whoever exercises sovereignty will tend toward an excess of domination—beyond this, there seems to be a rather complex, and most difficult to understand, relationship between a *new* democracy and an explosive exercise of domination beyond the borders of the state, an imperial *libido dominandi*. Some states, newly come to an exhilarating sense of unified national purpose, feel compelled to expend that recently generated energy on a course of foreign domination. (This century has witnessed the brutal examples of Germany, Japan, and Italy.) Jacqueline de Romilly, the great expositor of Thucydides, perhaps had this unconscious motivation in mind when she wrote of Athens that "moderate imperialism is the policy of moderate democracy and extreme imperialism the policy of extreme democracy."[24] It is a phenomenon full of complexities and contradictions—like the singing of the *Marseillaise* that accompanied the building of the French European Empire.

Almost all the limited data we have confirm that the Athenian people, particularly the lower classes who benefited most from employment in the fleet, overwhelmingly supported Athens' imperialist efforts. The few impulses toward moderation in these matters, like Nicias' objection to the Sicilian expedition, came from people in the aristocratic strata. As for that disastrous adventure, Thucydides tells us that "the idea of the common people and the soldiery was to earn wages at the moment, and make conquests that would supply a never-ending fund of pay for the future."[25]

There is no question but that landless and land-poor Athenians benefited from imperial conquest. One punishment against a state that unsuccessfully revolted against Athenian domination was to confiscate some of the best lands and either settle Athenian colonists on them or impose rents payable to specific Athenian citizens. When Athens was in the process of adding to her empire, Athenian colonists, called *klerouchoi*, were settled in the newly acquired territories as instruments of imperial control. Moses Finley estimates that as many as ten thousand Athenians, mostly from the poorer strata, so benefited during the course of the empire.[26] In a precapitalist, direct-democracy society—even in Rome where there was no true democracy though the *demos* did have some say in the politics of the state—a substantial part of the spoils of war and empire goes directly to the people.

Imperialist expansion can also be an efficient way to handle the problems of class conflict, a resolution with utilitarian and a psychological (irrational) dimension. The utilitarian considerations have been discussed above. Instead of trying to solve their problems of landlessness or hunger at the expense of the wealthy, the lower classes become partners in the exploitation and expropriation of other states. In his fourth-century work *To Philip*, Isocrates argued for imperialism against Persia as a way to solve problems of social conflict. Nineteenth-century England, too, was aware of the social benefits imperialism could bring to the mother country. Cecil Rhodes relates:

> I was in the East End of London yesterday and attended a meeting of the unemployed. I listened to the wild speeches, which were just a cry for "bread," "bread," "bread," and on my way home I pondered over the scene. . . . My cherished idea is a solution to social problems; i.e., in order to save the 40,000,000 inhabitants of the United Kingdom from a bloody civil war, we colonial statesmen must acquire new lands to settle the surplus population, to provide new markets for the goods produced by them in the factories and mines. The Empire, as I have always said, is a bread and butter question.[27]

Taking into consideration all their circumstances, it was logical that the lowest classes of the Athenian *demos* should embrace the opportunity to take their share of booty from this national piracy. Many of them, not prospering from agricultural endeavor, were at an economic dead end. They had seemingly renounced for all time the revolutionary measures of confiscation of land and cancellation of debts. They thus had no way to improve their economic position at the expense of the rich, a course both Plato and Aristotle assumed a radical democracy would take. Their only recourse was to seize the opportunity offered by the upper classes and become a partner in the tyranny over other *poleis*. No class will renounce the benefits of imperial domination until it can see its way to economic prosperity without it.

Aggression and domination are the irrational aspects of imperialist activity. People may live together in peace, Freud has said, as long as they have a means of projecting their aggression outward, beyond the borders of society.[28] When those who hold dominion within the *polis* can no longer exploit the economically disadvantaged due to the flourishing of democratic ideals and forms, they seek new areas outside the *polis* wherein to express their *libido dominandi*. The exploited class can now become exploiters. In addition, imperialist activity, especially in a direct-democracy state, can become a great unifier of society. As Plato noted, instead of being two states, one of the rich and one of the poor, rich and poor together can sail off to Sicily, flags flying, hearts throbbing to the melody of one united, conquering *polis*.

There is a peculiar, particular relationship between a new democracy and imperial expansion. The first stage of democratic advance is the great refusal to be a victim. Athenian democracy can most accurately be placed at this stage. *Having advanced no further*, freedom becomes conflated, as Thucydides expressed it, with "the rule over others."[29] Ruling others becomes a "necessary" expression of one's independence. It is very difficult to say why this should be so. An answer may lie in the peculiar ambiguities of child development wherein separation and individuation are achieved in a most irrational manner. At one point in development, the child cannot feel free of domination without expressing domination itself. We know many adults who have not advanced much further than this in their relationship to power. A whole society may be equally encumbered. How much further has our own liberal, democratic, bourgeois society come? We have institutionalized *universal* ideals of freedom and rights, but we remain enormously confused as to whether "universal" extends beyond the borders of our particular *polis*.

An ironic aspect of Athenian imperial domination was Athens' interference with the internal affairs of some of its subject states. In theory, the empire had been formed to counter the Persian Empire and Athens should have had no say in internal affairs of its allies as long as their foreign policy remained in accordance with the aims of the empire. On many occasions, however, "Athens infringed the internal political freedom of the allies. After Ephialtes' reforms of 462 and 461 Athens was self-consciously democratic, and although she sometimes tolerated oligarchies she often encouraged or *enforced* democracies in the allied states."[30] This is ironic because democracy is moral and imperial domination is immoral. That this moral contradiction could not have been comprehended by even the best of the Athenians tells us something significant about the Greek conception of power. Democracies were forcibly installed in the subject states because they would be more sympathetic to Athens and less inclined to revolt. It was not a matter of morals, but of *realpolitik*, like the morally contradictory support of fascist regimes by the United States as a cold war strategy. In Athens there was not the slightest criticism of any imperial design from any sector of society. There may have been disagreements about strategy, but the basic right of Athens to rule wherever she might was unchallenged.

One small bit of data supporting the intimate relationship of democracy to imperial expansion comes from Sicily in the middle of the fifth century. It is not that the tyrants of Sicily were uninterested in building empires, for they were, but the explosive energy with which Syracuse undertook to dominate the whole island after the overthrow of the tyrants and the installation of the democracy was extraordinary. Operating against both the non-Greek Sicels and the powerful Greek states, Acragas in particular, the Syracusian democracy became "the greatest state in Sicily. She claimed hegemony over many Greek states, and she exacted tribute from the Sicel towns. Her wealth enabled her to double her force of cavalry, maintain a fleet of 100 triremes, and build up financial reserves. Her aim was to win the whole of Sicily. Her methods resembled those of Athens, whose ambitions had already made themselves felt in the West."[31]

A fledgling democracy is clearly not the only road to empire. Rome, the champion of them all, was no democracy. Tyrants and monarchs of the Greek world—Pyrrhus of Epirus, Dionysius of Syracuse, Philip and Alexander of Macedon—were certainly bent upon empire, but the similarity of the explosion of energy between authoritarian leaders and the rising *demos* is striking. Nothing demonstrates more powerfully the nature of the people as a collectivized monarch, nothing emphasizes more compellingly the capacity of the *demos* to play the tyrant, than how quickly it assumes the mode of imperial domination.

The rise of democracy unleashes new energies into the world. Not all are productive, as we have observed in this reflection on imperialism, and as we shall see from our discussion of narcissism and individualism. The conscious moralization of democratic energy, which began with liberalism and the rise of democracy in the seventeenth century, still remains our greatest social task.

12

Narcissus–Dionysus

In Plato's dialogue, the *Symposium*, a group of friends and acquaintances meet for dinner and an evening's entertainment. Three prominent Athenians are there, Aristophanes, the comic playwright; Socrates; and Agathon, considered one of the most important writers of tragedy after Aeschylus, Sophocles, and Euripides, though none of his works survives. The year is 416 B.C. a year before the disastrous Athenian expedition to Syracuse. Agathon has just won his initial first prize in the dramatic competition and the evening is partly a celebration of the event. Plato deliberately sets a restrained, civilized, almost sublime, tone to the party. It is decided that there shall be no heavy drinking: "It was unanimously agreed that this was not to be a drunken party, and that wine was to be served merely by way of refreshment." [176E][1] It is further determined to send the flute girl away and spend the evening in discussion. Each participant in turn will give his companions a speech on the nature of Love. A potentially explosive topic, but a more humane, poetic, cultivated set of speeches cannot be imagined.

Serious talk of Love, in the Greek world, quickly turns to ruminations on beauty and what we in our new-found wisdom call narcissism, the love of self. An extraordinary speech that Plato assigns to Aristophanes expostulates what can almost be considered an Ur-myth of the narcissistic necessity. Human beings were, at one time, very different than they are today: double and complete. Four arms, four legs, two faces, two sets of genitals. They were globular, circular in shape, and psychologically, symbiotically content within themselves. There were three sexes: all male, all female, and a mixed male and female, possessing a set of genitals of each sex. Because they revolted against the gods, these creatures were rendered powerless by Zeus, who cut them in half, leaving two where one had been. The condition of symbiotic unity was never forgotten, however, and persists like a universal dream in each of us. With almost greater force than any other feeling, we long to be reunited with the other half from which we have been sundered. Those who were once double-male seek out a love of the same sex as do those who were double-female. Those originally hermaphrodite seek a love of the opposite sex who is, in effect, another self.

"So you see, gentlemen, how far back we trace our innate love for one another, and how this love is always trying to redintegrate our former nature, to make two into one, and to bridge the gulf between one human being and another. And so, gentlemen, we are all like pieces of the coins that children break in half for keepsakes—making two out of one . . . —and each of us is forever seeking the half that will tally with himself."[191D]

When one of these halves is lucky enough to meet his other, Aristophanes continues, they fall madly in love, never wanting to lose sight of the other. It is not sexual pleasure that binds them so close, however. "The fact is that both their souls are longing for something else—a something to which they can neither of them put a name, and which they can only give an inkling in cryptic sayings and prophetic riddles."[192C] If Hephaestus should offer to weld together these inseparable lovers, so they need never be separated again, continually enjoying a permanent reunion, then "no lover on earth would dream of refusing such an offer, for not one of them could imagine a happier fate. Indeed, they would be convinced that this was just what they'd been waiting for—*to be merged, that is, into an utter oneness with the beloved.*"[192E, italics added]

This is as powerful and accurate a description as has ever been given of the love of self and the love of the other-as-self—narcissism and narcissistic love. All the great young lovers of the world—Tristan and Isolde, Romeo and Juliet, Paolo and Francesca—embody and relive Aristophanes' myth.

All these lovers are beautiful. Beauty is the essence—and sexual beauty the problematic—in the narcissistic view of the world. Following Aristophanes, Socrates delivers a long discourse on the preservation of the beautiful ("And ugliness is at odds with the divine, while beauty is perfect harmony." [206C]), going beyond the superficiality of physical beauty and the shallowness of glamorous sex. It is a paean to sublimation, a moral ascent by means of repression and transformation of the sexual. A beautiful soul is a greater attraction than a beautiful body. One's heart can be quickened by the beauty of laws and institutions and, progressing further, by science and philosophy. At each step upward, beauty becomes more and more abstract, less and less particular. "Starting from individual beauties, the quest for the universal beauty must find him ever mounting the heavenly ladder, stepping from rung to rung—that is, from one to two, and from two to *every* lovely body, from bodily beauty to beauty of institutions, from institutions to learning, and from learning in general to the special lore that pertains to nothing but the beautiful itself—until at last he comes to know what beauty is."[211C]

This is one of the most dramatic of all Plato's dialogues. Just as Socrates finishes his speech to the applause of everyone but Aristophanes, there comes a knocking at the door and the sound of the flute and rough merriment in the street. Who enters? He who embodies the passionate narcissism of Aristophanes or the heavenly sublimation of beauty extolled by Socrates? Neither of these. He who crashes in on these cultivated philosophers extolling the virtues of Love brings an element we all share but that so far none has touched on: the Dionysian. Enter to them Narcissus–Dionysus, Alcibiades himself. First he is more than minimally drunk. Second, he wears a crown of ivy and violets, ivy for Dionysus, violets for Aphrodite.[2] Third, he brings raw, physical sexuality and, most important, anger and "sacred rage."[215D] In the years after the setting of this dialogue, as Plato and all his readers knew, Alcibiades would come close to being the ruin of Athens. The dramatic progression of the dialogue indicates that Narcissus and the holy sublimation of beauty cannot exist by themselves alone. Though we begin—and end—with the self and with beauty, we will be forced to deal with Dionysian frenzy and rage.

Alcibiades was without question one of the most remarkably talented people who ever lived. "In him," wrote the Roman Cornelius Nepos, "nature seems to have tried what she could do."[3] He was uncommonly beautiful at all stages of his life. He was an extraordinarily gifted orator, a superb general, and a genius at persuading and manipulating people, including Athenians, Persians, and Spartans. He had a sense of, and the capacity for, high drama in personal and political life that made people wild for him. In addition, he lacked a sense of boundaries to make a normal moral life possible. Like the great city that gave birth to him, he had a propensity toward self-destruction that ultimately brought him down to the final tragic conclusion to his life.

Alcibiades was Dionysus come to earth and so Plato most subtly exhibits him to us. Committed to the most radical expressions of individual desire, Dionysus–Alcibiades lived in a frenzy of acting-out, not in the calm of sublimation. As with Dionysus, no sharp gender lines are drawn between masculine and feminine—power is what is desired; it matters not which sex. Power includes the capacity for destruction and like the Dionysus in Euripides' *Bacchae*, Alcibiades drew out the self-destructive tendencies in people. After pages and pages in the *Symposium* devoted to the sublimation of the love of beauty in order to reach higher and higher human heights, Alcibiades tells a slightly comic, slightly crude, definitely de-sublimated story of how he attempted to seduce Socrates into physical sexual congress. He failed. Socrates' virtue remained intact. But though he failed to seduce Socrates, he did not fail to seduce Athens and Plato, sure of Socrates' virtue, he was attempting to transform Athens.

The great irony in the tale that Plato has Alcibiades tell is that it is the charismatic quality of Socrates' virtue and the unrivaled brilliance of his intellect that drive Alcibiades into a sexual frenzy—a "sacred rage." "From the moment I hear him speak I am smitten with a kind of sacred rage, worse than any Corybant, and my heart jumps into my mouth and the tears start into my eyes—oh, and not only me, but lots of other men." [215D–E] In an effort to justify his behavior, he elaborates on this feeling a little later, just before he tells the story of the attempted seduction. "I've been bitten by something much more poisonous than a snake; in fact, mine is the most painful kind of bite there is. I've been bitten in the heart, or the mind, or whatever you like to call it, by Socrates' philosophy, which clings like an adder to any young gifted mind it can get hold of, and does exactly what it likes with it. . . . and every one of you has had his taste of this philosophical frenzy, this sacred rage; so I don't mind telling *you* about it because I know you'll make allowances for me." [218A–B] How the great excitement over moral philosophy ("Socrates is the only man in the world that can make me feel ashamed." [216B]), how this intellectual frenzy and moral excitement is driven to climax in actual physical orgasm is truly a mystery, one of the many mysteries over which Dionysus presides.

Even the staid participants in the symposium are helpless against the human impulses toward de-sublimation. "And then, all of a sudden . . . a whole crowd of revelers came to the door, and finding it open . . . they marched straight in and joined the party. No sooner had they sat down than the whole place was in an uproar; decency and order went by the board, and everybody had to drink the most enormous quantities of wine." [223B] Dionysus triumphant! So much for the ascent of beauty, rung by rung.

The Birth of Radical Individualism

Plato has deliberately set before us a great ambiguity. After Aristophanes' magnificent paean to beauty and the power of infatuation and Socrates' sublime panegyric to all forms of sublimated beauty, the forced entry of Alcibiades brings the party to a raucous climax— Alcibiades, the most beautiful, capable, thrilling, brilliant, charismatic— and most destructive and self-destructive—force ever to walk the streets of Athens. The resplendent ideal of beauty and its infinite transformation and ennoblement are blown sky-high by the presence of this phallic, disruptive force. These two powerful elements, the ideal and its destruction, come together in the concept of radical individualism, of which Alcibiades was the perfect symbol. In radical individualism, culture united, on the one hand, deep, personal, intrapsychic conflicts over narcissism and, on the other, crucial social concerns of power, ambition, and domination. Radical individualism was, and is, like Alcibiades enormously attractive and profoundly potent with catastrophe: Dionysian, precisely.

Rarely does a long repressed human need-drive-instinct, once unleashed, return in a staid and circumspect manner. The return of the repressed is usually explosive, disruptive, and difficult to control. In no society does just enough—not too much—of the repressed needs return. Excess is an inevitable consequence of getting back in touch with repressed feelings. All moral advances in society are therefore accompanied by unwanted phenomena.

Individuality must be repressed in order that primitive and traditional-authoritarian societies can exist. When that repression is lifted—for causes that remain a mystery to us—as in the Archaic period of ancient Greece, individualism is expressed in an explosive, disruptive manner. It may take centuries for society to sort out the moral from the immoral forms of individualism; it may never succeed in that discrimination. One should not blame individualism for its excesses. The true culprit is the nature of repression and the costly mode by which human beings progress. Radical individualism is an exhilarating and deeply problematic phenomenon. The ancient Greek world was the first society in the West to experience that marvel. It is a question whether it ever existed outside the West. History demonstrates that every time traditional-authoritarian society breaks down, the virtues of individualism and the catastrophes of radical individualism appear simultaneously: in the twelfth century, the Renaissance, the modern world. The whole world is struggling today to retain the virtues of individualism, while controlling—need we say, repressing?—the uninhibited excesses of radical individualism. Mr. Gorbachev no less than Mr. Bush. Plato knew what the problem was, though he was deeply unsure of the solution. Alcibiades' life is so exciting, so revelatory of the human condition, because he was a walking objective correlative of this fundamental human predicament.

Between two essential modes of child rearing, authoritarian and permissive, there lie an almost infinite number of combinations of the authoritarian and the liberal. "Authoritarian" and "permissive" are both matters of degree, but there are times when it is accurate to describe a child-rearing regime as "permissive." If that is too pejorative a word, one may say "partaking of mutuality," with the true needs of the child acquiring as much importance as the many-times-corrupt needs of the parents. Lawrence Stone describes, in great depth, the advent of a much more permissive regime of child rearing in America and England at the end of the eighteenth century.[4] Our present century has also seen a dramatic rise in the mutual-permissive mode of caring for the young.

Two important human experiences correlate with the rise of mutual-permissive child rearing, one personal, one social: narcissism and democracy. Whenever a regime of authoritarian child rearing breaks down a more mutual, more permissive stance takes its place, a quantum leap in narcissistic phenomena results. This is demonstrated by Stone's data for the late eighteenth century and in our own century, almost all psychotherapists who have been practicing for the last thirty years have noted the vast increase in narcissistic disorders among their patients. The problems of narcissism have become a ready subject for psychology and sociology.

The breakdown of authoritarian child rearing and the beginnings of mutuality make democratic society possible. Though we would prefer individualism without narcissism, mutuality without excessive permissiveness, democracy without an exaggerated selfish egoism, historically, we have had no choice. The toad and the jewel in its head have been inseparable.

We have no firm data about child-rearing practices in ancient Greek society, especially for the early years. We can only speculate by observing the behavior of adults. We see the first democratic societies in history. We observe all the problems of narcissism, radical individualism, and unrestrained egoism. And we have Plato's trenchant critique of democracy which clearly lays the blame for social disorder on the permissive nature of society, particularly in the relationship of the young to their elders. He is admittedly writing a partisan critical tract, but he also seeks recognition and approbation from his readers. He must touch on a truth in which they are ready to acquiesce.

"That a father," he says, "habituates himself to be like his child and fear his sons, and a son habituates himself to be like his father and to have no shame before or fear of his parents—that's so he may be free. . . . As the teacher in such a situation is frightened of the pupils and fawns on them, so the students make light of their teachers, as well as their attendants. And, generally, the young copy their elders and compete with them in speeches and deeds while the old come down to the level of the young; imitating the young, they are overflowing with facility and charm, and that's so that they won't seem to be unpleasant or despotic."[5] This may be an exaggeration of Athenian society, but we all know family situations which fit this description. (In a world of authoritarian child rearing, like that of nineteenth-century Europe, Plato's description would seem absurd.) That he knew he could draw a smile of recognition from his audience meant that there was *a* truth, if not *the* truth, in the critique.

The essential ambiguity inherent in the rise of individualism and the breakdown of authoritarian religion and politics is reflected in the argument over the famous saying of Protagoras, as reported by Plato in *Theaetetus*: "Man is the measure of all things, of the things that are, how they are, and of the things that are not, how they are not."[6] Plato, the conservative, rejects this notion as egotistical and leading to a total moral and cognitive relativism. "Things are to me as they appear to me, and . . . they are to you as they appear to you."[7] This relativism can be overcome only by asserting the existence of a divinity beyond man. "For us, the god would be the measure of all things in the highest degree, and far more so than some 'human being,' as they assert."[8] Moral relativism, he claims, results from a radical narcissism in "extreme democracies," as expressed in the critical remark of Aristotle, quoted previously: "He ends with the view that 'liberty and equality' consist in 'doing what one likes.' The result of such a view is that . . . each man lives as he likes—or, as Euripides says, 'For any end he chances to desire.' "[9]

The critique of Protagoras' statement is spurious, however, equating the excesses of individualism with individualism itself. It does not follow that, if man is the measure, the moral center will not hold. There is as much reason to believe that a universal morality exists in the human psyche as it lies in the keeping of some pagan divinity. From what we know of Protagoras—that he taught "virtue," that he was appointed to draw up a code of law for the Athenian colony of Thurii[10]—it is probable that he held precisely this position. There is something deeply heroic in human beings taking full responsibility, including moral responsibility, for their own lives.

"Ripeness is all."[11] A free, democratic society gives birth to too many egoists (Alcibiades, for instance, never achieved ripeness), a disability exaggerated in a free-wheeling, capitalist environment wherein too many private vices are translated into public vices, rather than public virtues. If democratic society is to survive, it must learn to face egoism and somehow control it.

When children are no longer afraid to challenge their parents, either from the permissiveness or the mutuality in their upbringing; when the threat of castration is reduced to manageable proportions, so the child does not withdraw in intense anxiety from the oedipal challenge; when the goal of child rearing is no longer to beat the spirit out of the child but to have it express its spiritedness, the result is the creation of a new person and a new society. "The Athenians are addicted to innovation," Thucydides says, in a passage we have looked at before, ". . . they are adventurous beyond their power, and daring beyond their judgement. . . . They are swift to follow up success, and slow to recoil from a reverse. . . . A scheme unexecuted is with them a positive loss. . . . for they alone are enabled to call a thing hoped for a thing got, by the speed with which they act out their resolutions."[12]

These attributes are not an inevitable expression of human nature. Thucydides is deliberately contrasting the Athenians with their Spartan opponents. "Human nature" allows for two radically different forms of human beings and of society:

> On the one side is Spartan *apragmosynē*—a traditional conservatism, distrustful of all innovation, governed by an austere military discipline of restraint; a quietism of policy which verges, it seems, on apathy, but based upon the old Greek sense of a natural *dikē* [justice] of boundaries and behavior against which it was *hybris*, or *polypragmosynē* to trespass. On the other side is Athenian *polypragmosynē*, that divine, metaphysical restlessness and discontent, that enterprising meddlesome arrogance of mind and hand that made the Athenians both the bane and wonder of the Greek world. . . . [13] In political terms, *polypragmosynē* is the very pith and spirit of Athenian enterprise, its dynamic of *pleonexia*, the expansive *hybris* of energy and power in a spirited people; an *eros* or libido, a *libido dominandi*.[14]

One seemingly inevitable result of these remarkably "modern" phenomena is a fiercely competitive society. Individualism, once unrepressed and unleashed, must be expressed, and a characteristic mode of that expression is the intense need to triumph over one's opponent. The competitive spirit could be expressed against other *poleis*, either in warfare or in diplomatic triumph. An attempt at the sublimation of competitive aggression on the interstate level resulted in a heightened importance of the Olympian and other games (Nemean, Pythian, Isthmian). The competitive spirit also reigned supreme within the *polis*. It was difficult to keep it within bounds. Alvin Gouldner, commenting on Nietzsche's view that the Greeks turned almost every human activity into a contest, writes: "Yet it is the same contest system that also rends the *polis* and so lacerates its social order that at times it appears that, of all the Greek talents, by far the greatest is mutual destruction."[15] Alcibiades, our archetypical hero, practiced with great intensity all three forms of competitive exercise: foreign domination, the more sublimated triumph of the Olympian games, and the intra-*polis* struggle. Destruction and self-destruction were inherent in his behavior. Uncontrolled narcissism too easily transforms itself into a Dionysian enterprise.

There was—and is—a significantly effective way to sublimate (and, therefore, control) this unrestrained egoism and destructive competitiveness: so contrive that people struggle against each other for the honor of serving the commonwealth. Honor and glory—and their concomitant negatives, shame and dishonor—were of enormous importance in Greek society. Dodds's view that the society underwent a transformation from shame culture to guilt culture[16] is accurate for only a small part of the value system of the Hellenic world. Honor, glory, shame, and dishonor still reigned supreme in the *polis*.[17] "Every one of us," Plato has Socrates' mythical Diotima say in the *Symposium*, "no matter what he does, is longing for the endless fame, the incomparable glory that is theirs, and the nobler he is, the greater his ambition, because he is in love with the eternal."[18] One of Athens' greatest achievements was the sublimation and transformation of this narcissistic libido into a competition for the honor of advancing the commonwealth. To what degree the Dionysian impulses underwent the same sort of sublimation, how far the forces of destruction and self-destruction were subjected to control, remains an open question.

One of the most cogent statements of the Athenian ideal is placed by Plutarch, ironically enough, in the mouth of a Spartan, Charillus: "When someone asked him what he thought the best form of government, he said, 'That in which the greatest number of citizens are willing, without civil strife, to vie with one another in virtue.' "[19] The Athenians would, of course, differ from the Laconians on the question of what constitutes virtue, but neither would have denied that *philotimia*, love of honor, was virtuous. Athens recognized that an excessive love of honor, an excessive ambition, could prove disastrous to the state, but during the fourth century, the period of great democratic stability, the public decrees endorsed *philotimia* as a cardinal virtue, benefiting the commonwealth as a whole, as in the concept of *demosia philotimia*. Those who thus sought honor were the *philotimoi*, among the most highly regarded in the society.[20]

Athenian civic life was replete with occasions of recognition for someone who had served the *polis* with special honor—not connected with warfare. The local assemblies in the demes, or the national Assembly at Athens, could issue decrees honoring citizens, for example, for producing a particularly good performance at the theater, or bringing together an outstanding chorus, or achieving a diplomatic triumph. A higher and more costly honor was to have the decree inscribed on stone. The central Assembly awarded the highest honor of all when it decreed that a golden crown be given a particularly outstanding citizen. A decree from one of the local demes of Attica, Aixone, passed in the year 313/312, gives the flavor of these recognitions.

> On the proposal of Glaukides Sosippou. Since the *chorēgoi* [sponsors and producers of dramatic performances] Auteas Autokleous and Philox-enides Phillippou performed the choregy with a fine love of honor, the demesmen resolved to crown each of them with a golden crown worth one hundred drachmas in the theatre at the time of the comedies in the year after Theophrastus's archonship, in order that such a love of honor may also be shown by other *chorēgoi* who perform the choregy in the future. It was further resolved that the demarch Hegesileos and the treasurers should give them ten drachmas for a sacrifice, and that the treasurers should have this decree inscribed on a stone stele and set up in the theatre in order that Aixones may always make their Dionysia [theater festival] as fine as possible.[21]

The state of Athens lacked the complex system of taxation that is *de rigeur* in modern industrial societies; there was not, for instance, a graduated income tax. State expenditures for warfare and other demands represented a substantial part of what we designate the gross national product. The discrepancy between tax receipts and expenditures was made up by a system of "liturgies," apparently a transitional form between the primitive notion of gift (to the community) and the legal-rational idea of taxation. Concepts of honor, therefore, permeated the performance of these functions. A number of the richest people in the *polis* were designated each year to be financially and organizationally responsible for certain state activities: "the production of a chorus at the musical and dramatic festivals"; supervision of the gymnasium, the public sports ground open to all citizens; production of a banquet for a tribe at festivals; "the leadership of a public delegation to a foreign festival"; "the maintenance of a horse by a knight." More unexpected, from our point of view, was the "trierarchy": bearing all expenses for the maintenance and repair of a warship, and assuming the captainship thereof for the year.[22]

Though these liturgies were not voluntary, there was a definite amount of leeway in their execution. The person chosen could spend more than was required to get the job done, providing thereby an exceptional pleasure for the *demos*, and a substantial increase in honor for the liturgist. The two gold crowns were bestowed in Aixone for such services. And it was standard procedure in court cases for either the prosecutor or the defendant, both of whom had to plead their cases personally, to list in detail services done for the state, either as liturgist or in other capacities, to obtain the sympathy of the jury. The pleader usually claimed that, though required to do the liturgy, he performed it in such a manner as to produce a greater than usual benefit.

In his speech, *Defense Against a Charge of Taking Bribes*, Lysias has the defendant list, with prices, all the benefits he has bestowed on the state to prove that he could not possibly be guilty of the charge against him. "Appointed to produce tragic drama, I spent thirty minae and two months later, at the Thargelia, two thousand drachmae, when I won a victory with a male chorus; and . . . at the Great Panathenaea, eight hundred drachmae on pyrrhic dancers. Besides, I won a victory with a male chorus at the Dionysia . . . and spent on it, including the dedication of the tripod, five thousand drachmae; then . . . three hundred on a cylic chorus at the Little Panathenaea. In the meantime, for seven years I equipped warships, at a cost of six talents." The list goes on to specify nine other such occasions, emphasizing that "Of these sums that I have enumerated, had I chosen to limit my public services to the letter of the law, I should have spent not one quarter." The pursuit of honor in the Athenian state could be costly.

We can see how fiercely competitive the pursuit of honor could be in the Athenian *polis*, but this is clearly a sublimated, transformed mode of triumph: Far from rending the *polis*, it reinforced the sense of solidarity and community. It is not too much to say that, without this sublimated aggressive activity on the part of the elites of wealth, the stability of the democracy would have been impossible.

As final proof of the expansiveness of his generosity and public spiritedness, our defendant declares: "During the time when I had charge of a warship, my vessel was the best found in the whole armament. And I will tell you the surest evidence of that fact: at first Alcibiades—I would have given a great deal to prevent his sailing with me, as he was neither my friend nor my relative nor a member of my tribe [this speech was delivered after Alcibiades' final disgrace and death]—was aboard my ship. Now I am sure you must be aware that, being a commander who was free to do as he pleased, he would never have gone aboard any but the best found vessel, when he was himself to have his part in the danger."[23]

Dionysus

We thus return to that remarkable narcissistic, dionysian, godlike being who was certainly deaf to the voices of moderation and sublimation. With all his superhuman qualities, Alcibiades was only an extravagant manifestation of Athenian culture, lusting for honor, glory, triumph, and domination. To understand Alcibiades, we must understand both Narcissus and Dionysus.

Both Euripides and Nietzsche have used Dionysus to emphasize a fundamental human ambiguity: that great benefit and great evil may both flow from the same sources. Nietzsche argued that intellectual and artistic creativity—and destruction—arise from a common source. In *The Bacchae*, one of the most powerful and difficult plays ever written, Euripides seems to be saying that oppressive sexual repression cannot be lifted without simultaneously removing the inhibitions on destructive forces. Agave, who goes to the mountain with the women of Thebes to celebrate the uninhibited rites of the god Bacchus (Dionysus), ends up in a frenzy, tearing her own son apart. The play closes with the most horrible recognition scene ever written: the mother awakening from a trance and seeing what she had done. All this has been the god's doing.

For both Euripides and Nietzsche, Dionysus is equated with the energy of destruction, of others and of the self, as he is also equated with the highest human achievement, creativity, the capacity to transform one's life by playing alchemist to the self. It seems worth consideration that the fundamental, unsublimated narcissistic experience exhibits the same combination of potential for creation and destruction. This is precisely what Plato is saying to us in *Symposium*, that Narcissus–Dionysus is an ambiguous force we all must contend with. It seems reasonable to suggest that what lies behind the passionate criticism of the narcissism and radical individualism in our culture by Christopher Lasch and Robert Bellah is the correctly perceived fear that, should our narcissistic impulses maintain their totally uninhibited course, we will be overwhelmed, not by Narcissus, but by the destructive power of Dionysus.

The narcissistic experience is, in addition, vulnerable to corruption. Psychoanalytic theory talks of primary and secondary narcissism, and although different people use these expressions to describe different phenomena, on one point the theorists seem to agree, that the narcissistic experience goes through several stages. The stage of primary narcissism is perhaps one of self-confirmation: "I am beautiful because *I* say so. I need only the mirror to confirm that I am alluring and powerful." The secondary stage, the other person as mirror, becomes more problematic: "I am only beautiful if *you* say so." Other people do not even come close to having the mirror's reliability. They many times refuse to confirm one's beauty and power. We cannot, however, remain in the stage of primary narcissism; we must move on and become dependent on others. When they refuse to give us the confirmation of our worth that we require, an all-consuming rage is born, a rage that seeks domination over reality to force it to give the praise it has withheld. All conquerors are involved in narcissistic rape of the world.

The notion of worth, as the psyche evolves, extends beyond beauty and power and takes on a moral dimension. For those still caught up in a primitive condition of narcissism, however, moral worth becomes merely another means to beauty and power. So Socrates, for Alcibiades, is "the only man in the world that can make me feel ashamed [215B]," which leads to a "philosophical frenzy, this sacred rage [218B]," and ultimately to an ineluctable sexual passion, the whole manifesting a narcissistic polymorphous perversity.

Alcibiades exhibited in his life the quintessential Dionysian, narcissistic propensities for creativity and destruction. It was a life worth the telling.

A Brief Account of the Life of Alcibiades, the Son of Cleinias

He was raised in the house of Pericles, was a pupil and intimate of Socrates, and knew everyone of importance in Athens. Living with him in a democratic *polis* was like living with a captured lion. "A lion should not be raised in the city," Aristophanes wrote of him. "But if you raise him, you must cater to his ways."[24] Not everyone fell under the influence of his magnificent charm; some recognized his potential for becoming the ruin of Athens. One day, after he gave a particularly brilliant speech in the Assembly and was being mobbed by his admirers, "Timon the misanthrope" walked up to him purposefully, took him by the hand, and said: "Go on boldly, my son, and increase in credit with the people, for thou wilt one day bring them calamities enough."[25] The problem was that he was unbelievably attractive:

> Born in the most distinguished city, of a very high family, and by far the most handsome of all the men of his age, he was qualified for any occupation, and abounded in practical intelligence. He was eminent as a commander by sea and land; he was eloquent, so as to produce the greatest effect by his speeches; for such indeed was the persuasiveness of his looks and language, that in oratory no one was a match for him. He was rich, and, when occasion required, laborious, patient, liberal, and splendid, no less in his public than in his private life; he was also affable and courteous, conforming dexterously to circumstance; but, when he had unbent himself, and no reason offered why he should endure the labour of thought, was seen to be luxurious, dissolute, voluptuous, and self-indulgent, so that all wondered there should be such dissimilitude and so contradictory a nature in the same man.[26]

He was one of the great seducers of all time. Had he confined himself to sexual precocity—"In his adolescence he drew away the husbands from their wives, and as a young man the wives from their husbands."[27]—and been content with erotic dissolution, he would have been noteworthy enough, but he was determined to use his capacities for enchantment to dominate the whole of the world of power. His ability to assume various roles was extraordinary. "At Sparta," Plutarch writes, "he was devoted to athletic exercises, was frugal and reserved; in Ionia, luxurious, gay, and indolent; in Thrace, always drinking; in Thessaly, ever on horseback; and when he lived with Tissaphernes, the Persian satrap, he exceeded the Persians themselves in magnificence and pomp. Not that his natural disposition changed so easily, nor that his real character was so variable, but whenever he was sensible that by pursuing his own inclinations he might give offence to those with whom he had occasion to converse, he transformed himself into any shape, and adopted any fashion, that he observed to be most agreeable to them."[28]

After ten years of war between Athens and Sparta, the "Peace of Nicias" put a temporary halt to open hostilities. Several years of "cold war" followed, the conflict continuing with little direct confrontation between Athenian and Spartan forces. Though still committed to domination of the Hellenic world, Athens was clearly divided as to how belligerent to be toward the Lacedaemonians. Nicias headed the party of moderation. Alcibiades, just thirty years old, perceived a clear opening and quickly assumed the leadership of the more militant faction. Almost singlehandedly, he produced a diplomatic triumph, uniting Argos, Mantinea, and Elis (all states in the Peloponnese) in coalition against Sparta. The allies fought a crucial battle at Mantinea in 418, Athens sending only minimal aid. The Spartans, victorious, destroyed the coalition. Alcibiades later boasted, however, that the Laconians were significantly weakened. "Such are my aspirations, and however I am abused for them in private, the question is whether any one manages public affairs better than I do. Having united the most powerful states of Peloponnese, without great danger or expense to you, I compelled the Lacedaemonians to stake their all upon the issue of a single day at Mantinea; and although victorious in battle, they have never since fully recovered confidence."[29] People might question how wise he was. There could be no disagreement about his daring, his brilliance, or his power.

The statement just quoted comes from a speech delivered in the Assembly three years after Mantinea, the meeting that voted for the disastrous expedition to Sicily. Nicias had argued passionately and rationally against the project, attacking the golden boy of Athenian politics. "And if there be any man here, overjoyed at being chosen to command, who urges you to make the expedition, merely for ends of his own—especially if he be still too young to command—who seeks to be admired for his stud of horses, but on account of its heavy expenses hopes for some profit from his appointment, do not allow one to maintain his private splendour at his country's risk, but remember that such persons injure the public fortune while they squander their own."[30]

Alcibiades used Nicias' attack to trumpet his own virtue. "Athenians," he began, "I have a better right to command than others—I must begin with this as Nicias has attacked me. . . . The things for which I am abused, bring fame to my ancestors and to myself and to the country profit besides. The Hellenes, after expecting to see our city ruined by the war, concluded it to be even greater than it really is, by reason of the magnificence with which I represented it at the Olympic games, when I sent into the lists seven chariots, a number never before entered by any private person, and won first prize, and was second and fourth, and took care to have everything in a style worthy of my victory."[31] Lest we too quickly condemn Athenian politics for supposing that a chariot victory gave a person better judgment in state policies, let us remember that of the one hundred members of the U.S. Senate, one is there because he is a former astronaut, one because he is a former champion basketball player, and several because they were war heroes. No society has yet succeeded, if any has attempted the feat, in eliminating the narcissistic character of electoral politics. Whatever Alcibiades may have wanted for himself, he found a complementary response in the Athenian *demos*.

The matter under discussion was not horses and chariots, however, but whether to send a grand expedition to conquer Sicily in the West at a time when Athens could not even maintain control of its eastern empire. Alcibiades was largely responsible for the affirmative vote, the most disastrous decision the Athenian Assembly made during the war. Syracuse became the burial ground of thousands of Athenian troops, including the great general Nicias, and hundreds of Athenian triremes. To get the Assembly's approval, Alcibiades pulled out all the paranoid stops:

Men do not rest content with parrying the attacks of a superior, but often strike the first blow to prevent the attack being made. And we cannot fix the exact point at which our empire shall stop; we have reached a position in which we must not be content with retaining but must scheme to extend it, for if we cease to rule others, we are in danger of being ruled ourselves. . . . By sinking into inaction, the city, like everything else, will wear itself out, and its skill in everything decay; while each fresh struggle will give it fresh experience, and make it more used to defend itself not in word but in deed. In short, my conviction is that a city not inactive by nature could not choose a quicker way to ruin itself than by suddenly adopting such a policy, and that the safest rule of life is to take one's character and institutions for better and for worse, and to live up to them as closely as one can.[32]

Note the iron-cage antinomic paranoia: rule *or* be ruled; undertake reckless action *or* sink into an engulfing torpor; obey your nature whatever it may be *or* take the destructive consequences. The *demos* embraced the position with enthusiasm. It voted and assembled "by far the most costly and splendid Hellenic force that had ever been sent out by a single city up to that time."[33]

Shortly before the expedition was to depart a preternatural occurrence seriously disturbed the city's enthusiasm. Many of the statues of Hermes that stood as guardians before people's houses were mutilated one night. The true cause of this vandalism was never learned: whether it was a particularly vicious prank of some unusually wild club, an attempt to sabotage the euphoria over the Sicilian expedition, or part of a plot to overthrow the democracy. Many in Athens were convinced of this last possibility and Alcibiades' position was seriously compromised when testimony started to mount against him, not that he had participated in the mutilations, but that he and his friends had performed mock celebrations of the Eleusinian mysteries in private houses. These rites were of the highest order of sacredness and initiates were pledged not to reveal their nature. The mock celebrations represented the most acute form of sacrilege, in Athens punishable by death. Unfortunately for Alcibiades, many believed him capable of exactly this kind of behavior. The enemies of Alcibiades and of the Sicilian campaign loudly proclaimed that the mutilation of the Hermae and the profanation of the mysteries were parts of a scheme to discredit and overthrow the democracy, that Alcibiades intended to make himself tyrant.[34]

Alcibiades offered to stand trial immediately, but his enemies did not wish to bring him to court with the army and fleet, bound to be sympathetic to their commander, present in the city. It was decreed that the fleet should embark and a glorious armament sailed out of the Piraeus led by Alcibiades, who "stood on the poop of the ship with his golden shield and his device—a figure of *Eros*-armed-*with*-the-thunderbolt, as the great armada, sped on by high dreams and high hopes. . . , under the sign of an imperial and coercive Eros, sailed away to its miserable doom."[35]

After the fleet had departed, the ambivalence toward Alcibiades and the opposition to him grew in force. Either ironically or with poetic justice, his enemies turned the paranoid position against him. In addition to being suspected of wanting to overthrow the democracy, when a small force of Spartans advanced as far as the Isthmus of Corinth in pursuit of some matter concerning Boeotia, it was bruited about in Athens that the Laconians had come in response to a conspiracy with the absent commander. "In short, everywhere something was found to create suspicion against Alcibiades."[36] The official galley was sent to bring him home for trial and execution. Alcibiades agreed to return but, knowing what was in store, left the ship at a port in Italy and disappeared. The vessel returned to Athens, where he was condemned to death in absentia.

Needing a center of power and determined to revenge himself on the city that had betrayed him, Alcibiades offered Sparta his full cooperation and knowledge in the struggle against the Athenians. He set about to seduce the Spartans. "People who saw him wearing his hair close cut, bathing in cold water, eating coarse meal, and dining on black broth, doubted, or rather could not believe, that he ever had a cook in his house, or had ever seen a perfumer, or had worn a mantle of Milesian purple."[37] He even attempted to prove to the Laconians that he and they shared similar political views: "As for democracy, the men of sense among us knew what it was, and I perhaps as well as any, as I have the more cause to complain of it; but there is nothing new to be said of a patent absurdity. . . . For myself, therefore, Lacedaemonians, I beg you to use me without scruple for danger and trouble of every kind, and to remember the argument in every one's mouth, that if I did you great harm as an enemy, I could likewise do you good service as a friend, inasmuch as I know the plans of the Athenians, while I only guessed yours."[38]

Everything he chose to do he did with extraordinary success. Choosing the role of betrayer, he became one of the greatest betrayers of all time. His advice to the Spartans was superb. (1) Immediately send a general to Syracuse to aid that city in fighting the Athenian invasion. (2) Fortify the town of Decelea in Attica, thus establishing a permanent presence of Laconian arms less than twenty-five miles from the walls of Athens. (This proved a major problem for the Athenians as long as the war lasted.) (3) After Athens was so catastrophically defeated at Syracuse, its subject states in the islands and Asia Minor began to revolt. Alcibiades then had further advice for the Lacedaemonians. Raise and send a fleet to aid the rebelling cities. The flotilla sailed with Alcibiades aboard as minister without portfolio, his task to encourage the Ionia states to rise up against the Athenians.

Even at Sparta, however, he did not abandon his intimate alliance with Eros. For Alcibiades the *libido dominandi* was expressed in a multitude of ways, in many different parts of the body. He managed, while the Spartan king Agis was out of the country, to seduce the king's wife and impregnate her with a son. In public she called the child Leotychides and officially Agis was the father, but to her intimates she confided that the boy's name was Alcibiades. Alcibiades boasted that he did it, not out of insult or passion, but so his blood would run through the bodies of the future kings of the Lacedaemonians.[39]

Having left his seed in Sparta, Alcibiades sailed with the Laconian fleet to the islands and Asia Minor, urging the Athenian subject states to revolt. We do not know why but Alcibiades soon lost the confidence of the Spartans and King Agis (perhaps because of the latter's wife?) and word went out from Laconia that Alcibiades should be assassinated. Never one to be caught unawares, he received intelligence of the order and fled to the court of Tissaphernes, a Persian governor (satrap) in Asia Minor, a third center of power in the Aegean world.

Persian satraps had a reasonably wide latitude in pursuing foreign policy objectives, and Alcibiades quickly became the confidant and adviser of Tissaphernes. He urged the governor, who had now become the paymaster of the Spartan fleet, to play the Athenians and the Laconians off against each other to the point of exhaustion. Then the Persians could walk in and pick up the pieces of the Athenian Empire. Once again, it was sound advice. It obviously did not bother Alcibiades that, having betrayed Athens for Sparta, he was now betraying the Greek world for the "barbarian."

We need not retrace the steps, previously described, by which Alcibiades used his supposed influence with Tissaphernes to ingratiate himself again with the Athenian *demos*—events that led to the oligarchic coup of 411. The period from 411 to 407 was the most glorious of Alcibiades' contradictory life. As noted earlier, he did the state a great service when he convinced the troops and sailors on Samos not to sail against the oligarchs at Athens but to concentrate on the war in the Aegean. Appointed general by these same troops, he spent four years piling victory upon victory in Ionia and the Hellespont. He reversed Athens' disastrous position after the Sicilian debacle. Athens could again face Sparta with an equal chance of triumphing in the war.

The year 407 saw Alcibiades at the height of his power. He dared return to Athens where he had been condemned to death eight years before. Knowing he still had many enemies in the city, not sure of his reception, he sailed into the Piraeus at the head of his squadron, bringing a loot of one hundred talents and the report of victory after victory. "At first he stood motionless on the quarter-deck; then when he saw his friends there to escort him, he landed and walked up to the city."[40] It was a procession worthy of a great hero:

> As soon as he was landed, the multitude who came out to meet him scarcely seemed so much as to see any of the other captains, but came in throngs about Alcibiades, and saluted him with loud acclamations, and still followed him; those who could pass near him crowned him with garlands, and they who could not come up so close yet stayed to behold him afar off, and the old men pointed him out, and showed him to the young ones.[41]

Appointed supreme commander of the armed forces, he was formally absolved from the curse that had been laid on him. His death sentence and exile had resulted from the accusation that he profaned the mysteries of Eleusis. Now granted the honor of leading the sacred procession to Eleusis, he accomplished the task with high drama, performing a feat no one but Alcibiades could have dared and accomplished. Since the Spartans occupied Decelea (on the advice of Alcibiades) the Athenians had been unable to carry out the procession to Eleusis along the Sacred Way on land, and had instead gone by sea to avoid a confrontation with Spartan arms. Determined to reconcile himself with the goddesses Demeter and Persephone and to enhance his reputation for near-omnipotence, Alcibiades posted his troops along the Way and led the people of Athens to Eleusis and home again in perfect safety, the Spartan forces not daring to interfere. In the minds of most people—but not all—he had canceled out his treachery against Athens.

His reputation for omnipotence proved his undoing, however. The *demos* expected that he would deliver them and promptly win the war. "Certainly, if ever man was ruined by his own glory," Plutarch writes, "it was Alcibiades. For his continual success had produced such an idea of his courage and conduct that if he failed in anything he undertook, it was imputed to his neglect, and no one would believe it was through want of power. For they thought nothing was too hard for him, if he went about it in earnest. They fancied, every day, that they should hear news of the reduction of Chios, and of the rest of Ionia and grew impatient that things were not effected as fast and as rapidly as they could wish for them."[42]

The *demos* getting ready to eat the god they had created, Alcibiades obliged them by making a fatal mistake. Off Notium, he left the fleet in charge of a subordinate with instructions that under no circumstances was he to engage the Spartan fleet. This imperative was ignored and in the ensuing battle, the Athenians suffered a serious defeat. The *demos*, for the moment, remained characteristically ambivalent. In Aristophanes' *Frogs*, written shortly after the battle, we find this exchange:

DIONYSUS: Alkibiades is a baby who's giving
  our state delivery-pains. What shall we do with him?
  That's the first question.
EURIPIDES: How does the state feel about him?
DIONYSUS: It longs for him, it hates him, and it wants him back.[43]

Resolving their ambivalence, the *demos* renounced the leadership of this wondrous general for the second time. Accusations were brought against him by his seamen and some of the allied cities he had been looting. The election of generals for the coming year did not find Alcibiades included, and he lost the supreme command by special decree. Determined never to face an Athenian court, knowing the rage of a disappointed *demos*, Alcibiades fled into exile to a private fortress in the Chersonese, near Thrace, that he had prepared for just such an eventuality.[44]

The year 405 found the Athenian fleet encamped near Aegospotami in the Hellespont. The Spartan commander Lysander lay nearby with a great fleet. Each day the Athenian ships left their base and challenged Lysander, but he refused to engage. The Athenian troops grew careless and disorderly in their idleness. Alcibiades' castle was close by and one day he mounted his horse and rode down to where the Athenian generals were encamped. He cautioned them that they had chosen a most inauspicious spot, with no safe harbor and a great distance from a town for provisioning. He also pointed out the lack of discipline among the troops. He advised them to take the fleet to Sestos, but they disdained his advice. Tydeus, one of the generals, "with insulting expression, commanded him to be gone, saying, that now not he but others, had command of the forces."[45] A short time later, Lysander surprised the Athenian forces in their disorder and almost completely annihilated the Athenian fleet. The war was over.

After the great battle, Alcibiades, fearing the victorious Spartans, retreated inland to Bithynia, where he was robbed of much of his treasure. Undaunted, he determined to journey to the court of the great king of the Persians, Artaxerxes, imagining that he could win his confidence just as Themistocles—condemned to death in absentia at Athens—had ingratiated himself with the first Persian king of that name sixty years before. Alcibiades went first to the court of the satrap Pharnabazus, who treated him well but did not send him on to the king.

Meanwhile, the Thirty Tyrants had assumed their bloody power at Athens. Fearing the *demos* might call on Alcibiades to restore the democracy, they asked Lysander to eliminate him. Lysander communicated with Pharnabazus, who could not deny the request. Assassins were dispatched to the small village in Phrygia where Alcibiades was living with one of his mistresses. They set fire to his house; he escaped the inferno only to be killed by their darts and arrows. An alternative story of his death claims that neither Lysander nor Pharnabazus was involved. It reports that he debauched a young lady of a noble family and that her brothers murdered him in revenge.[46] It is a testament to Alcibiades' life that either story of his death—the grand heroic one wherein the whole Greek world was involved or the paltry tale of sexual debauch—could be the truth.

For all his genius, Alcibiades did nothing to transform the norms of Athenian society, either progressively or regressively. He left the moral state of society as he had found it. Like the self-made billionaire in an advanced capitalist society, he performed with superb success the task that many had set for themselves. In the famous funeral oration of Pericles-Thucydides, there is a sentence more often quoted (especially by humanist philo-Hellenes) than almost any other statement from the ancient world: "In short, I say that as a city we are the school of Hellas; while I doubt if the world can produce a man, who where he has only himself to depend upon, is equal to so many emergencies, and graced by so happy a versatility as the Athenian."

The singular fact is that almost nobody goes on to examine the rest of the passage. We would expect, from the great moral burden laid on this quotation, that Pericles goes on to cite the inventiveness of the Athenians in government, in philosophy, in expanding the possibilities of life. What we get instead is a remarkable paeon to power and domination. "And that this is no mere boast thrown out for the occasion," Pericles goes on to say, "but plain matter of fact, the power of the state acquired by these habits proves. For Athens alone of her contemporaries is found when tested to be greater than her reputation, and alone gives no occasion to her assailants to blush at the antagonist by whom they have been worsted, or to her subjects to question her title by merit to rule. Rather, the admiration of the present and succeeding ages will be ours, since we have not left our power without witness, but have shown it by mighty proofs . . . we have forced every sea and land to be the highway of our daring, and everywhere, whether for evil or for good, have left imperishable monuments behind us."[47]

Nothing underlines with greater poignancy the profound contradictions in Athenian society than the fact that the greatest pupil of the arch-democrat Pericles was his ward, Alcibiades, the son of Cleinias.

13

Warfare and Genocide

Ilf one reads Greek history unencumbered by the sentimental baggage of the "Glory that was Greece," one is immediately struck by the overwhelming importance of warfare to the political life of the *polis*. Almost every Greek state could be accurately described as a "warfare state." Athens, in its commitment to killing as an ordinary political activity, was no exception. An Athenian of military age, in two out of every three years, could expect to put on armor, take up his spear, and hope to thrust it into the body of an enemy before the enemy could thrust his spear into him. In the Greek world killing and being killed were events as intimate and frequent as automobile accidents today. Only the attendants at the emergency rooms of our large city hospitals see as much spilled blood in one year as the average citizen of the *polis*. The Athenian was acquainted with killing in a sense difficult for us to imagine, even with the statistics before us. Hornblower writes that, from the Persian struggles to the outbreak of the Peloponnesian War, 479-431, "Athens was at war, or Athenians were on campaign . . . virtually every year."[1] From the Persian Wars until the triumph of Philip in 338, Finley writes, "Athens was engaged in war on the average of two out of three years, and never enjoyed a period of peace for as long as ten consecutive years."[2] Comparable data from Sparta, Corinth, and Thebes would probably indicate the same situation there.

So much in Athens changed as the *mores* of the *polis* developed. Political life was profoundly different in the middle of the fourth century from what it had been in the fifth, except in regard for the constancy of warfare. An inscription of 459 commemorates those of the Erectheid tribe, "who died in the war, in Cyprus, in Egypt, in Phoenice, at Halieis, in Aegina, at Megara, *in the same year*."[3] A century later Isocrates, in a speech *On the Peace*, complains that "we undertake to wage war upon, one might almost say, the whole world."[4] The modern translator of the speech remarks that: "Between 363-355 B.C Athens made war on Alexander of Thessaly, King Cotys in the Thracian Chersonnese, Amphipolis, Euboea, Chios, Byzantium, and Potidaea—to mention only the chief campaigns."[5] And this at a time when there was no Athenian Empire to defend or extend. It is no exaggeration to say that killing and being killed were the business of the *polis*.

It is interesting to note an exception, at least, to this generalization. Megara in the fourth century was the Switzerland of ancient Greece and, except for one or two occasions, led a peaceful life, rejecting international entanglements, and concentrating on business affairs.[6]

The one value that was consistently respected by these small city-states was that *one's neighbor was one's enemy*. It was a rare exception when two neighboring *poleis* lived in peace, except in the case where one conquered or dominated the other. Herodotus explains that the state of Phocis took the Greek side in the Persian Wars because its neighbors, the Thessalians, had chosen to help the Persians. "If the Thessalians had backed the Greeks, I think the Phocians would have gone over to the Persian side."[7] In delineating the Phocian view of the Thessalians, Herodotus uses the word *echthros* (hatred). Similarly, in describing the history of the Greek colonies in Sicily and southern Italy in the sixth century, the modern historian Hammond notes: "As Greek colonies expanded, they came close to one another and their ambitions clashed. Syracuse destroyed her daughter-colony Camarina c. 550; in Italy a coalition of Croton, Sybaris, and Metapontium destroyed Siris c. 530; Croton in turn suffered a severe defeat at the hands of Locri and Rhegium and c. 510 destroyed Sybaris, the richest state in the West."[8] And Hornblower relates how, in the late 460s, Athens and Corinth became enemies after years of living together in peace. Athens and Corinth were not direct neighbors; two small independent states,

Megara and Aegina, lay between them. When the small states lost their independence the two large *poleis* faced each other directly. "When these minor states ceased to exist, or were annexed by one side or the other, the neighbour's neighbour became just a neighbour, and an enemy instead of a friend."[9]

If we eschew facile judgments about "human nature," we must consider two questions. Why does one's neighbor *inevitably* become one's enemy? Why are states so ready to shed blood in the settlement of disputes? Rather than a last recourse in the resolution of international differences, after all else has failed—arbitration, diplomacy, international conferences, even preferred friendship—warfare seems to be the first recourse. Kill first; talk afterward.

Is this tribal "lust to annihilate"[10] subject to sublimation or to significant transformation through the development of history? How different were Athens and Corinth and Croton and Sybaris from future nation-states? After the ancient world collapsed and the city-state form was born again in Italy in the eleventh century A.D., interstate warfare never ceased among the Italian city-states. As early as the middle of the eleventh century Milan and Pavia were at each other's throats. For the year 1059, the chronicler records: "The dissension arose because both cities were populous and ranked above the other cities in the kingdom [of Italy]. . . . They were neighbours and so each was ashamed to yield to the other. And so they mutually inflicted on each other killings, looting, fire and robbery."[11] And how different has been the 1870–1914–1939 history of the neighbors France and Germany?

One fact does seem to differentiate the Greek from the modern European world: the frequency with which the citizen was called to arms. This may tell us something significant about Greek society. Max Weber addressed this question and hypothesized that the ancient city-state, in its military organization, was of the structured type of a war-band: no permanent army; no significant mercenaries; no meaningful differentiation of military roles, except for a few elected or appointed generals; the whole citizen body was the fighting force.[12]

Many societies have exhibited this same form of military organization and activity. In traditional Africa, the Nuer and the Dinka fought each other every year, killing some, capturing some. In New Guinea, many cannibal or head-hunting tribes went on annual expeditions in search of victims. In these types of excursions, all the adult males of certain kin groups, which might be as large as the whole "tribe," became the military force. Many, if not most, societies in the "primitive," or "tribal," or "nonliterate" stage of development exhibited exactly this war-band type of behavior. Every adult male member of the society was a warrior; some form of battle, including a certain amount of killing, occurred annually; all nonkin neighbors were enemies.

Sophocles said that the last thing to grow old is anger. Warfare may be the last thing to mature and be transformed. Certain parts of society may make tremendous developmental progress while the warfare machine remains psychologically and sociologically "primitive." This may explain how the enormously sophisticated Greek society could remain in its military mentality at a basic level of development, Athens being no exception. No wonder Plato placed such emphasis on human reason and denigrated the passions. In such a society, it might seem that only reason was capable of developmental advance and moral tranformation, and that the passions must necessarily remain primitive. And if we are to argue against Plato in the attempt to establish that one of the primary tasks of reason is *not* to repress appetites, then we must establish that instinctual drives are capable of significant sublimation and transformation. Observing Greek society and seeing that even Athens became a genocidal state, it would be difficult to make such a pronouncement. After 2,500 years more of Western civilization, despite a desire to believe optimistically, one must remain agnostic in the face of such a fundamental question concerning the significant transformation of instincts.

The Greeks were not Nuer or Dinka, and Athenian society exhibited an ironic ambivalence in regard to man as a killing machine. In his antiwar plays, Euripides mounted the most severe criticism.[13] Herodotus observed that in warfare the order of nature was reversed: old people buried the young. Even the great warrior and imperialist, Pericles, noted the prodigious cost of imperial domination. In a funeral speech for young braves killed in action he remarked that it was "as if the spring had been taken out of the year."[14] This was just light ambivalence and rhetoric for Pericles however. His political activities ensured that Athens would live many years without spring.

In respects other than military *weltanschauung*, ancient Greece and Athens in particular was not a primitive, tribal society. This contrast between great sophistication in some areas and primeval behavior in others makes Greek society so difficult to understand. The independent city-states could not stop fighting each other, yet political theorists clearly saw this as a primary evil within the Greek world, and even offered sophisticated psychological and political remedies for the disease. Near the beginning of the fourth century, Isocrates published his speech *Panegyricus*. He observed, without any confusion, the nature of the Greek madness. "It is my opinion that if anyone should come here from another part of the world and behold the spectacle of the present state of our affairs, he would charge both the Athenians and the Lacedaemonians with utter madness, not only because we risk our lives fighting as we do over trifles when we might enjoy in security a wealth of possessions, but also because we continually impoverish our own territory while neglecting to exploit that of Asia."[15] Anticipating Freud's views on internal and external aggression, Isocrates' recommendation was to direct this unavoidable aggression outward, beyond the Greek world. The Greek states should unite in a loose confederacy, live with each other in peace, and pursue a holy war against the common enemy, the Persian Empire. It would become "the only war that is better than peace: more like a sacred mission than a military expedition."[16]

The Greek cities were also plagued by intense class conflicts that often erupted into bloody civil war. Athens, after the last oligarchic coup, was spared this disruption due to the stability of its democracy. Chapter 14 examines class conflict in detail, but we will look at it briefly here. In Italian city-states of the late medieval period, the intracity class conflicts were, if anything, even more violent and more persistent than those in the Greek *poleis*. Here again, historians and theorists observed the constant need to express primitive aggression, the only question being where it was to be exercised:

"War and hatred have so multiplied among the Italians," says the Florentine Brunetto Latini . . . writing about 1284, "that in every town there is division and enmity between the two parties of citizens." Even in the eleventh century Milanese chroniclers had remarked of their fellow citizens that "when they lack external adversaries they turn their hatred against each other." This well-founded observation was to become a commonplace for other cities too. Florence was built under the signs of Aries and Mars, says Malispini: "Our ancestors were always fighting battles and wars and when they had no other opponent they fought among themselves."[17]

As Isocrates deplored the fact that intercity strife prevented the Greeks from conquering Persia, so Italian observers bemoaned the circumstance that intracity conflict made it impossible for a city to conquer its neighbors. Bonvicino said of Milan: "If only envy could cease, they could love one another and take thought in all good faith for their fatherland. Then I firmly believe that they could easily make all Lombardy submit to their domination."[18]

Is the amount of raw, primitive aggressive energy a constant that must find some outlet in organized social killing of one sort or another? Is the only sociological question one of whether this killing occurs between classes in the same city, or between different *poleis* constantly warring against each other, or between city-states united against "the barbarian"? For the "modern" world—since the seventeenth century— the question is enormously complex with no simple answer. For the Greek world, the answer seems clear: Raw, primitive aggression was never significantly sublimated or transformed, merely displaced from one form of expression to another. The lust to annihilate never ceased to hold dominion over men's lives.

The failure of the moral faculty to develop did not mean there was no evolution in the forms and institutions of society. Tribal society knew nothing of the conquest of another people. There were no mechanisms for ruling others outside one's own society. Killing, raiding, pushing off the land, a certain amount of enslavement—yes, but no colonial or imperial policy. The mechanisms for imperial rule began to develop under the monarchies of Complex society and came to full flower in Archaic society in Egypt, Babylonia, Persia. Whether the construction of a complex imperial polity, like that of Rome or Persia, represents a true sublimation of primitive aggression or is merely another mode of expressing it, is an open question. The paranoidia of domination will be looked at in detail later, but it is appropriate to mention here that domination, through an imperial policy, through warfare, through killing other human beings, was a fundamental concern of the norms of ancient Greek society. Aristotle laments that "in most states, most of the laws are only a promiscuous heap of legislation;

but we have to confess that where they are directed, in any degree, to a single object, that object is always conquest."[19] To paraphrase a famous quote from Samuel Johnson, nothing seemed to concentrate the (legal) mind so much as the possibility of tyrannizing over others.

The insatiable dimension of conquest and domination is illustrated in an open letter Isocrates wrote to Philip of Macedon in 346, instructing him in the ways of the world, pointing out the failures of other Greek states, and urging him to avoid those errors and lead a crusade against the Persian. It was like trying to explain to a tiger how a tiger thinks:

> And as for the condition of the Thebans, surely you have not failed to note that also. They won a splendid victory [against Spartan hegemony] and covered themselves with glory, but because they did not make good use of their success they are now in no better case than those who have suffered defeat and failure. For no sooner had they triumphed over their foes than, neglecting everything else, they began to annoy the cities of Peloponnese; they made bold to reduce Thessaly to subjection; they threatened their neighbours, the Megarians; they robbed our city of a part of its territory; they ravaged Euboea; they sent men-of-war to Byzantium, as if they proposed to rule both land and sea; and, finally, they began war upon the Phocians, expecting that in a short time they would . . . prevail over all the treasures of Delphi. . . . But none of these hopes has been realized.[20]

Human beings have more difficulty accepting the aggressive dimension of their nature than the sexual. When, at the start of this century, Freud began to express the importance of sexuality (and infantile sexuality) for the psyche, resistance was enormous but it crumbled with remarkable speed and the latter part of this century has become an age of Freud and sexuality. With aggression, we remain back where Freud and sex were in 1905. We consistently refuse to see how pervasive and destructive are the aggressive drives. We hide the human blood that sustains domination with rhetoric: "splendid victor"; "covered themselves with glory"; "triumphed over their foes"; "reduced Thessaly to subjection"; "as if they proposed to rule both land and sea." The word "rule" is particularly useful. Thebes intended to rule; Athens ruled; Britannia rules. Those who refuse to accept that rule, pay with their blood and their lives. Nobody "rules" without being ready to use killing as a constant instrument of policy.

Genocide and Enslavement

A Very Short History of the Greek World,
511 B.C. to 188 B.C.

Item #1, 511 B.C. The best known event was the battle in which the men of Croton . . . won an overwhelming victory over Sybaris, followed by the complete destruction of that city. The event came as a shock to the Greek world, and the people of Miletus, attached to Sybaris by close truce relations, went into mourning.[21]

Item #2, 363 B.C. During [Epaminondas'] absence a plot was betrayed in which some Theban exiles and 300 leading men of Orchomenus planned to overthrow the democracy of Thebes. The Assembly of the Boeotian League decided to exact the full punishment for treachery, the terrible fate of *andrapodismos*: all males were killed, the women and children were enslaved, and the city was razed. On his return Epaminondas protested against the cruelty of his compatriots.[22]

Item #3, 188 B.C. The Achaean League, disregarding the Roman treaty with Sparta, had annexed Sparta by force in 188 B.C., torn down its walls and banished, enslaved or slain all opponents.[23]

The psychological overtones of the word "genocide" are those of a *complete* destruction—nobody is left to tell the tale—no victim, that is. Either it is a complete destruction of a people, or the total destruction of a particular *polis*, or the complete destruction of all the adult males. The totality of the killing gives it its genocidal character. The human impulse to kill one person is psychologically different from the impetus to kill *all*. Our culture, which has no problem with the killing involved in warfare—once we have performed the rather easy exercise of declaring the war "just"—pulls back in horror from genocide.

Not so the ancient Greeks. Genocide as a basic instrument of policy in intercity warfare was a fundamental norm of Greek society.* True, there were dissenting voices, like that of Epaminondas, but we have no record of anyone declaring during a debate that genocide is un-

---

*Josiah Ober (personal communication) argues that the Peloponnesian War was the great watershed in the use of genocide, that before it began the phenomenon was rare.

manly. In his account of the debate over the sentencing of Mitylene (probably reconstructed rather than literally recorded), Thucydides never has Diodotus declare that the genocide of the Mitylenians would be unmanly, unjust, forbidden by the gods, or unthinkable for a city such as Athens. Genocide was not only thinkable but doable. The Greeks even had a particular world—*andrapodismos*—to designate the execution of all adult males and enslavement of all women and children.[24] There are several examples of *andrapodismos* in our histories; and there were undoubtedly many more. The fact that such actions had a particular name (like our historical term "liquidate") indicates the frequency of their occurrence.

Even for the Greeks, nevertheless, there was a difference between normal warfare and genocide. Individual acts of warfare could be thought of as heroic. Genocide might be a necessary instrument of policy, but those ordering or performing the slaughter were not heroes and regret and condemnation after the fact were sometimes recorded. "In the fourth century the treatment of Melos and Scione was a stock illustration of the enormities of Athenian imperialism."[25] Such remonstrance did not, however, hamper the Athenian general Chares who, in 352, captured the city of Sestos, which had revolted from Athenian hegemony in 357 or 356. He killed or sold into slavery all its unfortunate inhabitants.[26]

In our own culture we clearly differentiate between warfare, which is legitimate, and massacre, which is not. The war in Vietnam was an heroic struggle against communist aggression, but My Lai was a massacre. The Israeli incursion into Lebanon was a valiant defense of the autonomy of a brave little country, but the slaughter allowed in one of the camps was a massacre and triggered street protests from almost one-fourth of the citizens of Israel. The crucial difference between heroic warfare and massacre is the killing of women and children. The destruction of male prisoners who cannot defend themselves, because they have no weapons or because they are bound, is also morally illegitimate, a massacre. The men, because of their condition, are reduced to women, helpless. Preoedipal aggression against women, children, or feminized men is shameful. Oedipal aggression against an armed, strong male opponent is heroic. It is of interest to note that in Picasso's picture "Guernica," which could be subtitled "All Warfare Is Massacre," the overwhelming emphasis is on women, children, and animals as victims. The Greek position approached ours: women and children were only enslaved, while all the males were slaughtered. A slight ambivalence was expressed about these genocidal occasions, but the practice was never abandoned.

> *Item #4, 427* B.C. And having, as they [the Spartans] considered, suffered evil at the hands of the Plataeans, they brought them in again one by one and asked each of them the same question, that is to say, whether they had done the Lacedaemonians and allies any service in the war; and upon saying that they had not, took them out and slew them all without exception. The number of Plataeans thus massacred was not less than two hundred, with twenty-five Athenians who shared the siege.[27]

About one very significant fact we have little information: how saleable as slaves would captured adult males have been, especially warriors? When, after a battle or siege, thousands of prisoners were slaughtered, were the perpetrators forgoing a substantial financial gain to satisfy their blood lust? Did Lysander, after slaughtering three thousand Athenians captured during the battle of Aegospotami, exclaim to himself: "It cost us a lot of cold cash to dispatch all those accursed Athenians, but it was worth it"? From Xenophon we know there was extended debate amongst the Spartans and their allies as to what course to take with the Athenian captives.[28] We are not told what the alternative to slaughter would have been, safe return to Athens or payment of ransom or enslavement.

We know that slave traders followed the armies, with plenty of cash to purchase slaves, but we don't know if sea battles presented tactical problems for them. We also have evidence that many prisoners were ransomed, but we lack details about the technique. Were the ransoms paid directly to the captors, or were the prisoners purchased by slave traders who then attempted to raise as much ransom money as possible, selling off those whom no one was willing to pay for?

And how complaisant a slave would a young adult warrior make? Women and children, yes, but a vigorous hoplite soldier? If slavery or slaughter were viable alternatives, why were adult males ever slaughtered to the man? It seems profligate of the Athenians, if adult male captives had financial value, to order the execution of all the adult male Mitylenians or to carry out such executions with the Melians and Scionians.

Diodorus gives us a description of the capture, by Dionysius of Syracuse in 398, of the city of Motya in Sicily, after a long siege. In Freeman's retelling: "Plunder was not thought of; slaughter was the one impulse; old and young, men, women, and children, every living soul of the hated race and his allies, were hewn down without mercy. . . . Such slaughter was in the eyes of Dionysius useless and mischievous; every human being that was slain lessened the value of the prize by the price which he would have fetched in the slave market. He first put forth an order bidding the slaughter to cease. But the rage of the Sikeliots [non-Greek allies of Dionysius] could not be controlled. . . . He then sent forth heralds to announce to the remnant of the people of Motya that all would be spared who took sanctuary in the temples. . . . This order did its work. The suppliants in the privileged temples were spared; and the soldiers . . . turned altogether from slaughter to plunder."[29] Dionysius, being more civilized than the "barbarian" Sikeliots, could sublimate his blood lust with capitalist profit.

The worst slaughters took place under two special circumstances: when a state revolted against an imperial power and was recaptured and especially after a city had sustained a prolonged siege and was finally invested. In the history of the world nothing seems to enrage human beings more, nothing seems to provoke more violent outrage and revenge, nothing is more likely to bring to the surface the most primitive human aggression, than a city that refuses to surrender and gives its besiegers great trouble in winning the day. This has been true not only of ancient Greece. The Albigensian Crusade in the thirteenth century, the Thirty Years War in the seventeenth, and thousands of other occasions demonstrate that the likeliest candidates for genocide are the residents of a beleaguered city—and the longer the city holds out, the more violent the terror that greets its collapse. The city must pay the full price for its arrogant resistance.

Such a primitive explosion of rage cannot be explained by rational considerations. The true horror in Thucydides' Melian debate—and it is one of the most horrible exchanges, fictional or actual, ever set down—is the ice-cold reason with which the Athenians assert their "tiger rights."[30] They intend to execute the most outrageous, most primitive act a "civilized" human being can commit, and they justify themselves with words, our tools for communing with each other. A greater perversion of thought and language is unimaginable. If the Sikeliotes or the Spartans or the Athenians ended up destroying their own property in a genocidal rage, it was because they had entered a stage of moral psychosis, where the only thing that mattered was Lear's great cry of vengeance: "Then, kill, kill, kill, kill, kill."[31]

To find the origins of such disorder, it is necessary to enter the most primitive part of the human psyche—not an easy or welcoming task. Some insight may be gathered by inquiring why it is that a besieged city, that refuses to be invested, that refuses to surrender and submit, that refuses to have its walls penetrated, elicits the primitive rage of the besiegers. "Surrender," "submit," "penetrated"—the sexual language is deliberate. A besieged city is like a woman's body that refuses to be entered. When the city is finally taken, the women are raped and the men slaughtered in an orgy of aggressive ravishment, the state of moral psychosis being uninterested in distinguishing between destruction and sexuality. It is not an oedipal act of killing father and raping mother. It is an uninhibited expression of preoedipal rage at the mother and the mother's body. It reverts to the place where the drives toward destruction are born. In this regressive, de-differentiated world, warfare becomes consumed by massacre.

The Greeks knew the difference between warfare and massacre; they expressed some ambivalence about the latter and censured the Athenians for their genocidal acts. It was remarkable, nonetheless, how easily the city-states resorted to massacre as an instrument of policy. Thucydides sees the horror of what the Athenians said and what they did to the Melians, but he has no cure for that human condition.

Item #5, the Peloponnesian War. On their arrival, the Athenians, afraid that Aristeus, who had been notably the prime mover in the previous affairs of Potidaea and their Thracian possessions, might live to do them still more mischief if he escaped, slew them all the same day, without giving them a trial or hearing the defence which they wished to offer, and cast their bodies into a pit; thinking themselves justified in using in retaliation the same mode of warfare which the Lacedaemonians had begun, when they slew and cast into pits all the Athenian and allied traders whom they caught on board merchantmen round Peloponnese. Indeed, at the outset of the war, the Lacedaemonians butchered as enemies all whom they took on the sea, whether allies of Athens or neutrals.[32]

When the Helots [serfs in Sparta] were felt to be specially dangerous, apparently in 424, the Spartans secretly and treacherously murdered two thousand of the best of them. The Spartans massacred all the free men they captured on the fall of Argive Hysiae in 417. The men of Byzantium and Chalcedon slaughtered the whole multitude of prisoners (men, women and children) they had taken on their expedition into Bithynia in c. 416/5.[33]

It is pitiful to read the defense by the knowledgeable contemporary historian de Ste. Croix of the moral capacity of the Athenian democracy: "The essential point is that the Athenians were certainly no more brutal, on the whole, in their treatment of the conquered than were other Greek states of their day."[34] The word "certainly" is sophistic. It implies that the Athenians were probably less brutal than the other *poleis*. All our evidence points in the opposite direction: Athens was as merciless as any and probably more barbarous than most. The "essential point" is that the great moral advance that was Athenian democracy did not sublimate brutality beyond the borders of the *polis*. Understanding this psychological capacity for splitting, on the level of the individual psyche, and of that of society, would make human history, especially in developmental perspective, much more comprehensible. Denial of that splitting—Athens was a glorious city; Athens was no more brutal than others—keeps us from comprehending the full, ambiguous, sometimes terrible truth.

Thucydides' genius made the genocide of Melos and the near-genocide of Mitylene exemplary tales in the ancient world, known to anyone of cultural accomplishment. There was a time in the modern Western world when all persons of education could tell these tales, but who could recall what the Athenians did to the Scionians, the Histiaeans, the Toronaeans, and the Aeginetans? Thucydides mentions the genocide of Scione *en passant*, as if it had no great significance: "About the same time this summer Athens succeeded in reducing Scione, put the adult males to death, and making slaves of the women and children, gave the land to the Plataeans to live in. She also brought back the Delians to Delos, moved by her misfortunes in the field and by the commands of the god at Delphi. Meanwhile the Phocians and Locrians commenced hostilities."[35] And so forth, to the reader's despair.

The Athenians, however, had reason to remember all they had done to others, after the battle of Aegospotami, with the war essentially over and Athens at the mercy of the Lacedaemonians and their allies. "It was at night that the Paralus arrived at Athens with tidings of the disaster, and a sound of wailing ran from Piraeus through the long walls to the city, one man passing on the news to another; and during that night no one slept, all mourning, not for the lost alone, but far more for their own selves, thinking that they would suffer such treatment as they had visited upon the Melians . . . after reducing them to siege, and upon the Histiaeans and Scionaeans and Toronaeans and Aeginetans [all having been subject to exile, enslavement, or massacre[36]], *and many other Greek peoples.*"[37] In the ancient world, retributive Nuremberg-type justice could be visited on the whole *polis*.

Essentially a fortunate city, Athens' good fortune held; its history would not cease with the fifth century. "When they arrived, the ephors called an assembly, at which the Corinthians and Thebans in particular, though many other Greeks agreed with them, opposed making a treaty with the Athenians and favoured destroying their city. The Lacedaemonians, however, said that they would not enslave a Greek city which had done great service amid the greatest perils that had befallen Greece [during the Persian Wars]."[38] None of this, remarkably enough, prevented the Athenians from committing genocide against Sestos in the fourth century.[39] The perception of high tragic drama in the real world, with themselves at the center of the tragedy, and the performance of instrumental-political *andrapodismos* were split off from each other in the Athenian mind. (Do not our cold-hot warriors who have talked so arrogantly of "winning" an atomic war suffer from the same pathological form of splitting?) Once again we ask the fundamental question: have we really moved beyond the Athenian affliction of paranoid self-destruction?

Item #6. After Philip and Alexander had established Macedonian hegemony over all of mainland Greece, when Philip was dead and Alexander king, the city of Thebes revolted. It was a fatal mistake. The city taken, "Alexander's hope . . . that so severe an example might terrify the rest of Greece into obedience, and also in order to gratify the Phocians and Plataeans [the enemies of Thebes], [he ordered] that, except the priests, and some few who had heretofore been friends and connections of the Macedonians, the family of the poet Pindar, and those who were known to have opposed the public vote for the war, all the rest, to the number of thirty thousand, were publicly sold for slaves; and it is computed that upwards of six thousand were put to the sword."[40]

Alexander's retribution against Thebes became a renowned instance of questionable vengeance. Such minor ambivalence, however, did nothing to stop the killing machine.

There are two remarkable passages, one in Plato, the other in Alexander's teacher, Aristotle, that may help us understand the origins of this man-destroying disease. In the *Euthydemus* of Plato, Socrates and Clinias are discussing the nature of various arts, talents, and gifts that humans possess and exercise. How happy does it make a person to practice these arts? "The general's art," Socrates asserts, "seems to be most certainly the art, which he who gets will be happy." Clinias demurs. "Why not?" "This art seems to me a sort of *hunting of men*," responds Clinias. The purpose of hunting is capture and the purpose of capture is ultimately eating. And the eating of men is problematic, at least for the Greeks. "No art of hunting," proceeds Clinias, "goes further than to hunt and to capture; but when they have captured what they hunted, they cannot use it; huntsmen and fishermen hand over to the cooks." Later Clinias adds: "And the same with the generals. As soon as they have hunted a city or an army, they hand it over to the politicians—for they do not know themselves how to use their captures—just as quail hunters hand over to the quail keepers."[41]

The argument has proceeded from handing over to the cooks to handing over to the "quail keepers," just as society evolved, somewhere in the dark past, from eating what was captured in war to enslaving it. Sometimes, however, the hunters (the generals) or the keepers (the politicians) are so enraged that they would eat raw those who have finally been subdued. Thus, Zeus to Hera:

> *Dear lady, what can be all the great evils done to you*
> *by Priam and the sons of Priam, that you are thus furious*
> *forever to bring down the strong-founded city of Ilion?*
> *If you could walk through the gates and through the towering ramparts*
> *and eat Priam and the children of Priam raw, and the other*
> *Trojans, then, then only might you glut at last your anger.*[42]

But she *cannot* eat them and the Greeks *could not* eat their victims, no matter how great their rage; so they slaughtered them instead.

The "rational" thing to do is to enslave the captured. Rational economics becomes an instrument of the sublimation of aggression. In the first book of *Politics*, Aristotle addresses the problem of household management and the art of acquiring what is needed to live, including slaves, a necessary instrument of management of the household (*oikos*). For Aristotle, what is just is always grounded in "nature." "Plants exist to give subsistence to animals, and animals give it to men." Both domesticated and wild animals (procured by hunting) serve man's purpose. "Accordingly, as nature makes nothing purposeless or in vain, all animals must have been made by nature for the sake of men." So far, so good, but Aristotle knows that men hunt more than animals: they also hunt other men. Then, with ambiguity of language and thought, Aristotle attempts to reconcile nature, warfare, hunting, slavery, and justice—an impossible task. What is important for us, however, is his clear belief that *some men and wild animals are being equated: they both may be justly hunted.* "It follows that the art of war is in some sense . . . a natural mode of acquisition. Hunting is a part of that art [whether of the art of war or the art of acquisition is unclear]; and hunting ought to be practised—not only against wild animals, but also against human beings who are intended by nature to be ruled by others [as slaves] and refuse to obey that intention—because war of this order is naturally just."[43]

After pausing to observe with awe the power of cultural norms to corrupt one of the greatest of minds, we ask what we can learn from this. The institutionalization of slavery—the hunting of men—may be the inevitable consequence for human beings of abandoning cannibalism. Societies committed to slavery may live closer to cannibalistic urges than we can imagine. At times of extreme regression, caused by extreme rage—the fury of the moment—cannibal impulses rise to the surface, but something in culture, completely internalized into the psyche, says we cannot eat the Mitylenians. Further enraged by this prohibition, we vote for slaughter.

The great question for the theory of social evolution is whether or not all "civilized" societies live equally close to the "natural" desires to hunt and eat men. Has a society living without slavery succeeded in putting its cannibal past far behind it? During the German holocaust in this century, those concentration camp victims who were not slaughtered were virtually slaves. In the terrible regression that ended with the genocide of the Jews and the Gypsies, slavery was first introduced and the holocaust followed. Had there been no holocaust, millions would still have been enslaved.

Slavery was a perfectly "natural" institution for the Greeks, legitimized by nature, universally accepted. Only an infinitely small number of insignificant voices was raised against it. The greatest moralists of the culture, Plato and Aristotle, accepted it as just. Perhaps a society that lives so comfortably with slavery inevitably practices genocide as an instrument of policy. In the last forty years, much historical research has attempted to illuminate the economic significance of slavery, but we have made little progress in understanding what it means psychologically to hunt and own men. When we succeed in comprehending that, we may well understand much better the genocidal, moral contradictions in Athenian life.

A Note on Social and Moral Evolution

This discussion of warfare, genocide, and slavery has inevitably raised the question of moral progress. The answer depends directly on the possibility of the transformation of instinct. To what degree, if any, are the aggressive drives capable of sublimation and transformation? Let us consider two important theoretical questions. First, is there such a thing as moral progress? Second, does modern democratic society represent a moral advance over ancient Athenian society?

Most people of general intellectual interest answer both these questions in the negative. Let us consider, therefore, a proposition most readers may be willing to accept: the presence of severe moral contradictions in Athenian society—and the continued existence of moral contradictions in our own democratic society. One cannot avoid the question of whether the moral contradictions in our present society are of the same order as those in Athens. From the moral point of view, has anything really changed, that is, progressed? From the psychological point of view, are we, as a society, significantly less paranoid than the Greeks?

My own position is clear. I have written four books attempting to establish that a theory of social *and* moral progress is a reasonable one. Twentieth-century democracy differs from Athenian democracy in three remarkably important ways, each with profound implications for the degree of the paranoid position within society and for the degree of justice within a necessarily ambivalent value system.

First, the abandonment of slavery means not only freedom for those who were, or were destined to become, slaves, but also freedom for a slave-owning class from the exercise of—and the incarceration within—a psychologically primitive mastery. The notion that human beings can hunt and own other human beings finds resonance only in a primeval part of the psyche. It represents a defense against anxiety appropriate to a child in a very early stage of development. In potentially reductionist psychoanalytic terms, the owning of other human beings is an attempt at mastery appropriate to the anal stage, with conflicting feelings about one's own feces. (I once knew a businessman of large wealth who enjoyed gaining power over politicians by the questionable expenditure of funds. He talked of "owning" certain public servants and would remark: "I have him in my pocket," and then give a few pats to his rear end. All ownership of other human beings resonates with that part of the anatomy.)

A sense of mastery is essential for all human beings. It gives great pleasure in itself, but is also, crucially, a means to defend against anxiety. And here the paranoia—paranoid position—nonparanoid developmental series becomes important. The more primitive (that is, in the direction of paranoia) the anxiety felt, the more primitive will be the defense to contain that anxiety. There is a great difference between asserting mastery by killing and eating one's neighbor, by hunting and enslaving "barbarians," or by dominating nature through industrialization. Each of these is an assertion of mastery, but each represents a different stage of psychological development. The domination of nature—though we have reached the point where its excesses threaten our existence—is, psychologically, a significant advance over the owning of other human beings. The abandonment of slavery is essential for a certain psychological, cultural, and moral advance.

The second crucial way in which twentieth-century democracy differs from that of Athens is its inclusion of women. In the ancient world there were three distinct human species: men, slaves, and women. In twentieth-century democracy, ideally at least, there is only one. The complex arguments offered by Horney, Dinnerstein,[44] and others about the masculine dread of women cannot be detailed here, but two things may be noted. One is that conflicts concerning paranoia and the paranoid position directly concern the anxiety men feel about feminine (that is, maternal) power. Second, overcoming that dread, to the point where men are willing to have women participate in the political process and, potentially, assume political power, and women are willing to take that power, is an extraordinary advance in psychic health and the great task of overcoming the paranoid position. The significant participation of women in the political process is a phenomenon of *twentieth-century democracy only*, never seen before in the history of the world. That we still await truly equal participation should not obscure the importance of this fact. Like giving up slavery, it was an achievement impossible for the Greeks. Any adequate theory of history must explain these two world-shaking advances.

The discussion of the third mode of difference between modern and ancient democratic societies is more conjectural. We have practically no data concerning child rearing in the ancient world, except for the widespread practice of infanticide amongst all social classes. Infanticide, slavery, and the severe inhibition of women probably produced in children decidedly paranoid defenses against anxiety. Discussions of infanticide have centered on the dead children and the psychological effect on the parents, but what of those older children who observed their newborn siblings killed either by their parents or by their parents' orders? It is almost impossible to imagine the dread such a circumstance must conjure up. There would be, as well, a sense of omnipotence in a wish come true: a potential rival for the affections of one's parents has disappeared from the earth. It is generally agreed that the practice of infanticide was widespread, not exceptional. How many of those who voted for genocide in the Assembly had seen their younger infant siblings destroyed?

Slavery, owning another human being, must have a debilitating effect on children. Certain primitive modes of dealing with aggression and anxiety must be overcome and sublimated for a child to develop into a mature adult. Certain impulses toward, and beliefs in, omnipotence must be abandoned. In our culture, the adult who believes he can—psychologically—own other people is pathological. In a slave society, children learn that one can live out that fantasy of omnipotence.

Last, the oppression of women must inevitably have a debilitating effect on child rearing. The child is taught that women (that is, mothers) are a second-rate species. The mothers revenge themselves on men by denigrating children (the play *Medea* is a deliberately exaggerated version of this syndrome). The denigration of women-mothers cannot advance the psychic health of children.

I am arguing that giving up infanticide, abandoning slavery, and allowing equality for women must have an enormously positive effect on the quality of child rearing within a society. This will be reflected in a decrease in the paranoid positions in the politics of the state. The work of deMause and Stone,[45] amongst others, has demonstrated that progressive changes in child rearing in the last four hundred years, especially in those countries that became the great democracies of the nineteenth and twentieth centuries, have been remarkable. A democratic society requires democratic child rearing. A nongenocidal democratic society requires nongenocidal child rearing.

Nevertheless, optimism must be tempered by the perception of political realities. In America, in the early 1950s—during the paranoid reign of Senator Joseph McCarthy—we came close to abandoning the open nature of our democracy and the paranoid impulses released by the cold war almost belie the notion that we are psychologically more mature than Athens. The precipitous moral retreat exhibited in our politics during the last ten years or so makes one doubt progress. Reasonable argument can be made on both sides of this issue but the general intellectual perception is pessimistic. In our modern world we are living on a fine edge, where, as Voltaire remarked, there is "a civil war in every soul."[46] One can not know whether his or her optimism or pessimism is justified.

14

Political Action with a Class Basis—Sometimes Violent, Sometimes Not

The disintegration of Marxist ideology in Europe as a ruling political philosophy neither invalidates nor confirms the usefulness of Marxism as a theoretical tool in the effort to understand society and human history. Certain essentially Marxist concepts have been helpful in shedding light on the history of Europe of the last four hundred years: ideas of class, class struggle, revolution, the rising bourgeoisie, the proletariat, and the perception of "capitalism" not only as an economic order but also as a system of domination. This four-hundred-year period has witnessed the rise of capitalism as the ruling economic system and the Marxist theory of history is a product of that historical development. For modern historians of the ancient world a fundamental question has been: How valuable is it to project current concepts of class struggle, the proletariat, and the bourgeoisie back on to the history of Greece and Rome which were precapitalist societies? Are they valid for the ancient world?

The *ultimate purpose* of such discussion should be, not to establish or reject the validity of Marxist concepts as such, but to understand ancient society. Before the Second World War, a serious effort was made to use Marxist categories to explain particular ancient historical phenomena. The class in the middle at the time of Solon—those here called "rich peasants"—were cited as a rising bourgeoisie. "Proletariat" designated the lower economic orders in Greece, and especially in the city of Rome. Hypotheses of "class" and "class struggle" were in the air.

After the war, a reaction set in, postulating that a backward projection of concepts from a capitalist to a precapitalist world had no validity. A serious thesis was expounded that not only was there no class struggle, but also there were no classes in the ancient world, in effect, that the development of various classes was, itself, the result of *capitalism*.

In the last ten years or so, a theoretical "postmodern" environment has prevailed, wherein all opinions are expressed and tolerated, a flexible, "anything goes" world of theoretical approach. In the early 1980s, G. E. M. de Ste. Croix, an historian of prodigious powers, published a conscious and deliberate Marxist interpretation of ancient history, an important book entitled *The Class Struggle in the Ancient Greek World*.[1] M. I. Finley, who trained and influenced a whole generation of ancient historians, propounded an entirely different theoretical position. Other historians struggled to attain a secure footing in this theoretical turmoil. W. Robert Connor, for instance, makes a brave try in his recent book on Thucydides. On page 39, he notes: "Since English 'factionalism' is too tame and 'civil strife,' 'civil war,' 'revolution,' 'class warfare' have the wrong connotations, I simply retain the Greek term, *stasis*, as a convenient label for this phenomenon." Such intellectual purity cannot be maintained; in the very next paragraph Connor writes: "another episode of class warfare—this one at Notium in Asia Minor—had preceded the account of the fall and punishment of Mitylene."[2]

It is not that Connor suffers from intellectual fuzzy-mindedness; his ambivalence arises because of the enormous amount of data that cries out, "class warfare." We are still not sure how to place it in an historical pre-capitalist context. Note the case of Mitylene whose revolt against Athens resulted in near-genocide. After the revolt, the Athenians invested the city; the promised Spartan aid did not materialize.

In the meantime the Mitylenians, finding their provisions failing, while the fleet from Peloponnese was loitering on the way instead of appearing at Mitylene, were compelled to come to terms with the Athenians in the following manner. Salaethus having himself ceased to expect the fleet to arrive, now armed the commons with heavy armour, which they had not before possessed, with the intention of making a sortie against the Athenians. The commons, however, no sooner found themselves possessed of arms than they refused any longer to obey their officers; and forming in knots together, told the authorities to bring out in public the provisions and divide them amongst them all, or they would themselves come to terms with the Athenians and deliver up the city.

The government, aware of their inability to prevent this, and of the danger they would be in, if left out of the capitulation, publicly agreed with Paches [the Athenian general] and the army to surrender Mitylene at discretion.[3]

The "people" of the ancient world threatening to turn their weapons against their aristocratic rulers has a nineteenth- and twentieth-century ring to it, a confusion perhaps originating in the fact that notions of "class struggle" do not much illuminate the history of the modern world, much less the ancient. The disorder certainly had a class basis, however; it is important to clarify exactly the form it took.

In weighing the problems, one need not accept or reject the Marxist historical interpretation as a whole. One may use certain concepts and find others unacceptable; theoretical clarity may lie in that direction.

My own approach finds the hypotheses of the existence of a "bourgeoisie" and a "proletariat" inaccurate. And yet I would argue that there were such things as classes in ancient society, and a form of "class struggle," but the latter must be accurately described. In studying the validity of this theoretical approach, this chapter attempts to illuminate the nature of ancient society.

In Mitylene, the *demos* and the *oligoi* avoided bloody violence. In many other Greek states, political conflict was a matter of living or dying. Diodorus writes of a short period of political activity in the Peloponnese around 375.

And the exiles from Corinth [democrats who had fled an oligarchic government], who, many in numbers, were living among the Argives, attempted to return, but though admitted into the city by some of their relatives and friends, they were denounced and surrounded, and, as they were about to be apprehended, fearful of the maltreatment their capture would entail, they slew one another. The Corinthians, having charged many of their citizens with assisting the exiles in the attack, put some to death and exiled others. Again, the city of the Megarians, when some persons endeavoured to overturn the government and were overpowered by the democracy, many were slain and not a few driven into exile. Likewise among the Sicyonians as well a number who tried to effect a revolution but failed were killed. Among the Phliasians, when many who were in exile had seized a stronghold in the country and gathered a considerable number of mercenaries, a battle was fought against the city party, and, when the exiles won the victory, over three hundred of the Phliasians were slain. Later, as the sentinels betrayed the exiles, the Phliasians got the upper hand and executed more than six hundred exiles, while they drove the rest out of the country and compelled them to take refuge in Argos. Such were the disasters that afflicted the Peloponnesian cities.[4]

It is remarkable in how many cases incessant Greek intercity warfare completely failed to keep violence out of intracity politics.

Alexander Fuks asserts that we have data verifying seventy-six cases of "social-economic conflict" and "social-economic revolution" from the time of the Persian Wars (490) to the middle of the second century. Most of the cases occurred from the fourth century to the second; he counts only about six occurrences from 490 to 404.[5] We have no way of knowing how many more social-economic conflicts occurred that we are not aware of. The phenomenon seems to have been widespread in the Greek world.

Perhaps a closer look at "social-economic conflict" and its relationship to "class" will lead us out of the Marxist versus non-Marxist theoretical woods. Political action, which in a democratic society necessarily includes voting, can proceed from various bases. First, there is the basis of the nation as a whole: a vote for or against war, for instance. Those in the United States who voted in Senate races, between 1968 and 1974 for candidates opposed to the war in Vietnam, were taking political action on a national basis, promoting what they thought best for the country as a whole. There is also an ethnic basis. Those Jews in the United States who vote for candidates perceived to be friendly to Israel are undertaking political action on an ethnic basis. When a working-class white person votes for Ronald Reagan believing that Reagan will endeavor to keep black people in their place (not in my neighborhood), such a vote is political action on a racial basis. A vote for a candidate because of his or her position on abortion has an ideological, or religious, foundation.

Last and most important for this discussion of ancient Greece, there is political action with an economic basis. To use an obvious modern example, if working-class people vote for Franklin D. Roosevelt because they believe he will promote their economic interests, and upper-class people vote against him because they fear he will harm their privileged position, such a vote is political action on an economic basis. And "class," it seems to me, means nothing more and nothing less than that. People who take similar political actions based on similarly perceived economic interests and positions represent a "class." If "class struggle" and "class warfare" smack too much of the modern world and Marxist theory to be accurate for ancient Greece, then Fuks's "social-economic" is a perfect replacement. "Social" because the activity occurs on a societal level, that is, politics, the activities of the *polis.* "Economic" because economic interests are the true dividing line of such action within the *polis,* that is, political action primarily determined by one's class interests.

Social-economic action—politics with a class basis—can be either violent (unlawful, revolutionary, murderous) or peaceful (lawful, legitimate, habitual). Fuks calls violent social-economic action "social-economic conflict," and his seventy-six cases all involve assassination, illegality, or revolution. Much, if not most, political action in a democratic society has a class, socioeconomic basis. Whether it grows violent or not is the crucial question.

A fundamental contradiction exists in all democratic societies, ancient and modern: Democracy implies *equality* in the political sphere, but private ownership of economic resources results in *inequality* in the economic sphere. The egalitarian values of the political world can challenge the legitimacy of economic inequalities. Some sort of social-economic conflict is therefore inevitable in every democratic society. The great achievement of Athens—an achievement that set it apart from almost all the Greek world—was to erect, after the terrors of the oligarchic coups, a political society with a socioeconomic basis that remained lawful and peaceful. There were rich and poor in Athens and their interests diverged many times, but from the fourth century on they did not kill each other over disagreements. There was a tacit understanding between the rich and the poor, the few and the many, the *oligoi* and the *demos*. The poor agreed not to use the political power of the radical democracy to dispossess the rich, not to confiscate and redistribute property. The rich agreed not to use their superior economic and social power to destroy the democracy. This *weltanschauung* came down from the time of Solon, who recognized that he could not fully reconcile the claims of the rich and the poor, that compromise was necessary, and that they could compete with each other on a lawful, nonviolent basis. It was a remarkable vision, and remains one of the fundamental values of our liberal, democratic, capitalist society.

How much political action within the *polis* was social-economic or class based? The convinced Marxist simplistically sees all political action of any significance as class inspired, in both the ancient and the modern worlds. Everything else has the quality of sham or false consciousness. The question is one of degree. If declaring that *most* political action in the *polis* has a social-economic basis makes one a Marxist, then, perforce, Plato, Aristotle, Isocrates, and even Machiavelli, are Marxists. All these thinkers saw social-economic conflict, violent or not, as the fundamental basis of political action in the city-state, the rich versus the poor. They believed violence was avoided in many cases only by the repressive success of the *oligoi*.

This perception of the oppressive, repressive nature of political activity goes far back in Greek culture. Hesiod, early in the seventh century, saw the relationship of the rich to the poor as that of a hawk to his prey:

> Thus said the hawk to the nightingale with speckled neck, while he carried her high up among the clouds, gripped fast in his talons, and she, pierced by his crooked talons cried pitifully. To her he spoke disdainfully: "Miserable thing, why do you cry out? One far stronger than you now holds you fast, and you must go wherever I take you, songstress as you are. And if I please I will make my meal of you, or let you go. He is a fool who tries to withstand the stronger, for he does not get the mastery and suffers pain besides his shame."[6]

What differentiated Greek society from those that had gone before was not the bifurcation of society along class lines, nor the incessant oppressive action of the rich against the poor—these go back to the origins of the state.[7] Greek society was truly remarkable in that, as early as the beginning of the seventh century the poor had found a voice. Even more remarkable, theirs was a permanent voice as subsequent centuries proved. The *demos*, once emergent, never returned to invisible status. According to Plutarch, this permanent division of the state became paramount in people's minds in the middle years of Pericles' leadership of Athens. "From the first there had been a kind of flow beneath the surface . . . but the rivalry and ambition of the two sides cut a deep wound in the state and caused it to be divided into two parts, one called the *demos* and one called the *oligoi*."[8]

The primary goal of Plato's political philosophy was to overcome the deleterious effects on the *polis* of this fatal intense conflict between the *demos* and the *oligoi*. Speaking of the numerous *poleis* in the Greek world, he contends: "Not one of them is a state but many states. For indeed any state, however small, is in fact divided into two, one the state of the poor, the other of the rich. These are at war with one another and in either there are many smaller divisions."[9] Not only are all states divided into classes, but class conflict is endemic. "If you approach them as though they were one, you'll be a complete failure; but if you approach them as though they were many, offering to the ones the money and the powers or the persons of the others, you'll always have the use of many allies."[10] "Class conflict" grows violent and becomes "class warfare," especially in a plutocracy where landless, penniless, unemployed, essentially disenfranchised men proliferate as they lose their property to the rich. Enraged at their condition, Plato says, and "hating the men who have acquired their property and conspiring against them and the rest of society, they long for revolution."[11]

One cannot dismiss this as the exaggeration of a younger and possibly too eager Plato, since the theme becomes central to the *Laws*, one of his last and most reflective works, which excised the "utopianism" of the *Republic* and presented a more realistic approach to politics. In the *Laws* Plato insists that most *poleis* do not deserve the name of "polity" because of the split along class lines. "These non-polities . . . I have often mentioned in our previous discourse—namely, democracy, oligarchy, and tyranny [that is, almost all existing states]. For none of these is a polity, but the truest name for them all would be 'factionstates'; for none of them is a form of voluntary rule over willing subjects, but a voluntary rule over unwilling subjects accompanied always by some kind of force."[12] If one of the great theoretical truths in Marxist social theory is a theory of domination, one may, ironically, inquire how much Marx owed to Plato. For the latter, the great discrepancy between wealth and poverty was the true cause of the pathology of the *polis*: "It is an old and true saying that it is hard to fight against the attack of two foes, especially when they are opposites. . . . And indeed the present fight is of the two and against the two—poverty [*penia*] and riches [*ploutos*], of which the one corrupts the soul of men with luxury, while the other by means of worries drives it into shamelessness. *What remedy is then to be found for this disease in a state gifted with understanding?*"[13]

Aristotle, much less passionately, much more "scientific" and "analytical" in tone, offers the same analysis: "A state is composed of two sections—the poor and the rich."[14] And a more complex analysis:

> The same persons, for example, may serve as soldiers, farmers, and craftsmen; the same persons, again, may act both as a deliberative council and a judicial court. Political ability, too, is a quality to which all men pretend; and everyone thinks himself capable of filling most offices. There is one thing which is impossible: the same person cannot be both rich and poor. This will explain why these two classes—the rich and the poor—are regarded as parts of the state in a special and peculiar sense. Nor is this all. One of these classes being small, and the other large, they also appear to be *opposite* parts. This is why they both form constitutions to suit their own interest [that of wealth in one case, and that of numbers in the other]. It is also the reason why men think that there are only two constitutions—democracy and oligarchy.[15]

Reading this and observing the plethora of data we have about social-economic conflict and social-economic violence, it is difficult to understand how Moses Finley, one of the most important and influential ancient historians of this century, could insist, at one point in his career, that there were no classes in ancient society, only a set of various and flexible "statuses."[16] Aristotle asserts and historical data confirm that "the poor" were one section of society, that they joined together to act politically and economically in their own interests, forming constitutions for that purpose, in circumstances often violent. If such a group of people are a "status" and not a "class," then the word "class" has no meaning, and there is not and never has been any such thing as a class either in the ancient or the modern world. Aristotle insists not only that there are classes, but also that the poorer classes are conscious of their interests in opposition to the wealthy class. The Marxist historian de Ste. Croix asserts that there was a "class struggle" in the ancient world and that it occurred between masters and slaves, that being the area in which the economic "surplus" was skimmed off by the wealthy; there was no significant surplus in the economic area between the rich and the free poor.[17] In fact, however, the conflict, the struggle, the banishments, the confiscations, the slaughters all occurred, not between slaves and masters, but between the rich and the free poor, between *oligoi* and *demos*. Call it what one will, that was the reality of the ancient Greek *polis*.

It is a rhetorical exaggeration to equate the *demos* and the poor. That the *oligoi* was composed almost exclusively of the rich there is no question. The *demos*, however, was a more conglomerate entity. Where we have the most data—in the accounts of the defeat of the two oligarchic coups in Athens and Samos—it is clear that those opposing the coups included not only the poor but also many, if not most, of the middling class (those neither rich nor poor) and several, if not many, of aristocratic birth and connection. Nobly born Pericles was the leader of the *demos* when the terms *demos* and *oligoi* became common currency to designate the two factions in society. Aristocrats and many of the middling class fought with, and became the leaders of, the people in Athens for ideological reasons. They believed in the validity and legitimacy of democracy. If political ideals had not cut across class lines democracy would have been impossible.

A political analysis based solely on class cannot explain the existence of democratic society. We know the situation in Athens. We would like to know more about the intricacies of political combinations in other areas of intense social-economic violence, such as Corcyra and Argos, but the information is not forthcoming. As far as we known, no *demos* composed almost entirely of the true, and not the metaphorical, poor ever created a mature, stable democracy. In Corinth in the fourth century, where the ruling oligarchy triumphed after an intense and prolonged period of what Finley calls "civil-war episodes,"[18] was it because most of the rich and the middling group either remained loyal to the oligarchy or were politically uninvolved? Political situations were always more complicated than Plato's and Aristotle's division into two factions would indicate. Plato does say, as noted, that the two are divided into many factions.

Disappointing as it is to proceed from Plato and Aristotle to the rather middling insights of Isocrates, perhaps the latter more truly represents the Hellenic mind than the two gods of Greek philosophy. We may learn from Isocrates the mind set of most elite Greeks. In about the year 366 B.C. he composed a speech that, supposedly, was to be delivered by Archidamos, a Spartan prince, soon to become king.

> They feel such distrust and such hatred of one another that they fear their fellow-citizens more than the enemy; instead of preserving the spirit of accord and mutual helpfulness which they enjoyed under our [Spartan] rule, they have become so unsocial that those who own property had rather throw their possessions into the sea than lend aid to the needy, while those who are in poorer circumstances would less gladly find a treasure than seize the possessions of the rich; having ceased sacrificing victims at the altars they slaughter one another there instead [we know of several incident in the fourth century of supplicants being violated during intracity violence][19] and more people are in exile now from a single city than before from the whole of Peloponnese.[20]

In a word, in the *polis* class hatred is endemic. The history of Italian city-states of the late medieval and Renaissance period overwhelms us with data on social-economic conflict, most often violent. Machiavelli succinctly sums it up: "The cause of all the ills that arise in cities is the serious and natural enmity which exists between nobles and *populari*, caused by the desire of the former to command and of the latter not to have to obey them."[21]

Athens—and possibly a few Greek *poleis* we know little about—was the great exception. By the fourth century it had learned how to express social-economic competition without resorting to civil violence, *under the necessary condition of a democratic society.* In almost all other city-states, either the *demos* was successfully repressed by the *oligoi* or social-economic violence made political stability impossible. For this purpose, we may define the *demos* as all those who do not naturally belong to an oligarchy, which is composed primarily of the very rich and the very high-born. The city-state was thus a form of society wherein the *demos* had found its voice, determined at times not to be a victim, but essentially incapable of seizing political power and establishing a democracy. Sometimes, as in Rome and early-modern Venice, the *demos* was successfully repressed almost permanently by a narrow aristocracy; there were other cities, especially among the Italian city-states, where civil violence was so incessant that only a resort to monarchy could restore order. In many situations, civil order was almost impossible and violent social-economic conflict ruled the *polis* for a long period of time.

Though its history extended, with interruptions, for more than two thousand years, the city-state was a transitional form for the *demos*. Transitional, because they had learned to refuse to be silent, unlike the people of ancient empires such as Persia and Egypt, where no polity included the people. Transitional, because it was only an intermediate step to power; the *demos* never achieved permanent power except in Athens. When the *demos* reached for power, the result was almost invariably a period of violent civil strife followed by repression (possibly a short period of democratic rule as in Syracuse) and some form of oligarchy or tyranny. Democracy was essentially an impossibility until the world of liberalism produced another significant transformation in human nature.

When violent civil strife occurs in the *polis* it is almost invariably a struggle for democracy, on both the political and economic levels. The *demos*, whatever sections of society it includes, strives for a political democracy; the poor, a portion of the *demos*, crave economic relief.

The struggle for democracy was unsuccessful in the city-state. Did the fault lie with "the people" who lacked the sophistication to assume and exercise power and too readily sold its soul to a would-be tyrant promising land and debt cancellation? Did the fault lie with an aristocracy that refused to compromise, or with the middling group of wealthy and not-so-wealthy nonnobles who would not ally themselves with the people and their democratic aspirations? In the struggle between the *oligoi* and the *demos*, the great unanswered question is still who composed the *demos*? Many members of the aristocracy and the nonnoble rich joined forces with the *demos* in Athens, throughout the fifth-century radicalization of democracy and in the civil war precipitated by the oligarchs in 411 and 404. Even the leaders of the non-*demos* faction—Aristides, Cimon, Thucydides the son of Melisias, Nicias—do not present a picture of radical oligarchs prepared to use violence to destroy the hated democracy. (Critias was the exception in the Athenian *oligoi*, not the rule.) What did Syracuse, for instance, lack that caused its struggle for democracy to fail—Syracuse and Argos and Corinth and Corcyra? That important question continues unanswered.

The Violent Struggle For and Against Democracy

Let us enlarge on two significant statements we have made. One that violent social-economic conflict was widespread in the Greek world, and two, that violence, once unleashed in political struggle within the *polis*, seems to have been limitless. The lust to annihilate did not start at the borders of the city-state; the internal politics of the *polis* could become murderous. Having already dealt at length with the Athenian coups of 411 and 404, we will treat here with six of Fuks's seventy-six cases, hoping this small sample may serve the interpretive purpose.

Corcyra, 427–425. In his history, Thucydides distinguishes between the fundamental cause of the great war, and its proximate cause. The basic reason, he tells us, was "the growth of the power of Athens, and the alarm . . . this inspired in Lacedaemon, [which] made war inevitable."[22] The particular events that triggered the war involved the city of Epidamnus, the island of Corcyra, Corinth (a major ally of Sparta), and Athens. Epidamnus, finding itself in trouble, appealed to its mother country, Corcyra, for aid, which was refused. Epidamnus then appealed to Corinth, which agreed to help after the Epidamnians delivered up their city. Corinth sent in troops and settlers, angering Corcyra and Corcyra and Corinth went to war. The Corcyraeans successfully appealed to Athens for an alliance, putting Athens in direct conflict with Corinth. And thus the great war began.

We retell this well-known story to emphasize that the Epidamnians' original trouble was a violent conflict between the nobles and the *demos*. Epidamnus was in a continual state of war with its barbarian neighbors, but that did not prevent strife within the *polis*. "The last act before the war was the expulsion of the nobles by the people. The exiled party joined the barbarians, and proceeded to plunder those in the city by sea and land; and the Epidamnians finding themselves hard pressed, sent ambassadors to Corcyra beseeching their mother country not to allow them to perish, but to make up matters between them and their exiles, and to rid them of the war with the barbarians."[23] Thus, the spark that set the whole Greek world aflame was a political struggle between *demos* and *oligoi*.

Ironically enough, it was Corcyra that suffered the most murderous intracity conflict early in the war. Thucydides takes this as a typical case, telling the story of the Corcyraean civil war in great detail. Four years after the war commenced, the rivalry between nobles and commons within Corcyra became intensified, each side allying itself with an antagonist in the war: the *demos* with Athens, the *oligoi* with the Lacedaemonians. So intense did the conflict become that both sides appealed to the slaves in the city, offering them freedom if they would come over and fight. The commons were successful in the struggle, and many of the *oligoi* took refuge in the sanctuary of Hera. A short time later, the *demos*, emboldened by the approach of an Athenian fleet, "slew such of their enemies as they laid hands on, dispatching afterwards as they landed them, those whom they had persuaded to go on board the ships. Next they went to the sanctuary of Hera and persuaded about fifty men to take their trial, and condemned them all to death. The mass of suppliants who had refused to do so, on seeing what was taking place, slew each other there in the consecrated ground. . . . During seven days that Eurymedon stayed with [the Athenian] sixty ships, the Corcyraeans were engaged in butchering those of their fellow-citizens whom they regarded as their enemies: and although the crime imputed was that of attempting to put down the democracy, some were slain also for private hatred, others by their debtors because of monies owed them. Death thus raged in every shape."[24]

As the war proceeded, Thucydides asserts, the violent intracity political struggle spread. "Later on, the whole Hellenic world was convulsed; struggles being everywhere made by the popular chiefs to bring in the Athenians, and by the oligarchs to introduce the Lacedaemonians."[25]

The civil war went on for two years in Corcyra. The nobles had left the island and established themselves on Mount Istone, from which base they continued to harass the government of the commons. With Athenian aid, the nobles were finally captured and gave themselves up to the discretion of the Athenian commanders. However, using certain ruses, the Corcyraean *demos* contrived to obtain custody of the prisoners whom they massacred. Thucydides here goes counter to his usual style.

He gives no detailed descriptions of Athenian genocide, but here we are told exactly how this massacre occurred. The shock is akin to that given by pictures of concentration camp survivors that have burned themselves into our memories. "The prisoners thus handed over were shut up by the Corcyraeans in a large building, and afterwards taken out by twenties and led past two lines of heavy infantry, one on each side, being bound together, and beaten and stabbed by the men in the lines whenever any saw pass a personal enemy; while men carrying whips went by their side and hastened on the road those that walked too slowly. As many as sixty men were taken out and killed in this way."[26]

When the prisoners remaining in the building learned what was happening, they refused to come out, whereupon the Corcyraeans mounted the roof and poured down roof tiles and arrows in a murderous rain. Many of the Corcyraean nobles preferred to take their own lives, some using spent arrows, some hanging themselves. Thucydides continues with a sentence reverberating with twentieth-century horror: "When it was day the Corcyraeans threw them in layers upon waggons and carried them out of the city."[27] All the women who had been taken captive were enslaved. *Andrapodismos* could become an instrument of political policy *within the polis*.

The civil war did not go on forever. "And so after terrible excesses the party strife came to an end, at least as far as the period of this war is concerned, for of one party there was practically nothing left."[28]

Corinth, 392–c. 350. In 392 civil strife in Corinth came to a climax. With the aid of Argos, Athens, and Boeotia, the democratic faction slaughtered 120 political opponents during a sacred festival, some actually at the altars. The leader of the *demos* merged the state with Argos to keep the oligarchs from returning to power. The oligarchs betrayed the walls of the city to Sparta and joined the Spartan forces. The democrats remained in power within the city, with the aid of Argos. Six years later, when as a result of the King's Peace Sparta returned the Corinthian exiles to power within the city, they promptly began to eliminate their democratic opponents.[29] By the middle of the century, "Corinth was a shadow of its past, battered by more than half a century of warfare and by several bitter civil-war episodes from which the ruling oligarchy, one of the most tenacious in Greece, emerged victorious."[30]

• • •

Argos, 370. Civil strife had a long history in Argos. Thucydides writes that, in the year 417, murderous conflict intensified when the oligarchs allied themselves with Sparta against the people.[31] The climax of terror occurred in the year 370. Diodorus relates:

> While these things were going on, in the city of Argos civil strife broke out accompanied by slaughter of a greater number than is recorded ever to have occurred anywhere else in Greece. Among the Greeks this revolutionary movement was called "Club-law," receiving this appellation on account of the manner of the execution.
>
> Now the strife arose from the following causes: the city of Argos had a democratic form of government, and certain demagogues instigated the populace against the outstanding citizens of property and reputation. The victims of the hostile charges then got together and decided to overthrow the democracy. When some of those who were thought to be implicated were subjected to torture, all but one, fearing the agony of torture, received a pledge of immunity, and as informer denounced thirty of the most distinguished citizens, and the democracy without a thorough investigation put to death all those who were accused and confiscated their property. But many others were under suspicion, and as the demagogues [the leaders of the *demos*] supported false accusation, the mob was wrought up to such a pitch of savagery that they condemned to death all the accused, who were many and wealthy. When, however, more than twelve hundred influential men had been removed, the populace did not spare the demagogues themselves. For because of the magnitude of the calamity the demagogues were afraid that some unforeseen turn of fortune might overtake them and therefore desisted from their accusation, whereas the mob, now thinking that they had been left in the lurch by them, were angry at this and put to death all the demagogues.[32]

Jacobin terror before Jacobins. Such outrageous behavior went too far for some Greeks and the Athenians performed a purificatory sacrifice in the Assembly after hearing of the slaughter.[33]

Heraclea Pontica, 364–281. The political life of the city of Heraclea Pontica, on the southern coast of the Black Sea, had been nothing if not turbulent. In 364 the adventurer Clearchus became tyrant of the city. Before that, four governments had fallen victim to revolution.[34] Democracy had ruled from time to time but in 364 a narrow oligarchy of 300 landowners were governing uneasily. Agitation for democracy, cancellation of debts, and land redistribution persisted. Hoping to repress this unrest once and for all, the oligarchs persuaded the agitated *demos* to agree to calling in an arbitrator. They selected Clearchus, once a member of the democratic faction, now exiled and serving as a military officer to a Persian satrap. The oligarchs had come to a secret agreement with this adventurer and when Clearchus arrived, with the aid of mercenary soldiers he repressed all democratic activity and assassinated the leaders of the democracy.

The *oligoi* had, however, underestimated the *libido dominandi* of their instrument. Playing on their fear, he convinced them to allow him to construct a fortified camp on the acropolis. Using the camp and his mercenaries, Clearchus made himself absolute tyrant of the city. Allying himself with a remnant of the *demos*, he confiscated the estates of members of the oligarchy, massacring many and exiling the rest, and even freeing their slaves. Clearchus controlled the only military force in the city and his tyranny went unchallenged. He was murdered in 353, but the tyranny continued until 281 when democracy was restored and descendants of the exiles returned.[35]

Alexander: Ephesus and Chios, 334. In 334 Alexander crossed the Hellespont to begin his conquest of Asia. His first task was to liberate the Greek cities of Asia Minor that had been conquered by the Persians. In many of the *poleis*, strife between democrats and oligarchs had interpenetrated foreign affairs. The Persians preferred oligarchies or tyrannies and in many cities members of the democratic faction had been exiled. Believing that democracies would favor his cause, Alexander decreed that all exiles should return and democratic governments be instituted in the liberated cities.

Alexander also desired, however, the support of united, peaceful states and he was unprepared when the restored democrats immediately began executing their oligarchic opponents. At Ephesus, when the democrats slaughtered the tyrant and his son, Alexander interceded at once and decreed that there be no more reprisals. At Chios he garrisoned the town to ensure that his amnesty was respected. Without the autocratic pupil of Aristotle, who had written that a king "must hold the balance even between the parties," the slaughter of the *oligoi* would have been prodigious.[36]

• • •

Sparta, 243–192. The history of Sparta in the last half of the third century presents a remarkable instance of the use of modern (revolutionary) political methods in the attempt to restore an ancient society. It was not a struggle for democracy as in the other cases discussed here, but involved violent political action to restore an ancient equality. It was revolution from above, fought by two kings and a usurper of the throne who had been guardian to a young king.

By the third century, Sparta no longer resembled the old "Lycurgan" polity of nine thousand equals dedicated to preserving a kinship society and oppressing many noncitizens with a garrison state. Equality was gone, replaced by the usual disparities of wealth, concentration of land in the hands of the few, and the psychological and political oppression of the many, including former Spartan citizens and equals, by a very narrow few. That such a situation should evolve is not surprising. What is extraordinary is the serious attempt made to reverse the process and restore the original "constitution of Lycurgus," obviously a treasured myth.

The first attempt was made by Agis IV, who became king in 244. A year later he introduced his plan of radical reform: cancellation of debts, redistribution of the land in equal lots, and extension of the rights of citizenship to all who had lost them because of poverty and also to resident aliens. When the Spartan Council rejected the plan, Agis deposed the ephors opposed to him and the other king, Leonidas, who fled into exile. When he burned all mortgages, however, he alienated his political allies, who had not expected such revolutionary action. They turned on him, brought Leonidas back from exile, and deposed and executed Agis. The revolution was dead—for the moment.[37]

Cleomenes III became king in 235. He was inspired with ideals of social reconstruction by his wife Agiatis, who had been the widow of Agis IV. He first devoted himself to military success abroad. When he returned home in 227, he engineered a political coup, made himself tyrant, and instituted the full revolutionary policy of Agis: land, debts, citizenship. But he could not disentangle himself from foreign military conflicts and was finally defeated by the Macedonians. He fled to Egypt, where he vainly tried to stir up a revolution in Alexandria and ended his life by suicide. His social reforms, dependent on his personal power, had a short life.[38]

The idea of social revolution did not die out, however; the third act of this drama was the most revolutionary and longest lasting of all. In 207 Nabis became guardian to the young king of Sparta, Pelops, who died shortly thereafter. Nabis seized the throne, surrounding himself with an armed guard of mercenaries and some citizens committed to social reform. He began violently to carry out the program of Agis and Cleomenes: "Spoliation, proscription, systematic destruction of the upper classes, confiscation of private fortunes (ostensibly for the State). Moreover, he enfranchised many Helots, who were made citizens, assigned land to those same Helots and to the poor, and distributed among mob-leaders and mercenaries the goods . . . of the proscribed."[39] He is even accused by Polybius, his foremost detractor in ancient times, of giving to the mob leaders the "wives and daughters of the proscribed"[40]—an accusation cast at many revolutionaries over the centuries. Nabis' revolution lasted for fifteen years, until he was assassinated in 192 in an oligarchic coup engineered with the aid of foreign enemies of Sparta.[41]

The concept illustrated here sharply differentiates the Greek world from the societies that had gone before (Persia, Egypt, Mesopotamia, even Israel)—the belief that political action could significantly transform the moral condition of the world. Except in Athens, all this valiant activity ended in failure. Democracy, equality could not endure. Oligarchy, tyranny, monarchy continued to rule the world. But it was a tragic failure: at one and the same time, nobly heroic and pitifully human.

The Betrayal of the City

The deadly ideological splits made inevitable by the modern world have made us acutely aware of the so-called "fifth column," people who betray a city or a country to an invading force, preferring to be ruled by foreigners with a kindred ideology rather than by fellow citizens with an antipathetical world view. We have become acquainted with a variety of quislings, of both "right" and "left." There have always been betrayers but this century has made treasonable action a widespread phenomenon of international politics. One may perhaps ironically praise those people who appear to care more for high ideals than for the petty emotions of a narrow, paltry patriotism. An ancient Greek would feel perfectly at home with them. The betrayal of the city, *almost always because of social-economic considerations*, was commonplace in the constant strife between *poleis*.

For Athens the evidence for this form of faithlessness in the years before the stability of the fourth century is plentiful. We have discussed the oligarchic coup in 411 when the Four Hundred were overthrown because of their determination to betray the city to Sparta. This, and the close alliance in 404 of the Thirty Tyrants with the Spartan commander Lysander, climaxed a long history of attempted treachery. Anton-Hermann Chroust summarizes for us:

Despite grave and even deadly dangers from without, civil dispute or party strife did not cease within the city. On the contrary, whenever the city was threatened by a hostile invasion, we nearly always find a faction within the city willing to betray it to the enemy in order to gain political hegemony, if necessary with the armed help of the foreign invader. Athens, as may be gathered from its checkered political history, was no exception to this general rule. This is fully borne out, among others, by the "conspiracy" of Cylon around the year 632, when with the assistance of his fellow "club members" and with the help of Megarian mercenaries he tried to seize Athens [Thucydides 1.126]; by the "reaction" engineered by the oligarch Isagoras and his partisans in the year 508/7, when the latter called upon the armed intervention of Sparta to suppress Cleisthenes and his "democratic" reforms [Aristotle, *Constitution of Athens*, 20.1–4; Herodotus 5.70 and 5.72–73]; by the conduct of Hippias, who in the year 490 was with the Persian army at Marathon in the hope of regaining political control over Athens with the help of his Asiatic friends [Herodotus 6.102; 6.115ff; 6.121ff]; by the "conspiracy" entertained by some Athenian oligarchs who on the eve of the battle of Plataea in 479 sought to overthrow the "democratic" regime at Athens by betraying the cause of the Greeks to the Persians [Plutarch, *Aristides*, 13]; by the "invitation" to march upon unsuspecting Athens and expel the democrats, extended to the Spartan army by some Athenian oligarchs shortly before the battle of Tanagara in 457 [Thucydides 1.107; Plutarch, *Cimon*, 17; Plutarch, *Pericles*, 10]; by the fact that in 431/30 Melesippus, the Spartan ambassador, was returned under strict guard so as to prevent any pro-Laconian oligarch in Athens from communicating with him [Thucydides, 2.12].[42]

It is a pitiful tale from Athena's city, the "school of Hellas." When present-day political theorists hold up to us the life of the *polis* as the great period when the sense of community and common purpose educated "men" to their political responsibilities, we wonder what history of Greece they have been reading. This is fantasy, born of the desire to flee the twentieth century into an imaginary past world where people and political life were whole and not fragmented as they are today. The truth is that political life in the *polis*, at least until Athens of the fourth century, was as treacherous as any we have known. Is it even legitimate to call the concern with enemies without and traitors within "paranoid?" The "paranoid view" is too often an accurate description of reality.

The ancient world was well aware of the pervasive inclination toward treachery. Aeneas Tacticus, a mid-fourth-century writer on military affairs, advises a city under siege to reduce or cancel interest on debts because debtors are potential betrayers.[43] Philip of Macedon is reported to have asked, when told that a city with strong walls was impregnable, whether gold could not overcome the fortifications.[44] Pausanias in the second century A.D. commented that "At no time was Greece wanting in people afflicted with this itch for treason."[45]

Class warfare always had the potential of inviting foreign intervention as a political maneuver. A few examples will suffice. (1) Around the time of the battle of Marathon, 490, the *demos* on the island of Aegina conspired to betray the island to an Athenian invading force. The plot was discovered and seven hundred democrats were executed by the ruling oligarchy.[46] (2) In 418, during the Peloponnesian War, a recent alliance between Athens and Argos was disintegrating and the Argives seeking an accommodation with Sparta. "They had before had a party in the town [Argos] desirous of overthrowing the democracy. . . . Their plan was first to make a treaty with the Lacedaemonians, to be followed by an alliance, and after this to fall upon the commons."[47] (3) In 382 a Spartan army was marching north and had encamped temporarily outside Thebes. Leontiades, the leader of the oligarchic faction in Thebes, seized this opportunity and surrendered the Theban acropolis to the Spartans, whereupon the Spartan commander arrested the leader of the *demos* and the oligarchs seized power. Three hundred democrats fled to Athens to live in exile.[48] (4) Early in the second century, the Roman general Flamininus defeated the Macedonian King Philip V and vastly increased Roman domination over Greece. Flamininus discovered that the wealthy Greeks were more than willing to support the Romans, whom they conceived of as a fierce bulwark against the despotism of Philip and the revolutionary impulses of the *demos*.[49]

The example above of the three hundred exiles fleeing to Athens accentuates an important phenomenon, one with which we are familiar: large bodies of political exiles finding refuge in neighboring countries. They could be of either the oligarchic or the democratic party and represented a formidable force ever-ready to ally themselves with a foreign power in the interest of retaking their city. In Athens, during the oligarchic coup of 404, thousands of political refugees found a haven in nearby *poleis* until they were strong enough to invade Attica and retake the city for the democracy.

The phenomenon contaminated the political life of the city. It had a long history. In the drama *Agamemnon*, written by Aeschylus and performed in 458, the character Aegisthus states: "Exiles feed on empty dreams of hope. I know it. I was one."[50] When Alexander crossed over to Asia in 334, he liberated the Greek cities that had been conquered by Persia. In most of them, the Persians had installed oligarchic polities, sympathetic to Persian hegemony. Alexander restored all political exiles to their cities; thousands, almost all of them of the democratic party, returned.[51]

The existence of a large group of political exiles seemed almost correlative with an advanced city-state. When the city-state was born again in Italy in the late Middle Ages, not only did fierce internal political struggles reappear, but the corresponding formidable groups of exiles as well. "In 1261, Milan's popular commune captured 900 Milanese noblemen, exiles who had made war on the city since 1254. The populace wanted them put to the sword, but the government resisted and the mob managed to catch and kill only a few, as they were being transferred from one prison to another. During the Emperor Henry VII's attack on Florence in 1312–1313, the Florentine exiles in his train were the most rabid in urging the use of violence, as Henry's forces ravaged and looted the lands surrounding the city."[52] Dante has made us familiar with the life of the exile from the *polis*.

What we learn from the savagery of these intracity politics is of crucial importance. The republican city-state was essentially an unstable, vulnerable form of polity. Something in the nature of the *polis* released intense political violence and very seldom did a stable, democratic society emerge. Freud's notion that projecting aggression outward—warfare—allows people within a society to love each other, does not accurately describe the *polis*. Intercity and intracity violence were constant, the one having, seemingly, no significant ameliorating effect on the other; the existence of a body of exiles and/or betrayers often intensified the two forms of destructiveness.

Athens, as we have said many times, was the great exception. Its history and the history of democracy subsequent to the rise of liberalism lead us toward an all-important question: What makes a mature, stable democracy, wherein people compete intensely with each other but forswear violence, possible? No simple answer will serve, be it "capitalism" or "liberalism" or "middle class" or "Protestant" or "nonparanoid" or whatever. When we reflect on the recent history of Poland, Russia, China, Argentina, Chile, Brazil, the Philippines, Uganda—and on through the roll call of nations—no moral and theoretical question could be of greater importance.

PART III

PROBLEMATICS WITHIN ANCIENT AND MODERN DEMOCRATIC SOCIETY

15

The People Reign but Elites Rule

T wo great inequalities render democratic society imperfect, and thereby restrict the extension of justice. The concept of justice, in democratic society, is inexorably intertwined with the idea of equality: *all* free people are entitled to whatever is considered a God-given right; *all* free citizens are entitled to one—and only one—vote on the destiny of the *polis*; *all* free people have the right to sit on juries wherein all vote equally. Anything condoning inequality is an anomaly and must be either legitimized or rationalized away. Two fundamental inequalities, nevertheless, lead to the perversion of democratic ideals of equality.

First, there is money. Every democratic society yet seen has been a monied society—not capitalist because it is not accurate to place Athens or eighteenth-century America under that rubric, but monied. A monied society is one in which a few extremely wealthy people are able, because of their economic position, to exert a more-than-equal influence on the politics of the state. In such societies, which would include all democracies, there is a direct relationship between wealth and political influence, between poverty and lack of political power.

Verifying the ironic comment that some are more equal than others, wealth is the creator of degrees of political "inequality."

Second, people differ significantly in their ability, their ambition, their cunning, their capacity and willingness to dominate over others. Without engaging the perennial argument as to how much these differences result from nurturing and social circumstances and how much from genetic differences, it seems clear that by the time people are adult, significant inequalities in regard to the capacity for political leadership are manifest. These inequalities account for the split between ruling and reigning that exists in even the most democratic of societies.

These two fundamental inequalities, combining with the nature of organizations and their inevitable drive toward efficiency of operation, lead to the creation of a political elite that rules even where the *demos* retains sovereignty. All organizations have a purpose, whether a trade union, a political party, an army, a church, or a state. Their activity is largely adversarial: union against owners, party against party, army against army, *polis* against *polis*. The outcome of these contests depends to a large extent on the capability of those making the strategic decisions. It is in the interest of an association—and, theoretically, for each of its members—to have tactical decisions made by the most competent members. This results in the creation of leadership; these leaders become organized into an elite and the elites more and more dominate over their constituents. "It is organization," Robert Michels writes, "which gives birth to the dominion of the elected over the electors, of the mandatories over the mandators, of the delegates over the delegators. Who says organization, says oligarchy."[1]

Michels undertook a study of trade unions and radical political parties—associations committed, at least in theory, to an increasing egalitarian enterprise—to demonstrate that even these most democratic organizations are undemocratically controlled by elites. "Thus the appearance of oligarchical phenomena in the very bosom of the revolutionary parties is a conclusive proof of the existence of imminent oligarchic tendencies in every kind of human organization which strives for the attainment of definite ends."[2] Michels points out that in the very beginning of the English trade-union movement, delegates to conventions were appointed in rotation or chosen by lot. With the growth of complexity within the organization, a certain degree of ability was required and this radical democratic approach was abandoned.[3]

Whenever a group of people who have been denied political and/or economic power begins the struggle to obtain that influence, a certain revolutionary fervor fuels the process. If the effort is successful, like the trade-union activity of the last two centuries or the recent movement by black people in America, almost all the members benefit to some degree, but the final result is the creation of a ruling elite, which not only openly fights the adversaries of the group, but also begins to assert a bureaucratic hegemony. The lack of democracy *within* the American trade-union movement, remarked by many, is an appalling and portentous phenomenon.

Even the most democratic state exhibits these symptoms. The rise of the "imperial Presidency" in the United States, as a consequence of the cold war, was merely an exaggeration of the tendency in every society to create an elite of rulers. Congress may struggle with the President to participate in foreign-policy decisions, but Congress has no more intention of sharing that power, if obtained, with the *demos* than the President has of sharing it with Congress. Elites of money, of birth, of power, of brains, of talent make the decisions and do the ruling. Elites are often divided amongst themselves and this gives the *demos* the opportunity to assert its sovereignty by choosing between elites and empowering one over the other. Since the demise of the direct democracy of the Athenian Assembly there has been no *demos* that has both reigned and ruled. The most stable democratic society is an open one wherein there is considerable social mobility, so that capable and ambitious people without the advantages of birth or money can attend an ivy-league school and rise into the elite. This ensures that they will not become revolutionaries to assuage their frustrated ambition, and raises the quality of leadership by securing the constant presence of fresh talent.

Ruling and reigning, however, are entirely different activities. Critics of democracy, like Michels, think they have finished once they have demonstrated the "oligarchic" tendencies in all societies, even the most democratic. To assert that the forms of rulership are essentially the same in all societies is not equivalent to saying that the status of sovereignty is identical in all societies. Democracy may share with oligarchy, aristocracy, monarchy, and tyranny the fact that elites are doing the ruling, but sovereignty in each of these societies differs profoundly.

"Democracy," Daniel Bell writes, "is a socio-political system in which legitimacy lies in the consent of the governed."[4] This is a reflection of Aristotle's concept of a citizen as a person capable of both ruling and being ruled, which implies that a citizen, when out of power, consents to being ruled. The concept of sovereignty includes the notion of both power and legitimacy. In monarchy, for instance, the kingship legitimizes the society, while the king exerts the final political power, modified by the realities of any complex society. In a democracy, the *demos* legitimizes the society and at least in theory holds the ultimate power. The *demos*, in a word, is sovereign. The discrepancies between the sovereignty of the *demos* and the realities of political power become a fundamental problematic in the theory of democratic society. The nature of organizations, the necessity of representative government, and the power of elites, all raise the question of how powerful, in reality, is the sovereign *demos*.

In the real world of political power elites, who do the ruling, often threaten the sovereignty of the people, who should be reigning, to the point where it becomes a real question of who is indeed sovereign. Can an ordinary member of an autocratic trade union really exercise sovereignty, even though there are national conventions and "chosen" delegates? The most radical critics of "bourgeois" democracy argue that the sovereignty of the *demos* is a fantasy, that money rules the bourgeois state and so-called democracy is a fiction imposed on a gullible people. It would be wrong if, in rejecting this radical critique of democracy as untrue, we fail to see the definite truth it contains. The "inevitable" existence of elites is a fundamental threat to the sovereignty of the *demos* in all democratic societies. Keeping the power of elites within reasonable bounds is essential if democracy is to survive.

It is not surprising to discover that this issue was perceived in ancient society and its importance clearly understood. In Plutarch, the differentiation between reigning and ruling is pronounced an absurdity by the near-mythical "Scythian" Anacharsis. He presumably stayed with Solon for a time and visiting the Assembly, "expressed his wonder at the fact that in Greece wise men spoke and fools decided."[5] Aristotle faced the question directly. " 'What body of *persons* should be sovereign?' ... 'What are the *matters* over which freemen, or the general body of citizens—men of the sort who neither have wealth nor can make any claim on the ground of goodness—should properly exercise sovereignty?' " An opponent of a radical or full democracy, Aristotle fears, not the excessive power of the elite, but the opposite: the immoderate power of the *demos*, the common citizen. Such *unter-menschen* should have "*some* share in the enjoyment of power" to keep them from revolt and civil strife. Solon, he argues, worked out the proper compromise, ensuring that the best people would rule society but the people would have a semblance of sovereignty. "The alternative [to civil strife] is to let them share in the deliberative and judicial functions; and thus we find Solon, and some other legislators, giving the people the two general functions of electing magistrates to office and of calling them to account at the end of their tenure of office, but not the right of holding office themselves in their individual capacity."[6] Advocates of moderate democracy would limit the sovereignty of the people, in the interest of having the best rulers possible.

In the stable, radical democracy of fourth-century Athens, there was a definite feeling that the potential conflict between ruling and reigning had been overcome, that Athens enjoyed the best of both worlds: able leaders and a sovereign people. "How can we find a more secure and just democracy than this," wrote Isocrates around 355, "which places the ablest in charge of affairs and gives the demos authority [*kurion*] over them?"[7] In his speech *Against Meidias*, one of the wealthiest men in Athens, Demosthenes, presents an elaborate elucidation of Madison's later view that faction, when it represents a minority interest, can be overcome by the republican principle, that is, majority rule. "All this [evidence for Meidias' wealth and power] is terrifying to each of the rest of you depending on the extent of your own individual fortunes. This is why you band together . . . since while individually you are weaker [than the rich] in terms of supporters or wealth or anything else, assembled together you are more powerful than any one of them and able to put a halt to their hubris [arrogance of power]."[8]

Josiah Ober[9] argues that the remarkable consummation of democratic effort in Athens was in part due to the direct nature of the democracy. Six to eight thousand people could attend an Assembly meeting—the people not only reigned but ruled. Leadership, which certainly existed to a significant degree, was held strictly accountable to the *demos* in a manner almost impossible for us to imagine in our huge, representative democracy. Ober's complex insight asserts that the large, direct Assembly might have been a necessary, but hardly a sufficient, cause of direct rule by the *demos*. An ideology that the *demos* must keep the reins of power prevailed in Athens; the *demos*, Ober insists, managed to control political discourse, which certified the right of the people to rule as well as to reign. Any leader who ignored, or tried to circumvent, this imperative was rendered politically impotent.

An ideological ideal may be observed more in the breach than the fulfillment. A comparison with Rome demonstrates how unique were Athenian ideology and achievement. The Roman constitution provided for popular assemblies, where "the people" were, in theory, sovereign. In his famous discussion of the "mixed" nature of the Roman constitution, Polybius points to these bodies as representative of the "democratic" element. In actuality, however, during the third and second centuries B.C. "the people" neither ruled nor reigned. "At elections the assemblies continued to elect to high office hardly any but representatives of the noble families . . . there was no important legislation during the period which had not first been shaped by senatorial discussion. . . . the people of Rome, though considering themselves sovereign, did not during this period assert their right to control taxation or to initiate financial legislation."[10] The ideology of a sovereign Roman people was a fiction that legitimized aristocratic rule and held society together.

Similarly, but with some differences, modern democratic societies preserve the fiction that the people rule as well as reign, though the cynical cliché that you can't sue City Hall would indicate the truth is known. When a group of previously impotent citizens—Irish, Italian, and Jewish first-generation politicians, for instance—becomes determined to participate in both reigning and ruling, the stability of the democratic order is temporarily disrupted until political power is granted the previously disenfranchised. The power to rule, however, ends up in the hands of new elites who have been created by these movements. The local "ward boss" becomes a wide-spread phenomenon. The *demos*, as far as ruling is concerned, remains almost as impotent as before.

Ruling and reigning, always matters of degree, are subject to political change. Ober's thesis is that, *to a large degree*, the people retained political power in Athens. He cannot find an equivalent situation in the historical record even after the rise of liberal democracy. If Athens was such a democracy, it was unique not only for its time, but maybe for all time. The local, direct democracy of the town meeting provides an exception where it exists, but in no case does it represent a whole society. In a modern democracy, social movements like those to preserve the environment or to end the war in Vietnam show a sovereign *demos* intent on increasing its share in ruling.

Since there is always tension between the manifestations of ruling and reigning, it is the task of the value system—a direct reflection of the spirit of society—to reconcile the conflict. In the stable, democratic society of fourth-century Athens, four fundamental value positions certified the existing political order. (1) Both *oligoi* and *demos* renounced violence as a political tactic. (2) The elites of money or political power renounced the idea of taking away the sovereignty of the people. (3) The *demos* did not question the legitimacy of great discrepancies of wealth, though the wealthy were required to contribute most heavily to the financial needs of civic life. (4) The *demos* was jealous of its power to both reign and rule and held political leaders to a strict accountability. The *demos* refused, unlike many other "peoples," to become passive and retreat into a childlike inactivity. We cannot be sure, however, *to what degree* it succeeded in keeping elites from ruling.

Modern democratic societies share with Athens the first three of these value concepts. The difference lies in the degree of ruling. Regardless of who rules, the *demos* must remain supreme. The governed must give its consent to the political order or the name "democracy" no longer applies.

In both ancient and modern times, there are those who argue that democracy is impossible, that the sovereignty of the people remains a fiction. The people *think* the *demos* reigns, but in actuality elites both rule and reign; severe Marxist critics argue that no real democracy is possible in a capitalist society. For such gainsayers, "democracy" is merely a name that disguises the true relationships in society. The Platonic dialogue of *Menexenus* (the authorship of which has been disputed) declares: "For in the main the same constitution then as now, an aristocracy, under which we now live and have always lived since then. A man may call it democracy, and another what he will. *But in truth it is an aristocracy with the approval of the majority.* We have always had kings: sometimes they were hereditary, sometimes elective."[11] Thucydides ascribed to Pericles and his fifteen-year rule of Athens the attributes of monarchy: "In short, what was nominally a democracy became in his hands government by the first citizen."[12]

Modern theorists have also emphasized this inevitable tension between ruling and reigning. In defining the relationship between these two modes of political action, we explicate the true nature of democracy. One crucial question is how the leadership elite controls its *demos*, how much it bends to, or manipulates, or goes around, or ignores the sovereignty of the people. Michels writes: "One of the most noted leaders of German socialism said in a critical period of tension between leaders and masses, that he must follow the will of the masses in order to guide them."[13] Compromise on some issues of sovereignty is necessary in order to maintain rulership. Max Weber believed that the sovereignty of the people ultimately prevailed, but that in the interim leaders assumed an autocratic stance. "In a democracy the people choose a leader in whom they trust. Then the chosen leader says, 'Now shut up and obey me.' People and party are no longer free to interfere with him. . . . Afterwards the people can sit in judgement. If the leader has made mistakes—to the gallows with him."[14] Significant variations on this scenario abound: the chosen leader stays in constant contact with the people, regularly seeking their advice; the leader is so successful in his autocratic mode that the *demos* loses the power to depose him. Each variation—and there are many—produces a different kind of social group, a different kind of society.

An interesting compromise resulting from the conflict between rulers and masses arises when the democratic leader takes the stance that he is both of the people and yet beyond the people, both attributes certifying his entitlement to rule. "The democratic leader," Leo Lowenthal writes, "usually tries to present himself as both similar to and different from his followers: similar in that he has common interests with them; different in that he has special talents for representing those interest."[15] Lowenthal demonstrates that the proto-fascist demagogue in America used this technique, to an exaggerated degree, to win the people over to his authoritarian leadership. Ober makes a similar observation about democratic leaders in fourth-century Athens: "The Athenian system for controlling elite politicians worked precisely because it was based on a series of contradictions. The orator had to be simultaneously of the elite and of the mass, and he was expected to prove his membership in both on a regular basis."[16]

An inevitable problematic arises from the psychology of power. All leaders, because they are rulers, tend to assume the attributes and privileges of authority, one significant privilege being the opportunity to domineer over one's "subjects." It is the rare political leader who forswears the occasion to become a ruler. The psychology of power also dictates that certain kinds of people seek leadership in the first place, usually those who cannot distinguish between leading and ruling. Revolutionary, supposedly radically egalitarian, parties end up being led by people who don't really understand equality. "Max Weber," Michels writes, "advised the German princes, if they wished to appease their terrors of socialism, to spend a day on the platform at a socialist congress, so that they might convince themselves that in the whole crowd of assembled revolutionists 'the dominant type of expression was that of the petty bourgeois, of the self-satisfied innkeeper.' "[17]

Lenin and Stalin, however, were of a different order of socialist ruler than the German variety derided by Weber. If an elite of rulers is inevitable in a revolutionary organization, social movement, or stable democratic society, then the crucial question becomes: what kinds of leaders? The *quality* of the elites need not be the same. One may compare, for instance, the political elite at the time of Madison-Adams-Jefferson with that in the years of Ulysses S. Grant's Presidency. Just as the existence of a monarchy does not tell us what kind of king rules, so the existence of a democracy cannot tell us what kind of political elite is in charge. It is a legitimate argument, for instance, whether the United States during the cold war suffered more from the erection of the Imperial Presidency or from the profoundly "un-royal" nature of those who filled that office. It is remarkable that among the six presidents elected between Truman and Bush, we have had one general, two paranoids, and a cowboy. This almost incredibly low level of psychological and intellectual capacity may present a greater threat to democratic society than the fact that a political elite rules the land.

Perceiving that the health and strength of a society may depend directly on the quality of its political elite, some thinkers and reformers have addressed themselves to the problem of creating the correct institutional framework for the education of this elite. Eric Havelock, who writes of the "liberal temper" in Greek society, considers one of the greatest achievements of Plato and Aristotle to be the insight that university education was vital to the health of a "liberal society." Ironically, these two thinkers, who were opposed to democracy, perceived the importance of creating an institution that would make democratic society possible, that would train a responsible political elite to rule where the people reigned. Of Plato and Aristotle, Havelock writes:

Their genius had made a social discovery of immense importance, a discovery the implications of which preoccupied them to the exclusion of almost all other interests. This was nothing less than the perception that a system of university education had now become socially indispensable for the progress of Western culture. For this they set themselves to devise the institutional forms, the curriculum, the techniques of instruction, and the necessary intellectual disciplines. As Rousseau rightly saw, the *Republic* is the greatest single treatise on education ever written. They made the mistake . . . of identifying the academic apparatus with the state apparatus. . . . They can be forgiven if, in their devotion to such a revolutionary conception, they failed to perceive the precise relationship which history would assign to such an institution in the society which it came into being to serve. . . . if modern democracies function with administrative efficiency and judicial objectivity, it is because they have adopted those instruments and techniques of training in the skills and service of government which were first articulated by the two masters of Greek idealist tradition.[18]

Whether Havelock is correct in the strength of the influence he attributes to Plato and Aristotle, there is no question that the importance of university training for political elites in a democratic society cannot be exaggerated. The relationship of university education to rule by elites is the same as the relationship of public education to the reign of the people: indispensable.

Even when the people reign, however, they may use their sovereignty to establish what can only be described as a perversion of democracy: They may abdicate their sovereign power and deposit it in the keeping of a charismatic ruler. Before the rise of fascism in the twentieth century, this tragic maneuver was referred to as "Bonapartism," since Napoleon III was the first king to be chosen by full democratic plebescite. "The Bonapartist interpretation of popular sovereignty was a personal dictatorship conferred by the people in accordance with constitutional rules."[19] Hohenlohe, German ambassador to France in 1874, was informed that the French were both *démocrate* and *authoritaire*, that the empire had the best form of government, satisfying both these contradictory impulses. Napoleon III remarked that his rule was "based on democracy, since all its powers were conferred by the people, whilst in organization it was hierarchical, since such an organization was essential to stimulate the capacities slumbering in the various degrees of society."[20]

The severest critics of democracy insist that these Bonapartist compromises are inevitable, that there is an iron law of oligarchy that rule by elites ultimately makes the sovereignty of the *demos* into a paltry thing. Writing before twentieth-century fascism transformed Bonapartism into a much more sinister and catastrophic institution, Robert Michels comments: "In practice . . . the election of the leaders, and above all their re-election, is effected by such methods and under the influence of suggestions and other methods of coercion so powerful that the freedom of choice of the masses is considerably impaired. In the history of party life it is undeniable that the democratic system is reduced, in ultimate analysis, to the right of the masses, at stated intervals, to choose masters to whom in the interim they owe unconditional obedience."[21] The final perversion of democracy—the final demise of democratic sovereignty—occurs when there is no selection at stated intervals, when there is a permanent abandonment by the *demos* of its right to reign. Hitler came to power, not in an illegal *putsch*, but in a legally conducted democratic election. Everything of importance in the world is a matter of degree: how much iron there is in the "iron law of oligarchy" depends, ultimately, on *what kind of demos* holds sovereignty.

The reign of the *demos* in a mature, sophisticated democracy need not be so passive as Michels assumes. The mass movement to end the war in Vietnam, the enormous public pressure on both sides of the abortion issue, the unforeseen power of the environmental movement all demonstrate that those who reign have more power to make rulers responsive than "oligarchic" theory would allow. I have postulated that the first phase of democratic society can be called the-great-refusal-to-be-a-victim. The degree to which the *demos* is active or passive in its own interests is an important indicator of the kind of democratic society that is possible. The activity or passivity of the people cannot be explained by any iron law. Something deep within the value system of society made possible the almost incredible response of Athens in the time of Solon and made a permanent reality of the democracy of Cleisthenes. If the people who reign choose not to rule, or to rule to a minimal degree, they have so chosen. If they have been coerced into making that decision, it is not by a "law" of oligarchy, but by the great human inclination to passivity and fear of activity. The fundamental question remains: to what degree is the *demos* ready to take responsibility for its own life?

The Power of Wealth Perverts the Democratic Ideal

The democratic ideal of equality makes significant discrepancies in wealth morally suspect and ambiguous. The question of legitimacy inevitably arises. "It is foolish to make laws on a basis of equality for all," writes Diodorus, describing an idealized Indian society, "but to make the distribution of property unequal."[22] Since no democratic society has ever entertained any real intention of doing away with these inequities, the moral contradiction continues, sometimes used as an impetus to political and economic reform, sometimes, as today, with no visible effect on society; at all times available to poets, moralists, and humorists for reference and comment. Not surprisingly, ancient Greek society was aware of the contradiction between the ideals of the "citizen" and the existence of the very rich. " 'Wealth makes the man'; and no poor man is noble or held in honor,"[23] Alcaeus wrote, close to the time of Solon.

The rise of the dream of communism seems an inevitable result of this contradiction. Someday, the dream promises, private property will disappear and all economic inequalities cease. Plato wrestled manfully with this vision. Before him, the communist ideal had become the concern of the comic poets. In *Ecclesiazusae*, Aristophanes' heroine passionately preaches:

> *Praxagora*. Let none contradict nor interrupt me until I have explained my plan. I want all to have a share of everything and all property to be in common; there will no longer be either rich or poor; no longer shall we see one man harvesting vast tracts of land, while another has not ground enough to be buried in, nor one man surround himself with a whole army of slaves, while another has not a single attendant; I intend that there shall be one and the same condition of life for all.[24]

It is impossible for large differences in wealth not to result in discrepancies in political power. Economic potency cannot be confined to the economic sphere and no democratic society has ever made a serious attempt to keep the power of riches insulated from political might. The rich always have more to say about the life of the *polis* than the poor.

Athens was no exception. Despite its direct democracy, despite the fact that the Athenian *demos* came as close as any people to ruling as well as reigning, the political power of wealth was as manifest in Athenian society as in our own. Attendance at the Athenian Assembly was open to all, but membership in the Council was restricted to five hundred citizens each year. A complicated procedure for selecting Council members, including a step involving a lottery, has convinced some historians that members of the Council were chosen at random. From a more critical look at the data recent historians have concluded that wealthy people were overrepresented in Council membership. "Active membership in the boule [the council]," writes P. J. Rhodes, "must have involved some financial sacrifice for most men, and it is likely enough that many poorer citizens will have been reluctant to abandon their normal occupation for a year."[25] Simon Hornblower asserts that, not only were those of the highest social class disproportionately present in the Council, but evidence also indicates that in certain crucial years, those with particular political interests could make sure they obtained Council membership.[26] The lottery step did not neutralize those with money or political influence.*

Mogens Hansen has estimated that the richest people in Athens, those who were responsible for the payment for liturgies, represented about 4 percent of the population, 1,200 citizens out of 30,000. Our data indicate that in the period from 355 to 322, of the eighty-two citizens known to have proposed decrees in the Assembly, twenty-three (or 28 percent) were members of the liturgical class.[27] In *every* monied society, money talks.

Beyond the normal legal conditions that allowed more political power to the rich, there were extralegal and even illegal pressures the wealthy could exert against the poor. On the local level of the deme, "when we catch a scent of it . . . the issue is the understandable reluctance of individuals voluntarily to testify in court against a member of a powerful local family."[28] The pressure was often not subtle at all. "Litigants did not rely solely upon this reluctance to antagonize men of wealth and power, but approached possible witnesses, either in person or through the agency of associates and friends, with definite threats. Thus Theocrines and his comrades are said to have visited the witnesses of his opponent, Epichares, and prevailed upon them by threats and persuasion not to testify."[29]

Even without the impediment to equal-justice-for-all presented by

---

*Josiah Ober (personal communication) seriously disputes that the rich were overrepresented on the Council. We cannot take it as proven.

the high cost of good legal assistance, the wealthy in Athens exercised
an advantage in the courts not available to every citizen. Allowing for
the usual exaggeration of court orations, Demosthenes' speech *Against
Meidias* is nevertheless enlightening:

> For, if I may add a word on this subject also, where the rich are con-
> cerned, Athenians, the rest of us have no share in our just and equal
> rights. Indeed we have not. The rich can choose their own time for
> facing a jury, and their crimes are stale and cold when they are dished
> up before you, but if any of the rest of us is in trouble, he is brought
> into court while all is fresh. The rich have witnesses and counsel in
> readiness, all primed against us; but, as you see, my witnesses are some
> of them unwilling to bear testimony to the truth.[30]

Anyone who has tried to sue a person with superior riches can testify
to the truth of Demosthenes' complaint. Equality before the law becomes an ambiguous notion when inequalities of wealth are factored
into the equation.

In addition to rights, honor is one of the great "goods" of democratic society. The poor were also poor in honor, since wealth, if it
could not buy happiness, could certainly buy public esteem. The ancient Greeks, as we have seen, were greatly concerned with honor, an
attribute the poor man had to forgo. Sholom Aleichem's character Tevye
opines that although being poor is no disgrace, it's no great honor
either. "Here we see," writes David Whitehead about Athens, "the
men and families which, for all the real extent of democracy and egal-
itarianism in its formal organization, in fact dominated deme society.
They . . . besides taking their turn as demarch and supplying the bulk
of proposers of decrees, were the natural choice of their fellow demes-
men when the need arose for particular individuals to spend their
time—and, as often as not, their money—on the community's behalf."[31] If thou wouldst have honor, first get thee riches. Or, as Hobbes
put it: "Covetousness of great Riches, and the ambition of great Hon-
ours, are Honourable; as signes of power to obtain them. . . . Riches
are Honourable; for they are Power."[32]

Hobbes's introduction of a concern for power in his discussion of
riches and honor accentuates a crucial problematic for democratic society: great wealth opens wide the possibilities for tyranny of the rich

over the poor and for the opposite, but rarely seen, side of the coin, a class revolt of the disadvantaged against the wealthy. The rich, because of their wealth and the power it brings, have the capacity to establish oligarchy. The poor, because of the potency of their numbers, have the capacity to overthrow a monied society. When people take their political stance solely on the basis of narrowly understood economic interests, class struggle is born.

For Plato and Aristotle, both oligarchy and class revolt were civic catastrophes. Both thinkers feared that great discrepancies of wealth made these calamities probable, and both offered prescriptions to ameliorate the devastation plutocracy brought to society. Aristotle rejects the communal ownership of property as untenable, at variance with human nature. The system of private ownership presenting great difficulties, however, he offers an equally utopian solution: a return to a more primitive state of society wherein kinship-friendship forms would soften the inflexible boundaries of private ownership. "The present system [of private property] would be far preferable, if it were adorned by customs [in the social sphere] and by enactment of proper laws [in the political]. It would possess the advantages of both systems, and would combine the merits of a system of community of property with those of the system of private property. . . . for property *ought* to be generally and in the main private, but common in one respect [that is, in use]. When everyone has his own separate sphere of interest, there will not be the same ground for quarrels. . . . And on such a scheme, too, moral goodness [and not, as in Plato's scheme, legal compulsion] will ensure that the property of each is made to serve the use of all, in spirit of the proverb which says 'Friends' goods are goods in common'. Even now there are some states in which the outlines of such a scheme are so far apparent, as to suggest that it is not impossible. . . . In these states each citizen has his own property; but when it comes to the use of this property, each makes a part of it available to his friends, and each devotes still another part to the common enjoyment of all fellow-citizens. In Sparta, for example, men use one another's slaves, and one another's horses and dogs, as if they were their own. . . . [T]he better system is that under which property is privately owned but is put to common use; and the function proper to the legislator is to make men so disposed that they will treat property in this way."[33]

One cannot blame Aristotle for failing to solve a problem that no human society has yet resolved. Private property—and the inevitable disparities of wealth—are a continuing problematic for the health of the *polis*. Nothing indicates that the abandonment of private property is a solution to the problem, but to deny that private property and disparities of riches attenuate the vitality of the commonwealth is to remain naive about the nature of society.

Even Plato, criticized as antidemocratic and conservative and at his most extreme, reactionary and proto-totalitarian, repeats again and again that riches subvert virtue. "Isn't it by now plain," says Socrates in the *Republic*, "that it's not possible to honor wealth in a city and at the same time adequately to maintain moderation among the citizens, but one or the other is necessarily neglected."[34] In the *Laws* Plato says: "But it is impossible for someone to be both unusually good and unusually rich."[35]

The *Laws* as a prescription for society is a deliberate attempt to avoid the "utopianism" of the *Republic*. On the question of wealth and property, Plato begins by describing an ideal condition, obviously unobtainable by human beings: "if women are common, and children are common, and every sort of property is common; if every device has been employed to exclude all of what is called the 'private' from all aspects of life," such a society will constitute "the extreme as regards virtue." Unfortunately, "Such a society is inhabited, presumably, by gods or children of gods . . . and they dwell in gladness, leading such a life."[36]

Though the highest life is not attainable for mortals, reform of present-day society is possible, and the virtuous nature of the *polis* can be substantially improved if we abolish the extreme disparities of wealth that threaten the stability of the commonwealth: "If . . . the city must avoid the greatest illness, which has been more correctly termed 'civil war' than 'faction,' then neither harsh poverty nor wealth should exist among any of the citizens. For both these conditions breed both civil war and faction."[37]

The solution lies in not allowing either great wealth or poverty. Poverty is prevented by giving each citizen a basic allotment of land from which he can never be severed. Great riches are prevented by limiting the total wealth of any citizen to four times the value of the basic allotment. Anything above this would be subject to confiscation.[38] This scheme allows for competitive and acquisitive impulses—some would attempt to accumulate the fourfold capital—without seriously disrupting the ideal of equality.

It is fascinating that when some forward-looking twentieth-century reformers attempted to deal with the gross absurdities of capitalist society, they rediscovered Plato's scheme of moderate inequalities of wealth and economic reward. Some cooperative enterprises in Catalonia, Spain, for instance, wishing to maintain incentive, individual expression, and a sense of equality, have established that no worker can earn more than a certain number of times the wages of the lowest paid laborer.[39] Whether this is a "utopian" prescription, it is impossible to know at this time. The graduated income tax and the welfare state have taken us in the direction of a more virtuous *polis*, but it seems remarkable, almost incredible, that the stretch limousine and people sleeping in the streets have become two of the most powerful images of our current society.

When liberalism introduced the second stage of democratic society in the seventeenth and eighteenth centuries, the marriage of capitalism and liberal democracy produced some strange progeny. In the ancient world even the most conservative of thinkers like Plato and Aristotle were seriously bothered by the extremes of wealth and poverty, but the main concern of later liberal thinkers was whether the poor were entitled to vote.[40] The enthronement of individualism buried the deep concern for the commonwealth and the common health of the *polis* that had been second nature to any thinking person in the ancient democratic world. The loss of this deep commitment to community has caused some modern thinkers to exaggerate the virtue of the *polis*, ignoring its conflicts and profound contradictions. If the second stage of democracy—liberal, bourgeois, capitalist—is to be transformed into something more just, it will have to learn what was obvious to those who lived in the *polis*: great wealth is a problematic for democratic society—great poverty is a catastrophe.

16

The Boundaries of Justice and the Tribal Bond

A Justice Expires at the Frontier of the Polis

Although he devoted his whole life to thinking and writing about justice, and urging us toward its enactment, Plato never solved the problem of its boundaries. Of all the people in the world, how many are to be treated justly? Not everyone—not barbarians and slaves, for example. Where, then, is it just to set the frontier of justice?

In the first book of the *Republic*, devoted to explicating the meaning of justice, Plato declares that no society, no small group—even one dedicated to unjust activity—can exist without just action within the group. "Do you believe," Socrates asks his sounding board Thrasymachus, "that either a city, or an army, or pirates, or robbers, or any other tribe which has some common unjust enterprise would be able to accomplish anything, if its members acted unjustly to one another?" "Surely not." . . . "For surely, Thrasymachus, it's injustice that produces factions, hatreds, quarrels among themselves, and justice that produces unanimity and friendship."[1]

Justice is a primary mode of social cohesion; it holds all groups, including large societies, together. So important is this idea to his argument, that Socrates repeats and elaborates it directly: "For we don't

290

speak the complete truth about those men who we say vigorously accomplished some common object with one another although they were
unjust; they could never have restrained themselves with one another
if they were completely unjust, but it is plain that there was a certain
justice in them at least not to do injustice to one another at the same
time that they were seeking to do it to others; and as a result of this
they accomplished what they accomplished, and they pursued unjust
deeds when they were only half bad from injustice, since the wholly
bad and perfectly unjust are also perfectly unable to accomplish anything."[2]

At once, we are in the middle of a dilemma. If justice, by definition,
is inherent in *every* group or *polis*, on what basis do we describe some
groups (robbers, pirates) as unjust? By the manner in which they treat
other groups or *poleis*? By the manner in which they treat those within
the group, but excluded from the boundary of justice? Describing an
action as just or unjust becomes intricately involved with where the
boundary of justice is drawn, who is within and who without. Reich-
marshal Heinrich Himmler understood perfectly Plato's notion that
even robbers and pirates require justice. He set his boundaries as narrow as possible: "We must be honest, decent, loyal and comradely to
members of our own blood and nobody else."[3]

For political thinkers and political actors in the ancient Greek world,
the critical line of differentiation was the boundary of the *polis*. Almost
all discussion on the question of justice revolves around the problem
of where to draw the line *within* the *polis*, that is, who is to be excluded
from participation in the political life of the city. Justice between *poleis*
is of no concern, the assumption being that it is impossible. Wise and
unwise action, yes, but justice nowhere enters the discussion of foreign
relations. Socrates, in Xenophon's recollections, drew this distinction.
We have no way of knowing how accurately it records Socrates' thinking, but it perfectly reflects the Greek mind. "Lying occurs among men,
does it not?" Socrates begins. "Yes it does," "Under which heading,
then, are we to put that?" "Under the heading of injustice, clearly."
And so on through deceit and doing mischief and selling into slavery.
"Then we shall assign none of these things to justice, Euthydemus?"
"No, it would be monstrous to do so."

Euthydemus has been thinking only of actions *within* the *polis*, but
Socrates has a broader view. "Now suppose a man who has been

elected general enslaves an unjust and hostile city, shall we say that he acts unjustly?" "Oh no!" And on again through deceiving enemies when at war, and stealing and plundering their goods. Quickly realizing where he has arrived, Euthydemus explains his previous confusion. "But at first I assumed that your questions had reference only to friends." "Then I propose to revise our classification," Socrates goes on, and now pronounces the Greek view which had held dominion since the time of Homer, a view that drew the ordinary citizen much closer to the pirate than he would have liked to think: "It is just to do such to enemies, but it is unjust to do them to friends, towards whom one's conduct should be scrupulously honest."[4]

This time-honored, simple solution did not end the moral problems, however. The question remained: within the *polis*, who was a friend and who an enemy? Women, slaves, and foreign-born noncitizens did not exist as political persons and therefore did not enter this question. Rich citizens and poor citizens, however, did inhabit the *polis*. Were they to treat each other as friends or enemies? If as friends, then justice would rule the state; if as enemies, then tyranny or political violence would prevail. Plato, believing that justice should be sovereign within the *polis*, perceived that the war between the rich and poor was the main obstacle to that end. To repeat, he wrote: "For indeed any state, however small, is in fact divided into two, one the state of the poor, the other of the rich. These are at war with one another."[5] Unlike the inevitable war of one *polis* against another, intracity warfare was intolerable to Plato and must be overcome: unlike foreign warfare, it was a violation of justice. The fundamental *telos* of Plato's philosophy was the elimination of strife within the state and the establishment of a just society, the restoration of the fractured *polis* to a single polity.

He faced directly the problem of the boundary of justice in the opening pages of his monumental *Laws*. Kleinias, the Cretan, is praising the ancient lawgiver of Crete and is challenged by the Athenian Stranger, Plato's spokesman: "The definition you seem to me to have given for a well-governed city is that it must be ordered in such a way as to defeat the other cities in war. . . . Well, is it the case that this definition is correct for cities, in relation to cities, but that another would be correct for a neighborhood, in relation to another neighborhood?" The Cretan, however, is a moral absolutist and refuses to draw the boundary of justice anywhere. As cities are at war with all cities, so all neighborhoods are at war; even households, in relation to other households, are agonistic. Kleinias carries the argument to its ultimate absurdity, insisting that as "all are enemies of all in public . . . in private each is an enemy of himself."[6] Thus there is no justice, only interests and warfare, a perfect Hobbesian before his time. Rejecting this view, the Athenian Stranger will spend the rest of the book constructing a society, not of universal justice, but of justice *within* the city-state. The *polis* remains the boundary of the universal.

Beyond the generally accepted notion that justice expired at the border of the *polis*, there was a tentative project on the part of some advanced thinkers to establish the view that all Greeks should treat all other Greeks as friends. This was never seriously considered except under the notion of Greeks as a unit opposed to barbarians, that is, those not speaking the Greek language. The most succinct statement of this occurs in Book V of Plato's *Republic*. Socrates first asserts that since we have two different names, war and faction, for two different forms of strife, one must refer to what is alien and one to what is one's own: "Now the name faction is applied to hatred of one's own [that is, those who should be treated with justice], war to the hatred of the alien." So far, the age-old enemy–friend dichotomy, but Socrates immediately takes a leap beyond the *polis*. "I assert the Greek stock is with respect to itself its own and akin, with respect to the barbaric, foreign and alien." Warfare between Greeks and barbarians is no violation of justice. Injustice occurs only when those who should be friends war with each other; therefore, "when Greeks do any such thing to Greeks, we'll say that they are by nature friends, but in this case Greece is sick and factious, and their kind of hatred must be called faction."[7] This extension of the boundary of justice beyond the *polis*, seemingly based on reason, is really dependent on what the philosopher arbitrarily considers "by nature" and what not. When justice is on the road to universality, this occurs "by nature." When the definition of friend is a narrow one, that, too, is "nature's" work. All of us, including the great philosophers, draw the boundary of justice where we will and legitimate its frontier by a capricious appeal to "nature."

Plato's intrinsic concern for the problem of the limits of justice was forcefully adumbrated in the work of Thucydides, as the historian Jacqueline de Romilly has pointed out.[8] The inherent contradiction of placing a confine on justice is not consciously addressed but a careful reading of the text reveals a deep, ironic split in Thucydides' mind about how human beings should treat one another.

Thucydides' reputation as a cold-hearted, "scientific" historian, devoted to the exigencies of *realpolitik*, and totally unsentimental about the role of morality or justice in human affairs, stems primarily from his treatment of certain crucial incidents during the Peloponnesian War, the surrender of Plataea and the genocide of Melos, for instance. The city of Plataea, in Boeotia, was an ally of Athens during the war, fighting both its neighbor Thebes and the Spartans. In the fifth year of the war, the city was invested by its enemies and finally surrendered at discretion. The Plataeans pleaded for their lives, trying to justify their alliance with Athens. The Thebans insisted on "justice" and vengeance: "Vindicate, therefore, Lacedaemonians, the Hellenic law which they have broken; and to us, the victims of its violation, grant the reward merited by our zeal." They would have them all dead. "The Lacedaemonian judges . . . having, as they considered, suffered evil at the hands of the Plataeans, they brought them in again one by one and asked each of them the same question, that is to say, whether they had done the Lacedaemonians and allies any service in the war; and upon their saying that they had not, took them out and slew them all without exception. The number of Plataeans thus massacred was not less than two hundred, with twenty-five Athenians who had shared in the siege. The women were taken as slaves." A year later the city was razed to the ground and an inn and a chapel to Hera erected over the barren foundations. Thucydides explains the action: "The adverse attitude of the Lacedaemonians in the whole Plataean affair was mainly adopted to please the Thebans, who were thought to be useful in the war at that moment raging. Such was the end of Plataea, in the ninety-third year after she became the ally of Athens."[9]

Since this is the first description of genocide in the *History* (the Mitylenean genocide was aborted, as we saw), we long for the historian to say something—anything—to help us understand this phenomenon. Thucydides had not previously been averse to psychological analysis, discussing fear, the lust for power, vanity, ambition, the desire to rule rather than be ruled. In this case of slaughter, an act of warfare, of hatred between *polis* and *polis*, we get no comment, no reflection. It is considered self-explanatory. The next sentence reads: "Meanwhile, the forty ships of the Peloponnesians . . . were caught in a storm off Crete."[10]

In the case of the genocide of Melos by Athens the issue of justice is openly raised in the debate on the destruction of the city that Thucydides composed. The Athenians will not allow the Melians to talk of right or justice, only of practicality and interests. The Melians, however, insist on raising issues of justice in a vain attempt to get the Athenians to listen: "As we think . . . it is expedient . . . that you should not destroy what is our common protection, the privilege of being allowed in danger to invoke what is fair and right, and even to profit by arguments not strictly valid if they can be got to pass current. And you are as much interested in this as any, as your fall would be a signal for the heaviest vengeance and an example for the world to meditate on."[11]

The call for justice does not, however, evoke a positive response in the Athenians. We will take our risks, they answer, about the fall of our empire. Even the evocation of the gods cannot convince the Athenians of any universal application of justice: "Of the gods we believe, and of men we know, that by a necessary law of nature they rule where they can." And the Athenians insist the Lacedaemonians are no different. "Of all the men we know they are most conspicuous in considering what is agreeable honourable, and what is expedient just."[12]

There is no justice, only interests that sometimes hide themselves under its name. The advocate of reasonable punishment in the Mitylenean debate, Diodotus, expressed these very sentiments. "I have not come forward either to oppose or to accuse in the matter of Mitylene; indeed, the question before us as sensible men is not their guilt, but our interests. Though I prove them ever so guilty, I shall not, therefore, advise their death, unless it be expedient."[13]

It would be reasonable to conclude that Thucydides is in full agreement with his polemical Athenians about the nonexistence of justice as a motive force in the actions of men. Remarkably, however, between the descriptions of the destruction of Plataea and the annihilation of Melos, the historian tells the story of civil war in Corcyra and seems to enter a different world, where the human emotions of pity and compassion play an essential role and the laws of right and justice are violated only at enormous human cost. Wherefrom this great reversal of sentiment?

The *demos* and the *oligoi* on the island of Corcyra (modern Corfu) entered into one of the most violent, most pitiless engagements of civil strife, exaggerated as Thucydides tells it, by the great war and the concomitant opportunity to involve Athens and Sparta as participants. Thousands were brutally killed. In the description of these events, we no longer hear the scientific historian, the cold practitioner of rational *realpolitik*, but the morally outraged voice of the tragic poet. "Death thus raged in every shape; and, as usually happens at such times, there was no length to which violence did not go; sons were killed by their fathers and suppliants dragged from the altar or slain upon it; while some were even walled up in the temple of Dionysus and died there. So bloody was the march of the revolution, and the impression which it made was the greater as it was one of the first to occur."[14]

Thucydides was the first to note that at times of civil chaos perversion of language is one of the first things to occur: it becomes unrecognizable. He makes no attempt to contain his repulsion at this violation of human dignity:

> Words had to change their ordinary meaning and to take that which was now given them. Reckless audacity came to be considered the courage of a loyal ally; prudent hesitation, specious cowardice; moderation was held to be a cloak for unmanliness; ability to see all sides of a question inaptness to act on any. Frantic violence became the attribute of manliness; cautious plotting, a justifiable means of self-defense. The advocate of extreme measures was always trustworthy; his opponent a man to be suspected. To succeed in a plot was to have a shrewd head, to divine a plot a still shrewder; but to try to provide against having to do either was to break up your party and to be afraid of your adversaries. . . . even blood became a weaker account than self-preservation. Oaths of reconciliation, being only proffered on either side to meet an immediate difficulty, only held good so long as no weapon was at hand.[15]

Justice was exiled; moral chaos prevailed. "In their acts of vengeance they went to greater lengths, not stopping at what *justice or the good of the state demanded. . . . Thus religion was in honour with neither party*; but the use of fair phrases to arrive at *guilty ends* was in high reputation."[16] How could the man who wrote the cold-blooded Melian debate suddenly speak with the agonized voice of the great moralist Euripides? "Corcyra gave the first example of the savage and pitiless excesses into which men who had begun the struggle not in a class but in a party spirit, were hurried by their ungovernable passions."[17]

We do not know when, and in what order, the *History* was composed, but the passage that follows can only send a shiver through us who have read the Melian debate and know how close Athens came to annihilation at the end of the war. "Indeed men too often take upon themselves in the prosecution of their revenge to set the example of doing away with those general laws to which all alike can look for salvation in adversity, instead of allowing them to subsist against the day of danger when their aid may be required."[18]

Thucydides is *not* preaching a sermon to Athens, *not* castigating its tragic commitment to interests, expediency, and the abandonment of justice. He is engaged in the most extraordinary—to the Greek mind, the most ordinary—psychological and moral splitting. *Within* the *polis* and *between poleis* are two different worlds, to be judged by two different standards. We recall that the horror of the Corcyraean massacre, including the piling of the corpses on carts, is described in detail whereas the genocide of Melos is told in one sentence and never fleshed out. Justice and religion, "those general laws to which all alike can look for salvation," have validity only when citizens engage citizens. To make war on another *polis* is to be transformed into a different form of human being, almost a separate species. Thucydides has no intention of reconciling these two species, for he cannot. Nor yet can we.

In addition to the obdurate boundary that persisted around each *polis*, there was another line of demarcation that engaged the Greek mind: the frontier between Greeks and barbarians. Barbarians were all those who did not speak Greek, both culturally and politically less developed peoples on the periphery of the Greek world and the rulers of the Persian Empire. Though they did not say so in so many words, the Greeks, like the ancient Hebrews, considered themselves a chosen people. Greek culture was superior to other cultures; to be Greek was to be a special kind of human.

Thucydides again provides us with a remarkable example of splitting in regard to moral perception and judgments. The *History*, as many ancient and modern commentators have noted, is full of the most destructive kinds of human behavior about which the author renders not one word of condemnation or outrage. He does not, however, consistently maintain an emotion-free stance. His most unambivalent expression of horror at human destructiveness occurs when he describes the actions of a group of "barbarians." A company of Thracians, a people living in a tribal, not a *polis*, society, had been engaged by the Athenians to assist in the war effort. Short of funds, the Athenians dismissed them and sent them back to Thrace under the command of an Athenian general, who was instructed to inflict on the enemy whatever injury he could during the journey. The troops stormed the city of Mycalessus, allied with Sparta. Their savage behavior evoked the full condemnation of the historian, who, in this instance, has no reluctance to render judgment on the immoral acts of these not-quite-human people:

> The Thracians bursting into Mycalessus sacked the houses and temples, and butchered the inhabitants, sparing neither youth nor age, but killing all they fell in with, one after the other, children and women, and even beasts of burden, and whatever other living, creatures they saw; the Thracian race, like the bloodiest of barbarians, being ever so when it has nothing to fear. Everywhere confusion reigned and death in all its shapes; and in particular they attacked a boys' school, the largest that there was in the place, into which the children had just gone, and massacred them all. In short, the disaster falling upon the whole town was unsurpassed in magnitude, and unapproached by any in suddenness and horror.[19]

The establishment of a hierarchy of horror, wherein some unnecessary killings are more horrible than others, enables "civilized" people to deny their own "barbarisms" and maintain their self-regard.

The Greeks used this hierarchy philosophically to justify the ownership of human beings. Aristotle regards it as a first principle, to be stated, not argued. "This is why our poets have said, 'Meet it is that barbarous peoples should be governed by the Greeks'—the assumption being that barbarian and slave are by nature one and the same."[20] Nature is once again called on to justify what appears to us grossly unnatural. Is there a universal standard that can set the boundary of justice, placing some outside of it? Is the erection of any line of demarcation necessarily arbitrary?

The Greek world was nonetheless a "modern" world and therefore, as Marx has said of modernism, pregnant with its opposite.[21] The culture as a whole did not question the "natural" split between Greek and barbarian though it was challenged by a few. In an extraordinary series of remarks, the sophist Antiphon not only delegitimates the moral

distinction between Greek and barbarian but relates this mode of splitting to the lack of equality within the *polis*. A remarkable statement of
a universal concept of justice, it disturbed the value system of Greek
culture not one iota.

> ... *but if a man*
> *be of a lowlier family*
> *we feel no awe for him and show him no veneration.*
> *This is a case where*
> *in our {social} relations with each other*
> *we have 'barbarized' ourselves.*
> *For by nature all of us in all things are constituted alike*
> *both barbarian and Hellene.*
>
> *There is evidence available*
> *in the {area} of those {resources} which by nature are essential to all human*
> * beings . . .*
> *. . . and in this {area} barbarian and Hellene among us are not definable*
> * separately*
>
> *For we all use our mouths and nostrils*
> *to draw breath in and out of the atmosphere*
> *and we all*[22]

Such a radical view had no chance to prevail. Much more typical of
the attempts to overcome the limitations of the *polis* frontier were the
"progressive" views of Isocrates, who would have all Greeks friends
with each other, sharing justice and uniting in attacking the true enemy, the vast barbarian empire. "I have led the way in discourses
which exhort the Hellenes to concord among themselves and war against
the barbarians, and which urge that we all unite in colonizing a country
so vast and so vulnerable that those who have heard the truth about it
assert with one accord that, if we are sensible and cease from our
frenzy, we can quickly gain possession of it without effort and without
work, and that this territory will easily accommodate all the people
among us who are in want of all the necessities of life. And these are
enterprises then, which, should the world unite in search, none could
be found more honourable or more important or more advantageous

to us all."[23] Ironically, when Alexander within twenty-five years accomplished this conquest, the Greek world was united only by the tyranny of Macedonian kings, its fragmented self totally vulnerable to Roman conquest.

In spite of the efforts of the philosophical elite, Antiphon, Isocrates, and Plato, to cross the frontier of the *polis* and create a pan-Grecian justice, the society and its political and intellectual leaders fully accepted the concept that justice expired at the boundary of the state. Commenting on a motion to remove the treasury of the Athenian Empire from Delos to Athens—an act that distinctly declared the confederacy an instrument of Athenian imperial policy and not a voluntary defensive alliance—Aristides, surnamed "the Just," declared the act "not just but expedient."[24] Demosthenes may have been echoing Thucydides on the Athenians' declaration to the Melians, when he asserted "The rights of individuals within a state are impartially guaranteed by the law of the weak and strong alike; but on the international plane the strong lay down what rights the weak are to enjoy."[25]

In an intense expression of emotional splitting, Democritus makes a passionate plea for moral concern: "When the powerful have the heart to provide those who have nothing, and to help them and fulfill their needs, here at last is pity, and an end to isolation, and comradeship, and mutual aid, and harmony of mind among citizens, and other good things too numerous to tell." Reading this, we might assume we have come to a remarkable place, one of republican virtue and Christian charity. But the words "among citizens" give us a clue and Democritus soon enlightens us as to how liberated he is from the standard *mores* of the society: "From unity of mind [*homonia*] come great achievements: only with this can cities crush their enemies."[26]

This psychological, emotional, and ethical splitting is still a fundamental moral ambiguity for humankind. The greatest moralists among us have preached the extension of virtue within the *polis*; justice between states remains in a moral limbo. When the city-state reappeared in Italy at the beginning of the modern era, almost nothing had changed from the time of Isocrates and Democritus in regard to this dilemma. Describing that "Machiavellian moment" in the history of the West, J. G. A. Pocock elaborates on Machiavelli's view of virtue within the republic. "Its justice was spatially and temporally finite; toward other republics it could display only a *virtù militarie*, and its ability to do this was determinative of its ability to maintain civic virtue internally. Virtuous republics were at war with one another."[27]

The question persists: To what degree, if any, have we overcome this pathological view of reality? We have created nation-states that have extended the notions of friend, citizen, and justice to 250 million people. At the borders of these states, do we cease to be any more liberated than Thucydides, that great historian of what, "by nature," humans can and cannot do?

The Tribal Band and the Tribal Bond

What has been written above—the original formulation of the problem of the boundaries of justice—contains a fundamental flaw. Plato is wrong when he states that justice exists even among pirates, and the quote from Himmler does not illustrate narrow boundaries of equity. What holds a society of pirates together, or a band of Nazis, is not justice, but kinship—a tribal bond, not an abstract concept of rights. *Justice is the attribution of rights that I claim for myself to others whom I do not know, do not meet on a face-to-face basis, and to whom I am unrelated either in actual, fictional, or metaphorical kinship.*

A tribal bond is a replication and extension, not a transformation, of the bonds of kinship: comradeship, relatedness, an acute sense of in-group belonging, conflicted love, and an intense sense of out-group exclusion. Kinship and the kinship system hold the hunting-gathering band together and the primitive (nonliterate, tribal) society. When the state is invented and becomes a social reality, nonkinship forms of social cohesion become as important as kinship forms, loyalty and obedience to the king being foremost.[28] What happens to kinship forms of cohesion under state circumstances is of crucial importance; some attempt will be made here to illuminate that tension.

If justice has nothing to do with holding a group of pirates together, what does? Fairness, yes. Expectable behavior, yes. A reasonably stable, and assumed legitimate, hierarchy. This says nothing, however, of rights or the attribution of rights to unrelated or unknown others. Himmler's "honest, decent, loyal and comradely" is about kin and *eros* and requires no abstract notion of rights. It requires only, as Himmler says, "our own blood." Justice is a complex and *abstract* concept. Blood represents a very low level of abstraction.

The ideas of citizen and citizenship play a crucial role in the transition from kinship to nonkinship forms of social cohesion, since they straddle both notions. On the one hand, citizenship, like kinship, sharply defines who is within and who without society, a frontier of inclusion guarded with passionate concern. This was especially so in the Greek *polis*. All observers have noted the insularity of Greek concepts of citizenship. We can understand this insularity if we recognize the kinship substratum that underlies it. Greek citizenship was extremely narrowly conceived, because Greek kinship notions (for reasons that remain hidden to us) exhibited intense "stranger anxiety." Anything beyond a small group of kin provoked the paranoid fear of the foreign.

Citizenship, on the other hand, already on the way to abstract commonality, lends itself perfectly to the great moral and psychological leap necessary for the invention of rights. Once we have a concept of citizen, it is an easy step to the attribution of rights to all citizens. Jones quotes Demosthenes as arguing that, "in a democracy each man considers that he himself has a share in equality and justice [that is, each citizen has the same rights]," and "for as everyone has an equal share in the rest of the constitution, so everyone is entitled to an equal share in the laws."[29] By "everyone" Demosthenes meant "all citizens in my *polis*," but the abstract concept of rights had emerged, and it contained within itself its own developmental logic. As so often, Euripides saw where the moral future—if there was to be a moral future—might lead us: "Though a wise man live far from my own land, though I never set eyes upon him, I count him as a friend,"[30] combining the kinship perception of friend with the nonkin perception of never-seeing, under the abstract commonality of wisdom. Citizenship and justice are those transformations of the feelings of kinship that take us beyond kinship.

For all the complex development of the state, however, the tribal band and the tribal bond that holds it together, never disappear or become unimportant. A modern, democratic, advanced industrial society of 250 million people still depends, to a greater degree than we like to admit, on the bonds of the tribe to make it cohere. Despite the extension of justice within the *polis* to include the poor, women, and minority peoples—a movement of enormous historical importance—

kinship, in the form of the tribal band, remains a fundamental, and perhaps irreducible, form of social cohesion for the nation-state.

Warfare and the intense emotional feelings it engenders reduce even the most complex state to a tribal society. The emotional level of the superpatriotic English during the "triumphant" Falkland Island War or of jingo America on the "glorious" invasion of Grenada differs in no degree from that of the Nuer on their yearly excursion against the Dinka. "Our own blood" rallies round to engage *their* blood in tribal strife. One of the most pitiful experiences of the twentieth century was the complete failure of the international socialist movement at the beginning of World War I to substitute loyalty to an abstract idea, a transnational conception of justice, comradeship, and socialism, for the tribal bond of the nation-state. After bravely announcing that French workers and German workers would never kill each other in the service of capitalist profits, almost all those workers and their leaders marched off to annihilate each other in one of the bloodiest wars ever fought. Blood spilled in the service of the tribal bond is sacred, however; it will take a moral and psychological revolution to transform that deep religious commitment. No matter how well developed the concept of justice may be within a society, at the border of the *polis*, the tribal bond is supreme.

Having left our parents' protection, we look to the tribe to assuage our anxieties. It becomes the common repository of our interests and we are ready to defend it against the interests of other *poleis*. No matter how we may differ among ourselves, we must join together to sustain American interests against evil-empire Russia or unfairly competitive Japan. Like the kinship system, the state defines us, preserves us, defends us against threatening others. The security of the kin is a fundamental defense against the paranoid anxiety of being left totally without protection. It is almost impossible to live without it.

Some tribal bands are more vicious than others; some more aggressive and conquering; some more retiring. The relative viciousness or expansiveness of a tribe has nothing to do with its commitment to justice. In the modern world, the Swiss tribe became a snail and the French tribe a lion, not because one was more just than the other, but because they took different roads to self-preservation in a Thucydidian jungle world of no justice. The study of nonliterate societies has revealed an extraordinary range of aggressive stances. Some were cannibals; other had given up cannibalism for head-hunting; some only practiced incessant warfare; some types of warfare involved extensive torture of prisoners: some societies were relatively peaceful, more concerned with defense than aggression; a few were the terror of the world. All, however, remained tribes, held together by the tribal bond. Modern nation-states present the same variegated picture. We have the Russians and the Swedes; the French and the Dutch; the Germans and the Swiss. Tribes all.

Size seems to make no difference. No matter how large a tribe may grow, the tribal bond does not weaken. That would jeopardize the existence of the state. Isocrates' call for Greek *poleis* to stop fighting each other, unite together, and conquer the barbarian is in no way an exhortation to transform the tribal bond. It is a program for the formation of a larger tribe than had ever been seen in the Greek world. If the new confederacy were to hold together permanently, it would be by the same bonds of kinship that preserved the individual *polis*.

The theoretical notion of boundary thus contains three different moral, psychological, and political problems. (1) What determines the boundaries of justice within the *polis*? (2) What happens to justice at the border of the *polis*? (3) What determines the size of the *polis*? Since all three problems are concerned with boundaries, we might think them psychologically related. Historically, they are autonomous, one from the other. The problems of the creation of the nation-state, a polity of millions of citizens, seem almost completely unrelated to the question of the boundaries of justice within the state; whether, for instance, women are included in citizenship or not. The construction and maintenance of nation-states are beyond the parameters of this book, but they seem to have little, if anything, to do with the problematics of justice.

Regarding the boundaries of justice within the *polis*, crucial to the theory of democratic society is the idea, often touched on here, that a polity can accurately be called "democratic" and yet be profoundly exclusionary. Three categories of people have traditionally been excluded from moderate democratic polities: poor men, women, and what I prefer to call "internal barbarians": slaves, racial minorities, and, in the case of Athens, a significant number of *metics*, foreign-born permanent residents. These "barbarians" are excluded from the rights of citizens because though they are within the *polis*, they are outside the kin. They cannot enter the tribal band and participate in the tribal bond; they are the barbarians safely ensconced within the gates.

The exclusion of women from citizenship is its own case, with its own deep psychological disabilities that must be overcome before women grow insistent that they be included and men are willing to take such a terrible risk. It is remarkable how recent is the participation of women in the democratic process, beginning faintly at the end of the nineteenth century and becoming universal as an ideal only in the twentieth. Women were allowed to vote in national elections in France only after the Second World War.[31] It seems inarguable that the effort toward full equality for women is intricately related to the movement of democratic universalism of the last two centuries.

For ancient Greek society, and for all city-states in the history of the West, the moral frontier, the great struggle for exclusion or inclusion, was the relationship of the free, male poor to citizen rights. We have discussed this previously, but it is pertinent to add here that on the psychological level, the question of including the poor is determined by whether they are to be considered members of the tribal band or merely another branch of internal barbarians. For radical oligarchs, the poor were no better than barbarians. The free poor may be citizens but have no or little power as in Rome. Though the phrase had to wait for the twentieth century, such people were truly "second-class citizens," existing on the very borders of the tribe.

The ideal of democratic universalism—the concept that no adult is to be excluded from the boundary of justice *within* the *polis*—is the product of the last two hundred years of human history. Athens, its achievements and its inadequacies, has been the focus of this work, but it is important to reiterate that the democracy of our Founding Fathers, though differing from state to state, was generally not one iota more inclusive than the radical Athenian democracy, and in regard to the poor substantially less democratic. The poor, women, slaves, and other internal barbarians such as free blacks and native Americans, had no citizen rights in eighteenth-century America and were outside the boundary of justice. It is only the moral revolution of the nineteenth and twentieth centuries that has brought us the kind of democracy we take for granted. The tribal band as a paranoid defense is the great hindrance to the advance of universal ideas of justice, and only when it is overcome and transformed to a significant degree will an all-inclusive ideal of democracy be possible. It was a moral transformation of which Athens was incapable. Nor should we ignore the ambiguities and contradictions that have plagued our last two centuries. We have witnessed an incredible repression of sexuality in women in the nineteenth century, two world wars, and the full implications of totalitarian society. Nothing in human history indicates that Athens was the only great paradoxical society.

We come last to the problem of justice at the border of the *polis*. To what extent, if any, have we ceased to be a tribe at the boundary of the state? Is it possible for an abstract concept of justice to transcend the frontier of the *polis*? Or does the irreducible necessity of the tribal bond negate such a possibility? A certainty of answer being most problematic, it may be helpful, nonetheless, to argue a little on both sides of the issue.

It is debatable whether we can assert any advance over Athens. Dresden, and Hiroshima, and the bombing of the hospitals in Hanoi, make even our claim to a nongenocidal society questionable. One may also argue that the relative viciousness of foreign policy measures (including warfare and acts of imperialism) reflect only the relative viciousness of the initiator and have nothing to do with justice. Ranking the four great European imperialist countries from 1880 to 1914—Britain, France, Belgium, and Germany—in terms of the relative savagery of their acts of warfare and imperialist repression, Britain would come out "most civilized" and Belgium and Germany "most barbarous." Does that result show differences in the degree of commitment to justice for "barbarians," or does it mean that one tribe has chosen to abandon cannibalism and another has not?

To argue the more optimistic view, must not the great movement from the exclusionary democracy of the eighteenth century to the universal ideal of justice now prevailing in democratic society have had an effect on the way nations treat each other? Slavery has been abandoned; women have been included in the polity; the poor are entitled to rights and participation in deciding the fate of the *polis*; in the ideal, at least, there are to be no more internal barbarians. Within the *polis*, this represents an almost incredible transcending of the paranoid position. It must affect the whole tenor of foreign policy decisions. Martin Luther King argued that the racist war in Vietnam was a manifestation of the same racism within America, that the struggle against the war in Indo-China and for civil rights at home was the same struggle. Sweden, one of the most universally democratic countries of the world, is attempting civil responsibility on an international scale. Jimmy Carter urges America to foster human rights all over the globe. Gorbachev simultaneously abandons the Russian Empire and promotes democracy at home. The democratic revolution of the last two hundred years may have moved the moral frontier to the very boundary of the *polis* itself. The split in the human regard for justice, so brilliantly and tragically manifested by Thucydides, may be on the verge of transcendence. There shall be, perhaps, no more barbarians.

17

Gain, Honor, Wisdom

Searching for an answer to the question of why one society is capable of becoming a stable democratic polity and another is not, we have confronted the seemingly inexplicable concept of the spirit of society. "Society" is a collectivized, generalized concept. In Greek thought the polity was the sum of the individuals composing it, the spirit of the *polis* reflected the individual spirits of the men who embodied it. In Thucydides' powerful description of the difference between the Athenian and the Spartan approaches to reality, he appears to be simultaneously describing individual men and a collectivized *weltanschauung.*

It was *equally* apparent to all thoughtful and critical Greek thinkers that the spirit of each man in the *polis* was the result of the educational aspects of life in the polity. Psyche and society were each the cause of the other. We have lost sight of this insight in our scientist, positivist world, which prefers the logical approach of either/or to the metaphorical view of both/and. Considering the psyche aspects of mutual causability, we see that the nature of political men determined the nature of the *polis.* All the great—and non-great—political thinkers of the Greek world knew that the study of society must begin with an analysis of the nature of the soul. The attempt of some "rationalist" modern theorists to understand society without first postulating a psychology would have been incomprehensible to the Greek mind. What is it, then, that drives a man?

The Hellenic mind loved to organize and analyze in threes. Plato took from Pythagoras the concept of a tripartite soul consisting of Reason, Spirit, and Appetite and constructed his ideal society of three classes: Guardians, Soldiers, and ordinary people.[1] Aristotle, as noted, conceived of basically three types of society depending on power being held by one, by the few, or by the many: monarchy, aristocracy, and polity, with their respective perversions, tyranny, oligarchy, and democracy.

In response to the query "What drives a man?"—what is it that the soul craves—here, too, there existed the time-honored judgment that all humans could accurately be divided into three categories: "lovers of wisdom, lovers of honour, lovers of gain."[2]*

Though the world has changed profoundly since Plato wrote the *Republic*, great value can still be found in this psychological descriptive rubric. The analysis of the lovers of gain, honor, and wisdom may tell us much about the spirit of democratic society.

To ask what the soul craves is to address the question of ambition. The goals of ambition are both an end in themselves and a means. Honor is an intrinsic good and a means toward an even greater good, the defining of the self. If we take "gain" in its most positive sense, providing a decent livelihood for oneself and one's family, the thing desired is a goal unto itself, but also a crucial means toward the establishment of self-esteem.

The greatest anxiety that people—especially men—face is the dissolution of the self, the existence of which is problematic and cannot be taken for granted. Reflecting on Descartes' famous dictum about existence, the phrase *ergo sum*, "therefore I am," indicates that "I am" is an achieved, not a given, position. People may differ from Descartes as to what defines their existence—his *cogito* is not for everyone—yet the goal of affirming the self is universal; only the means differ. We can observe the overwhelming negative impact on a man when he loses his primary mode of self-definition: Ajax gone mad when his honor is

---

*When the twentieth century experienced the greatest advance in psychological insight since the ancient world, the magical analytic power of the number three still prevailed: Freud subsumed all psychic action under a tripartite psyche: ego, id, and superego.

traduced, or the disintegration of a steady, stable worker unemployed through no fault of his own. Philosophers have therefore promoted wisdom as the highest good, the most enduring mode of the establishment of the self. Unlike gain or honor, it cannot be taken away by others.

The construction of the self is a fragile thing. The defenses created against self-dissolution are extraordinarily vulnerable. Society plays a crucial role in these complex processes, always providing modes for the defining of the self; the soul is never left to its own devices. Any "advanced" or "complex" society creates intricate notions of the self, but these intricacies are a sign of vulnerability. To understand the tensions within any "modern" society one must take into account the tenuousness of self-definition.

We receive from Thucydides, Plato, and Aristotle the clear message that the Greeks had succeeded in creating a complex society, allowing for an almost infinite variety of human response and achievement. The school of Aristotle collected over 150 different constitutions of Greek city-states in an effort to understand the *polis* in all its variety. Theory attempted to reduce the intensely variegated to its simplest components, but it was always encountering the nonconformities of the real world. The reduction of all ambition to the categories of gain, honor, and wisdom made no provision for variation in the intensity, the degree of appetite. What could explain, for example, the extraordinary power of Athenian ambition elaborated at length by Thucydides? "Born into the world to take no rest themselves and to give none to others."[3] How born into the world? Can we take the Athenian superspiritedness as a given, or does it allow for explanation? Thucydides could go no further than naming it. Two hundred years of anthropology, sociology, political theory, and psychology have moved us only a bit closer to explanation. A few theorists might surmise that something in the nature of Athenian child rearing made intense aspiration inevitable. But what that something was, and how it got there, remains one of the great psychosociological mysteries.

The schema gain–honor–wisdom prompts us to consider the connections between society and the psyche, since each category resonates in both the culture as a whole and the individual soul. To represent the concept visually, imagine the Greek view as a three-step pyramid. The overwhelming number of people would occupy the bottom stage:

gain. A goodly number, especially in a *polis* placing emphasis on this attribute, would occupy the second stage of honor. Only a few would occupy the third stage. The pyramid image implies a moral ascent. Those committed to gain see only self-interest. Honor serves the highest aspirations of the commonwealth. Wisdom entails subjecting the accepted values of the community to moral critique.

Only the philosophers and the tragic poets conceived of a world superior to honor. The great political leaders of the *polis* only went so far as to urge an emphasis on honor as opposed to gain. "For it is only the love of honour that never grows old," says Pericles/Thucydides in the celebrated funeral oration, "and honour it is, not gain, as some would have it, that rejoices the heart of age and helplessness."[4] Almost eighty years later Demosthenes said "Athenian democracy, never eager to acquire riches, coveted glory more than any other possession in the world. . . . Once they possessed greater wealth than any other Hellenic people, but they spent it all for the love of honour; they . . . recoiled from no peril for glory's sake. Hence the People inherits possessions that will never die . . . yonder Propylaea, the Parthenon, the porticoes, the docks."[5]

The statesman urged the pursuit of honor in opposition to gain or riches, and the philosopher, the teacher of morality, pressed the pursuit of wisdom rather than honor. "You are an Athenian," declared Socrates in Plato's *Apology*, "and belong to a city which is the greatest and most famous in the world for its wisdom and strength. Are you not ashamed that you give your attention to acquiring so much money as possible, and similarly with reputation and honor, and give no attention or thought to truth and understanding and the perfection of your soul?"[6]

Each of these three goods satisfies a particular appetite of the soul. Yet, although they have been conjoined in one formulation, within the psyche they are almost completely autonomous one from the others. In the ancient world gain was not a subject of discussion. It was assumed to be a basic, universal, uninteresting need, especially in contrast with honor or wisdom. The advent of capitalism raised gain to an equal, or perhaps more important, human appetite. The transition from aristocratic to capitalist society downgraded honor and elevated acquisition within the priorities of ambition. This perception of moving in a downward direction on the soul's tripartite pyramid has made sensitive observers uneasy with capitalist morality, despite its success in providing the material goods of the world. That the market succeeds in transforming private vices (gain and greed) into public goods has been preached, in one form or another, for hundreds of years, as a legitimization of capitalist morality. Honor and wisdom remain outside this formulation.

The pursuit of gain is not necessarily undertaken in the most logical manner, though it seems the most natural, least complicated of appetites. Max Weber's great work on capitalism and the Protestant ethic demonstrated that the foremost achievement of the capitalist mentality was to organize the pursuit of gain and that this rationality is an achieved position to which most societies did not aspire.[7] The capitalist *weltanschauung* did nothing for honor and wisdom, except overshadow them in the turmoil of the race for acquisition. Weber's "iron cage"— "specialists without spirit, sensualists without heart"[8]—is a metaphor for a world wherein the rational pursuit of gain has eclipsed all other appetites. Democracy cannot survive in such an umbrageous world, where the soul's felicity must be satisfied by a single gratification. To leave almost all social decisions to the market is to prescribe a moral disaster.

This moral reductionism on the part of modern capitalist society has caused some theorists to long for the "glories" of the world of the *polis*, and to exaggerate its moral and political virtue. "To live in a *polis*," writes Hannah Arendt, "meant that everything was decided through words and persuasion and not through force and violence. In Greek self-understanding, to force people by violence, to command rather than persuade, were . . . characteristic of life outside the *polis* . . . life in the barbarian empires of Asia."[9] Twenty-five pages of Thucydides will convince even the most casual reader of the patent absurdity of these remarks, but Arendt, a self-consciously moral person, was struggling to free herself from the iron cage of a society that had reduced almost all honor to a function of gain and hardly knew what wisdom was. Perceiving that in the ancient world honor and wisdom (justice) were held in higher regard than profit, that human beings are not necessarily doomed "by nature" to live in an acquisition-obsessed society, Arendt looked to a mythical past to justify an optimistic transformation of the future.

It is no exaggeration of the truth to claim that the world of the *polis* greatly esteemed honor. It was still very much an aristocratic world; there had been no triumph of the bourgeoisie despite the importance of wealth in society. Like all aristocratic societies, therefore, it remained obsessed with shame. This can be traced to the beginning of the Archaic world, in the works of Homer[10] and remained a fundamental concern of Greek "manliness." In a society where shame is a characteristic anxiety, honor will be a characteristic defense against it. When shame threatens the dissolution of self-esteem, honor restores and maintains the cohesion of the estimable self. The satisfaction of the soul's appetite is both an end in itself and a means to the preservation of the vulnerable self. Aristotle brought shame and honor together in delineating the former: "Let shame then be defined as a kind of pain or uneasiness in respect to misdeeds, past, present, or future, which seem to tend to bring dishonour."[11]

Estimable in itself, honor has an ambiguous relationship to wisdom and morality. Though superior to gain as an activity of the soul, honor can be false in an inflexible definition of what is "manly," oftentimes resulting in unwise or unjust action. In the Athenian Assembly that voted the doomed expedition to Sicily, Nicias argued vehemently against the invasion and the mental heroics that Alcibiades used to stir the citizens to vainglory. "I, in my turn, summon any of the older men that may have such a person sitting next to him, not to let himself be shamed down, for fear of being thought a coward if he do not vote for war, but, remembering how rarely success is got by wishing and how often by forecast, to leave to them the mad dream of conquest."[12] The *demos*, come to power, inherits the aristocratic commitment to a pathological notion of manliness. "These colors don't run," cried the bumper sticker that urged us to sustain the slaughter in Vietnam, reflecting the remarkable continuity of human response: "In my view," wrote Demosthenes in the fourth century, "shame at what has been done is the greatest compulsion upon free men."[13]

Honor is inadequate as a moral guide because it is *external* to the soul; like its counterpart shame, it depends on the opinion of others. Aristotle pronounced it the greatest of *external* goods.[14] Justice and morality require internalization, a conscience independent of the current values of society. Demosthenes demonstrates this externality of honor and exercises uncommon intellectual gymnastics when he treats of interests, gain, shame, honor, and justice all in one sentence. "If everyone

[else] has set out to do what is right, it is shameful if we alone are unwilling to do it, but when everyone else is bent on doing wrong, I do not think it is justice, but unmanliness, for us alone to put up a screen and talk about rights and take no action; for I observe that any nation is accorded its rights in proportion to its strength at the time."[15] "Everyone else" is essential to the notion of honor; wisdom may find one standing absolutely alone.

One of the most powerful of ambiguities in the human condition arises when honor fuses with the tribal bond: the genesis of glory and death in defense of the fatherland. Such glory represents the finest emotion that many people, and many nations, are capable of: the sacrifice of the self for an ideal greater than oneself. Many injustices and self-destructive acts, however, are committed under that corruptible banner. The battle of Marathon *and* the invasion of Sicily; World War II *and* Vietnam; Stalingrad *and* Afghanistan. Only wisdom can judge between a just and an unjust war; only wisdom can subject honor and glory to critique.

These glorious deaths have evoked, in both the ancient and the modern worlds, some of the finest rhetoric ever, rendering the comfort that "these dead shall not have died in vain." An official epitaph erected in Athens in 432, before the great war began, declares simply: "This city and Erechtheus' people are longing for the men, the sons of the Athenians, who died fighting in the front line at Potidaia; they staked their lives as the price of valour, and brought glory to their country."[16] Grander and more elaborate is Pericles/Thucydides' tribute to the Athenian dead: "In the business before them they thought fit to act boldly and trust in themselves. Thus choosing to die resisting, rather than to live submitting, they fled only from dishonour, but met danger face to face, and after one brief moment, while at the summit of their fortune escaped, not from their fear, but from their glory. . . . For heroes have the whole earth for their tomb; and in lands far from their own, where the column with its epitaph declares it, there is enshrined in every breast a record unwritten with no tablet to preserve it, except that of the heart. These take as your model, and judging happiness to be the fruit of freedom and freedom of valour, never decline the dangers of war."[17]

Some died in the struggle for democracy; some in the defense of Greek liberty when threatened by the Persian Empire; and some fell defending Athenian imperial interests against other Greeks who were protecting their own freedom. The grand rhetoric did not distinguish the cause. Plutarch tells of the Romans asserting dominion over Greece in the second century. Some of the conquerors meditate on the history of the Hellenes: "Courage and wisdom are, indeed, rarities amongst men, but of all that is good, a just man it would seem is the most scarce. Such as Agesilaus, Lysander, Nicias, and Alcibiades, knew how to play the general's part, how to manage a war, how to bring off their men victorious by land and sea; but how to employ that success to generous and honest purposes, they had not known. For should a man except the achievement at Marathon, the sea-fight at Salamis, the engagements at Plataea and Thermopylae [opposing the Persian invasion] . . . Greece fought all her battles against, and to enslave, herself; she erected all her trophies to her own shame and misery, and was brought to ruin and desolation almost wholly by the guilt and ambition of her great men."[18] The tribal bond demands that honor and glory be won at the expense of whomever one may meet at the tribal boundaries, no matter how narrowly or how spaciously these frontiers may be drawn.

Honor is concerned with the *highest, accepted* values of the community and service to the community is of its essence: to train a tragic chorus, to complete successfully a diplomatic mission, to win an Olympic victory, to outfit a warship, to die fighting for the *polis*. From ancient to modern times, nothing has changed in the performance of honorable acts and the receipt of honor, except the specifics: now one can endow hospitals or university chairs, win a Nobel prize, be an astronaut. The community still rewards with honor those who live up to its highest ideals. Those ideals are determined, however, by something that has nothing to do with honor, except insofar as honor is a positive value within the *polis*. The pursuit of honor takes the values of society as given, not attempting to enlarge or transform them. In Athens, where competition had a heightened value, the result was, ironically, a fierce competition for honor.

Only wisdom can subject the values of society to criticism and transform the conception of what is honorable or dishonorable. Only wisdom can change our view of Teddy Roosevelt, for instance, from that of a grand hero charging up San Juan Hill into that of a banal imperialist. Our present liberal, bourgeois democracy has a profoundly ambivalent relationship to the moral enlargement of the system of values.

Nothing is as unpredictable as the attempt to determine where our society will stand even five years from now on the great moral issues of our time—racism, equality between men and women, vast economic disabilities. One thing seems certain: the degree of honor within society will have nothing to do with the future enlargement or contraction of the frontier of morality and justice. It is invigorating to live in a society that values honor more than gain, the latter being the most uninteresting of human appetites but wisdom, justice, and morality are a different order of human concern.

A society may take great moral strides and then become incapable of any further forward movement. In the fourth century after the establishment of the stable, radical democracy Athens was incapable of any further extension of justice, either to those disenfranchised within the *polis*, or to Greeks and barbarians beyond the frontier. Its philosophers, however, particularly Plato and Aristotle, expounded on the necessity of going beyond honor (service to the *polis*) to wisdom (a thorough critique of the culture's values). Though we may disagree with the particulars of this philosophic assessment, the concept that society can and should be subject to radical moral critique is one of the greatest gifts bequeathed to us by Greek society. The political application of this principle changed the world in the nineteenth and twentieth centuries.

However, even wisdom, the highest good, is subject to perversion. Aristotle's view that each basic form of society has its perverted form can be applied to this other tripartite analyses. Do gain, honor, and wisdom have corrupt modes? What is the relationship between each ideal form and its perversion? Aristotle linked the basic political configurations and their corresponding perversions by number. Kingship and Tyranny are governments by One; Aristocracy and Oligarchy by the Few; and Polity and Democracy by the Many. The overriding moral differentiation is whether sovereignty is exercised for the common good or for narrow personal interest, the latter being the malignant or immoral form.[19]

How do gain, honor, and wisdom fare in this analysis? The corruption of gain is greed; of honor, narcissism; of wisdom, ideology. Each debased form carries the fulfillment of the soul's craving to excess, degrading a normal appetite into an addiction. The differentiation between the ideals and their perversions echoes Aristotle's analysis of societal forms: is the pursuit undertaken for the sake of others, as well as for self? For honor and wisdom, the answer may be clear, but gain also is almost always undertaken to provide for others (family and other dependents) as well as for self. This appears especially to be so when one begins, as did Aristotle, with the *oikos*, the economics of the household. Gain is an essential human activity, not an addiction.

Greed, narcissism, and ideology are egotistical pursuits. Engulfed by them, people lose their sense of reality. Greed, as we generally understand it, in the capitalist sense, was not problematic in ancient Greek society, hardly existing as a social problem. The one insatiable craving was for power over others—the paranoidia of domination. This voracious pursuit of power will be treated at length in the final chapter; we may leave it for now.

Ideology as a perversion of wisdom was nonexistent in the political life of the city-state. People did not annihilate each other for wrong views of the world. Only in thought—Plato's suggestion, for instance, that all those over ten years of age be transported out of the city in order to create a new society[20]—were the potential catastrophes of ideology adumbrated. It is logical that Plato's should be the first voice of ideology: He was the great link between ancient pagan culture and the Hebrew-Christian world view. Neo-Platonism played a crucial role in the conversion of ancient society to Christianity, an enormously important step in moralizing the world. And yet—in one of the great ironies of moral progress—the ancient Hebrews invented the idea that it was just to exterminate a people because they believed in the wrong god. No Egyptian, Assyrian, Persian, Greek, or Roman society ever undertook such a crusade or such a hounding of heretics. It seems that, once human beings discover the possibility of transforming the world morally, they feel obliged to do so. Any form of violence seems legitimate to save people from themselves or to create a new, ideal society. In this tragic century we have seen the suffering that the near-psychotic pursuit of ideology can bring. And ideology is the perversion of wisdom because perpetrators of ideological catastrophes insisted on annihilating millions in the pursuit of the highest ends: wisdom, justice, and morality. To name it is not necessarily to understand it. We could comprehend the malignant nature of political life far better if we could penetrate to the depth of this ideological perversion of wisdom. To see it as "paranoid" is only a beginning.

Narcissism, the perversion of honor, was the greatest problematic in the Greek world. It was endemic in Athenian society. We have seen it in the life of Alcibiades. Themistocles, hero of the battle of Salamis which freed Greece from Persian domination in 480, was born in c. 528, more than seventy-five years before Alcibiades. Before the days of his military triumphs, he tried to use the Olympic Games to enhance his personal glory, but met with resistance from a more conservative public. "When he came to the Olympic games, and was so splendid in his equipage and entertainments, in his rich tents and furniture . . . he displeased the Greeks, who thought that such magnificence might be allowed in one who was a young man and of great family, but was a great piece of insolence in one as yet undistinguished, and without title or means of making any such display."[21] Such overweening ambition may become a threat to the democratic polity. Self-interested glorification knows not where to stop, having no limits and limits are the essence of democratic life. After years of political success at Athens, during which he ostracized several political opponents, Themistocles was himself ostracized, condemned to death in absentia, and escaped execution only by fleeing to the court of the Persian king.[22]

Greed, narcissism, and ideology are fundamental threats to the democratic spirit. Democracy and the individualism it liberates may allow individuals to grow in such reckless expression of egoistic appetite that the democracy itself becomes vulnerable. Because they represent paranoid defenses against the threat of paranoia, these perverted appetites are violations of the democratic spirit. The insatiable pursuit of money, self-glorification, or ideological power has an addictive quality at variance with the democratic view that all people are real and have rights. A certain amount of greed and self-glorification are admissible in democratic society, without its fabric being threatened. The greatest threat is ideology: the idea that *The Truth* is knowable and ownable and must be imposed on others, by force if necessary, in the interest of a perverted conception of righteousness and justice. Critics of mass culture, the puerile nature of television, and the pervasive narcissistic quality of advertising sometimes write, in exaggeration, as if the commitment to designer jeans could truly destroy our culture. They are perceiving a more frightening threat, that the uncontrolled perversion of gain and honor may lead to the perversion of wisdom, that a soul that craves greed and grandiosity will ultimately demand ideology in a desperate attempt to restore a fractured self.

We gain insight when we designate greed, narcissism, and ideology "perversions." The word "perversion" originates in the psychology of sexuality, describing the pursuit of a corrupt or distorted sexual satisfaction. The broader implications in the concept are that, whereas authentic sexual experience can satisfy, perversions have an obsessive, compulsive character that ultimately makes true gratification impossible. A person may be driven, over and over again, to return to the perverse experience, but true satiation never results. Just so the pursuit of greed and grandiose narcissism can never satisfy. The void in the middle of the soul is never filled. Alienation and despair follow the repetitive and hollow experience. Political vulnerability results because such alienation and despair often drive some—even many—to seek escape from their "iron cage" through an ideological transformation of the world. History has demonstrated that when enough people choose the perverted political way out, democracy is destroyed and many millions of citizens along with it.

Capitalism, it seems, has won the great struggle with communism. How solid or how hollow the victory will be depends on the degree to which it can control and sublimate greed and self-glorification. And ideology—the great adversary of democracy—waits, always, in the wings.

18

Education for the Political Life: Small–Town Democracy

"Without local institutions," Alexis de Tocqueville wrote in his analysis of American democracy, "a nation may give itself a free government, but it has not got the spirit of liberty."[1] De Tocqueville considered local democracy so important that he began his lengthy analysis with a description of democracy in the townships of America. In regard to ancient Athens all extant written evidence of its political life reveals strangely little on the politics at the township level. "No ancient commentator on the Athenian democratic system," declares David Whitehead, "informs us that the demes [the townships of Attica] played a crucial role therein."[2]

The picture we get of Athenian democracy from Thucydides, Aristophanes, Xenophon, and their ilk is of a boisterous Assembly of 5,000 to 6,000 impetuous citizens voting on whether or not to go to war, execute generals, or commit genocide. The fourth-century orators (Desmosthenes, Aeschines) present a more stable and responsible picture but still one of central democracy by multitudes. The day-to-day government of the towns was a virtually unexplored area until this century. However, an extraordinary picture of town politics has been revealed, particularly since 1945, confirming de Tocqueville's intuition: The democratic spirit thrived in the demes of Attica. The central democratic government did not arise full grown from the head of Zeus. It owed much to township democracy.

There were 139 to 140 demes in Attica, some much larger or smaller than the average. The population of Athens varied significantly over the years, but estimates set the average number of citizens at about 30,000,[3] giving an average deme membership of about 220. In the deme almost everyone knew everyone else on a face-to-face, daily-contact basis, a far different situation than in the city.

Each deme had its own full-participation, direct-action assembly open to every citizen. The percentage of the total citizen body attending was probably much higher than at the central Assembly in Athens, where the inhibition of walking twenty to twenty-five miles each way to attend, and the sense that 1 vote in 6,000 could not matter much, kept many from exercising their political rights. It is generally agreed that in the deme assembly each attendee had the right to vote on all issues, as in the New England town meetings. We do not know who was allowed to speak, nor for how long, but this information is also lacking for the national Assembly at Athens. We know a great deal about attendance at the national Assembly, about voting procedures and the chairmanship, but we don't know what kept discussions from getting out of hand. From the speeches that remain to us, it is clear that those with political power (Demosthenes, Cleon) could address the Assembly, but how the debate was limited we do not know. We know even less about the deme assemblies but those with superior wealth and more than usual personal force probably had greater influence, since this is true for almost all such institutions. That deme politics was a school of democracy, with all its strengths and faults, seems a more than reasonable assumption.

The activities of a deme were many and complex. Whitehead calls it "a *polis* in microcosm."[4] First and foremost, citizenship in the city-state at large was determined at the deme level. A man reaching the age of political maturity was certified as a legitimate member of the *polis* in the deme of which his father had been a citizen. Family connections with particular demes were established at the time of Cleisthenes, in 508. Descendants of those original deme citizens remained politically attached to their demes, regardless of where they eventually lived; the citizenship of all sons of citizen fathers had to be attested to in the original deme of residence. Contested cases of citizenship were decided first under deme auspices.

The use of the deme name to identify a person, either in place of or with the patronymic, or father's name, grew with the emerging democratic spirit:[5] So-and-so of Rhamnus, instead of So-and-so the son of. . . . Those with strong aristocratic connection continued to use the patronymic as an indication of high status.

Connecting deme and national politics, members of the Council (five hundred in all) were elected annually from the demes on a proportional basis. The deme of Eleusis sent eleven councillors each year; the largest deme, Acharnai, twenty-two; very small demes, like Pambotadai and Sybridai, alternated with each other, each electing one member of the Council every other year.[6] This smacks of "representative democracy" in Athens, supposed to exemplify pure direct democracy. The problem is that our data fail us at this point. We have no indication whether those elected to the Council were given instructions at the deme level on how to vote. We do not know whether the councillors owed their election to their stand on certain issues. We cannot know, therefore, whether this was a case of representative government or merely a broad, democratic way of choosing a Council.

Every deme annually selected an executive officer, the *demarchos*. Evidence indicates that originally he was elected, but by the fourth century the demarch was selected by sortition,[7] though we do not know how. It may have been by lot from a chosen group of people. It seems unlikely that the names of all men, rich and poor, literate and illiterate, capable and incapable, were thrown into the lottery. The question is unanswerable to date.

We do not know to what extent the demarch was responsible for religious and other festivities of the deme, but the amount of communal activity was remarkable. "The demes always provided a rich and varied religious diet for their members, and this is nowhere more evident than in the surviving portions of deme *fasti* or calendar of recurring festivals and sacrifices."[8] The communal celebrations cost money and the performance of the calendar forced each deme to maintain a complex budgetary system. "The costs of cult—upkeep of temples and shrines, offering of regular sacrifices, celebration of recurrent festivals—surely represented . . . the major object of regular expenditure, and indeed the fundamental *raison d'être* of the budget as a whole."[9]

The same kind of interpenetration of religion and political life—the "civil religion" if you will—pertained on the deme level as in the central polity of Athens. Many demes had local cults, involving permanent temple structures. Some were self-sufficient, but others were maintained by the deme government, which appointed priests or priestesses. The demarch might be in charge of cult money, collecting rent from leased sacred land. He might also attend to the maintenance of temples and their precincts. It was common practice for the demarch to play a significant role in offering sacrifices. In Eleusis and Myrrhinous, for instance, it was his responsibility to distribute the sacrificial meat.[10] The burial of the unclaimed dead—those unattended by relatives or, in the case of slaves, masters—was, by law, the duty of the demarch.[11]

The great theater of Athens, where the magnificent festival of Dionysus was celebrated, was not the only such structure in Attica. We know of seven and evidence indicates seven more demes that had their own theaters,[12] host, among other festivals, to the rural Dionysia at which theatrical triumphs from the city were performed. It is a moving experience to sit today, looking at the sea, in the amiable theater at Thorikos, over twenty-five miles from Athens (a four- to six-hour walk), and ruminate on how rich and complex life was in the townships of ancient Attica. A democracy as powerful and enduring as Athens did not survive on city air alone.

The *demarchos* also had more mundane, secular tasks to perform. In many demes, he supervised the inscribing and erection of the stone stelai that recorded the decrees of the deme assembly. It is interesting that some demes dated their documents by reference to the incumbent demarch and not to the eponymous Archon of the government of Athens, the accepted procedure of the national polity. Some demes used the name of a local priest or priestess, ignoring the central calendar.[13] We have strong evidence that the theoric fund—state allowances, originally made to poorer citizens to enable them to attend the theater, later distributions from the central government to all citizens—was distributed on a deme-by-deme basis, probably by the *demarchos* himself.[14] This must have been a reasonably complex affair. We don't know how the amount for each deme was decided, how the distribution took place, about deme members living in other, distant demes; or what forms of corruption were possible. We know, however, that such "welfare state" measures must have led to some "bureaucratic" modes of operation. We are no longer dealing with a simple, centralized city-state.

The annual budget of the township was a complex one; much of the deme's activity involving the collection and expenditure of funds. An office most often mentioned in the documents is that of *tamiai*, treasurers. Many demes owned land collectively and derived income by renting it out. A decree from the deme of Aixone states, "it is resolved to elect men who, with the demarch and the tamiai and the lessee of land from the deme, will sell to the highest bidder the rights to olive trees on it; and the names of the three men chosen are appended."[15] The deme could also lend out—at interest—its own or temple funds over which it had some control. Ordinary expenditures would routinely be handled by town officials, but sometimes an extraordinary expenditure required a special appointment. A decree from Acharnai makes reference to " 'elected men' who have reported what it will cost to build altars for Ares and Athena Areia."[16]

Regardless of the time or form of government, human beings appear reluctant to pay their debts and force may be necessary to preserve the sacredness of a contract. In a speech written by Demosthenes, Euxitheus recollects his year as *demarchos* in Halimous and the enemies he made by insisting that rents and other monies due the deme be paid. The demarch was also called on to collect bad debts from individuals and enforce the obligations of citizens to the central state.[17]

My family summers in a small township in New England, where the population increases a hundredfold in the summer, but where the year-round inhabitants number only about 700 with approximately 500 voters. Many of the permanent citizens are active in the political and economic life of the town: selectmen, assessors, building inspectors, garbage-dump supervisors, and members of the planning board, zoning board, board of health, school committee, finance committee. A hint of corruption appears every so often; factions form; money talks; lawsuits abound. But the direct democratic process reigns supreme. Many important decisions are made in the full-town meeting. An unusually large number of citizens make it their business to know what goes on in town. It is remarkable how much the demes of Attica, though dimly perceived, resonate with the knowledge and experience of this modern community.

The key to responsible democratic government is accountability. Without it, corruption reigns. The failure of a community to police its officers and to curb the normal amount of corruption and arrogance can only lead to degradation of a polity. (When the city of New York decentralizes its Board of Education and creates thirty-two separate, local school boards, thirty-two different mechanisms for holding officials accountable have to be put in place; otherwise the quality of education quickly suffers and the taxpayers' money floats away.) In its central government and on the deme level Athens spent an extraordinary amount of time and energy on holding officials accountable, usually at the end of their term of office. The health of the *polis* largely depended on this. Whitehead describes the intricate nature of deme oversight:

> What is envisaged is a meeting of the deme assembly, early in the administrative year, with the new demarch presiding over the euthynai of his predecessor. Various specialists are to be sworn in by the demarch, to perform the examination itself: a *euthynos*, a *logistēs*, and an unspecified number of *synēgoroi*. The duties of the *synēgoroi* apparently include some sort of preliminary vote; however, the vote which really matters is that of the ten "elected men," who are sworn in by the demarch in front of their fellow demesmen and who vote in a secret ballot. If a majority of the ten are satisfied, the *euthynos* destroys the accounts and the proceedings are at an end. If not, they impose a fine— but in that event the ex-official has the right of appeal (*ephesis*) to the assembly as a whole; after checking that at least *thirty demesmen* are present, the presiding demarch administers an oath to them and distributes votes, and this final "court of appeal" may either reverse the decision of the ten or else confirm their vote of condemnation and increase the fine originally imposed by 50 percent in consequence.[18]

Corruption and the fight against it were continuous on the deme level. It is amusing to observe that some demes developed a reputation for being amenable to the sale of what was not supposed to be purchasable: citizenship within the *polis*. They became the butt of the comic poets, just as our comedians could get a quick laugh by referring to the assumed political dishonesty of Jersey City or Cook County, Illinois. "Today a slave, tomorrow a Sounian" ran a joke of the second quarter of the fourth century.[19] The deme of Potamos was equally infamous for its flexible civic virtue in regard to illegal citizenship as the comic poet Menander noted.[20] In his court speech *Against Eubulides* Demosthenes details the corruption in the deme of Halimous. Two foreigners, Anaximenes and Nikostratos, were enrolled as Halimousioi illegally after paying bribes of five drachmas each to the conspirators.[21] Despite this publicity, the deme maintained its easy approachability. Several years after Demosthenes' speech, an ex-slave and metic Agasikles was impeached for a successful fraudulent attempt to obtain full citizenship from the same deme.

Citizenship was not the only thing for sale. We have evidence that some of the townships, during the first half of the fourth century, "had begun . . . to 'sell' opportunities to hold sortitive city offices." As a result the central government took away from the demes the privilege of filling those places, though they could still fill council seats.[22] Some citizenship cases involved dirty politics. Euxitheus, who is the complainant in the case *Against Eubulides*, asserts that in Halimous, where he was a citizen, Eubulides and his father, the current demarch, conspired to remove Euxitheus from the citizenship roll, claiming that the written record had been lost. A vote of the deme assembly, held under oath but under questionable circumstances, excluded ten men, including Euxitheus, from citizenship. Euxitheus claimed that Eubulides initiated the action for revenge against him and that coconspirators were bribed to readmit the others expelled.[23] The trial for which the speech was delivered took place at the Heliastic court in Athens, where, we assume, since the records do not tell us, Euxitheus' rights were restored to him.

When we contemplate the democracy of the central Athenian government, a direct polity with an Assembly of 6,000 citizens, some of them walking more than twenty miles to attend a session, juries of 1,000 or 2,000, offices filled by lottery, votes for war or peace taken in huge meetings more closely resembling an army than a voting body, we may reflect that this is "not us," that it is truly *ancient* society. The polity in the townships, on the other hand, has a familiar ring. The style of democratic participation and even the brand of petty and not-so-petty corruption echos our own experience. Mr. Dooley would have felt perfectly at home in Halimous; the rascals have ever been among us.

We have a single, unfortunately brief, reference in an ancient source to the feeling people had for their demes. After the outbreak of the Peloponnesian War, Sparta invaded Attica. The city was secure behind its walls, but the countryside was wasted, and Pericles moved all the country folk into the city, making it an island of refuge. The uprooted were not happy with their displaced-persons status, and Thucydides tells us "Deep was their trouble and discontent at abandoning their houses and the hereditary temples of the ancient constitution, and at having to change their habits of life and to bid farewell to *what each regarded as his native city.*"[24]

There is no political analysis from Aristotle or anyone else on what action on the deme level meant for the democratic spirit of the society. We can now see enough, however, to postulate that there may have been great similarities between ancient Athens and nineteenth-century America as to the *meaning* of the township democracy. If we resort to the comparative method, de Tocqueville may teach us much about Athens in his paean to township politics.

> The New Englander is attached to his township because it is strong and independent; he has an interest in it because he shares in its management; he loves it because he has no reason to complain of his lot; he invests his ambition and his future in it; in the restricted sphere within his scope, he learns to rule society; he gets to know those formalities without which freedom can advance only through revolutions, and becoming imbued with their spirit, develops a taste for order, understands the harmony of the powers, and in the end accumulates clear, practical ideas about the nature of his duties and the extent of his rights.[25]

There is one passage in Euripides that gives a picture of a sturdy, right-thinking, democratic yeoman which resembles the laconic, upright, steady New Englander of the last century. How much does the practice of township democracy contribute to these characteristics?

> *But at last*
> *someone stood up to take the other side.*
> *Nothing much to look at, but a real man;*
> *not the sort one sees loafing in the market*
> *or public places, ma'am, but a small farmer,*
> *part of that class on which our country depends;*
> *an honest, decent, and god-fearing man,*
> *and anxious, in the name of common sense,*
> *to say his bit.*[26]

It seems unlikely that our yeoman learned this commitment to the democratic spirit—the right and *the obligation* to say his bit for the just decision—only through the central government in Athens. Political and social action in the deme may have more to do with the spirit of society than we have imagined.

Some tantalizing questions arise about the relationship of political action and ambition on the township and the central-government level. Did an ambitious, rising politician learn his political ropes in deme politics? Was success at the township level the avenue to political recognition in the central government (as some of our successful politicos proceed up the ladder from county to state to Washington)? We cannot know but the answer appears to be negative. It seems that the central government in the city and political life in the 139 to 140 demes occurred on two different levels with little interaction between the two, especially among the political leaders. We know the names of forty demarchs, but only two certainly held office in the central government. Of the 250 citizens known to have held the office of general in the fifth and fourth centuries, not one was active in the demes. And of the 157 known proposers of laws or decrees in the central Assembly between 403 and 322 only 3 or 4 can be proven to have participated in deme politics.[27]

Central political life apparently operated independently of township politics, with no need to draw its rising stars therefrom. This may represent a social and economic hierarchical pattern. The rich and those of noble houses would tend to concentrate their efforts in the city. Their sons and nephews would provide the fresh new political talent. In the demes, the local nobility and rich peasants probably held dominant positions, but the middling and lower-class citizens no doubt had their say, as in New England townships.

A more important question, because its answer would shed light on the origins of democracy, is that of the historical development of the deme democracy. Cleisthenes put the final configuration on the distribution of demes, but he did not create the demes, many of which, like Eleusis, must have descended from small city-states or villages that merged at some point in the dark past to form the *polis* of Athens. What was local political life like at the time of Solon and of the tyranny of the Pisistratidai? It is possible that, though the central government became a tyranny, democracy still flourished in the townships. It is even possible that local democracy waxed and developed during the tyranny of Pisistratus and this evolution prepared the way for the central democratic reforms of Cleisthenes in 508 after the fall of the tyrants. We are asking, but cannot know, how much, if at all, the development of local democracy contributed to the establishment of democratic forms in the central government.

Must a healthy democratic state originate on the local level? What would a comparative study of England and Germany, for instance, reveal? The former led the modern world in democratic action; the latter encountered formidable difficulties in establishing and maintaining a free society. How much did differences in township life in the eighteenth century contribute to these two different developments? Was it not unreasonable to anticipate success for democracy in this century in traditional Africa with its almost complete lack of democratic life on the local level? For ancient Athens, the answers may never come; only the central state is visible to us before the fifth century. We have the obligation, however, to look at the modern world, to inquire of the multitude of states that have struggled for democratic forms and failed, how much this failure results from the fact that democracy is almost impossible to impose from above. The "miracle" of Athenian democracy may have had its genesis in the lowly, almost invisible, demes.

The Guardians of the Democratic Spirit: Education and Law

There is a remarkably important, but unfortunately condensed, passage in Aristotle's *Politics* about the nature of social and moral development. Having declared in a famous pronouncement that "man is a political animal"—a phrase Barker renders more profoundly as "man is by nature an animal intended to live in a *polis*,"[28]—Aristotle remarks a few paragraphs later that, "there is therefore an imminent impulse in all men toward an association of this order. But the man who first *constructed* such an association, was none the less the greatest of benefactors. Man, when perfected, is the best of animals; but if he be isolated from law and justice he is the worst of all."[29]

It is in our nature to live in a *polis*; human nature dictates political life. But, surprisingly enough, people and the *polis* are *not* coterminous. Humans existed before the *polis*, which had to be invented, or, in Aristotle's word, "constructed." The creation of the *polis* is an historical event despite the fact that humans are destined by their nature to live in one. For law and justice there is also "an imminent impulse in all men" but the system of education must be invented and constructed. The surprisingly Hegelian notion is that although many things of great value are imminent in human nature, only the advance of history makes them a reality.

It is a fundamental theory of this book on Athenian democracy that the democratic impulse is "imminent in all humans." Those who first constructed a democratic society were "the greatest of benefactors" but it need not necessarily have happened, intrinsic though the impulse is in human nature. Aristotle knew of many men who did not live in a *polis*—barbarians and even some Greeks such as the Thessalians and Aetolians. Aristotle knew that there was a pre-*polis* time in Greek history. The historically contingent nature of democratic society has influenced me to declare its first construction miraculous. Without a certain kind of education and a particular sacred regard for law, two essential instruments for overcoming the paranoid position, the democratic spirit would never have come alive. The Athenians, well aware of these contingencies, knew that without education and law the *polis* could not exist.

It is remarkable that many of the great thinkers of Liberalism and the Enlightenment, many of whom prided themselves on their liberation from the absurd fictions of traditional religion, nevertheless had complete faith in one of the most fantastic notions ever fobbed off on humankind, that society can be, and is, held together by a rational perception and balance of interests, by a social contract. Nothing so rational ever held any society together. The forms of social cohesion inevitably have a more primitive genesis. There is always something religious or sacred in the tribal bond. No legal-rational contract ever made people willing to die for each other. And without that spirit, there is no *polis*. *Why* so many intelligent people have believed in the absurdity of the contract theory since the seventeenth century is a challenge. Aristotle perceived the vacuity in such a notion almost two thousand years before the rise of Liberal thought. His assertions against contract theory quote another thinker, indicating that the idea was already in the air in the fourth century. Aristotle knew, as we are just beginning to rediscover, that education for justice, no matter how widely or narrowly justice may be defined, holds the *polis* together:

The conclusion which clearly follows is that any polis which is truly so called, and is not merely one in name, must devote itself to the end of encouraging goodness. Otherwise, a political association sinks into a mere alliance. . . . Otherwise, too, law becomes a mere covenant—or (in the phrase of the Sophist Lycophron) 'a guarantor of men's rights against one another'—instead of being as it should be, a rule of life such as will make the members of a polis good and just.[30]

Through the centuries advocates of Liberalism have not been averse to education for what they considered goodness and justice. They have always preached the virtues of the Liberal position, a strange combination of humane justice and absurd fantasies: on the one hand, equality and the universality of rights, and on the other, the superrational social contract theory of society, wherein private vices become public virtues and the market solves all human problems. Aristotle lived in a slave, not a capitalist, society and, therefore, although his thought was beclouded by the existence of slavery, he saw what the true end of political action should be, unconfused by capitalist perceptions. In Philip Rieff's terms, *homo politicus* had not yet given way to *homo oeconomicus*.[31] Aristotle viewed political education as one of the primary tasks of society:

The greatest, however, of all the means we have mentioned for ensuring the stability of constitutions . . . is the education of citizens in the spirit of their constitution. There is no profit in the best of laws, even when they are sanctioned by general civil consent, if the citizens themselves have not been attuned, by the force of habit and the influence of teaching, to the right constitutional temper.[32]

In the perception of Plato and Aristotle, though not in the actuality of Athenian political life, our nineteenth-century ideal of free, universal education had already taken shape. Though placed by most in the antidemocratic camp, these two thinkers clearly saw what was essential for a stable, modern democratic society. "No father," Plato wrote, "shall either send or keep away his son as a pupil from school at his own whim, but every Tom, Dick and Harry, so to speak, must as far as possible, be compelled to receive education." Aristotle echoed the thought: "The system of education must also be one and the same for all . . . it cannot be left, as it is at present, to private enterprise, with each parent making private provision for his children."[33] The discussion first elaborated by these great Greek humanists continues today in the controversy over the variant qualities of public education due to discrepant local taxing capacities.

Although overcoming the paranoid position is "imminent in all men," it takes a large dose of guidance and indoctrination to ensure the viability of the democratic spirit. The true *telos* of teaching in a democratic society is to enable people to live their political lives without exaggerated recourse to paranoid defenses. All discussion about the nature of the educational curriculum—particularly intense these days—is an argument about *means*. The *end* of education in a free society is the creation of an environment in which the democratic spirit may thrive. Any morally valid changes in curriculum must serve that end.

The other guardian of the democratic genius is law. Not law narrowly defined, since even the most totalitarian societies have "laws," but a special relationship to law. As early as Solon in the beginning of the sixth century, a particularly "sacred" view of law was evident:

> These are the lessons which my heart bids me teach the Athenians, how that lawlessness brings innumerable ills to the state, but obedience to the law shows forth all things in order and harmony and at the same time sets shackles on the unjust. It smooths what is rough, checks greed, dims arrogance, withers the opening blooms of ruinous folly, makes straight the crooked judgement, tames the deeds of insolence, puts a stop to the works of civil dissention, and ends the wrath of bitter strife. Under its rule all things among mankind are sane and wise.[34]

It is significant that Solon does not credit a just man, or a good man, or even a law-abiding man with his "order and harmony" but the law itself, and the obedience that is its due.

A peculiar psychological relationship exists between citizens and the law. Everyone knows that laws are made by the people and yet one must treat them with a certain reverence, as if they are not created by humans, but given. In a well-ordered society, we are told, the law, not the people, should be sovereign, a double vision similar to the feeling for the gods. Athena was reverenced as a god although her persona was constructed by human beings. Our Bible calls it sacrilegious to worship idols, the creations of our own hands, yet there is apparently nothing more reverent than worshipping the gods themselves, the creations of our moral imaginations.

Demosthenes wrote eloquently on the seemingly contradictory aspects of the law. "Of 'the three most important factors which maintain and preserve democracy,' " he insisted, "the first is law."[35] Hypereides, an orator contemporary with Demosthenes, declared: "in a democracy the laws shall be sovereign."[36] Demosthenes further supports this thesis when he contrasts oligarchy and a free democratic society: "Under oligarchic government everybody is entitled to undo the past, and to prescribe the future transactions according to his own pleasure; whereas the laws of a free state prescribe what shall be done in the future, such laws having been enacted by convincing people that they will be beneficial to those who live under them."[37]

The declaration of the sacred nature of the law has a deep rhetorical impact but logically there is something amiss. The laws can be changed, and only people, not gods, can make that change. "And what is the strength of the laws?" Demosthenes asks. "If one of you is wronged and cries aloud, will the laws run up and be at his side to assist him? No; they are only written texts incapable of such action. Wherein resides their power? In yourselves, if only you support them and make them all-powerful to help him who needs them. So the laws are strong through you and you through the laws."[38] However, Aristotle's basic criticism of the worst form of democracy is that, under it, "the people, not the law, is the final sovereign. This is what happens when popular decrees are sovereign instead of the law; and that is a result which is brought about by leaders of the demagogue type."[39]

The confusion in this argument results from the two different ways the words "law" and "people" are used. A double vision in regard to the law is necessary for a free society. On the one hand, the law is sacred; it must be sovereign; no person may set himself above the law; a just citizen will reverence the laws of the *polis*; they are given, not enacted. On the other hand, there can be no final arbiter of what the law means or should be except the *demos* itself; the spirit of the *demos* is the final cause of a just society; if that spirit does not reverence the law, some form of naked power will rule. A free society requires the *demos* to remain without arrogance in the exercise of its sovereignty.

This conflict between the sovereignty of the people and the sovereignty of the law is resolved in all basically free societies by the creation of a distinction between the constitution (the fundamental law of the *polis*) and decrees-laws-enactments by legislators. The psychological split necessary to preserve both freedom and stability is resolved by attributing to the constitution the required psychological dimensions of sacred, given, ultimately sovereign, and reserving to the people the day-by-day power of decrees and enactments. Not that there should be no provision for changing the constitution, but it must be slow, difficult, filled with the sense of treading on sacred ground.

Athenian judicial conduct and conscious thought made precisely that distinction. "In Athens in the fourth century," writes Raphael Sealey, "a distinction was drawn between 'laws' (*nomoi*) and 'decrees' (*psēphismata*). Both laws and decrees were upheld by the courts. . . . Laws had greater authority than decrees, and if a decree was known to contravene a law or some laws, the decree was declared invalid by a court. The procedure for changing the laws, whether by adding to them or canceling some of them, was slower and more difficult than the procedure for passing or repealing decrees."[40] From 403 to 399 the Athenians completely revised the basic law code (the constitution) and by 382 had worked out a procedure for amending that constitution:

> Three safeguards attached to that procedure are conservative in spirit. First, when the assembly voted that any of the four categories of law needed to be revised, it also elected five men to defend the current laws. Second, even after a new law had been passed by a board of lawgivers, it could be challenged as "inexpedient" before a *dikastērion* [jury-court]. The third safeguard was the rule that the old law overrode the newly passed law, if the latter did not repeal the old law explicitly.[41]

The same conservative spirit (sovereignty of law over sovereignty of *demos*) informed a particular clause of the United States Constitution. What were to be the grounds for impeaching a President? George Mason argued that "maladministration" should be sufficient. This would obviously open the door to a hostile Congress attempting to remove a President with whom it simply disagreed. The final adoption of the phrase "high crimes and misdemeanors" made of the impeachment process a sacred, not a secular, experience[42]—one not to be taken lightly, but with a certain degree of fear and trembling. It was revealing to watch the House of Representatives during the impeachment debate after the Watergate scandal involving President Richard Nixon. They called on all the powers of righteousness for the preservation of the Republic to overcome their anxiety and perform their constitutional task. They were considering no ordinary decree. Changing the constitution of the *polis* stimulates the same reverential feelings.

The split between the practical and the sacred aspects of law creates a logical division between conservatives and progressives. The conservative stresses the constitutional, sacred and traditional, aspects of the law; the progressive believes the *demos* should be free to move as its majority vision dictates. Aristotle was the great conservative. Barker comments: "If we ask ourselves . . . 'What has been, and still is, the nature of the legacy which the *Politics* bequeathed to the common thought of Europe?', the answer may almost be compressed in a single word . . . 'constitutionalism.' "[43] Aristotle criticized the demagogues of Athens (Cleon and others)—as also did those who feared the power of the *nouveaux riches* leaders of the *demos*—because they disregarded the traditional, constitutional, here called "sacred," dimension of the law, and attempted to reduce it to what-the-people-want. Aristotle, being a true conservative and not a reactionary, objected as strenuously to oligarchy, in which the law was also traduced by a small group of self-appointed tyrants.

The person of liberal temperament sees the sacred and traditional aspects of the law as maintaining—at the least—inherited privilege and—at the worst—the dominance and tyranny of a politically and economically empowered minority, a situation that must be transformed if the *polis* is to move forward. A healthy democratic society must have room for both points of view. Should either fail in its viability, the democracy becomes endangered. Athens in the fourth century fully comprehended this reality.

Was this most complicated truth learned only at the level of the central government in the city? The experience of education and law in day-to-day deme life may have been the greatest teacher of all.

19

The Instability of the Republican City-State

Introduction

I t seems prudent to present the argument of this chapter succinctly right at the start. The historical periods covered in this chapter are so far-reaching that only rather cursory data supporting its propositions can be presented. Anyone acquainted with the history of ancient Greece and of other city-states observes many striking similarities in their value systems and institutions, even though they come from radically separate historical eras. It is important to emphasize those congruences and to ask what they might mean.

We are concerned here only with Mediterranean city-states in three historical periods: those of ancient Greece, the Roman Republic, and Italy in the late medieval and early-modern world. The states of the Low Countries in the late Middle Ages, or of the Hanseatic League, for example, are outside the purview of this survey.

We are discussing *Republican* city-states, societies without a monarch. The forms of social cohesion are crucial to any society: what holds the social system together, what makes individuals adhere to each other in their political animality. In a functioning monarchy, loyalty to the king, with his charismatic appurtenances, and fear of his punishing power

are essential forms of social cohesion. In a Republican state these motivations are lacking. Citizenship, the transformed energy of kinship,
holds the *polis* together. Domination and terror also make a sizeable
contribution in oligarchic and aristocratic governments to the stability
of society. Even in authoritarian societies, the lack of a monarch makes
a significant difference. The psychology of kingship and the way in
which it binds society are unique phenomena. Though Sparta had a
king—two at a time—it was still a Republican society because the
kings were more hereditary executive-generals than monarchs; the essence holding the Spartan garrison state together was not monarchical
sentiment but kinship-citizenship. The Republican city-state can be
transformed into a monarchical state (the Medici became the kings of
Florence, for instance) creating a different form of society. The universal impulse of all Republican city-states to evolve in the direction of
monarchy is a topic of this chapter, but the Republican state is our
subject and is what we refer to with the words "city-state," unless
otherwise indicated.

The city-state was fundamentally an unstable form of society. Athens in
ancient Greece and Venice in Italy were the exceptions to the otherwise
valid observation that the city-state was vulnerable to dissolution. Three
potent political attributes tending toward instability were present in
almost all such societies:

1. Socioeconomic conflict. The rich versus the poor. The struggle
of wealthy nonnobles against inherited nobility and the seemingly inevitable tendency for the conflicts to become violent.

2. Almost constant interstate warfare.

3. Internecine struggle among members of the aristocracy for leadership of the *polis* which could develop into the bloodiest of civil wars.

The psychological power of monarchy derives, ultimately, from a
particular view of paternal potency. Once the king—the father—is
removed, the locus of psychological-political power becomes indeter-
minate. Freud was wrong in the fable he told in *Totem and Taboo* wherein
the brothers in prehistoric times, after killing and eating the father,
shared out the women and lived together in equality, subsequently re-
evoking the father's presence in the totem feast. That fable was a metaphorical description of the revolutionary birth of a democratic state.
The history of the city-state demonstrates that once the father is removed and the possibilities of equality become real, the brothers begin

to war with each other, either seeking sibling equality or determined to become the new father and the new tyrant. There is no longer a father with the power to command the sons to stop slaughtering each other. Unless a stable democratic state eventually prevails, or the monarchy is reborn, the fraternal killing never seems to stop.

Since almost all city-states were incapable of democratic resolution of their conflicts, monarchy proved to be the *telos* of the *polis*. Not only did the *polis* society of ancient Greece ultimately get swallowed up by Hellenistic monarchies, but the clear signs of monarchical transformation were already apparent, even at Athens, in the fourth century before Philip and Alexander conquered the Hellenic world. Once the Roman Empire had reached enormous size, and had ceased to be a safety-valve for intra-*polis* rivalry, the city-state of Rome indulged in a series of civil wars to determine who should be the new monarch of the *polis* and the emperor of the Empire. In the Italian city-states, the experiment with *polis* life over several hundred years did not succeed, and the *Signorie*, in city after city, put an end to Republican politics. Machiavelli was not the first to announce that only an enlightened and ruthless prince could put an end to political chaos. He stands at the end of a long line of observers who despaired of the Republican city-state. Since a stable, democratic society appeared impossible to him, monarchy became the alternative to anarchy and impotence.

In Greece, Rome, and Italy we observe characteristic political phenomena apparently inevitable in the history of the city-state:

1. Citizen soldiers give way to mercenaries, often leaving the state at the mercy of home-grown generals or foreign mercenary captains (*condottieri*). Republican politics yields to a clash of armies.

2. An attempt is made to end the violence of the socioeconomic struggles by appointing an arbitrator, chosen either from the *polis* or from outside the city, or, as in Rome, by appointing a temporary dictator. The historical line runs all the way from Solon to the *podestas* of early-modern Italy.

3. In their struggle with each other for supreme power in the state, aristocrats make instrumental alliances with lower socioeconomic classes to strengthen their political position.

4. As soon as the aristocratic faction or a rising tyrant no longer needs the help of "the people," they are dispensed with, and the *demos* discovers for the thousandth time that it has been used. It does not learn how to use others.

5. Whenever a rising socioeconomic class succeeds in attaining political power, almost its first act is to take measures to prevent those below it from acquiring the same power. The *arrivistes* often ally themselves with their former opponents to keep the *demos* powerless, putting an end to democratic aspirations.

The Republican city-state was a transitional phenomenon. If it did not evolve into a mature democratic society, as it rarely did, it either moved toward monarchy or remained in an almost constant state of warfare and civil conflict. Monarchy holds. The Republican order, on the contrary, is fragile indeed. The stability of the monarchical system rests on its effective defense against paranoid anxieties. All monarchies attribute psychological omnipotence to the king, a crucial factor protecting his subjects from unnameable psychic stress. Scholars cite Venice as the exception to the otherwise valid observation that Italian city-states were profoundly unstable. But this example may confirm, rather than contradict, the concept that in predemocratic societies monarchical omnipotence is essential for political stability. Venice had no king, but a narrow group of high nobles, a sort of collectivized monarchy, ruled with all the charismatic trappings and corresponding terror of the monarchical office. A Doge was elected for life, practiced many of the rituals associated with kingship, and even—in a famous ceremony—married Venice to the sea.

The Republican city-state in its typical form, forsook monarchy, a fundamental defense against the threat of paranoia, only to fail to develop adequate new defenses. The failure to arrive at a mature democratic society indicated that the paranoid position had not yet been overcome. Trapped in this transitional state society became violent and unstable.

The Republican City-State: Greece, Rome, Italy

A multitude of commentators have remarked on the instability of the Republican city-state. N. G. L. Hammond, author of an important recent general history of ancient Greece, concluded with this indictment after five hundred pages of detailed history: "The turmoil in and between the Greek states was ultimately due to the failure of the city-state as a political form to meet the spiritual, social, and economic needs of the citizens."[1]

When we turn to Roman history, we find the general intellectual view suffers from distortion. Under the unfortunate influence of Gibbon, most people believe the fall of the Roman Empire is the most important sociological problem of Roman history. Far more important to the history of human society is understanding the total collapse of the Roman Republic in the years from 133 (the tribunate of Tiberius Gracchus) to 27 (the consolidation of Augustus Caesar's power as de facto emperor). "Why the fall of the Republic occurred exactly when and how it did," states the Oxford History of the Classical World, "is secondary to the main question: why did leading members of the Roman governing class, who themselves had most to gain from the existence of the Republic, destroy it, thereby committing political suicide."[2]

Theodor Mommsen, the great historian of Republican Rome, confirms the point being made here: either monarchy or democracy could have provided the stability that the Republic lacked. Not a sociological analysis, it remains a pungent observation on the problematic in the polity. "In the Rome of this epoch the two evils of a degenerate oligarchy and a democracy still undeveloped but already cankered in the bud were interwoven in a manner pregnant with fatal results. According to their party names, which are first heard during this period, the 'optimates' wished to give effect to the will of the best, the 'populares' to that of the community; but in fact there was in Rome of that day neither a true aristocracy nor a truly self-determining community. Both parties contended alike for shadows, and numbered in their ranks none but enthusiasts or hypocrites. . . . The Commonwealth would beyond doubt have been a gainer, if either the aristocracy had directly introduced a hereditary rotation [that is, eliminated all popular dimension in the choosing of magistrates] . . . or the democracy had produced from within it a real demagogic government."[3] Thus Rome, far from being an exception, was, according to Mommsen's description, typical of the Republican city-state.

When we pass on to the Italian city-states, the demonstration is even simpler. Nobody can read even briefly the history of Italian *poleis* without being struck by the enormity of human political incompetence. If man is driven by his nature to live in a *polis*, it appears that nature fails him when it comes time to make that *polis* liveable. Note, for example, this forty-year period: "At Brescia, in 1196, there was a confrontation between the guilds and the order of knights. A similar clash took place at Piacenza in 1198, and another at Milan during the years 1198 to 1201. Assisi saw violent class and factional disturbances between 1198 and 1202. Padua also experienced the like in 1200, Cremona in 1201, Lucca in 1203, and Sienna in 1212. Even little towns, such as Monetpulciano in 1229 and Pistoia in 1234, rang with the clangor of the bloody altercations between the middle and upper classes."[4] Venice's famed stability may be explained by the fact that its *polis* history began two hundred years earlier than that of most other states. Venice suffered at the end of the tenth century what Brescia, Padua, Lucca, and others experienced at the end of the twelfth. It recovered from political chaos, established a small aristocracy as a collective *signori*, and became the very symbol of political stability. At the end of the tenth century, however, it was a typical city-state: "The factions broke out again under new names; this time the parties were Morosini and Colopini, and once again Venice's mercantile expansion was hindered by domestic war. Deaths, mourning, tears and exile: the tragic cycle continued."[5]

The historian Daniel Waley sums up the Italian city-state experience as follows: "The existence of republican forms of government in the Italian city-states was intensely precarious. These institutions were so constantly under pressure or even in full crisis that there is little reason to be puzzled at their failure to survive in most of the cities. The factionalism discussed . . . suffices on its own to explain why, in most cities, the regime of a single individual was able to secure acceptance before the end of the fourteenth century. Clearly the occasional survival of republicanism as an exception needs more explaining than do the triumphs of the *signori*."[6]

James Madison and Alexander Hamilton, prominent spokesmen at the time of the founding of the American Republic, were keenly aware of the history of the Republican city-state. Intensely conscious of the vulnerability of Republican forms, they were determined to safeguard this new union against the catastrophes of past history. That past history provided them with a powerful argument: should the individual states remain virtually independent and not united in one federation, the history of Greece and Italy was bound to be repeated. Nothing so powerfully calls to mind George Santayana's dictum that he-who-does-not-remember-the-past-is-condemned-to-repeat-it as this passionate argument from the pen of Hamilton:

A Firm Union will be of the utmost moment to the peace and liberty of the States as a barrier against domestic faction and insurrection. It is impossible to read the history of the petty Republics of Greece and Italy, without feeling sensations of horror and disgust at the distractions with which they were continually agitated, and at the rapid succession of revolution, by which they were kept in a state of perpetual vibration, between the extremes of tyranny and anarchy. If they exhibit occasional calms, these only serve as short-lived contrasts to the furious storms that are to succeed. If now and then intervals of felicity open themselves to view, we behold them with a mixture of regret arising from the reflection that the pleasing scenes before us are soon to be overwhelmed by the tempestuous waves of sedition and party-rage. If momentary waves of glory break forth from the gloom, while they dazzle us with a transient and fleeting brilliancy, they at the same time admonish us to lament that the vices of government should pervert the direction and tarnish the lustre of those bright talents and exalted endowments, for which the favoured soils, that produced them, have been so justly celebrated.[7]

The political violence that made the existence of the Republican city-state impossible differed in quality and degree in the three historical periods under consideration here. In Greece, it was the struggle between classes, the civil war over democracy and oligarchy, as well as inter-*polis* warfare that threatened the existence of the state. The destructive element in Rome was a pathetic (because without moral content), violent competition among aristocrats. "The political life of the Roman Republic," writes Ronald Syme, an historian of the collapse of Rome, "was stamped and swayed, not by parties and programmes of a modern and parliamentary character, not by the ostensible opposition between Senate and People, *Optimates* and *Populares*, *nobiles* and *novi homines*, but by the strife for power, wealth and glory. The contestants were the *nobiles* among themselves."[8] The Italian city-states had the misfortune of combining all the destructive forces into one fractured *polis* phenomenon: social-economic struggle, incessant interstate warfare, and murderous competition among aristocrats.

We need not repeat what has been said concerning the destructive power of social-economic struggle and inter-*polis* warfare. We have not, however, considered the violent conflict of aristocrats among themselves, which played a role in the Greek *polis*, proved so damaging to

Italian city-states, and destroyed the Roman Republic. This warfare was not about democracy, or equality, or freedom, or "class struggle"; it was simply a rage for power among the leaders of society who seemed not to know what else to do with their lives. Those not engaged in the struggle were powerless to prevent this political suicide.

Though political violence was endemic in Rome from 133 until the destruction of the Republican state and formation of the Empire, there were two particular periods of extended civil war among aristocratic factions. The first centers around the rivals Marius (c. 157–86) and Sulla (c. 138–78). The second period developed into a contest for the monarchy and had two stages, the first involving the ambitions of Julius Caesar, Pompey the Great, Cicero, and Cato the Younger. The second witnessed the final triumph of Octavius Caesar over Cicero, Brutus, the younger Pompey, and Antony.

It is striking that these Roman aristocrats, after four hundred years of sophisticated, "civilized" Republican history, could not—would not—figure out a way to compete with each other without destructive violence. Romans massacred Romans as if their opponents were the lowliest barbarians, nonpeople. In 87 Marius took Rome. "He then entered, and with him the reign of terror. It was determined not to select the individual victims, but to have all the notable men of the Optimate party put to death and to confiscate their property. The gates were closed; for five days and five nights the slaughter continued without interruption; even afterwards the execution of individuals who had escaped or been overlooked was of daily occurrence, and for months the bloody persecution went on throughout Italy. . . . His revenge was not satisfied even with the death of his victim; he forbade the burial of the dead bodies: he gave orders . . . that the heads of the *senators* slain should be fixed to the rostra of the Forum."[9] He did not eat their bodies; he was too civilized for that.

Five years later it was Sulla's turn to play headhunter. Returning with an invincible army after extraordinary military success in the East, "Sulla secured all the approaches to Rome and entered the city unopposed. Meantime Marius [the Younger] had imitated the ferocity of his father. Realizing that Rome was lost, he ordered the *praetor urbanus*, L. Junius Brutus Damasippus, before evacuating the city to put to death most of the notable men of the other party. . . . In the proscriptions of Sulla Italy endured the consummation of her sufferings. The execution of the captured Marian leaders and the butchery of the Samnite prisoners were followed by continual murders in the city. . . . At length one of [Sulla's] own partisans questioned him in the Senate as to his intentions. His response was the issue of a series of proscription lists, by which he outlawed all who had in any public or private capacity aided the cause of his opponents. . . . Rewards were offered to those who murdered or betrayed any of these outlaws."[10]

It seems almost incredible to us, who have witnessed this kind of slaughter in this century under the banner of ideological purification, that this butchering had no moral or political thrust. "Populares" and "Optimates" were merely names under which "the best" people could rally, and possibly look for allies; they could just as well have been yellows and purples. It is hard to know which is worse, ideological or meaningless slaughter. No wonder thoughtful people, abhorring such behavior, cried out for a king to put a stop to the chaos.

Cicero, the last of the aristocratic Republicans, never became a monarchist; he probably could not espy anyone in the chaotic politics of Rome, except for himself, worthy of the position of monarch. Cicero believed the Republican solution lay in a restoration of the "concord of the orders," that is, a harmony among the classes. The memory of Sulla's terror had burned itself into his imagination,[11] and when he criticized his sometime ally Cato the Younger for an unwise political action, he commented that Cato was behaving "as if he were living in Plato's Republic and not in the cesspool of Romulus."[12] To such an abyss had the once proud Republican city-state descended. No one has yet succeeded in telling us why.

We who live in an intensely competitive society, who daily witness acute rivalry in sports, business, and politics, do not find competition for power among aristocrats to be unusual. For theoretical understanding, however, we would be wiser if we could explain the phenomenon and not consider it a given of some hypothetical "human nature." Nothing is more important for the future of *our* society than the question of how much competition is necessary in human relations. To what degree is the competitive drive capable of sublimation and transformation? What immediately strikes us in reading about the ancient city-states is not the competitive nature of political life—we easily comprehend that—but that the rivalry became so murderous. Losers in the political struggle lived short lives.

One bizarre, but possibly archetypical, example of the human need for murderous competition comes from the ancient world but not strictly from a city-state. So illustrative is it of a wild, irrational, completely amoral impulse in the human psyche that it may help toward understanding why Roman aristocrats slaughtered each other with such ease. In the later Roman Empire of the fifth and sixth centuries A.D., the population of many cities divided themselves into two factions, the Blues and the Greens. Originating in the competitive chariot races of the hippodrome, the violence of these factions, and their hatred for one another, became a fundamental ingredient in the instability of Byzantine political life, at times actually threatening the reign of the Emperor himself. In the sixth century A.D. the historian Procopius described the phenomenon:

> The populace in every city has from time immemorial been divided into Blues and Greens, but it is only recently that for the sake of those names . . . they lavish their money, expose their persons to the most cruel tortures and are willing to die a dreadful death. They fight with their opponents, not knowing what the struggle is about, though they understand full well that, even if they defeat their adversaries in a fight, their fate will be to be put into prison forthwith and after the extremest tortures to be executed. The enmity which they feel towards their neighbours is irrational, but it persists without end for all time. It overrides the bonds of kinship or friendship, even if those who quarrel about these colours are brothers or the like. They care for nothing human or divine beside victory in this contest, whether a sacrilege is committed against God or the laws or the constitutions are overturned by domestic or foreign foes. . . . Even women share in this contagion, not only supporting their husbands, but if it so happens opposing them—though they never go to the theatre and have no other motive. In short I can only describe it as a psychopathic condition.[13]

When the city-state was born again some five hundred years later in Italy, this "psychopathic condition" appeared to be the normal human condition. Guelphs and Ghibellines were the names, not Blues and Greens, under which Italian aristocrats played this murderous game. "In the later twelfth century . . . in commune after commune, the nobility was torn by homicidal rivalries."[14] "After 1250, from Umbria to the Alps, there was a dramatic escalation in the strife between political blocs: the alignments became sharper, the sides more uncompromising, the wars bloodier and more expansive. . . . In a number of cities— Perugia, Bologna, Pisa, Genoa—the ferocity of party and sometimes class conflict persisted thereafter. Mass exile became commonplace; so also the wholesale confiscation of enemy properties, the razing of houses, and the formation of exile armies."[15]

Let us emphasize that these murderous conflicts were almost wholly without a moral or class dimension, though sometimes social-economic conflict played a role. What this almost-fantasy, almost-nightmare political life could mean for a prominent individual living through this dream, is demonstrated by the following note John Ciardi appends to his translation of lines 32 to 51 of Canto X of Dante Alighieri's *Inferno*:

> Farinata degli Uberti was head of the ancient noble house of Uberti. He became leader of the Ghibellines of Florence in 1239 and played a large part in expelling the Guelphs in 1248. The Guelphs returned in 1251, but Farinata remained. His arrogant desire to rule singlehanded led to difficulties, however, and he was expelled in 1258. With the aid of Manfredi of Sienna, he gathered a large force and defeated the Guelphs at Montaperti on the River Arbia in 1260. Re-entering Florence in triumph, he again expelled the Guelphs, but at the diet of Empoli, held by the victors after the battle of Montaperti, he alone rose in open counsel to resist the general sentiment that Florence should be razed. He died in Florence in 1264. In 1266 the Guelphs once more returned and crushed forever the power of the Uberti, destroying their palaces and issuing special decrees against persons of the Uberti line. In 1283 a decree of heresy was published against Farinata. [That is, they were hounding him even in hell.][16]

If we were in the position of Madison and Hamilton and had only the Republican histories of Greece, Rome, and Italy before us, and knew nothing of the nineteenth and twentieth centuries A.D., we might conclude that Athenian democracy, which experienced only two short internally motivated oligarchic coups in four hundred years and knew hardly any murderous aristocratic rivalry, was not only "miraculous" but impossible. The previous history of Republics must have given Madison and Hamilton great pause. It took courage for an historically sophisticated person to imagine that another Republic could long survive.

Unlike Madison, Hamilton was ambivalent about Republicanism, and monarchically inclined. When expressing this side of his ambivalence, he placed himself within the time-honored political tradition that conceived of a Republican state as leading to chaos or impotence, the only possible solution being some form of monarchy. All three historical periods under review here strongly exhibited an inclination toward monarchy as the answer to social-economic conflict and intra-aristocratic slaughter. In some cases the Republican city-state did yield to a monarchy: in Rome after catastrophic civil wars; in Italy, in city after city, following almost unrelieved civic strife.

In Greece in the fourth century, the great age of Athenian democracy, many believed that only a king could end the incessant inter-*polis* slaughter and lead Greece to triumph over Persia. Even in Athens, some elite men's minds inclined toward monarchy. "Not only is the century marked by the figures of actual monarchs—Dionysius I of Syracuse, Jason of Pherae, Philip and Alexander: it is also a century of monarchist opinion. Plato writes of philosopher kings in the *Republic*, and of the 'young tyrant' in the *Laws*: Xenophon, half a Socratic and half a soldier, preaches the virtue of a wise sovereign, such as Cyrus, ruling a state organized in the fashion of an army: Isocrates longs for the coming of the commander-in-chief who shall lead a united Greece to the East. . . . This monarchism found its plea and alleged its justification, in the need which was often proclaimed for a strong hand that should not only repress civic strife in Greece, but should also guide all its cities in union to the common war against barbarism."[17]

It is fascinating to observe the attempt to equate the new kings with the gods, an impulse indicating a longing in people's souls not satisfied by the Republican city-state. Not only the "rational" desire to end civil strife and conquer the barbarian but also the deep irrational need for an omnipotent father ordering our lives provided the energy toward monarchy. After Clearchus seized power as a tyrant-king in Heraclea Pontica in 364, he announced that he was the son of Zeus and entitled to divine honors. When he appeared in public he was preceded by an attendant carrying an eagle, the symbol of his divine father. He rouged his face and wore the costume used in tragedy to indicate a monarch: "elevated shoes, purple robes, gold crown, and sceptre."[18] Two years after the battle of Chaeronea (338) when Philip of Macedonia had succeeded in dominating Greece, he began his invasion of Asia and celebrated that event and the wedding of his daughter with a festival to which all Greece was invited. After a lavish banquet in the evening games were to be celebrated the next day. "While it was still dark," Diodorus writes, "the multitude of spectators hastened into the theatre and at sunrise the parade formed. Along with lavish display of every sort, Philip included in the procession statues of twelve gods wrought with great artistry and adorned with a dazzling show of wealth to strike awe in the beholder, and along with these was conducted a thirteenth statue, suitable for a god, that of Philip himself, so that the king exhibited himself enthroned among the twelve gods."[19]

In both the Hellenistic monarchies that followed the conquests of Alexander and in the Roman Empire which succeeded to the Republic, the king was worshipped as a god. The Republican city-state may have provided people with a freedom that, ultimately, they found unbearable. How much easier to cuddle up under the care and tyranny of a king. The twentieth century was not the first to witness a precipitous flight from freedom. Knowing how frightening liberty can be, the amazing thing is that human beings begin a journey toward it in the first place.

Isocrates, who lived to be ninety-eight and had an impact on political life for almost sixty years until his death in 338, exhibited a similar ambivalence about freedom. A sometime supporter of a responsible and limited democracy, Isocrates formulated a classical statement on the advantages of a monarchical polity in the speech *Nicocles* (sometime between 372 and 365). The arguments are familiar to us, but Isocrates was one of their inventors. "Now oligarchies and democracies seek equality for those who share in the administration of them; and the doctrine is in high favour in those governments that one man should not have the power to get more than another—a principle which works in the interests of the worthless! Monarchies, on the other hand, make the highest award to the best man, the next highest to the next best, and in the same proportion to the third and the fourth and so on. . . . Then again, men who live in oligarchies or democracies are led by their mutual rivalries to injure the commonwealth; while those who live in monarchies, not having anyone to envy, do in all circumstances so far as possible what is best."[20]

Isocrates became infatuated with Philip of Macedon. Philip was going to end the debilitating strife in Greece and lead the Greeks in the conquest of Asia. Isocrates was ready to bargain away the freedom of the city-state in return for the charismatic protection *and aggressive conquest* of a divine father. Philip, like twentieth-century fascism, promised order, the end of unbearable freedom, and the enslavement of those outside the reborn kinship system. Isocrates wrote to Philip: "Be assured that a glory unsurpassable and worthy of the deeds you have done in the past will be yours when you shall compel the barbarians . . . to be serfs of the Greeks, and when you shall force the king who is now called Great to do whatever you command. For then will naught be left for you except to become a god."[21]

The Roman Republic, unlike the Greek city-states, needed no foreign influence (for the Macedonians were not, strictly speaking, considered Greeks) to assist it on its compulsive path of self-destruction. L. Cornelius Sulla, though he twice overwhelmed the city of Rome with his armies (88 and 83 B.C.), though he was dictator and took the lives of a large number of Roman aristocrats, nevertheless refused to become a king, and died in retirement after voluntarily giving up political power. The Republic might still be saved from its self-destructive impulses. The suicidal course prevailed, however, and by the crucial year 52 the rivalry between generals had become so acute and so murderous that "The impending war was not a struggle possibly between republic and monarchy—for that had been virtually decided years before—but a struggle between [Pompey] and Caesar for the possession of the crown of Rome."[22]

By that same year, thoughtful, concerned Republicans realized that they had very few options left:

> . . . and the ill-government of Rome, where all who were candidates for office publicly gave money, and without any shame bribed the people, who, having received their pay, did not contend for their benefactors with their bare suffrages, but with bows, swords, and slings. So that after having many times stained the place of election with blood of men killed upon the spot, they left the city at last without a government at all, to be carried about like a ship without a pilot to steer her; where all who had any wisdom could only be thankful if a course of such wild and stormy disorder and madness might end no worse than in a monarchy, and that they ought to take that remedy from the hands of the gentlest physician, meaning Pompey [that is, not Caesar], who, though

in words he pretended to decline it, yet in reality made his utmost efforts to be declared dictator. Cato perceiving his design, prevailed with the senate to make him sole consul, that with the offer of a more legal sort of monarchy he might be withheld from demanding the dictatorship.[23]

After Caesar had destroyed Pompey and Caesar's assassination had been avenged by Antony and Octavius, these last two fought to the death for the crown. Of this struggle "One thing was clear," Syme tells us, "monarchy was already there and would subsist, whatever principle was invoked in the struggle, whatever name the victor chooses to give to his role, because it was for monarchy that the rival Caesarian leaders contended."[24] Republican liberty was dead. It was replaced by "a civil war in which men fought, not for principle, but only for a choice of masters."[25]

Thus was born the Roman Empire, led by absolute rulers for almost five hundred years in the West, and for an additional millennium in the new Rome at Constantinople. Whereas the question of the decline and fall of the Empire has become the stuff of history, the self-destruction of the Republic purveys the essence of tragedy and the tragic flaw, if you will, can be found in the fractured nature of the Republican city-state.

In the Italian city-states the dissolution of Republican liberty and its replacement by a monarchical system occurred in two stages. In the earlier period, a serious attempt was made to preserve Republican forms through the appointment of an arbitrator and governor chosen from outside the city and, therefore, uncontaminated by city politics. Such was the institution of the *podesteria*. From late in the twelfth century, and lasting for about one hundred years as an important institution, the *podesteria* was established to end intra-aristocratic strife and class-based political conflict. Competition for high office had become murderous. The Genoese chronicler announces for the year 1190:

Civil discords and hateful conspiracies and divisions had arisen in the city on account of the mutual envy of many men who greatly wished to hold office as consuls of the commune. So the *sapientes* and councillors of the city met and decided that from the following year the consulate of the commune should come to an end and they almost all agreed that they should have a podesta.[26]

The word *podestà* comes from the Latin *potestas* (power). A noble citizen from another city, not a neighboring one, who had been trained in the law, usually held the office for six months or a year. Many of the most successful practitioners moved from city to city. Guglielmo Pusterla of Milan had no fewer than seventeen different terms as *podestà*. Early in the thirteenth century, the *podesteria* was the rule, rather than the exception, in the Italian communes. He was not a temporary dictator and he still had to pay great attention to the power of the Council in the city where he presided. Gradually the councils became more powerful and by the fourteenth century, where he still existed, the *podestà* was no more than a "chief justice with police powers."[27]

The *podesteria* gave way to tyrant-monarchs, the *signorie*. This transformation appears to have occurred when the political conflict within the city-states changed from intraaristocratic to interclass rivalry. An arbitrator might settle things between nobles, but only a tyrant could keep the peace when the passions of class conflict were released. Machiavelli describes the process in a passage that reads, eerily, almost like a description of the Greek *polis*:

> For in every city these two opposite parties are to be found, arising from the desire of the populace to avoid the oppression of the great, and the desire of the great to command and oppress the people. And from these two opposing interests arises in the city one of three effects: either absolute government, liberty, or license. The former is created either by the populace or the nobility, depending on the relative opportunities of the two parties; for when the nobility see that they are unable to resist the people they unite in exalting one of their number and creating him prince, so as to be able to carry out their own designs under the shadow of his authority. The populace, on the other hand, when unable to resist the nobility, endeavour to exalt and create a prince in order to be protected by his authority.[28]

Whatever the solution, the Republican state is destroyed. Waley argues that more *signorie* arose through antipopular moves than from actions against the magnates, but both forms of tyranny were widespread.[29] Unfortunately for the *popolo*, almost all the princes became tyrants of the people rather than monarchs for the people. Real democracy never seemed a viable option for the Italian city-states, despite its inclusion among Machiavelli's three alternative modes. The other two, license and absolute government, were the true possibilities. The institution of the *signoria* arose to prominence with remarkable speed. From about 1250 to 1300 it swept all of northern Italy. "The significant title of 'permanent lord' seems first to have been granted at this time, to Buoso da Dovara at Soncino in 1255. By the 1280's the *signoria* had become the normal constitutional form over the entire northern plain; from the sub-Alpine regions in the west . . . right across to the Veneto [including, especially, Milan where] . . . except for brief periods the greatest city of Lombardy was never to return to republicanism."[30]

With a knowledge of this history and an accurate perception of the vulnerability of Republican government, Alexander Hamilton, when in his Republican mode, argued for the possibility of a stable democracy. "From the disorders that disfigure the annals of those republics, the advocates of despotism have drawn arguments," he wrote, "not only against the very principles of civil liberty. They have decried all free government, as inconsistent with the order of society, and have indulged themselves in malicious exaltation over its friends and partisans." The absolutist conclusions are wrong, however: "Happily for mankind, stupendous fabrics reared on the basis of liberty, which have flourished for ages have in *a few* [italics added] glorious instances refuted their gloomy sophisms."[31]

Hamilton lists the *institutional* forms that will make responsible Republicanism possible: legislative checks and balances, courts and judges, representative government. "These are either wholly new discoveries or have made their principal progress toward perfection in modern times. They are means, and powerful means, by which the excellencies of republican government may be retained and its imperfection lessened or avoided."[32] A justly cautious statement. Hamilton could not be sure these institutional means would do the trick. The argument of this book is that without the additional crucial factor of a democratic spirit suffused throughout the *demos*, no institutional means can ensure a stable democratic society. We should not be surprised by the fragility of democratic society when we consider how extraordinarily difficult it has been to achieve.

The Demise of the Citizen Soldier

One important social-political development took place in all three historical periods of Republican government under discussion here. Early Republican city-states were dependent on citizen soldiers. To be a citizen, in fact, was almost synonymous with being a soldier. As the Republics matured, they became less dependent on citizen soldiers and made more use of mercenary armies. This process created serious threats to Republican life. It seems no coincidence that, when the bourgeois cities of Northern Europe in the early modern period made their move for power under Republican auspices, and when the American Republic was born, citizen militias played a crucial role in both political developments. American democracy might not have been possible without the state militias. The Greek *poleis*, including Athens, the Roman Republic, and the Italian city-states, all began their Republican existence as citizen-militia states. How much their increasing dependence on mercenaries contributed to the demise of Republican politics is an important question.

H. W. Parke, an authority on Greek mercenary armies, believes the development was crucial in the breakdown of the Republican state. "The prevalence of Greek mercenary soldiers in the Mediterranean world of the fourth century was at once a symptom and a secondary cause of the downfall of the city-state. In the mercenary's development out of the earlier citizen soldier can be seen part of that great process of transition which led from the [*polis*] to the Hellenistic monarchy as the chief unit of political life. Also the hired soldier provided the means whereby democracy could be violently subdued under autocracy, and the individual gifted to rule could maintain himself supreme over the community or aggregate of communities."[33]

As an example of the use of mercenary soldiers in the establishment of a tyranny-monarchy, Parke relates the story of Clearchus at Heraclea Pontica. Having been introduced into the city to serve political ends, Clearchus opted to satisfy his own tyrannical ambitions. In control of the mercenary forces, with hardly any citizen militia to oppose him, he engineered his coup without difficulty. Aeneas Tacticus, a fourth-century writer on military matters, comments that this occurs when one faction "brings in more mercenaries than is expedient into their city. They brought about the death of their opponents, but then they destroyed themselves and their city through the tyranny of the Mercenary leader."[34]

A standing army was more efficient than a militia of citizens. It could fight all year-round, whereas the citizen army had to return periodically to its farms. "I am told," Demosthenes writes, "that in the Peloponnesian War the Spartans and everybody else fought for four or five months in the summer; they would invade, ravage the countryside with a citizen hoplite army and go home again. But now Philip leads an army not just of hoplites but of light-armed troops, cavalry, archers, mercenaries, and he campaigns summer and winter through."[35] Parke concurs that the true superiority of the Macedonian army that conquered Greece lay in the fact that it was a standing army.[36] No citizen militia could approach its efficiency.

When a traditional society is transformed into a "modern" one, an inevitable result is that traditional constraints on change of all kinds are lifted and efficiency becomes a value in the society: military, industrial, or bureaucratic. A traditional kinship culture has values that contradict instrumental efficiency; kinship will prevail over contract, paternalism over the legal-rational. We see this clearly in the juggernaut of the capitalist system which overrides all personal values in the pursuit of profit: personal loyalty must give way to the bottom line. Other historical instances of "modernization" show the same phenomenon at work, including fifth and fourth century Greece. The old traditional-kinship-farm-based military system could not compete with the efficiency of a standing army. Philip of Macedon destroyed the classical form of the *polis*.

Another phenomenon leading to this denouement is the decreasing desire of the citizen to engage in warfare as the Republican state matures, wealth increases, and a "soft" culture grows. Whether this is related to the growth of narcissism and self-indulgence, or is the result of a psychological development beyond the tribal, head-hunting stage, or is a combination of these—and something more—I cannot say. In Athens and Sparta, in Rome, in Milan and Florence, however, we can see just this development. "Never have I suggested," wrote that epitome of Republican virtue, Demosthenes, "that we should ourselves remain inactive, idle, and helpless, and only learn by report that so-and-so's mercenaries have won a victory. For that is what happens now."[37]

Athens indeed moved in the direction that became standard proce-dure in the early-modern Italian city-states. Three important Athenian generals of the middle fourth century, Iphicrates, Chabrias, and Chares eventually led mercenary armies and achieved a certain independence from control by the central government. "Moreover, Chares ignored the home authorities so completely, that when in 346 Philip was marching on the Chersonese a motion was proposed in the [Assembly] 'to sail with all speed and look for the general put in command of the force.' The Athenian [*strategos*] had become a roving *condottiere*, over whose movements his city had little control."[38]

Philip's Macedonia was a monarchy, and the mercenary elements within its army were compatible with, and would not corrupt, the polity. In a Republican state, however, if a situation like that of Chares were allowed to develop to maturity, the *polis* could be in jeopardy. That is what happened in the Roman Republic. See this analysis of developments from the time of Marius (c. 100):

Thus the effect of the change in the method of recruitment was to constitute the legions of men who made soldiering a profession and whose natural reluctance to lose their livelihood left them indifferent to the nature of the cause in which they fought. When the war for which they were recruited was ended, it was all to the good if their general found some other excuse for keeping his army together, and it mattered nothing to the troops if the excuse was no more than a selfish and treasonable struggle for the general's own political advance-ment. . . . The long and continuous service rendered by the legionnaires after the time of Marius demanded a system of pensions as its reward, and such a system did not yet exist. To meet the need nothing more than a haphazard expedient was devised: when an army was to be demobilized, a *lex agraria* was passed to provide the veterans with allotments of land. But to secure the passage of such a bill, as was revealed most clearly by the experience of Pompey in 60 B.C., all the influence of the *imperator* himself—and more—was needed: if the vet-erans were not to be cast destitute upon the street, they must follow their commander to the bitter end. Such was the most potent cause of the tie which united generals to their armies during the last decades of the Republic; and the union was of the most disastrous consequences to Rome. Indeed, it made possible the civil wars. . . . Sulla sought a [solution] in vain, and it was left for the genius of Augustus [as Emperor], by instituting the *aerarium militaire* to make the State itself responsible for pensions.[39]

Why, with all its capacity for genius in so many fields, could the Roman Republic not find an answer to a not insoluble problem? Why must it await the return of the monarch-father?

The Italian city-states followed the same developmental path from citizen militia to *condottiere*. In their early Republican development, they created the institution of the *popolo*, mainly the instrument of wealthy craftsmen and educated professional elements.[40] "In its fully evolved form the Popolo retained a military organization."[41] The *popolo* had its own captain and as many as 1,000 or 2,000 citizen soldiers in readiness to do battle with the nobility. In effect, the Republican state was constituted as a citizen army.[42] By the time of Machiavelli in the sixteenth century A.D., the *popolo* was dead and mercenary generals constituted a major threat to political stability. Machiavelli had no use for mercenary soldiers or their leaders, the *condottieri*: "Mercenary captains are either very capable men or not; if they are, you cannot rely upon them, for they will always aspire to their own greatness, either by oppressing you, their master, or by opposing others against your intentions; but if the captain is not an able man, he will generally ruin you."[43]

That this problem is not merely of historical interest is the tragedy for democratic life. In the modern world of the twentieth century, military leaders and military dictators demonstrate, in country after country, that a stable democratic society is an enormously difficult achievement, that tyranny continues a powerful and yet pathetic alternative to chaos.

The *Demos* Seduced and Abandoned

The history of the Republican city-states repeatedly tells the pitiful tale of the *demos*: Like so many attractive yet powerless heroines of nineteenth-century novels, it refused to take power into its own hands but deposited its potential and its faith in the keeping of one man, or a small group of men, who quickly progressed from savior to betrayer. The experience was often noted by observers of the city-state. "Now when a people goes so far as to commit the error of giving power to one man," writes Machiavelli, "so that he may defeat those whom they hate, and if this man be shrewd, it will always end in his becoming their tyrant. For with the support of the people he will be enabled to destroy the nobility, and after these are crushed he will not fail in turn to crush the people; and by the time that they become sensible of their own enslavement, they will have no one to look to for succor."[44] In the first Federalist paper, Hamilton, with more history to look back on, said the same thing more succinctly: "Of those men who have over-turned the liberties of republics the greatest number have begun their career, by paying an obsequious court to the people, commencing Demagogues and ending Tyrants."[45] And if we now recall V. I. Lenin, a man who also overthrew a burgeoning republic, we see the same phenomenon in both the modern nation-state and the ancient city-state.

For ancient Greece we give two typical examples. When Clearchus became tyrant of Heraclea Pontica in the mid-fourth century, it was with the support of the lower classes in society, who expected that they would benefit from his imperium. Not surprisingly, nothing significant changed. "The main result of Clearchus' becoming tyrant was a change at the top of society in which their new masters became also the new owners of the estates. The poor, as the rapid return of the debt problem shows, shared only to an insignificant degree, if at all, in the redistri-bution of the confiscated land."[46] When Agathocles in Sicily overthrew the oligarchy in 317, he made great pretense of helping the poor who were his main support. Neither democracy nor communism resulted, however, but only the usual tyranny.[47]

In the Roman Republic, the history of the "class struggle," or the Conflict of the Orders, as far as the poorer citizens were concerned, for a period of four hundred years can be summarized in one sentence: "Instead of working towards thoroughgoing constitutional reforms, the Roman lower classes tended to look for, and put all their trust in, leaders whom they believed to be, so to speak, 'on their side'—men who in the Late Republic were called *populares*—and to try to put them in positions of power."[48] These men "on their side" were either high aristocrats competing with their peers for political power or rich ple-beians aspiring to noble status. Neither group had any real interest in social justice (except for the Gracchi, who were assassinated by those in power). The rich plebeians used the people until they attained their aspired positions, whereupon they oppressed those below them who strove for full equality—a phenomenon repeated many times in the Italian city-states. Livy comments on the state of affairs at the end of the third century: "For the plebian nobles had already been admitted to the same rites as the others and had begun to look down on the *plebs* from the moment they themselves had ceased to be looked down on by the patricians."[49]

The crucial fact was that the lower economic classes never insistently or consistently demanded radical reform. The goal of the Conflict of Orders, "never was to change social conditions radically or substantially to democratize political life at Rome. Certainly none of the participants [*including, most important, the lower classes*] thought of introducing the Athenian model of radical democracy."[50] In short, the people trusted in others, and got in return what most people receive when they do: two parts relief and eight parts betrayal.

The third act of this repetitious tragic drama, the Italian city-states, requires only a change of locale and historical period. The theme remains essentially the same. Each social and economic class fought only for its own narrow interests; no overriding conception of justice and peaceful competition prevailed; the Republics were destroyed almost as quickly as they were formed. The word *popolo* first referred to the organization of the rising, high bourgeoisie with enough economic and political power to challenge the nobility. "But once their political authority was secure, they swiftly mobilized resources of government— legislation and armed force—to block the formation of guilds among the lower classes or to keep them feeble and subjugated."[51] The high bourgeoisie were often unable to retain exclusive political control. In Milan in the early thirteenth century, two political associations were formed. Bankers, merchants, and lesser knights joined the Motta, artisans and small shopkeepers the Credenza of St. Ambrose. After 1225, the two associations formed a united front to fight the nobility, but when they gained political power, a civil war broke out between them. The defeated Motta were driven from the city and the nobility ultimately returned to power.[52] Fratricide, it seems, makes necessary the return of the fathers.

The more complicated story of Perugia in the fourteenth century demonstrates the impotence of a *demos* with no ideology, democratic or otherwise, to institutionalize after taking power. The city's merchants and rich guildsmen were organized into an association named the Ras-panti, which controlled the city for several decades. The largely exiled nobility, however, joined forces with Papal mercenaries and besieged the city in 1369. The burdens of the siege fell largely on the lower classes and, headed primarily by workers in the wool industry, they revolted twice (in 1370 and 1371) against the Raspanti, who refused to listen to their demands. The last time the working classes drove the Raspanti from the city, naturally clearing the way for the return of the nobility and the Pope's forces. After four years of oppression under these rulers, popular resentment exploded again. The nobility was forced into exile, with the predictable result that the Raspanti returned and "again bypassed the wool-working 'rabble' who had no program, no political experience, and no sense of sustained organization."[53] In this Hobbesian environment no democracy, certainly no radical de-mocracy, could exist. The life of the Republican city-state gave every evidence of being nasty, brutish, and short.

We are thus confronted with two fundamental series of questions: first, those facing Madison and Hamilton. Is a stable Republican society possible? If so, under what circumstances? What is required to over-come and transform the catastrophic history of Republican states? Sec-ond, the question of the nineteenth and twentieth centuries: what makes a stable radical democracy possible, one in which even the poor are included in the *demos*?

As late as the mid-nineteenth century A.D., for an historical model of a stable, radical democracy one had to turn to Athens of the fourth century B.C. With radical democracy once more on the political agenda in the nineteenth century it was logical for historians and political theorists to shift their interest from ancient Rome and Sparta to ancient Athens. George Grote's *A History of Greece* (1846–1856), a profoundly influential work, held up Athens, not Sparta, as the ideal Greek state. It sought to reconcile the radicalism of the French Revolution, so fright-ening to so many English theorists, with democratic stability. Grote believed Cleisthenes was a great hero-statesman who had created "the grand and new idea of the sovereign people composed of free and equal citizens—or liberty and equality, to use words which so profoundly moved the French nation half a century ago."[54]

What can Athens teach us? A stable Republican society requires a simple, but enormously difficult, psychological maneuver: the renunciation of violence as a political means within the *polis*, the sublimation of primitive aggression into intense, nonviolent competition. What destroyed Republican societies was not the competition for power between Optimates and Populares, between Motta and St. Ambrose, but the ease with which political contests degenerated into tribal warfare. The confiscations, the banishments, the executions, the assassinations, the civil wars: these made Republican life impossible. Hamilton and Madison may have believed that their representative government, their checks and balances, had solved the problem of Republican instability. Not so. The lightning speed with which the Weimar Republic was destroyed in 1933 A.D. demonstrated just how much a sophisticated constitution could do to contain a polity hell-bent on violence. What made Republican life possible in America was a people committed to the rejection of political violence. The powerful opponents of democratic society—violent anarchists, terrorists, oligarchs, and fascists—understand this. They attempt to accelerate the use of violence and turn the whole political process into a pure contest of force. No Republican society is brought down without the substantial augmentation of terror.

From the point of view of psychological analysis, what seems necessary to accomplish the transformation to nonviolent competition is to overcome the anxiety of living without a father, without a king. The presence of a king suppresses the use of force among the brothers, not only because he forbids and punishes it but also because he is present. His absence raises the level of psychic anxiety, which people attempt to diminish by a resort to violence. Huddling under the comfort and security of a monarch quiets the psyche. Many observers have commented on the increase of disquietude during an interregnum, the transition from a monarch to his successor. How much more uncertain is a society where no king rules?

Capitalism has played an important role in the process of sublimation from violence to competition. This is not to say that capitalism is either necessary (there was no capitalism in Athens), or sufficient (there are a plethora of tyrannical capitalist societies) for the transformation, but capitalism with its ideal of and opportunities for nonviolent competition can be of great assistance in turning potential oligarchic terrorists into captains of industry. Joseph Schumpeter observed that a capitalist society is the first in which a man can establish his manliness without killing someone.[55] Capitalism by itself cannot solve the problem of violence and terror—the assassination of union leaders and strikers attests to that—but it would be wrong to argue that it has played no role in making a stable Republican society possible.

Our second question concerns the conditions necessary for a stable radical democracy. An enduring Republicanism is a major factor. Not to kill one's political opponent is to grant him his right to life. It assumes a reciprocity that guarantees an opponent the same right to compete for power as one automatically grants to oneself. Once killing has been renounced between Federalists and Republicans, it is most difficult to legitimize it in regard to lower classes, when they make their move.

The ideal of universal rights is vital to a viable Republicanism. Athenian democracy never achieved it but Pericles and Demosthenes strongly implied their belief in universal rights. Once liberal people of wealth raise the banner of rights in their struggle against monarchy, the long path to a radical, full democracy is laid out.

All this remains descriptive, not analytical. What religious and moral development, what changes in values and improvements in child rearing produced a society Madison could be optimistic about—one in which a Republican state could survive? This question delineates our most important theoretical task and though no answer may be forthcoming here, it seems important to have propelled the question as far as possible.

20

Democracy and the "Paranoidia" of Greed and Domination

Everything important is a matter of degree. Crucial to an understanding of democratic society and its problematics is the capacity to distinguish between a normal-average-expectable-sensual-bourgeois manifestation of the paranoid position and a radical-extremist-murderous-oligarchic-totalitarian expression of the same. Pericles—a radical democrat *and* a fierce imperialist—is not Critias—an oligarchic terrorist *and* a fierce imperialist. Secretary of State Dean Rusk—who helped to project us into Vietnam—is not identical to those generals who would solve all problems in Asia by "nuking the Chinks." The extremist paranoid position pushes very close on the border of paranoia and may cross the border. Whether the radical-extremist position, or the average-expectable one, prevails will determine the nature of a society.

It is, many times, difficult to distinguish between these two positions, especially when the moderate one flirts with moral catastrophe, as in the game of brinkmanship played with hydrogen bombs. Morally and psychologically, the difference may be obscure. Thucydides' Melian debate, which preceded the genocide, strikes us with horror: We cannot tell whether the Athenians are cold, calculating, *realpolitik*, normal paranoids or whether they are close to going mad; whether we are in the presence of radical evil or the "banality of evil." (Hannah Arendt, who

362

gave us the latter expression, faced the same intellectual confusion and horror in dealing with the reality of Adolf Eichmann in Jerusalem.) Though it may sometimes be difficult to distinguish between the normal and the radical expression, in the vast majority of cases the distinction is perfectly clear.

Extremist manifestations of the paranoid position are incompatible with a democratic society, as the fascist and totalitarian regimes of this century have cruelly demonstrated. The normal, expectable expressions—imperialism, racism, sexism, aggressive warfare—are compatible with the democratic societies that have existed so far. The foremost struggles in our present society lie within the parameters of this moral contradiction. This last chapter is an attempted explication of the relationship of the normal paranoid position to a stable, democratic society, especially in the case of ancient Athens.

Though I have distinguished between the paranoidia of greed and the paranoidia of domination, it may be helpful to think of these as manifestations of a single paranoid defense, especially in the ancient Greek world, where the insatiable lust for power and conquest was considered a form of greed. Thucydides writes of the murderous class warfare brought on by the Peloponnesian War: "The cause of all these evils was the lust for power arising from greed and ambition; and from these passions proceeded the violence of the parties once engaged in contention."[1] Diogenes Laertius relates the proverbial tale of Dionysius the Stoic who was seized and dragged off to Philip, after the latter had won the battle of Chaeronea. Dionysius, asked by Philip who he was, replied: "A spy upon your insatiable greed."[2] Domination, not money, drove Philip on.

Ancient society regarded devouring greed for power and domination as a fundamental problematic. There is a marvelous cautionary tale in Plutarch's life of Pyrrhus, the king of Epirus (present-day Yugoslavia and Albania), who attempted to conquer Rome and gave the expression "Pyrrhic victory" to our language. Cineas, a close associate of the king, asks him what he will do if he succeeds in conquering Rome. Why then, answers Pyrrhus, all of Italy will fall to us. What then? inquires Cineas. "Sicily next holds out her arms to receive us," answers the enthusiastic monarch. "But will the possession of Sicily put an end to the war?" Clearly not; Libya and Carthage are the next logical victims. Controlling Italy, Sicily, and North Africa, Cineas insists, will make the conquest of Macedon and all of Greece a simple matter. "And when all these are in our power what shall we do then?" "We will live at our ease, my dear friend," responds the smiling king, "and drink all day, and divert ourselves with pleasant conversation." "And what hinders us now, sir, if we have in mind to be merry, and entertain one another, since we have at hand . . . all those necessary things?"[3]

There are people—and they are responsible for much of world history—who cannot make merry until they have made trial of the world and conquered it. But conquest requires warfare and warfare necessitates killing in the thousands and hundreds of thousands. In the sanitized tale of Cineas and Pyrrhus, we smell no blood and do not see the severed limbs and heads on the battleground. Since we all live to some extent in the same fantasy as Pyrrhus, it is reasonably easy for us to comprehend his ambition. What is difficult to comprehend is that some men are willing to do all that is necessary to accomplish that fantasy. The normal, expectable paranoid position is a very strange place.

Thucydides' *History* is the greatest text written on the powerful, ultimately self-destructive, impulses toward greed and domination. The whole work can be taken as an explication of the paranoid position and the force it exerts on the politics of the state. Ironically, in his obsessive attempt to prove how rationally the Athenians could behave in the jungle world of international politics, he demonstrates just how mad they were. The catastrophic Sicilian expedition toward the end of the Peloponnesian War was the great paranoid, self-destructive moment for Athens. Thucydides believed its failure lay not with the original plan of conquest, conceived and promoted by Alcibiades, but with the error the Athenians made in removing Alcibiades from command. Their fear and jealousy of him "caused them to commit affairs to other hands, and thus before long to ruin the city."[4] There was nothing wrong with the initial plan of conquest: "This failed not so much through miscalculation of the power against whom it was sent, as through a fault in the senders in not taking the best measures afterwards to assist those who had gone out."[5] This is a remarkable statement since his narrative tells us that those at home responded with vigor and alacrity to all the requests for aid from the forces in Sicily. The catastrophe occurred because the original plan of invasion was based on a paranoid fantasy. Thucydides himself was a victim of the paranoid position.

And Alcibiades, who presumably could have saved the Athenian state, showed no shame in announcing to the Spartans, with whom he sought refuge: "We sailed to Sicily first to conquer the Siceliots, and after them the Italiots also, and finally to assail the empire and city of Carthage. In the event of all or most of these schemes succeeding, we were then to attack Peloponnese . . . and after this to rule the whole of the Hellenic name."[6] And all this succeeding, they could then live at their ease and drink all day and divert themselves with pleasant conversation—for Alcibiades was most gifted in these arts as well.

Such grandiosity is a disease of the mind, but it is not a manifestation of psychosis. It represents the normal psychopathology compatible with a complex, advanced society: the average, expectable paranoid position. That one remarkable, disordered individual could give reality to such dreams of glory is not so extraordinary. The ease with which he imposed his fantasy on a large majority of the people demonstrates, however, how fragile is the health of the democratic state:

> Alcibiades . . . seemed to look upon Sicily as little more than a magazine for the war. The young men were soon elevated with these hopes, and listened gladly to those of riper years, who talked wonders of the countries they were going to; so that you might see great numbers sitting in the wrestling grounds and public places, drawing on the ground the figure of the island and the situation of Libya and Carthage.[7]

A few saw the fantasy for what it was. Socrates and the astrologer Meton, we are told, "never . . . hoped for any good to the commonwealth from this war."[8]

Grandiosity was not only an Athenian disease. The city-state of Argos, one of the most powerful near-neighbors of Sparta, had a thirty-year treaty of peace with Sparta, which both observed scrupulously. When the treaty expired during the tenth year of the Peloponnesian War, Argos began negotiating with Corinth and other allies of Sparta who were dissatisfied with the Lacedaemonians for making a peace treaty with Athens (which did not, however, stop the war). In one of those simple sentences of his that tell us so much, Thucydides declares: "Argos came into the plan the more readily because she saw that war with Lacedaemon was inevitable, the truce being on the point of expiring; and *also because she hoped to gain the supremacy of Peloponnese.*"[9] For thirty years a piece of paper had maintained peace between these two powers, and now war became "inevitable." The quest for supremacy takes the lives of many youths.

How much more comforting the world would be if we could lay the blame on the likes of Alcibiades, who suffered from a severe narcissistic disorder with delusions of grandiosity. Thucydides was ambivalent about Alcibiades, admiring his daring, courage, and intelligence but critical of his impetuosity and lack of judgment. Thucydides had no reservations about Pericles, however. Pericles is his great hero. Pericles was as insatiable in his pursuit of domination as anyone, but in Thucydides' view he never lost control over a rational and considered judgment, never got carried away by illusion into committing error. Thucydides believed Athens should dominate the Greek world, that it should fight a war with Sparta—and win—and extend its domination to a greater and greater extent. He admired Pericles because the statesman shared these dreams and was ready to use whatever "rational" means were necessary to fulfill them. Thucydides would no doubt deny that morality and justice should be considered.

Thucydides elucidates the mind of the great democratic statesman in a remarkable speech he ascribes to him. It touches directly on three of the most important tenets of the normal paranoid creed: that offense is the best defense; that slavery is the only alternative to the pursuit of dominance; that the domination of others is a good in itself and worth any sacrifice, even the eventual loss of power:

> To lose what one has got is more disgraceful than to be baulked in getting. . . . Besides, to recede is no longer possible, if indeed any of you in the alarm of the moment has become enamoured of the honesty of such an unambitious part. For what you hold is, to speak somewhat plainly, a tyranny; to take it perhaps was wrong, but to let it go is unsafe. And men of these retiring views . . . would quickly ruin a state . . . such qualities are useless to an imperial city, though they may help a dependency to an unmolested servitude. . . . Even if now, in obedience to the general law of decay, we should ever be forced to yield, still it will be remembered that we held rule over more Hellenes than any other Hellenic state, that we sustained the greatest wars against their united or separate powers, and inhabited a city unrivalled by any other in resources and magnitude. These glories may incur the censure of the

slow and unambitious; but in the breast of energy they will awaken emulation, and in those who must remain without them an envious regret.[10]

Who among us would be unwilling to fight and die for such a cause? Considering the self-destructive dimension in the paranoid position, it can be emphasized that "the general law of decay" did not go unmentioned in this paean to glory.

Two thousand three hundred and two years after Pericles' oration, Benjamin Disraeli, Prime Minister of England and a fierce advocate of imperialism, delivered a famous speech in the Crystal Palace in London. The question, Disraeli told his listeners, is "whether you will be content to be a comfortable England, modelled and moulded upon Continental principles and meeting in due course an inevitable fate [the general law of decay], or whether you will be a great country—an imperial country—a country where your sons, when they rise, rise to paramount positions, and obtain not merely the esteem of their countrymen, but command the respect of the world."[11] Militant heroism or a life not worth living! Disraeli did not invent those paranoid binary opposites. How profoundly important the paranoid position seems to be during the first two phases of democratic society (ancient democracy and modern liberalism).

Thucydides' ideal, embodied in Pericles, is a man committed to the paranoid view, in all its greed for power, who maintains his equilibrium and judgment. Intoxication with domination was a fundamental problematic in Greek society. What George Nolan says of Isocrates, of the fourth century—"He accepts the recognized law of Greek ethics, that power begets folly, folly begets insolence, and insolence begets ruin,"[12]—was first propounded by Thucydides in the fifth century: "Human nature being what it is, man allows himself to be so carried away by success that he conceives immoderate desires. This law is used by Thucydides to explain all political mistakes in his work, and those of Athens in particular."[13]

People lose their judgment for good reason when caught up in this vortex of desire. The pursuit of greed and domination is not rational, as indicated by the speed with which it becomes excessive. The Greeks were unable to talk of ambition and desire without immediately moving to greed and extravagance. To admit to desire was to become vulnerable to the pangs of insatiability. The Greek word was *pleonexia*, which Arrowsmith renders as "untrammelled freedom and power, the danger of insatiable greed."[14] This erotic, libidinal dimension in the pursuit of power haunted Athenian political life. "Now this Eros is not only metaphysical and sexual and material; it is also profoundly political. . . . And this political stress—this theme of political passion— is expressed as a part of the pervasive language of Eros. . . . Politics itself was, to the mind of the period, so pervasively passionate that it could naturally be brought under the rubric of Eros. Or rather Eros, specifically and indeed commonly, was applied, from Aeschylus to Plato and Aristotle, to activities and traits which we would normally classify as political: ambition, the love of glory, envy, lust for power, partisan zeal, greed for money and conquest."[15] To Shakespeare's lunatics, lovers, and poets, who "are of imagination all compact,"[16] it seems we must add those in love with conquest of the world.

Euripides understood the erotic origins of the *libido dominandi*: in *Iphigeneia at Aulis* Agamemnon asks, "What *Aphrodite* has made this Greek army so passionately mad to sail against the barbarians?"[17] When Thucydides describes the debate that preceded the doomed sailing against Sicily, he uses the language of desire. Nicias, arguing against the expedition, urges the *demos* not to "fall sick of a *fatal passion*." But the Athenians "were not delivered of their passion for the voyage, instead they *desired* it more eagerly . . . a *passion* seized upon all." The young men were caught up in a "longing" to see distant lands, and the *"excessive desire for more"* quieted even those who had their doubts.[18] Plutarch adds that the young men were *"carried away on the wings of such hopes"* by Alcibiades who made for himself, as the expedition sailed forth to disaster, a golden shield "bearing no ancestral device, but *Eros armed-with-the-thunderbolt*."[19] Thucydides, who knew when he wrote the words how miserably the tale would end, says in summary: "Eros afflicted them all alike to sail forth."[20]

Under the calm, organized, compulsively rational exterior of Pericles and Disraeli lies the eros of domination. Man is an animal driven by his nature into projecting his personal conflicts on to the state, in good part to control them and keep them from disorganizing the psyche. The average, normal paranoid person is not content to express his or her psychic disorder, and erect defenses against it, only in terms of mother, father, spouse, and children. The whole world becomes the screen on to which are projected all one's hopes, anxieties, despairs.

The normal paranoid is not psychotic and the screen therefore contains elements, albeit distorted, of the real world: the Russians, the Jews, the blacks really are "out there."

This projective maneuver, moreover, advances in the direction of psychic health, a fact crucially important to its staying power. It frees the psyche from the necessity of dealing with manifestations of disorder on a *personal* basis. It allows progress from near-psychosis to neurosis. Note Hofstader's important insight: "Although they both tend to be overheated, oversuspicious, overaggressive, grandiose, and apocalyptic in expression, the clinical paranoid sees the hostile and conspiratorial world in which he feels himself to be living as directed specifically *against him*; whereas the spokesman for the paranoid style finds it directed against a nation, a culture, a way of life whose fate affects not himself alone but millions of others."[21] Disraeli and Pericles are *not* Hitler and Stalin; there is no comparison between them in the degree of psychic distress and disorder, or in their capacity for world destruction. They are alike in one crucial regard: *they are all using the political world in an attempt to resolve their own psychic conflicts.* The neurotic inhabits a better world than the near-psychotic, but to say that is not to call neurosis health.

The normal, expectable paranoid position is compatible with a stable democratic society, but that society will also be compatible with imperialism, aggressive warfare, racism, abject poverty. To transform our present liberal, bourgeois, capitalist democracy into a more humane society, to establish the third stage of democratic society, we must go beyond Pericles. The imperialism, the glory, the workaholic activity in the interest of the state, all indicate that the parasite of the paranoid position continued to gnaw at his vitals. The coming of "the good society"[22] awaits the cessation of such compulsion.

Another factor makes the transformation difficult. In projecting paranoid conflicts onto the *polis*, a psychic splitting occurs. The paranoid needs are laid on the state which becomes a surrogate, acting out our disordered conceptions of reality. This leaves the individual psyche a bit freer to concentrate on sobriety, harmony, and reality. Isocrates perceived in this mode of splitting the ruin of the state: "If you will go over these and similar questions in your minds, you will discover that arrogance and insolence have been the cause of our misfortunes while sobriety and self-control have been the source of our blessings.

But, while you commend sobriety in individual men and believe that those who practise it enjoy the most secure existence and are the best among your fellow-citizens, you do not think it fit to make the state practise it."[23]

The paranoidia of greed and dominance and the projection of psychic disorder on to the state constitute a mechanism of defense that the ego erects to save itself from dissolution. When we recognize that we must abandon these powerful and effective measures of psychic defense if we are to reform and transform our society, we begin to perceive how difficult is the task.

Domination or Slavery

Those who see *only two alternatives* in the human condition, slavery or domination, will necessarily equate freedom with domination over others. They will be little interested in justice and equality. "Who rules?" will be the primary concern. Ancient Athenian society was profoundly ambivalent on the question of to *what extent* freedom should be equated with domination. So is our present democratic society. No President of the United States since the Second World War, with the possible exception of Jimmy Carter, has appeared to believe otherwise than if we cease to rule, we will be defeated and enslaved. A presidential candidate not committed to that position is unelectable and Carter paid that price.

"If we cease to rule others," Thucydides' Alcibiades says in urging the Sicilian campaign, "we are in danger of being ruled ourselves." Brilliant speaker that he was, he had a direct line to the paranoid catechism: "Men do not rest content with parrying the attacks of a superior, but often strike the first blow to prevent attack being made. And we cannot fix the exact point at which our empire shall stop; we have reached a position in which we must not be content with retaining but must scheme to extend it, for, if we cease to rule . . ."[24]

Though Alcibiades was the great antihero of Athenian democratic history, exhibiting and practicing almost unimaginable grandiosity, he did not invent the slavery-or-domination dogma, but adopted it for his own purposes. Thucydides' sober hero Pericles delivered a speech before the war commenced. The Peloponnesians had made certain demands on the Athenians, but a careful reading of the text indicates that the issues could have been negotiated, that war was not "inevitable." What was inevitable, it seems, was the ringing paranoid rhetoric that labeled as slaves those seeking an alternative to the war—destined to last twenty-seven years and bring Athens to the brink of ruin:

> Make your decision therefore at once, either to submit before you are harmed, or if we are to go to war, as I for one think we ought, to do so without caring whether the ostensible cause be great or small, resolved against making concessions or consenting to a precarious tenure of our possessions. For all claims from an equal, urged upon a neighbour as commands, before any attempt at legal settlement, be they great or be they small, have only one meaning, and that is slavery.[25]

If the only alternative to domination is slavery, then a life without dominating is a life not worth living. We admire the slave who rises in revolt, risking his life for freedom. Alcibiades and Pericles, in a strange but powerful way, were risking their lives for freedom-domination to avoid slavery and for them also it was heroic. It is a bizarre view of the world, but it does explain why people were willing to die for such a premise. This hyphenating of freedom with domination caused David Hume to assert, of ancient society: "These people were extremely fond of liberty, but seem not to have understood it very well."[26] The subsequent history of democratic societies demonstrates that most of them also have but a vague understanding of freedom, refusing to renounce domination as an essential quality.

Fear—panic at losing one's autonomy and being overwhelmed—drives the process. From the moment we announce we are free of domination, we live in fear someone will take our independence away. Enslave, dominate, oppress, and the illusion is created that one's freedom is secure. Thucydides gives fear central importance as a motivation for political action. Note the speech he gives the Athenians on their arrival in Sicily: "Now, as we have said, fear makes us hold our empire in Hellas, and fear makes us now come . . . to order safely matters in Sicily, and not to enslave any but rather to prevent any from being enslaved."[27] The catastrophe occurred because they feared the wrong thing. As Nicias warned them in the Assembly debate about the projected Sicilian expedition, they should have been apprehensive about their own illusions of omnipotence, their own unambivalent commitment to the grandiose. They submitted instead to a deep, irrational, paranoid anxiety about their selfhood, and resorted to the time-honored paranoid defense: "Conquer or die!"

Athenian society was extraordinary in its ambivalence on this issue (much like our own society over the war in Vietnam). With his brilliant portrait of Alcibiades, Thucydides also presents the calm, rational, non-paranoid arguments of Nicias against the invasion. The vote in the Assembly was overwhelming to proceed, but Athens was remarkably capable of recovery from its worst excesses. The paranoidia of domination and greed and the insistent possibility of excess were its temptations and problematics. Alvin Gouldner has succinctly described the condition: "The Greek self was a coin on one side of which was inscribed, 'Avoid control of self,' and on the other read, 'Impose control on others.' There is, then, a painful dilemma in the Greek conception of the person: it disposes individuals to do unto others as they would not be done unto themselves; it leads them to behave toward others in a manner that outrages their strongest sentiments."[28]

The same may be said of our own liberal, capitalist, bourgeois democracy, especially in its foreign policy and in its most exaggerated capitalist modes. If fear drives us to Sicily, nothing will change until that fear comes under control. We have lived for the last forty years with 35,000 missile warheads without fear accelerating to panic. The normal, expectable paranoid position has held its ground. Would it be asking too much of humanity to give *it* up?

Of Statues and Hemlock

The greatness of Athens lies in its pervasive ambivalence on this central question of the paranoid position. Its commitment to normal, expectable paranoid propositions and the constant threat of a more radical stance have been documented here at length. Athens was also, however, capable of the most extraordinary investment in real freedom and liberation from paranoid imperatives, a deep inconsistency that has caused many lovers of democracy to express their ambivalence about Athens. "There are particular moments in public affairs," writes James Madison, "when the people stimulated by some irregular passion, or some illicit advantage . . . may call for measures which they themselves will afterwards be most ready to lament and condemn. In these critical moments, how salutary will be the interference of some temperate and respectable body of citizens . . . to suspend the blow meditated by the people against themselves, until reason, justice, and truth can regain their authority over the public mind? What bitter anguish would not the people of Athens have often escaped, if their government had contained so provident a safeguard against the tyranny of their own passions? Popular liberty might then have escaped the indelible reproach of decreeing to the same citizens, the hemlock on one day, and statues on the next.''[29]

Let us, therefore, erect a statue to Pericles: If we may believe Thucydides, he gave voice to extraordinary insights on the renunciation of the paranoid world view. Nowhere in the history of the world until then had any sentiments come close to his remarkable vision:

> The freedom which we enjoy in our government extends also to our ordinary life. There, far from exercising a jealous surveillance over each other, we do not feel called upon to be angry with our neighbour for doing what he likes, or even to indulge in those injurious looks which cannot fail to be offensive, although they inflict no positive penalty. But all this ease in our private relations does not make us lawless as citizens. Against this fear is our chief safeguard, teaching us to obey the magistrates and the laws. . . . If we turn to our military policy, there also we differ from our antagonists. We throw open our city to the world, and never by alien acts exclude foreigners from any opportunity of learning or observing . . . trusting less in system and policy than to the native spirit of our citizens.[30]

That this was no mere rhetoric to decorate the occasion was demonstrated with extraordinary force some twenty-seven years later. Athens had lost the great war; her empire was gone; her citizen body had been reduced by 30 or 40 percent; two oligarchic counterrevolutions had prevailed within the last seven years of the conflict and had executed 1,500 to 2,000 citizens; the city had come within an inch of being annihilated by the war's victors. Despite these catastrophic experiences, the *polis* responded with remarkable maturity, renouncing revenge, proclaiming an amnesty to all but a few, determined above all "to bind up the nation's wounds."[31] Abraham Lincoln could be charitable in the expectation of complete victory, but Athena's city was a beaten dog of a *polis*. The depths of their despair, however, seemed to bring out the best in them. "In fact, it appears," wrote Aristotle, a critic of democratic society, "that their attitude both *in private and in public* in regard to the past disturbances was the most admirable and the most statesmanlike that any people have ever shown in such circumstances."[32]

In subsequent years, those who had participated in the oligarchic terrors were freely admitted into the democratic life of the *polis*, serving as jurors, ambassadors, and generals,[33] an extraordinary amnesty that made possible the fourth moral and psychological transformation of the *polis*—to the stable, mature, radical democracy of the fourth century. The first transformation had occurred at the time of Solon with the establishment of social equity and compromise as the basis of politics. The second was the beginning of true democracy with Cleisthenes. Ephialtes and Pericles brought about the third transformation, a radical democracy that included the poor. This state was vulnerable, however, to oligarchic backlash and a grandiose imperialism. The radical democracy of the fourth century experienced no such internal threat.

Our own American democratic society has also witnessed several fundamental transformations of the polity. The first involved democratic developments in various states that culminated in the founding of the Republic. The second was the nineteenth-century establishment of a radical democracy, vaguely associated with the person of Andrew Jackson. The third transformation eliminated slavery and attempted to bring former slaves into the political process. The fourth, which culminated after the First World War, brought women into the life of the *polis*. The fifth stage of democratic evolution saw the erection of the welfare state, the beginnings of capitalism with a human face. The last, a product of the 1960s, produced the civil rights movement and specific civil rights legislation that attempted to fulfill promises of equality made a hundred years before.

These remarkable moral transformations were accomplished, not by gods or heroes, but by ordinary mortals: normal, average, sensual, and expectably paranoid people. Many argue that it is utopian to anticipate a further transformation of democracy. Despite the evidence of human progress in the past, they insist, we have come to the end of political evolution, to the end of history itself. The burden of proof would seem to lie with them. But the history of democratic society, ancient and modern, demonstrates that humans have accomplished astonishing things. In our present moment of ambivalent dispiritedness, the tribulations and the triumphs of Athens speak to us.

Notes

Chapter 1
The Great Paradoxical Society: Ancient Athens

1. William Scott Ferguson, *Hellenistic Athens* (London: Macmillan & Co., 1911), passim.
2. Plutarch, *Dion*, V, 185, trans. Dryden-Clough.
3. Thucydides, V, 90–91, trans. Crawley.
4. Quoted in S. C. Humphreys, *Anthropology and the Greeks* (Boston: Routledge and Kegan Paul, 1978), p. 17.
5. "Speech at the Anniversary of the People's Paper," in Robert C. Tucker, ed., *The Marx-Engels Reader,* 2d edition (New York: W. W. Norton, 1978), p. 577. Reference to this speech originally encountered in Marshall Berman, *All That Is Solid Melts into Air* (New York: Penguin Books, 1988).
6. Aristotle, *Rhetoric*, I, IV, 7, Loeb translation.
7. Eric Havelock, *The Liberal Temper in Greek Politics* (New Haven: Yale University Press, 1957), p. 320.
8. Aristotle, *Politics*, III, chap. 7, trans. Ernest Barker (Oxford: Oxford University Press, 1958).

Chapter 2
Democracy and the Paranoid Position

1. Sigmund Freud, "Analysis Terminable and Interminable," *Standard Edition*, vol. 23 (1937): p. 235.

2. Richard Hofstader, "The Paranoid Style in American Politics," in *The Paranoid Style in American Politics and Other Essays* (New York: Alfred A. Knopf, 1966), p. 4.

3. Ibid., p. 3.

4. Aristophanes, *The Wasps*, trans. Douglas Parker (Ann Arbor: University of Michigan Press, 1961). I have changed Parker's word "dictatorship" to "tyranny," which is literally what the Greek says.

5. David Shapiro, *Neurotic Styles* (New York: Basic Books, 1965), p. 83.

6. Hofstader, "Paranoid Style," p. 33n.

7. Shapiro, *Neurotic Styles*, p. 73.

8. Ibid., p. 68.

9. Hofstader, "Paranoid Style," p. 32.

10. Lacey Baldwin Smith, *Treason in Tudor England* (Princeton: Princeton University Press, 1986), p. 186.

11. Quoted in Theodor Mommsen, *The History of Rome*, trans. William Dickson, vol. 3 (New York: Charles Scribner's Sons, 1900), p. 298.

12. Hofstader, p. 4.

13. Ibid., pp. 29–30.

14. Ibid., p. 28.

15. Personal communication, 1969, aides to Senator Thomas Eagleton.

16. Thucydides, VI, 84, trans. Crawley.

17. Thucydides, VI, 18, trans. William Arrowsmith, in "Aristophanes' *Birds*: The Fantasy Politics of Eros," *Arion*, New Series, 1/1, p. 143.

18. Thucydides, VI, 87, trans. Crawley.

19. Simon Hornblower, *The Greek World 479–323 B.C.* (New York: Methuen and Co., 1983), p. 69.

20. J. A. O. Larsen, "Freedom and Its Obstacles in Ancient Greece," *Classical Philology* 57 (1962): p. 431, quoting F. W. Walbank.

21. Aristotle, *Politics*, V, C2, 2, trans. Ernest Barker, *The Politics of Aristotle* (Oxford: Oxford University Press, 1958).

22. Thomas Hobbes, *Leviathan*, I, 11 (New York: Macmillan, 1986).

23. Plato, *The Laws*, 831B–832D, cited in Alexander Fuks, *Social Conflict in Ancient Greece* (Jerusalem: The Magnes Press, The Hebrew University; Leiden: E. J. Brill, 1984), p. 140.

24. *Isocrates*, vol. I, editor's introduction, p. xxxiii, Loeb translation.

25. Hobbes, *Leviathan*, I, 11.

26. Isocrates, *On the Peace*, 91–93, Loeb translation.

27. Personal communication, Professor Andrew Katz.

28. Lloyd deMause, *Foundations of Psychohistory* (New York: Creative Roots, 1982), pp. 139–40, 183–84.

Chapter 3
The Founding Miracle: Crisis and Possibility

1. P. A. Brunt, *Social Conflicts in the Roman Republic* (New York: W. W. Norton, 1971), p. 36.

2. *Cambridge Ancient History*, vol. IX, 1951, p. 303.

3. Solon, Frag. 2, in Kathleen Freeman, *The Work and Life of Solon* (London: Humphrey Milford, 1926), pp. 207–8.

4. Aristotle, *The Constitution of Athens*, 2, in A. Andrews, "The Growth of the Athenian State," chap. 43 in the *Cambridge Ancient History*, 2d edition, vol. III, part 3, 1982, p. 378.

5. Livy, Book II, 23 and 24, Loeb translation.

6. Kurt A. Raaflaub, *Social Struggles in Archaic Rome* (Berkeley: University of California Press, 1986), p. 208.

7. Eli Sagan, *At the Dawn of Tyranny* (New York: Alfred A. Knopf, 1985), p. 284.

8. W. J. Woodhouse, *Solon the Liberator* (New York: Octagon Books, 1985), p. 17.

9. Ivan M. Linforth, *Solon the Athenian* (Berkeley: University of California Press, 1919), p. 48.

10. Richmond Lattimore, *Greek Lyrics* (Chicago: University of Chicago Press, 1960), p. 22.

11. Livy, Book II, 23, Loeb translation.

12. Woodhouse, *Solon*, p. 122.

13. Solon, Frag. 2, in Freeman, *Solon*, pp. 207–8.

14. Aristotle, *Constitution of Athens*, V, 1–2, trans. Kurt von Fritz and Ernest Kapp (New York: Hafner Press, 1974).

15. Plutarch, *Solon*, XIII, 3. Loeb translation.

16. Livy, Book II, 23, Loeb translation.

17. M. I. Finley, *Economy and Society in Ancient Greece* (New York: Viking Press, 1982), p. 162 (italics added).

18. Livy, Book II, 28, Loeb translation.

19. Aristotle, *Constitution of Athens*, XI, 2, trans. J. M. Moore (Berkeley: University of California Press, 1975).

20. Ibid., VI, 1.
21. Alexander Fuks, *Social Conflict in Ancient Greece* (Jerusalem: The Magnes Press, The Hebrew University; Leiden: E. J. Brill, 1984), p. 19.
22. G. E. M. de Ste. Croix, *The Class Struggle in the Ancient Greek World* (Ithaca: Cornell University Press, 1981), p. 299.
23. Fuks, *Conflict*, p. 29.
24. Edward P. Cheyney, *The Dawn of a New Era, 1250–1453* (New York: Harper and Brothers, 1936), p. 97.
25. Stanley M. Burstein, "Greek Class Structures and Relations," in Michael Grant and Rachel Kitzinger, eds., *Civilization of the Ancient Mediterranean*, vol. I (New York: Charles Scribner's Sons, 1988), p. 538.
26. Raaflaub, *Struggles*, pp. 206–7.
27. Ibid.
28. E. A. Freeman, *The History of Sicily*, vol. IV (Oxford: Oxford University Press, 1894), p. 381.
29. Plutarch, *Solon*, in Woodhouse, *Solon*, p. 25.
30. Aristotle, *Constitution of Athens*, VI, 4.
31. Ibid., X, 1, 2, trans. Moore.
32. Lattimore, *Lyrics*, p. 22.
33. Livy, Book II, 29, Loeb translation.
34. Raaflaub, *Struggles*, p. 227.
35. Aristotle, *Politics*, 1306(a) 10, quoted in N. G. L. Hammond, *A History of Greece to 322 B.C.* (Oxford: Oxford University Press, 1967), p. 146.
36. de Ste. Croix, *Struggle*, p. 359.
37. M. I. Finley, *Early Greece* (New York: W. W. Norton, 1981), p. 119.
38. Eric Havelock, *The Liberal Temper in Greek Politics* (New Haven: Yale University Press, 1957), p. 145.
39. Lattimore, *Lyrics*, p. 22.
40. Linforth, *Solon*, pp. 33–35.
41. Brunt, *Conflicts*, pp. 76–77.
42. de Ste. Croix, *Struggle*, p. 288.
43. Stanley Mayer Burstein, *Outpost of Hellenism: The Emergence of Heraclea on the Black Sea* (Berkeley: University of California Press, 1976), p. 37.
44. Livy, Book VI, 11, Loeb translation.
45. C. N. Cochrane, *Christianity and Classical Culture* (New York: Oxford University Press, 1977), p. 18.
46. de Ste. Croix, *Struggle*, pp. 340–41.
47. Aristotle, *Constitution of Athens*, 12, in Linforth, *Solon*, p. 135.
48. Solon, Frag. 2, in Freeman, *Solon*, p. 208.

Chapter 4
The Founding Miracle: Compromise, Reconciliation, and Continuing Strife

1. Ivan M. Linforth, *Solon the Athenian* (Berkeley: University of California Press, 1919), p. 46.

2. Plutarch, *Solon*, XIV, 2, Loeb translation.

3. Aristotle, *Constitution of Athens*, II, trans. J. M. Moore (Berkeley: University of California Press, 1975).

4. Solon, quoted in C. Hignett, *A History of the Athenian Constitution to the End of the Fifth Century B.C.* (London: Oxford University Press, 1952), p. 96.

5. Solon, quoted in W. G. Forrest, *The Emergence of Greek Democracy, 800–400 B.C.* (New York: McGraw-Hill, 1979), p. 173.

6. Plutarch, *Solon*, trans. Dryden-Clough, vol. I, p. 168.

7. Plutarch, *Solon*, XV, 2, Loeb translation.

8. M. I. Finley, *Economy and Society in Ancient Greece* (New York: Viking Press, 1981), p. 157.

9. Aristotle, *Constitution of Athens*, VI, 1, trans. J. M. Moore

10. Richmond Lattimore, *Greek Lyrics* (Chicago: University of Chicago Press, 1960), p. 22.

11. Aristotle, *Constitution of Athens*, VII. Also Stanley M. Burstein, "Greek Class Structures and Relations," in Michael Grant and Rachel Kitzinger, eds., *Civilization of the Ancient Mediterranean*, vol. I (New York: Charles Scribner's Sons, 1988), p. 539.

12. Aristotle, *Constitution of Athens*, VII.

13. Hignett, *History of Athenian Constitution*, p. 101.

14. Ibid., p. 96. Also E. S. Stavely, *Greek and Roman Voting and Elections* (Ithaca: Cornell University Press, 1972), p. 26.

15. Hignett, *History of Athenian Constitution*, p. 96.

16. Ibid. Also Stavely, *Greek and Roman Voting*, p. 26.

17. Hignett, *History of Athenian Constitution*, p. 101.

18. Stavely, *Greek and Roman Voting*, p. 33.

19. Hignett, *History of Athenian Constitution*, p. 101.

20. Aristotle, *Constitution of Athens*, IX, trans. J. M. Moore

21. Forrest, *Emergence of Greek Democracy*, p. 172.

22. Aristotle, *Constitution of Athens*, IX, trans. J. M. Moore

23. Stavely, *Greek and Roman Voting*, p. 98.

24. Thucydides, *The Peloponnesian War*, II, 37, trans. Crawley (italics added).

25. Aristotle, *Politics*, Book III, chap. VII, 2–5, trans. Ernest Barker, *The Politics of Aristotle* (Oxford: Oxford University Press, 1958).

26. Thucydides, *Peloponnesian War*, II, 37.
27. Eli Sagan, *Freud, Women, and Morality* (New York: Basic Books, 1988), passim.
28. J. Walter Jones, *The Law and Legal Theory of the Greeks* (Oxford: Oxford University Press, 1956), p. 22.
29. Mogens Herman Hansen, *The Athenian Assembly in the Age of Demosthenes* (New York: Basil Blackwell, 1987), passim.
30. Demosthenes, *Against Timocrates*, 170–71, Loeb translation.
31. Plutarch, *Solon*, trans. Dryden-Clough, vol. I, p. 177.
32. Aristotle, *Constitution of Athens*, XIII, 1, trans. J. M. Moore
33. Ibid., XIII, 2.
34. Forrest, *Emergence of Greek Democracy*, p. 166.
35. Aristotle, *Constitution of Athens*, XIII, 2, trans. J. M. Moore.
36. Lauro Martines, *Power and Imagination* (New York: Alfred A. Knopf, 1979), p. 47.
37. Plato, *Republic*, Book IV, 422e, trans. Alan Bloom (New York: Basic Books, 1968).
38. Hignett, *History of Athenian Constitution*, p. 124.
39. Aristotle, *Politics*, Book III, chap. VII, 5, trans. Barker.
40. Ibid., Book V, chap. X, 3–4.
41. M. I. Finley, *Early Greece: The Bronze and Archaic Ages* (New York: W. W. Norton, 1981), p. 103.
42. G. Glotz, *The Greek City and Its Institutions* (London: Routledge and Kegan Paul, 1950), p. 110.
43. M. I. Finley, *Politics in the Ancient World* (Cambridge: Cambridge University Press, 1983), pp. 46–47.
44. Marvin Goldwert, *Democracy, Militarism, and Nationalism in Argentina, 1930–1966* (Austin: University of Texas Press, 1972), p. 96.
45. G. E. M. de Ste. Croix, *The Class Struggle in the Ancient Greek World*, (Ithaca: Cornell University Press, 1981), p. 279.
46. N. G. L. Hammond, *A History of Greece to 322 B.C.*, 2d edition (Oxford: Oxford University Press, 1967), p. 150.
47. Ibid., p. 198.
48. *The Oxford Classical Dictionary*, 2d edition (Oxford: Oxford University Press, 1970), article on "Pisistratus," p. 836.

Chapter 5
The Spirit of Society: Citizenship, Freedom, and Responsibility

1. Aristotle, *Politics*, III, chap. IV, 15, ed., trans. Ernest Barker (Oxford: Oxford University Press, 1958).
2. Quoted in Hannah Fenichel Pitkin, *Fortune Is a Woman* (Berkeley: University of California Press, 1984), p. 83.
3. William L. Bouwsma, *Venice and the Defense of Republican Liberty* (Berkeley: University of California Press, 1968), p. 6.
4. Marshall Berman, *All That Is Solid Melts into Air* (New York: Penguin Books, 1988), p. 284.
5. Simon Hornblower, *The Greek World 479–323 B.C.* (New York: Methuen, 1983), p. 69.
6. Thucydides, VI, 92.4, quoted in Peter Krentz, *The Thirty at Athens* (Ithaca, Cornell University Press, 1982), p. 75.
7. William Linn Westermann in M. I. Finley, ed., *Slavery in Classical Antiquity, Views and Controversies* (New York: Barnes and Noble, 1968), p. 30.
8. Demosthenes, XXI, 67, quoted in A. H. M. Jones, "The Athenian Democracy and its Critics," *The Cambridge Historical Journal*, XI, 1 (1953): 4.
9. Isocrates, *Lochites*, 1, Loeb translation.
10. Plato, *Republic*, VIII, 562c, trans. Alan Bloom (New York: Basic Books, 1968).
11. Aristotle, *Politics*, VI, chap. 2, 1–4, trans. Barker.
12. Ernest Barker, *Greek Political Theory* (London: Methuen, 1977), p. 98.
13. Shakespeare, The *Merchant of Venice*, III, 1, 58.
14. J. Walter Jones, *The Law and Legal Theory of the Greeks* (Oxford: Oxford University Press, 1956), pp. 90–91.
15. Thucydides, *The Peloponnesian War*, II, 37, trans. Crawley.
16. Aristotle, *Politics*, V, chap. IX, 15–16, trans. Barker
17. Demosthenes, XX, 106.
18. J. M. Moore, editor's comment in Aristotle, *Constitution of Athens* (Berkeley: University of California Press, 1975), p. 55.
19. N. G. L. Hammond, *A History of Greece to 322 B.C.* (Oxford: Oxford University Press, 1967), p. 426 (italics added).
20. Euripides, *The Trojan Women*, trans. Richmond Lattimore (Chicago: University of Chicago Press, various editions), lines 1322–23 and 1331–32.
21. Ibid., translator's introduction, note 1.
22. Plato, *Republic*, VIII, 562e–563d, trans. Bloom
23. Charles Wirszubski, *Libertas as a Political Idea at Rome* (Cambridge: Cambridge University Press, 1968), p. 8.

24. Robert N. Bellah, et al., *Habits of the Heart* (Berkeley: University of California Press, 1985); Christopher Lasch, *The Culture of Narcissism* (New York: W. W. Norton, 1979).

25. Aristotle, *Politics*, V, chap. IX, 16, trans. Barker

26. Thucydides, II, 38, trans. Crawley.

27. Plato, *Republic*, VII, 558c, trans. Bloom.

28. Aristotle, *Politics*, III, chap. IX, 4, trans. Barker.

29. William Arrowsmith, "Aristophanes' *Birds*: The Fantasy Politics of Eros," *Arion*, New Series, 1/1, p. 126.

30. Ibid., p. 129.

31. Ibid., p. 127, translating Thucydides I, 70ff.

32. James Madison, *Federalist* 57. *The Federalist*, Jacob E. Cooke, ed. (Middletown: Wesleyan University Press, 1961), p. 387.

33. Aristotle, *Politics*, V, chap. IX, 12, trans. Barker.

34. Provenance unknown.

35. Thucydides, II, 41, trans. Crawley.

36. Aristotle, *Politics*, V, chap. II, 2, trans. Barker.

37. W. S. Ferguson in *Cambridge Ancient History*, vol. V (1953), pp. 332–33.

38. [Pseudo-Plutarch], *Lives of the Ten Orators, Lysias*, 835e–836a.

39. Donald Kagan, *The Fall of the Athenian Empire* (Ithaca: Cornell University Press, 1987), pp. 256–57.

40. Aristotle, *Constitution of Athens*, 39, 6, see also note 133 on p. 184. trans. Kurt von Fritz and Ernst Kapp (New York: Hafner Press, 1974).

41. C. Hignett, *A History of the Athenian Constitution to the End of the Fifth Century B.C.* (London: Oxford University Press, 1952), p. 295.

42. Aristotle, *Constitution of Athens*, 40, 2, trans. von Fritz and Kapp.

43. Hignett, *Athenian Constitution*, p. 295.

44. Krentz, *The Thirty*, p. 117.

45. Aristotle, *Constitution of Athens*, 40, 2–3, trans. von Fritz and Kapp.

46. Isocrates, *Areopagitigus*, 62, quoted in Claude Mosse, *Athens in Decline*, trans. Jean Stewart (London and Boston: Routledge and Kegan Paul, 1973), p. 62.

47. Krentz, *The Thirty*, p. 18.

48. M. I. Finley, *Economy and Society in Ancient Greece* (New York: Viking Press, 1982), p. 66.

49. William Scott Ferguson, *Hellenistic Athens* (London: Macmillan and Co., 1911), passim.

50. *Cambridge Ancient History*, vol. IX (1951), p. 244.

51. P. J. Rhodes, *The Athenian Boule* (Oxford: Oxford University Press, 1985), p. 86.

Chapter 6
The Health of the Democratic *Polis*

1. M. I. Finley, *Economy and Society in Ancient Greece* (New York: Viking Press, 1982), p. 173.
2. A. H. M. Jones, *Athenian Democracy* (Baltimore: Johns Hopkins University Press, 1986), p. 5.
3. Ibid.
4. David Whitehead, *The Demes of Attica, 508/7–Ca. 250 B.C.* (Princeton: Princeton University Press, 1986), p. 319.
5. P. J. Rhodes, *The Athenian Boule* (Oxford: Oxford University Press, 1985), p. 3n. Also personal communication from Josiah Ober.
6. Quoted in ibid., p. 214.
7. Ibid., pp. 211–12.
8. Jones, *Democracy*, p. 61.
9. Jennifer Tolbert Roberts, *Accountability in Athenian Government* (Madison: University of Wisconsin Press, 1982), pp. 17–18.
10. Mogens Herman Hansen, *Eisangelia: The Sovereignty of the People's Court in Athens in the Fourth Century B.C. and the Impeachment of Generals and Politicians* (Odense [Denmark]: Odense University Press, 1975), p. 13.
11. Roberts, *Accountability*, p. 174.
12. Plato, *Protagoras*, 320d–323c, trans. W. K. C. Guthrie (italics added).
13. Ibid., 324e.
14. Simon Hornblower, *The Greek World 479–323 B.C.* (New York: Methuen, 1983), p. 37; Victor Ehrenberg, *From Solon to Socrates* (London: Methuen, 1968), p. 141.
15. Rhodes, *Boule*, p. 210.
16. C. Hignett, *A History of the Athenian Constitution to the End of the Fifth Century B.C.* (London: Oxford University Press, 1952), p. 215.
17. E. S. Stavely, *Greek and Roman Voting and Elections* (Ithaca: Cornell University Press, 1972), p. 33.
18. Rhodes, *Boule*, p. 13; Hignett, *History of Athenian Constitution*, p. 215.
19. Martin Ostwald, *From Popular Sovereignty to the Sovereignty of Law* (Berkeley: University of California Press, 1986), p. 80.
20. Aristotle, *Constitution of Athens*, XXVIII, 2–3, trans. Moore.
21. Thucydides, II, 65–66, trans. Crawley.
22. Aristotle, *Constitution of Athens*, XXVIII, 1, quoted in W. Robert Connor, *The New Politicians of Fifth-Century Athens* (Princeton: Princeton University Press, 1971), p. 141.
23. Connor, *New Politicians*, p. 153.
24. Ibid., p. 155.

25. Aristotle, *Constitution of Athens*, XXVIII, 4, trans. Moore.
26. Thucydides, II, 66, trans. Crawley.
27. Aristotle, *Constitution of Athens*, XXVIII, 3, trans. Moore.
28. Connor, *New Politicians*, p. 139.
29. M. I. Finley, "Athenian Demagogues," *Past and Present* 21 (1962): 3–24, passim; Connor, *New Politicians*, passim.
30. Mogens Herman Hansen, *The Athenian Assembly in the Age of Demosthenes* (New York: Basil Blackwell, 1987), p. 48.
31. Jones, *Democracy*, p. 33.
32. Ibid., p. 34.
33. Victor Ehrenberg, *The People of Aristophanes* (New York: Schocken Books, 1962), p. 108.
34. Hignett, *History of Athenian Constitution*, p. 214.
35. Thucydides, II, 39, trans. Crawley.
36. Connor, *New Politicians*, pp. 144–46.
37. Quoted ibid., pp. 144–46.
38. Quoted ibid., p. 147.
39. Ostwald, *Sovereignty*, pp. 202–3.
40. Aristotle, *Politics*, IV, chap. XI, 4–7, trans. Barker.
41. Robert N. Bellah, et al., *Habits of the Heart* (Berkeley: University of California Press, 1985); Christopher Lasch, *The Culture of Narcissism* (New York: W. W. Norton, 1979).

Chapter 7
Moderate Antidemocratic Movements and Oligarchic Death Squads: The Coups of 411 and 404

1. Andrew Lintott, *Civil Strife and Revolution in the Classical City, 750–330 B.C.* (London: Croom Helm, 1982), p. 135.
2. William James McCoy, "Theramenes, Thrasybulus and the Athenian Moderates," Ph.D. diss., Yale University (1970), pp. 3–4.
3. Xenophon, *Hellenica*, II, chap. III, 48, Loeb translation.
4. Ibid.
5. Thucydides, VIII, 55, trans. Crawley.
6. Ibid., 65.
7. Thucydides, VIII, 68, trans. McCoy, in McCoy, "Theramenes."
8. Donald Kagan, *The Fall of the Athenian Empire* (Ithaca: Cornell University Press, 1987), p. 157.
9. W. S. Ferguson in *Cambridge Ancient History*, vol. V, pp. 332–33.
10. Ibid.
11. Thucydides, VIII, 87, trans. Crawley.
12. Ibid., VIII, 92.

13. Ibid., VIII, 68.

14. Lysias, quoted in McCoy, "Theramenes," p. 176.

15. *The Oxford Classical Dictionary*, 2d edition (Oxford: Oxford University Press, 1970), article on "Critias," p. 299.

16. N. G. L. Hammond, *A History of Greece to 322 B.C.* (Oxford: Oxford University Press, 1967), pp. 443–44.

17. Peter Krentz, *The Thirty at Athens* (Ithaca: Cornell University Press, 1982), p. 130.

18. Ibid., p. 60.

19. Ibid.

20. Hammond, *History*, pp. 444ff.

21. Lysias, *Against Eratosthenes*, 6–7, quoted in Claude Mossé, *Athens in Decline* (London and Boston: Routledge and Kegan Paul, 1973), p. 7.

22. Mossé, *Decline*, p. 7.

23. Lysias, *Against Agoratus*, 39–42, Loeb translation.

24. *Lysias*, Loeb translation, translator's note pp. 278-281.

25. McCoy, "Theramenes," passim; Antony Andrewes, "Theramenes" in *Oxford Classical Dictionary*, p. 1060.

26. Shakespeare, *Macbeth*, I. iv. 7.

27. Xenophon, *Hellenica*, II, chap. 3, 20–23, Loeb translation.

28. Ibid., II, chap. 3, 37–40.

29. Hammond, *History*, p. 445.

30. Plato, *Apology*, 32 c–d, trans. Tredennick.

31. Xenophon, *Hellenica*, II, chap. 4, 8–10, Loeb translation.

Chapter 8
Antidemocratic Thought, the Beginnings of Totalitarian Theory, and the Origins of Political Terror

1. Speech at Harvard University, 1947.

2. Plato, *Republic*, VIII, 558c, trans. Bloom.

3. Demosthenes, XXI, 67, quoted in A. H. M. Jones, "The Athenian Democracy and Its Critics," *The Cambridge Historical Journal*, xi, 1 (1953): 4.

4. William James McCoy, "Theramenes, Thrasybulus and the Athenian Moderates," Ph.D. diss., Yale University (1970), p. 4.

5. Peter Krentz, *The Thirty at Athens* (Ithaca: Cornell University Press, 1982), p. 109.

6. P. J. Rhodes, *The Athenian Boule* (Oxford: Oxford University Press, 1985), p. 217.

7. McCoy, "Theramenes," pp. 3–4.

8. Herodotus, 3.81, quoted in Krentz, *The Thirty*, p. 22 (italics added).

9. "Old Oligarch," [Ps-Xenophon] *Constitution of Athens*, I, 5–7, quoted in M. M. Austin and P. Vidal-Naquet, *Economic and Social History of Ancient Greece* (Berkeley: University of California Press, 1977), p. 189.

10. Plato, *Gorgias*, 515e, trans. Woodhead (italics added).

11. Plato, *Republic*, VIII, 557a, trans. Bloom.

12. Jones, "Critics," p. 17.

13. Plato, *Letter VII*, 324b–d, trans. Post.

14. Stanley M. Burstein, "Greek Class Structures and Relations," in Michael Grant and Rachel Kitzinger, eds., *Civilization of the Ancient Mediterranean*, vol. I (New York: Scribner's Sons, 1988), p. 20.

15. "Old Oligarch," [Ps-Xenophon] *Constitution of Athens*, I, 9, quoted in Austin and Vidal-Naquet, *Social History*, p. 190.

16. "Old Oligarch," [Ps-Xenophon] *Constitution of Athens*, I, 13, translated in J. M. Moore, *Aristotle and Xenophon on Democracy and Oligarchy* (Berkeley: University of California Press, 1975).

17. Xenophon, *Memorabilia*, III, chap. 7, 5–6, Loeb translation.

18. Andocides (?), fragment 4 Blass, quoted in Martin Ostwald, *From Popular Sovereignty to the Sovereignty of Law* (Berkeley: University of California Press, 1986), p. 327.

19. Cicero, *For Flaccus*, 15–18, quoted in P. A. Brunt, *Social Conflicts in the Roman Republic* (New York: W. W. Norton, 1971), p. 125.

20. Aristotle, *Politics*, III, chap. V, 3 and 5, trans. Barker.

21. Brunt, *Social Conflicts*, p. 125.

22. Talcott Parsons, *The Evolution of Societies* (Englewood Cliffs, N.J.: Prentice-Hall, 1977), p. 13.

23. Ernest Barker, *Greek Political Theory* (London: Methuen, 1977), pp. 239–40.

24. Thucydides, II, 37–38, trans. Crawley.

25. Ibid., II, 41 (italics added).

26. Plato, *Republic*, VII, 540d–541a, trans. Bloom.

27. Eli Sagan, *At the Dawn of Tyranny* (New York, Alfred A. Knopf, 1985), passim.

28. E. R. Dodds, *The Greeks and the Irrational* (Berkeley: University of California Press, 1951), pp. 223–24. Based on Plato, *The Laws*, 907d–909d.

29. Ibid., p. 224.

30. Aristotle, *Politics*, V, chap. IX, 15; Isocrates, *Areopagiticus*, VII, 37; Plato, *Republic*, VIII, 557b. All cited in Jones, "Critics," p. 3.

31. Plutarch, *Agesilaus*, trans. Dryden-Clough, vol. III, p. 337.

32. Moore, *Aristotle and Xenophon*, pp. 67–121.

33. Xenophon, *Politeia of the Spartans*, II, 13–14, trans. Moore, *Aristotle and Xenophon*.

34. Plutarch, *Agesilaus,* trans. Dryden-Clough, vol. III, p. 305.

35. Plutarch, *Lycurgus,* 25, quoted by Moore, *Aristotle and Xenophon,* p. 103.

36. Aristotle, *Politics,* VIII, chap. IV, 1, quoted by G. E. M. de Ste. Croix, *The Origins of the Peloponnesian War* (Ithaca: Cornell University Press, 1972), p. 91.

37. T. W. Adorno, et al., *The Authoritarian Personality* (New York: Harper, 1950); Hannah Arendt, *Eichmann in Jerusalem* (New York: Viking Press, 1963).

38. Eli Sagan, *Freud, Women, and Morality* (New York: Basic Books, 1988), p. 116.

39. Aristotle, *Politics,* V, chap. II, 6, trans. Barker.

40. Xenophon, *Hellenica,* II, 3, trans. in Raphael Sealey, *The Athenian Republic* (University Park: Pennsylvania State University Press, 1987), p. 134.

41. Aristotle, *Politics,* V, chap. II, 2, trans. Barker.

42. Krentz, *The Thirty,* p. 130.

43. Livy, II, chap. XXXIV, 9–10, Loeb translation (italics added).

44. Plutarch, *Coriolanus,* trans. Dryden-Clough, vol. II, p. 17.

45. Barry Goldwater, acceptance speech, Republican National Convention, 1964.

46. Jessica Benjamin, *The Bonds of Love* (New York: Pantheon Books, 1988), p. 33 (italics added).

47. Livy, II, chap. LVIII, 5–6, Loeb translation.

48. Livy, II, chap. LVIII–LXI, Loeb translation

49. Aristotle, *Politics,* V, chap. IX, 10–11, trans. Barker.

50. Percy Bysshe Shelley, "The Mask of Anarchy: Written on the Occasion of the Massacre of Manchester," lines 1–13.

51. Shakespeare, *A Midsummer Night's Dream,* V. i. 17.

Chapter 9
Clubs, Factions, Political Parties, and Mass Action

1. W. Robert Connor, *The New Politicians of Fifth-Century Athens* (Princeton: Princeton University Press, 1971), p. 32.

2. Plato, *Laws,* 856B, trans. in George Miller Calhoun, *Athenian Clubs in Politics and Litigation* (Rome: "L'erma" di Bretschneider, 1964), p. 126.

3. Thucydides, VIII, 66–67, trans. Crawley (italics added).

4. Plutarch, *Pericles,* trans. Dryden-Clough, vol. I, p. 303.

5. Connor, *New Politicians,* p. 118.

6. Josiah Ober, *Mass and Elite in Democratic Athens* (Princeton: Princeton University Press, 1989), passim.

7. Calhoun, *Clubs*, p. 30.

8. Raphael Sealey, *A History of the Greek City States, ca. 700–338 B.C.* (Berkeley: University of California Press, 1976), p. 360.

9. Quoted in Calhoun, *Clubs*, p. 24.

10. Ibid., p. 36.

11. Thucydides, VII, 28, trans. Crawley.

12. Thucydides, VIII, 54, quoted in Calhoun, *Clubs*, p. 97.

13. Erich S. Gruen, *The Last Generation of the Roman Republic* (Berkeley: University of California Press, 1974), passim.

14. Calhoun, *Clubs*, p. 47.

15. Calhoun, *Clubs*, p. 48, citing Xenophon, *Memorabilia*, II, chap. IX, 5–8.

16. Demosthenes, LIV, *Against Conon*, 33–35, Loeb translation.

17. Calhoun, *Clubs*, p. 1.

18. Calhoun, *Clubs*, p. 137, quoting Plutarch, *Nicias*.

19. Ober, *Mass and Elite*, passim.

Chapter 10
The Eating of the Gods

1. Jennifer Tolbert Roberts, *Accountability in Athenian Government* (Madison: University of Wisconsin Press, 1982), pp. 142–43; C. Hignett, *A History of the Athenian Constitution to the End of the Fifth Century B.C.* (London: Oxford University Press, 1952), pp. 164–66.

2. George P. Murdock, *Our Primitive Contemporaries* (New York: Macmillan, 1934), pp. 394–96.

3. Eli Sagan, *At the Dawn of Tyranny* (New York: Alfred A. Knopf, 1985), p. 161.

4. Plutarch, *Aristides*, trans. Dryden-Clough (italics added), vol. II, p. 218.

5. Plutarch, *Themistocles*, trans. Dryden-Clough, vol. I, p. 233.

6. Isocrates, *Antidosis*, 142–43, Loeb translation.

7. Plutarch, *Aristides*, trans. Dryden-Clough, vol. II, p. 219.

8. Aristophanes, *Knights*, 1139–60, anonymous prose translation.

9. Roberts, *Accountability*, p. 143.

10. Kratinos, fragment 71 Kock, quoted in S. C. Humphreys, *Anthropology and the Greeks* (Boston: Routledge and Kegan Paul, 1978), p. 229.

11. Jules Henry, *Jungle People* (Richmond: J. J. Augustin, 1941), p. 108.

12. Sagan, *Dawn*, passim.

13. Norman Cohn, *The Pursuit of the Millennium* (New York: Oxford University Press, 1980), passim.

14. W. Robert Connor, *The New Politicians of Fifth Century-Athens* (Princeton: Princeton University Press, 1971), p. 25.

15. K. J. Maidment, translator's note, pp. 546–47, *Minor Attic Orators*, vol. I, Loeb translation.

16. Roberts, *Accountability*, p. 153.

17. Ibid.

18. *The Oxford Classical Dictionary*, 2d edition (Oxford: Oxford University Press, 1970), article on "Eisangelia," pp. 375–76.

19. Donald Kagan, *The Fall of the Athenian Empire* (Ithaca: Cornell University Press, 1987), p. 352.

20. In narrating this crucial incident, I follow Kagan's (ibid, p. 352ff.) brilliant reconstruction of the history.

21. Ibid., p. 360.

22. Ibid., p. 367.

23. Ibid., p. 371, quoting Xenophon, *Hellenica*, I, chap. VII, 11.

24. Xenophon, *Hellenica*, I, chap. VII, 12, Loeb translation.

25. Ibid., I, chap. VII, 15.

26. Ibid., I, VII, 24–29.

27. Ibid., I, chap. VII, 34–35.

28. Ibid.

29. Kagan, *Fall*, p. 374.

30. Ibid.

31. Mogens Herman Hansen, *Eisangelia: The Sovereignty of the People's Court in Athens in the Fourth Century B.C. and the Impeachment of Generals and Politicians* (Odense [Denmark]: Odense University Press, 1975), p. 90.

32. W. Kendrick Pritchett, *The Greek State at War*, vol. II (Berkeley: University of California Press, 1974), pp. 113–14.

33. Ibid., p. 31n., citing Polybius, I, chap. II, 5.

34. Thucydides, VII, 48, trans. Crawley (italics added).

35. Demosthenes, *The First Philippic*, IV, 47, cited in Hansen, *Eisangelia*, p. 59.

36. Hansen, *Eisangelia*, pp. 64–66.

37. Roberts, *Accountability*, p. 174.

38. Ibid., p. 177.

39. Hansen, *Eisangelia*, p. 65.

Chapter 11
The *Demos* as Tyrant

1. Xenophon, *Hellenica*, I, chap. VII, 2, Loeb translation.

2. Xenophon, *Memorabilia*, I, chap. II, 40–46, trans. G. E. M. de Ste. Croix, *The Class Struggle in the Ancient Greek World* (Ithaca: Cornell University Press, 1981), p. 415.

3. Aristotle, *Politics*, IV, chap. IV, 26–28, trans. Barker.

4. James Madison, *The Federalist 10. The Federalist*, Jacob E. Cooke, ed. (Middletown: Wesleyan University Press, 1961), pp. 60–61.

5. Ibid.

6. Ibid., pp. 61–62 (italics added).

7. Ibid., p. 62.

8. Ibid., pp. 64–65.

9. *Cambridge Medieval History*, vol. I, p. 244.

10. Thucydides, III, 35, trans. Crawley.

11. Ibid., III, 36.

12. Ibid., III, 37.

13. Ibid., III, 49.

14. Thucydides, IV, 65, quoted in Jennifer Tolbert Roberts, *Accountability in Athenian Government* (Madison: University of Wisconsin Press, 1982), p. 9.

15. Plutarch, *Precepts of Statecraft*, Moralia 821B, Loeb translation.

16. Isocrates, *Antidosis*, 133, Loeb translation.

17. Isocrates, *On the Peace*, 52, Loeb translation.

18. Isocrates, *Nicocles*, 21–22, Loeb translation.

19. Aristotle, *Constitution of Athens*, 28, 3, quoted in Martin Ostwald, *From Popular Sovereignty to the Sovereignty of Law* (Berkeley: University of California Press, 1986), p. 228.

20. Plutarch, *Precepts of Statecraft*, Moralia, 801A–801B, Loeb translation.

21. Isocrates, *Panathenaicus*, 132–33, Loeb translation.

22. Thucydides, V, 90, trans. Crawley.

23. Ibid., III, 45.

24. Jacqueline de Romilly, *Thucydides and Athenian Imperialism* (New York: Barnes and Noble, 1963), p. 64.

25. Thucydides, VI, 24, trans. Crawley.

26. Moses Finley, in P. D. A. Garnsey and C. R. Whittaker, eds., *Imperialism in the Ancient World* (Cambridge: Cambridge University Press, 1978), p. 115; N. G. L. Hammond, *A History of Greece to 322 B.C.* (Oxford: Oxford University Press, 1967), pp. 305–6.

27. Robert Heilbroner, *The Worldly Philosophers*, 6th edition (New York: Simon & Schuster, 1986), p. 196.

28. Sigmund Freud, "Civilization and Its Discontents," *Standard Edition*, vol. 21, p. 120 (1930).

29. Thucydides, III, 45, trans. Crawley.

30. P. J. Rhodes, *The Athenian Empire* (Oxford: The Clarendon Press, 1985), p. 39 (italics added).

31. Hammond, *History*, p. 377.

Chapter 12
Narcissus-Dionysus

1. All quotes from *Symposium*, trans. Michael Joyce.

2. Martha C. Nussbaum, *The Fragility of Goodness* (Cambridge: Cambridge University Press, 1986), p. 193.

3. Cornelius Nepos, trans. John Selby Watson, in *Justin, Cornelius Nepos, and Eutropius* (London: George Bell and Sons, 1876), p. 334.

4. Lawrence Stone, *The Family, Sex and Marriage in England 1500–1800* (New York: Harper & Row, 1977), passim.

5. Plato, *Republic*, 562e–63b, trans. Bloom.

6. Plato, *Theaetetus*, 152a, in Plato's *Laws*, trans. Thomas L. Pangle, p. 525, n. 17.

7. Plato, *Cratylus*, 386a, trans. Benjamin Jowett.

8. Plato, *Laws*, 716c, trans. Pangle.

9. Aristotle, *Politics*, V, chap. IX, 16, trans. Barker.

10. *Oxford Classical Dictionary*, 2d edition (Oxford: Oxford University Press, 1970), article on "Protagoras," p. 890.

11. Shakespeare, *King Lear*, V. ii. 11.

12. Thucydides, I, 70–71, trans. Crawley.

13. William Arrowsmith, "Aristophanes' *Birds*: The Fantasy Politics of Eros," *Arion*, New Series, 1/1, pp. 126–27.

14. Ibid., p. 129.

15. Alvin W. Gouldner, *Enter Plato* (New York: Basic Books, 1965), p. 60.

16. E. R. Dodds, *The Greeks and the Irrational* (Berkeley: University of California Press, 1951), chap. 2.

17. Eli Sagan, *The Lust to Annihilate* (New York: Psychohistory Press, 1979), chap. 5.

18. Plato, *Symposium*, 208d–208e, trans. Michael Joyce.

19. Plutarch, *Moralia*, 232c, Loeb translation.

20. David Whitehead, *The Demes of Attica, 508/7–Ca. 250 B.C.* (Princeton: Princeton University Press, 1986), pp. 242–43.

21. Ibid., p. 235.

22. *Oxford Classical Dictionary*, article on "Liturgy," p. 613.

23. Lysias, *Defense Against a Charge of Taking Bribes*, 1–7, Loeb translation.

24. Aristophanes, *Frogs*, 1431–32, cited in Arrowsmith, *"Birds,"* p. 134n.

25. Plutarch, *Alcibiades*, trans. Dryden-Clough, vol. I, p. 389.

26. Cornelius Nepos, pp. 334–35, trans. Watson.

27. Diogenes Laertius, *Lives of Eminent Philosophers*, IV, 7, 49, quoted in

Michael Foucault, *The Use of Pleasure* (New York: Vintage Books, 1986), p. 188.

28. Plutarch, *Alcibiades*, trans. Dryden-Clough, vol. I, pp. 297–98.

29. Thucydides, VI, 17, trans. Crawley.

30. Ibid., VI, 13.

31. Ibid., VI, 16.

32. Ibid., VI, 18–20.

33. Ibid., VI, 31.

34. Ibid., VI, 28–30.

35. Arrowsmith, *"Birds,"* p. 141, citing Plutarch, *Alcibiades*, 17.

36. Thucydides, V, 62, trans. Crawley.

37. Plutarch, *Alcibiades*, trans. Dryden-Clough, vol. I, p. 397.

38. Thucydides, VI, 90–93, trans. Crawley.

39. Plutarch, *Alcibiades*, trans. Dryden-Clough, vol. I, p. 398.

40. N. G. L. Hammond, *A History of Greece to 322 B.C.* (Oxford: Oxford University Press, 1967), p. 413.

41. Plutarch, *Alcibiades*, trans. Dryden-Clough, vol. I, p. 411.

42. Ibid., p. 414.

3. Aristophanes, *Frogs*, 1422–25, trans. Richmond Lattimore.

44. Hammond, *History*, p. 414.

45. Plutarch, *Alcibiades*, trans. Dryden-Clough, vol. I, p. 416.

46. Ibid., pp. 417–19.

47. Thucydides, II, 41–42, trans. Crawley.

Chapter 13
Warfare and Genocide

1. Simon Hornblower, *The Greek World 479–323 B.C.* (New York: Methuen, 1983), p. 122.

2. M. I. Finley, *Economy and Society in Ancient Greece* (New York: Viking Press, 1982), p. 88.

3. Quoted in *Cambridge Ancient History*, vol. VI, p. 509 (italics added).

4. Isocrates, *On the Peace*, 44, Loeb translation.

5. George Norlin, translator, in *Isocrates*, vol. II, p. 35n., Loeb translation.

6. *Cambridge Ancient History*, vol. VI, p. 58.

7. Herodotus, VIII, 30, trans. in Hornblower, *Greek World*, p. 15.

8. N. G. L. Hammond, *A History of Greece to 322 B.C.* (Oxford: Oxford University Press, 1967), p. 200.

9. Hornblower, *Greek World*, p. 16.

10. Friedrich Nietzsche, "Homer's Contest," in *The Portable Nietzsche*, Walter Kaufman, ed., trans. (New York: Viking Press, 1954), p. 32.

11. Daniel Waley, *The Italian City-Republics* (New York: McGraw-Hill, 1969), p. 119.

12. In this description I follow S. C. Humphreys, *Anthropology and the Greeks* (Boston: Routledge and Kegan Paul, 1978), p. 160.

13. Eli Sagan, *The Lust to Annihilate* (New York: Psychohistory Press, 1979), chaps. VII and VIII.

14. Aristotle, *Rhetoric*, I, 7, Loeb translation.

15. Isocrates, *Panegyricus*, 133–34, Loeb translation.

16. Ibid., 182.

17. Waley, *City-Republics*, p. 164.

18. Ibid., pp. 219–20.

19. Aristotle, *Politics*, VII, chap. II, 9, trans. Barker.

20. Isocrates, *To Philip*, 53–54, Loeb translation.

21. Victor Ehrenberg, *From Solon to Socrates* (London: Methuen, 1968), p. 114; based on Herodotus 6, 21.

22. Hammond, *History*, p. 506.

23. *Cambridge Ancient History*, vol. VIII, p. 363.

24. Hammond, *History*, pp. 418 and 506.

25. Raphael Scaley, *A History of the Greek City States ca. 700–338 B.C.* (Berkeley: University of California Press, 1976), p. 351.

26. *Cambridge Ancient History*, vol. VI, p. 219.

27. Thucydides, III, 68, trans. Crawley.

28. Xenophon, *Hellenica*, II, chap. I, 31–32.

29. E. A. Freeman, *The History of Sicily*, vol. IV (Oxford: Oxford University Press, 1894), pp. 82–83.

30. Aldous Huxley, as quoted in Ernest Barker, *Greek Political Theory* (London: Methuen, 1977), p. 83.

31. Shakespeare, *King Lear*, IV. vi. 191.

32. Thucydides, II, 68, trans. Crawley.

33. G. E. M. de Ste. Croix, "The Character of the Athenian Empire," *Historia* (Weisbaden) III (1954): p. 15.

34. Ibid., p. 16.

35. Thucydides, V, 32, trans. Crawley.

36. Xenophon, vol. I, 104–5, Loeb translation, translators note, pp. 104–105n.

37. Xeophon, *Hellenica*, II, chap. II, 3, Loeb translation (italics added).

38. Ibid., II, chap. II, 19–20.

39. *Cambridge Ancient History*, vol. VI, p. 219.

40. Plutarch, *Alexander*, trans. Dryden-Clough, vol. IV, p. 13.

41. Plato, *Euthydemus*, 290b–290d, trans. W. H. D. Rouse (italics added).

42. Homer, *Iliad*, Book IV, 31–36, trans. Lattimore.

43. Aristotle, *Politics*, I, chap. VIII, 11–12, trans. Barker. Stanley Burstein and Josiah Ober have helped me understand this passage.

44. Dorothy Dinnerstein, *The Mermaid and the Minotaur* (New York: Harper & Row, 1977); Karen Horney, "The Dread of Women," *International Journal of Psychoanalysis* 13 (1932): 348–60.

45. Lloyd deMause, ed., *The History of Childhood* (New York: Psychohistory Press, 1974); Lawrence Stone, *The Family, Sex and Marriage in England 1500–1800* (New York: Harper & Row, 1977).

46. Quoted in George Rudé, *Europe in the Eighteenth Century* (Cambridge: Harvard University Press, 1972), p. 138.

Chapter 14
Political Action with a Class Basis—Sometimes Violent, Sometimes Not

1. G. E. M. de Ste. Croix, *The Class Struggle in the Ancient Greek World* (Ithaca: Cornell University Press, 1984).

2. W. Robert Connor, *Thucydides* (Princeton: Princeton University Press, 1984), pp. 39n. and 39.

3. Thucydides, III, 26–27, trans. Crawley.

4. Diodorus, XV, 40, Loeb translation.

5. Alexander Fuks, *Social Conflict in Ancient Greece* (Jerusalem: The Magnes Press, The Hebrew University; Leiden: E. J. Brill, 1984), p. 17.

6. Hesiod, *Works and Days*, 203ff, Loeb translation.

7. Eli Sagan, *At the Dawn of Tyranny* (New York: Alfred A. Knopf, 1985), passim.

8. Plutarch, *Pericles*, 11, trans. in Jennifer Tolbert Roberts, *Accountability in Athenian Government* (Madison: University of Wisconsin Press, 1982), p. 149.

9. Plato, *Republic*, 422E–423A, trans. in Fuks, *Conflict*, p. 80.

10. Ibid., 423A, trans. Bloom.

11. Ibid., 555D–555E, trans. in Fuks, *Conflict*, p. 89.

12. Plato, *Laws*, 832B–832C, trans. in Fuks, *Conflict*, p. 133.

13. Ibid., 919B–919C, trans. in Fuks, *Conflict*, p. 134 (italics added).

14. Aristotle, *Politics*, V, chap. XI, 32, trans. Barker.

15. Ibid., IV, chap. IV, 18–19.

16. M. I. Finley, *The Ancient Economy* (Berkeley: University of California Press, 1973), especially chap. 2.

17. de Ste. Croix, *Class Struggle*, passim.

18. M. I. Finley, *Ancient Sicily*, rev. ed. (London: Chatto and Windus, 1979), p. 95.

19. Isocrates, vol. I, 386–87, Loeb translation, translators note.

20. Isocrates, *Archidamus*, 67, Loeb translation.

21. Machiavelli, *Istorie fiorentine*, III, 1, quoted in Daniel Waley, *The Italian City-Republics* (New York McGraw-Hill, 1969), p. 165.

22. Thucydides, I, 24, trans. Crawley.

23. Ibid., I, 25.

24. Ibid., III, 80–81.

25. Ibid., III, 82.

26. Ibid., IV, 48.

27. Ibid., IV, 49.

28. Ibid.

29. N. G. L. Hammond, *A History of Greece to 322 B.C.* (Oxford: Oxford University Press, 1967), pp. 460 and 467.

30. M. I. Finley, *Sicily*, p. 95.

31. Thucydides, V, 76, 81–82.

32. Diodorus, XV, 57–58, Loeb translation.

33. Plutarch, *Moralia*, 814B.

34. Stanley M. Burstein, *Outpost of Hellenism: The Emergence of Heraclea on the Black Sea* (Berkeley: University of California Press, 1976), p. 90.

35. Stanley M. Burstein, "Greek Class Structures and Relations," in Michael Grant and Rachel Kitzinger, eds. *Civilization of the Ancient Mediterranean*, vol. I (New York: Charles Scribner's Sons, 1988), p. 543; Burstein, *Heraclea*, pp. 49–51.

36. *Cambridge Ancient History*, vol. VI, p. 371.

37. Fuks, *Conflict*, pp. 31–32; *Oxford Classical Dictionary*, article on "Agis IV," p. 27.

38. *Oxford Classical Dictionary*, article on "Cleomenes III," p. 250.

39. *Cambridge Ancient History*, vol. VIII, p. 147.

40. Ibid.

41. *Oxford Classical Dictionary*, article on "Nabis," p. 719.

42. Anton-Hermann Chroust, "Treason and Patriotism in Ancient Greece," *Journal of the History of Ideas*, XV (1954): 283–84.

43. Aeneas Tacticus, 14.1, cited in M. I. Finly, *Economy and Society in Ancient Greece* (New York: Viking Press, 1982), p. 86. Also de Ste. Croix, *Class Struggle*, p. 298.

44. Diodorus, XVI, 54.

45. Pausanias, VII, 9–10, quoted in Will Durant, *The Life of Greece* (New York: Simon & Schuster, 1939), p. 295.

46. G. E. M. de Ste. Croix, "The Character of the Athenian Empire," *Historia* (Weisbaden) III (1954): p. 30; based on Herodotus, VI, 91–93.

47. Thucydides, V, 76, trans. Crawley.

48. Hammond, *History*, p. 469.

49. *Cambridge Ancient History*, vol. VIII, p. 197.

50. Aeschylus, *Agamemnon*, line 1668, Lattimore translation.

51. *Cambridge Ancient History*, vol. VI, p. 371.

52. Lauro Martines, *Power and Imagination* (New York: Alfred A. Knopf, 1979), pp. 97–8.

Chapter 15
The People Reign but Elites Rule

1. Robert Michels, *Political Parties*, trans. Eden and Cedar Paul (Gloucester: Peter Smith, 1978) [1915, 1st English publication], p. 401.

2. Ibid., p. 11.

3. Ibid., p. 28.

4. Daniel Bell, *The Cultural Contradictions of Capitalism* (New York: Basic Books, 1978), p. 14.

5. Plutarch, *Solon*, trans. Dryden-Clough, vol. I, p. 158.

6. Aristotle, *Politics*, Book III, chap. XI, 6–8, trans. Barker.

7. Isocrates, *Areopagiticus*, 27, cited and translated in Josiah Ober, *Mass and Elite in Democratic Athens* (Princeton: Princeton University Press, 1989), p. 336.

8. Demosthenes, *Against Meidias*, 21, 140, cited and translated in Ober, *Mass and Elite*, pp. 240–41.

9. Ober, *Mass and Elite*, passim.

10. *Cambridge Ancient History*, vol. VIII, p. 358.

11. Plato, *Menexenus*, 238c–238d, cited and translated in A. H. M. Jones, "The Athenian Democracy and Its Critics," *The Cambridge Historical Journal*, II, 1 (1953): 1–26, p. 7 (italics added).

12. Thucydides, II, 66, Crawley translation.

13. Michels, *Political Parties*, p. 165.

14. Walter Struve, *Elites Against Democracy* (Princeton: Princeton University Press, 1973), p. 147n., quoting a conversation between Weber and General Ludendorff.

15. Leo Lowenthal and Norbert Gutterman, *Prophets of Deceit*, reprinted in

Leo Lowenthal, *False Prophets: Studies on Authoritarianism* (New Brunswick: Transaction Books, 1987), p. 129.

16. Ober, *Mass and Elite*, p. 135.

17. Speech of Weber, October 2, 1907, cited in Michels, *Political Parties*, p. 305n.

18. Eric Havelock, *The Liberal Temper in Greek Politics* (New Haven: Yale University Press, 1957), p. 20.

19. Michels, *Political Parties*, p. 215.

20. Ibid., pp. 217n.–18n.

21. Ibid., p. 222.

22. Diodorus, II, 39.5, quoted in G. E. M. de Ste. Croix, *The Origins of the Peloponnesian War* (Ithaca: Cornell University Press, 1972), p. 138.

23. Quoted in Chester G. Starr, *The Economic and Social Growth of Early Greece, 800–500 B.C.* (New York: Oxford University Press, 1977), p. 193.

24. Aristophanes, *Ecclesiazusae*, anonymous prose translation.

25. P. J. Rhodes, *The Athenian Boule* (Oxford: Oxford University Press, 1985), p. 5.

26. Simon Hornblower, *The Greek World 479–323 B.C.* (New York: Methuen, 1983), p. 118.

27. Mogens Herman Hansen, *The Athenian Assembly in the Age of Demosthenes* (New York: Basil Blackwell, 1987), p. 65.

28. David Whitehead, *The Demes of Attica, 508/7–Ca. 250 B.C.* (Princeton: Princeton University Press, 1986), p. 300 (italics deleted).

29. George Miller Calhoun, *Athenian Clubs in Politics and Litigation* (Rome: "L'erma" di Bretschneider, 1964), pp. 84–85.

30. Demosthenes, *Against Meidias*, 112, Loeb translation.

31. Whitehead, *Demes*, p. 240.

32. Hobbes, *Leviathan*, chap. 10.

33. Aristotle, *Politics*, Book II, chap. V, 5–8, trans. Barker.

34. Plato, *Republic*, Book VIII, 555c, trans. Bloom.

35. Plato, *Laws*, Book V, 743a, trans. Pangle.

36. Ibid., Book V, 739c–739e.

37. Ibid., Book V, 744d.

38. Ibid., Book V, 744e–745a.

39. Personal communication, Ernest Callenbach.

40. C. B. Macpherson, *The Political Theory of Possessive Individualism* (New York: Oxford University Press, 1988), passim and index under "The Poor" and "Poverty."

Chapter 16
The Boundaries of Justice and the Tribal Bond

1. Plato, *Republic*, Book I, 351c–351d, trans. Bloom.

2. Ibid., 352c.

3. Quoted in Hannah Arendt, *The Origin of Totalitarianism* (New York: Harcourt Brace Jovanovich, 1973), p. 377.

4. Xenophon, *Memorabilia*, IV, chap. II, 13–16, Loeb translation.

5. Plato, *Republic*, 422e–423a, translated in Alexander Fuks, *Social Conflict in Ancient Greece* (Jerusalem: The Magnes Press, The Hebrew University; Leiden: E.J. Brill, 1984), p. 80.

6. Plato, *The Laws*, 626b–626d, trans. Pangle.

7. Plato, *Republic*, Book V, 470b–470c, trans. Bloom.

8. Jacqueline de Romilly, *Thucydides and Athenian Imperialism* (New York: Barnes and Noble, 1963), passim.

9. Thucydides, III, 67–68, trans. Crawley.

10. Ibid., III, 69.

11. Ibid., V, 91.

12. Ibid., V, 105–7.

13. Ibid., III, 44.

14. Ibid., III, 81–82.

15. Ibid., III, 82.

16. Ibid. (italics added).

17. Ibid., III, 84.

18. Ibid.

19. Ibid., VII, 29–30.

20. Aristotle, *Politics*, I, chap. II, 4, trans. Barker.

21. Quote in Marshall Berman, *All That's Solid Melts into Air* (New York: Penguin Books, 1988), p. 20.

22. Antiphon, FVS6 87B44; 2.352.B 23ff., quoted in Eric Havelock, *The Liberal Temper in Greek Politics* (New Haven: Yale University Press, 1957), p. 256.

23. Isocrates, *Panathenaicus*, quoted in Fuks, *Social Conflict*, pp. 41–42.

24. Plutarch, *Aristides*, trans. Dryden-Clough, vol. II, p. 240.

25. Demosthenes, VI, *The Liberty of the Rhodians*, 28, translated in K. J. Dover, *Greek Popular Morality in the Time of Plato and Aristotle* (Berkeley: University of California Press, 1974), p. 311.

26. Quoted in H. C. Baldry, *The Unity of Mankind in Greek Thought* (Cambridge: Cambridge University Press, 1965), pp. 57–58.

27. J. G. A. Pocock, *The Machiavellian Moment* (Princeton: Princeton University Press, 1975), p. 213.

28. Eli Sagan, *At the Dawn of Tyranny* (New York: Alfred A. Knopf, 1985), passim.

29. A. H. M. Jones, *Athenian Democracy* (Baltimore: Johns Hopkins University Press, 1986), p. 45.

30. Euripides, fragment, quoted in Baldry, *Unity of Mankind*, p. 36.

31. Robert A. Dahl, *Democracy and Its Critics* (New Haven: Yale University Press, 1989), p. 235.

Chapter 17
Gain, Honor, Wisdom

1. Ernest Barker, *Greek Political Theory* (London: Methuen, 1977), p. 56.

2. Plato, *Republic*, Book IX, 581c, trans. Jowett. Bloom and Shorey (in Hamilton and Cairns) translate "honor" as "victory." In the whole passage there is an ambiguous interchange and relationship between the Greek words *"nikē"* (victory) and *"timē"* (honor). [My appreciation to Josiah Ober.] In the Greek world, honor was one of the goods, as Aristotle put it, that one could fight over. Honor was many times won at the expense of someone else. Victory and honor, therefore, were not all that different. For the analysis undertaken in this chapter, I prefer "honor" since "victory" can easily be merely a means to "gain," and "honor" means something very special in English.

3. Thucydides, I, 70, trans. Crawley.

4. Ibid., II, 45.

5. Demosthenes, *Against Androtion*, 76, Loeb translation.

6. Plato, *Apology*, 29d–29e, trans. Tredennick.

7. Max Weber. *The Protestant Ethic and the Spirit of Capitalism*, translated by Talcott Parsons (New York: Charles Scribner's Sons, 1958), passim.

8. Ibid., p. 182.

9. Hannah Arendt, *The Human Condition* (Chicago: University of Chicago Press, 1958), pp. 26–27.

10. Eli Sagan, *The Lust to Annihilate* (New York: The Psychohistory Press, 1979), passim.

11. Aristotle, *Rhetoric*, II, chap. VI, 2, Loeb translation.

12. Thucydides, VI, 14, trans. Crawley.

13. Demosthenes, IV, 10, cited and translated in K. J. Dover, *Greek Popular Morality in the Time of Plato and Aristotle* (Berkeley: University of California Press, 1974), p. 228.

14. Cited in A. R. Hands, *Charities and Social Aid in Greece and Rome* (Ithaca: Cornell University Press, 1968), p. 49.

15. Demosthenes, XV, 28f., cited and translated in Dover, *Popular Morality*, p. 311.

16. Victor Ehrenberg, *The People of Aristophanes* (New York: Schocken Books, 1962), p. 311.
17. Thucydides, II, 43–44, trans. Crawley.
18. Plutarch, *Flamininus*, trans. Dryden-Clough, vol. II, p. 318.
19. Aristotle, *Politics*, III, chap. VII, 2 and 5, trans. Barker.
20. See Chapter 8.
21. Plutarch, *Themistocles*, trans. Dryden-Clough, vol. I, p. 215.
22. *Oxford Classical Dictionary*, p. 1053, article on "Themistocles."

Chapter 18
Education for the Political Life: Small-Town Democracy

1. Alexis de Tocqueville, *Democracy in America*, trans. George Lawrence (New York: Doubleday and Co., 1969), p. 63.
2. David Whitehead, *The Demes of Attica, 508/7–Ca. 250 B.C.* (Princeton: Princeton University Press, 1986), p. xviii.
3. P. J. Rhodes, *The Athenian Boule* (Oxford: Oxford University Press, 1985), p. 3n.
4. Whitehead, *Demes*, p. xviii.
5. Ibid., p. 71.
6. Simon Hornblower, *The Greek World 479–323 B.C.* (New York: Methuen, 1983), p. 112.
7. Whitehead, *Demes*, p. 59.
8. Ibid., p. 44.
9. Ibid., p. 164.
10. Ibid., pp. 127–28.
11. Ibid., p. 137.
12. Ibid., p. 219.
13. Ibid., p. 60.
14. Ibid., p. 110.
15. Ibid., p. 145.
16. Ibid.
17. Ibid., p. 125, referring to Demosthenes, *Against Eubulides*, 57, 63–64.
18. Ibid., p. 119 (italics added).
19. Ibid., p. 292.
20. Ibid.
21. Ibid., p. 296, citing Demosthenes, *Against Eubulides*, 57, 59.
22. Ibid., p. 291.
23. Ibid., p. 105, citing Demosthenes, *Against Eubulides*.
24. Thucydides, II, 17, trans. Crawley (italics added).

25. de Tocqueville, *Democracy*, p. 70.

26. Euripides, *Orestes*, 916–22, trans. Arrowsmith.

27. Whitehead, *Demes*, pp. 317–18.

28. Aristotle, *Politics*, I, chap. II, 9, trans. Barker.

29. Ibid., I, chap. II, 15.

30. Ibid., III, chap. IX, 18.

31. Philip Rieff, ed., *Sigmond Freud: Therapy and Technique* (New York: Collier Books, 1963), editor's introduction, pp. 8–11.

32. Aristotle, *Politics*, V, chap. IX, 11–12, trans. Barker.

33. Quoted in A. R. Hands, *Charities and Social Aid in Greece and Rome* (Ithaca: Cornell University Press, 1968), p. 124.

34. Solon, fragment 2, translated in Kathleen Freeman, *The Work and Life of Solon* (London: Humphrey Milford, 1926), p. 208.

35. Demosthenes, *Against Leochares*, 4, quoted in A. M. H. Jones, *Athenian Democracy* (Baltimore: Johns Hopkins University Press, 1986), p. 53.

36. Hypereides, III, 5, quoted in Jones, *Democracy*, p. 53.

37. Demosthenes, *Against Timocrates*, 76, Loeb translation.

o38. Demosthenes, *Against Meidias*, 224, Loeb translation.

39. Aristotle, *Politics*, IV, chap. IV, 25, trans. Barker.

40. Raphael Sealey, *The Athenian Republic* (University Park: Pennsylvania State University Press, 1987), p. 32.

41. Ibid., p. 45.

42. Jennifer Tolbert Roberts, *Accountability in Athenian Government* (Madison: University of Wisconsin Press, 1982), p. 168.

43. Aristotle, *Politics*, translator's introduction, p. lxi, trans. Barker.

Chapter 19
The Instability of the Republican City-State

1. N. G. L. Hammond, *A History of Greece to 322 B.C.* (Oxford: Oxford University Press, 1967), p. 525.

2. Miriam Griffin in *The Oxford History of the Classical World* (Oxford: Oxford University Press, 1986), p. 470.

3. Theodor Mommsen, *The History of Rome*, trans. William Dickson (New York: Charles Scribner's Sons, 1900), vol. III, p. 303.

4. Lauro Martines, *Power and Imagination* (New York: Alfred A. Knopf, 1979), p. 41.

5. *Cambridge Medieval History*, vol. IV, I (Cambridge: Cambridge University Press, 1966), p. 267.

6. Daniel Waley, *The Italian City-Republics* (New York: McGraw-Hill, 1969), p. 221.

7. Alexander Hamilton, *Federalist 9. The Federalist*, Jacob E. Cooke, ed. (Middletown: Wesleyan University Press, 1961), pp. 50–51.

8. Ronald Syme, *The Roman Revolution* (Oxford: Oxford University Press, 1960), p. 11.

9. Mommsen, *Rome*, vol. IV, pp. 66–67 (italics added).

10. *Cambridge Ancient History*, vol. IX, pp. 274 and 276.

11. Ibid., p. 277.

12. Cited by Miriam Griffin in *Oxford History*, p. 467.

13. Procopius, *Persian Wars*, I, chap. XXIV, 2–6, cited in A. M. H. Jones, *The Later Roman Empire, 284–602* (Baltimore: Johns Hopkins University Press, 1986), vol. II, p. 1019.

14. Martines, *Power*, p. 24.

15. Ibid., pp. 97–98.

16. John Ciardi, translation of Dante Alighieri, *The Inferno* (New Brunswick: Rutgers University Press, 1954), p. 101.

17. *Cambridge Ancient History*, vol. VI, p. 512.

18. Stanley Mayer Burstein, *Outpost of Hellenism: The Emergence of Heraclea on the Black Sea* (Berkeley: University of California Press, 1976), pp. 60–61.

19. Diodorus, XVI, 92, Loeb translation.

20. Isocrates, *Nicocles*, 15–16, 18, Loeb translation.

21. Isocrates, *To Philip, II*, 5, Loeb translation.

22. Mommsen, *Rome*, vol. V, p. 169.

23. Plutarch, *Julius Caesar*, trans. Dryden-Clough, vol. IV, p. 117.

24. Syme, *Revolution*, p. 258.

25. Ibid., p. 294.

26. Waley, *City-Republics*, p. 66.

27. Ibid., pp. 68–71.

28. Niccolo Machiavelli, *The Prince*, trans. Luigi Ricci (New York: The Modern Library, 1950), chap. IX.

29. Waley, *City-Republics*, p. 232.

30. Ibid., pp. 237–38. Sentence order changed.

31. Hamilton, *Federalist 9*, p. 51.

32. Ibid.

33. H. W. Parke, *Greek Mercenary Soldiers* (Oxford: Oxford University Press, 1933), p. 20.

34. Cited in ibid., p. 98.

35. Demosthenes, *Third Philippic*, IX, 48ff., cited in Simon Hornblower, *The Greek World, 479–323 B.C.* (New York: Methuen, 1983), p. 157.

36. Parke, *Mercenary*, p. 159.

37. Demosthenes, *Third Olynthiac*, 35, Loeb translation.

38. Parke, *Mercenary*, p. 57, quotation from Parke, p. 144.

39. *Cambridge Ancient History*, vol. IX, pp. 136–38.

40. Waley, *City-Republics*, p. 183.

41. Ibid., p. 185.

42. Ibid.

43. Machiavelli, *Prince*, chap. XII.

44. Niccolo Machiavelli, *The Discourses*, trans. Luigi Ricci (New York: The Modern Library, 1950), Book I, chap. 40.

45. Hamilton, *Federalist 1*, p. 6.

46. Burstein, *Heraclea*, p. 59.

47. *Oxford Classical Dictionary*, article on "Agathocles," p. 25.

48. G. E. M. Ste. Croix, *The Class Struggle in the Ancient Greek World* (Ithaca: Cornell University Press, 1981), p. 340.

49. Livy, 22. 34. 7–8, cited in Kurt Raaflaub, ed., *Social Struggles in Archaic Rome* (Berkeley: University of California Press, 1986), p. 366.

50. J. Von Ungern-Sternberg, ibid., p. 355.

51. Martines, *Power*, p. 186.

52. Ibid., p. 67.

53. Ibid., pp. 133–34.

54. Cited in Mogens Herman Hansen, "Was Athens a Democracy?" *Historisk-filosofiske Meddelelser* 59 (Copenhagen: The Royal Danish Academy of Sciences and Letters, 1989), p. 27.

55. Joseph Schumpeter, *Capitalism, Socialism, and Democracy* (New York: Harper and Bros, 1947), passim.

Chapter 20
Democracy and the "Paranoidia" of Greed and Domination

1. Thucydides, III, 82, trans. Crawley.

2. Diogenes Laertius, VI, 43–44, Loeb translation.

3. Plutarch, *Pyrrhus*, trans. Dryden-Clough, vol. II, pp. 349–50.

4. Thucydides, VI, 16, trans. Crawley.

5. Ibid., II, 66.

6. Ibid., VI, 90.

7. Plutarch, *Alcibiades*, trans. Dryden-Clough, vol. I, p. 390.

8. Ibid.

9. Thucydides, V, 28, trans. Crawley (italics added).

10. Thucydides, II, 63–65, trans. Crawley.

11. Quoted in Theodore H. Von Have, *The World Revolution of Westernization* (New York: Oxford University Press, 1987), p. 16.

12. Isocrates, vol. I, p. xxxiii, Loeb translation, translator's introduction.

13. Jacqueline de Romilly, *Thucydides and Athenian Imperialism* (New York: Barnes and Noble, 1963), p. 322.

14. William Arrowsmith, "Aristophanes' *Birds*: The Fantasy Politics of Eros," *Arion*, New Series, 1/1, pp. 119–67, 134.

15. Ibid., pp. 131–33.

16. Shakespeare, *A Midsummer Night's Dream*, V. i. 8.

17. Quoted in Arrowsmith, *Birds*, p. 134.

18. Ibid., pp. 134–35.

19. Translated by Arrowsmith, ibid., p. 141.

20. Thucydides, 6.24.3, trans. W. Robert Connor, *Thucydides* (Princeton: Princeton University Press, 1984), p. 167.

21. Richard Hofstader, *The Paranoid Style in American Politics and Other Essays* (New York: Alfred A. Knopf, 1966), p. 4.

22. Robert Bellah, et al., *The Good Society* (New York: Alfred A. Knopf, 1991).

23. Isocrates, *On the Peace*, 119, Loeb translation.

24. Thucydides, VI, 18, trans. Crawley.

25. Ibid., I, 140.

26. David Hume, "On the Populousness of Ancient Nations," quoted in M. I. Finley, "Athenian Demagogues," *Past and Present* 21 (1962): 3–24, 20.

27. Thucydides, VI, 84, trans. Crawley.

28. Alvin Gouldner, *Enter Plato* (New York: Basic Books, 1965), p. 102.

29. James Madison, *Federalist* 63. *The Federalist*, Jacob E. Clarke, ed. (Middletown: Wesleyan University Press, 1961), p. 425.

30. Thucydides, II, 37–39, trans. Crawley.

31. Abraham Lincoln, "Second Inaugural Address," 1865.

32. Aristotle, *Constitution of Athens*, 40.2, trans. Kurt von Fritz and Ernst Kapp (New York: Hafner Press, 1974) (italics added).

33. Peter Krentz, *The Thirty at Athens* (Ithaca: Cornell University Press, 1982), p. 117.

Bibliography

Ancient Texts

Except as indicated below or as cited in the notes, I have used the translations of ancient works from the Loeb Classical Library published by Harvard University Press, Cambridge. The phrase "Loeb translation" indicates this usage.

Individual Translations

Aristotle. *Politics.* Edited and translated by Ernest Barker. Oxford: Oxford University Press, 1958.

Plato. *The Laws.* Translated, with notes by Thomas L. Pangle. New York: Basic Books, 1980.

———. *The Republic.* Translated, with notes by Alan Bloom. New York: Basic Books, 1968.

———. *The Collected Dialogues.* Edited by Edith Hamilton and Huntington Cairns, translated by various hands. Princeton: Princeton University Press, 1961.

Plutarch. *Lives.* The translation called Dryden's corrected from the Greek and revised by A. N. Clough. 5 vols. Philadelphia: The Nottingham Society, 1910.

Thucydides. *The Peloponnesian War.* Translated by R. Crawley. Various editions.

Standard Reference Works

Cambridge Ancient History. Cambridge: Cambridge University Press. Vol. V, 1927, reprinted 1953. Vol. VI, 1927, reprinted 1953. Vol. VII, 1928, reprinted 1954. Vol. VIII, 1930, reprinted 1954. Vol. IX, 1932, reprinted 1951.

Cambridge Medieval History. Cambridge: Cambridge University Press. Vol. I, 1911, reprinted 1975. Vol. IV, Part I, 1966.

The Oxford Classical Dictionary, 2d edition. Oxford: Oxford University Press, 1970.

The Oxford History of the Classical World. Oxford: Oxford University Press, 1986.

Other Works

Adorno, T. W., Else Frenkel-Brunswik, Daniel S. Levinson, and R. Nevitt Sanford. *The Authoritarian Personality.* New York: Harper and Bros., 1950.

Aeschylus. *Agamemnon.* Translated by Richmond Lattimore. Chicago: University of Chicago Press, various editions.

Andrews, A. "The Growth of the Athenian State." In the *Cambridge Ancient History*, 2d edition, Vol. III, pt. 3. Cambridge: Cambridge University Press, 1982.

Arendt, Hannah. *The Human Condition.* Chicago: University of Chicago Press, 1958.

————. *The Origins of Totalitarianism.* New York: Harcourt Brace Jovanovich, 1973.

————. *Eichmann in Jerusalem.* New York: Penguin Books, 1977.

Aristophanes. *The Wasps.* Translated by Douglas Parker. Ann Arbor: University of Michigan Press, 1961.

————. *Four Plays by Aristophanes.* Translated by Arrowsmith, Lattimore, and Parker. New York: New American Library, 1984.

Aristotle. *Constitution of Athens.* Translated by Kurt von Fritz and Ernst Kapp. New York: Hafner Press, 1974.

————. *Constitution of Athens.* Translated by J. M. Moore. Berkeley: University of California Press, 1975.

Arrowsmith, William. "Aristophanes' *Birds*: The Fantasy Politics of Eros." *Arion*, New Series, 1/1 (1979): 119–67.

Austin, M. M., and P. Vidal-Naquet. *Economic and Social History of Ancient Greece.* Berkeley: University of California Press, 1977.

Baldry, H. C. *The Unity of Mankind in Greek Thought.* Cambridge: Cambridge University Press, 1965.

Barker, Ernest. *Greek Political Theory.* London: Methuen and Co., 1977.

Bell, Daniel. *The Cultural Contradictions of Capitalism.* New York: Basic Books, 1978.

Bellah, Robert N., Richard Madsen, William M. Sullivan, Ann Swidler, and Steven M. Tipton. *Habits of the Heart.* Berkeley: University of California Press, 1985.

Benjamin, Jessica. *The Bonds of Love.* New York: Pantheon Books, 1988.

Berman, Marshall. *All That Is Solid Melts into Air.* New York: Penguin Books, 1988.

Bouwsma, William J. *Venice and the Defense of Republican Liberty.* Berkeley: University of California Press, 1968.

Brunt, P. A. *Social Conflicts in the Roman Republic.* New York: W. W. Norton, 1971.

Burstein, Stanley Mayer. *Outpost of Hellenism: The Emergence of Heraclea on the Black Sea.* Berkeley: University of California Press, 1976.

———. "Greek Class Structures and Relations." In Michael Grant and Rachel Kitzinger, eds., *Civilization of the Ancient Mediterranean*, Vol. I. New York: Charles Scribner's Sons, 1988.

Calhoun, George Miller. *Athenian Clubs in Politics and Litigation.* Rome: "L'erma" di Bretschneider, 1964.

Cheney, Edward P. *The Dawn of a New Era, 1250–1453.* New York: Harper and Bros., 1936.

Chroust, Anton-Hermann. "Treason and Patriotism in Ancient Greece." *Journal of the History of Ideas* XV (1954): 280–88.

Ciardi, John. Translation of Dante Alighieri: *The Inferno.* New Brunswick: Rutgers University Press, 1954.

Cochrane, C. N. *Christianity and Classical Culture.* New York: Oxford University Press, 1977.

Cohn, Norman. *The Pursuit of the Millennium.* New York: Oxford University Press, 1980.

Coniff, Michael, ed. *Latin American Populism in Comparative Perspective.* Albuquerque: University of New Mexico Press, 1982.

Connor, W. Robert. *The New Politicians of Fifth-Century Athens.* Princeton: Princeton University Press, 1971.

———. *Thucydides.* Princeton: Princeton University Press, 1984.

Dahl, Robert A. *Democracy and Its Critics*. New Haven: Yale University Press, 1989.

deMause, Lloyd, ed. *The History of Childhood*. New York: Psychohistory Press, 1974.

———. *Foundations of Psychohistory*. New York: Creative Roots, 1982.

de Romilly, Jacqueline. *Thucydides and Athenian Imperialism*. New York: Barnes and Noble, 1963.

de Ste. Croix, G. E. M. "The Character of the Athenian Empire." *Historia* (Weisbaden) III (1954): 1–41.

———. *The Origins of the Peloponnesian War*. Ithaca: Cornell University Press, 1972.

———. *The Class Struggle in the Ancient Greek World*. Ithaca: Cornell University Press, 1981.

de Tocqueville, Alexis. *Democracy in America*. Translated by George Lawrence. New York: Doubleday & Co., 1969.

Dinnerstein, Dorothy. *The Mermaid and the Minotaur*. New York: Harper & Row, 1977.

Dodds, E. R. *The Greeks and the Irrational*. Berkeley: University of California Press, 1951.

Dover, K. J. *Greek Popular Morality in the Time of Plato and Aristotle*. Berkeley: University of California Press, 1974.

Durant, Will. *The Life of Greece*. New York: Simon & Schuster, 1939.

Ehrenberg, Victor. *The People of Aristophanes*. New York: Schocken Books, 1962.

———. *From Solon to Socrates*. London: Methuen and Co., 1968.

The Federalist. Jacob E. Cooke, ed. Middletown: Wesleyan University Press, 1961.

Ferguson, William Scott. *Hellenistic Athens*. London: Macmillan and Co., 1911.

Finley, M. I. "Athenian Demagogues." *Past and Present* 21 (1962): 3–24.

———, ed. *Slavery in Classical Antiquity, Views and Controversies*. New York: Barnes and Noble, 1968.

———. *The Ancient Economy*. Berkeley: University of California Press, 1973.

———. *Ancient Sicily*, revised edition. London: Chatto and Windus, 1979.

———. *Early Greece*. New York: W. W. Norton, 1981.

———. *Economy and Society in Ancient Greece*. New York: The Viking Press, 1982.

———. *Politics in the Ancient World*. Cambridge: Cambridge University Press, 1983.

Forrest, W. G. *The Emergence of Greek Democracy, 800–400 B.C.* New York: McGraw-Hill Book Co., 1979.

Forster, E. M. *Two Cheers for Democracy*. New York: Harcourt Brace and Co., 1951.

Foucault, Michael. *The Use of Pleasure*. Translated by Robert Hurley. New York: Vintage Books, 1986.

Freeman, E. A. *The History of Sicily*, Vol. IV. Oxford: Oxford University Press, 1894.

Freeman, Kathleen. *The Work and Life of Solon*. London: Humphrey Milford, 1926.

Freud, Sigmund. *Civilization and Its Discontents, Standard Edition*, Vol. 21, 1930, pp. 59–145.

———. "Analysis Terminable and Interminable," *Standard Edition*, Vol. 23, 1937.

Fuks, Alexander. *Social Conflict in Ancient Greece*. Jerusalem: The Magnes Press, The Hebrew University. Leiden: E. J. Brill, 1984.

Garnsey, P. D. A., and C. R. Whittaker, eds. *Imperialism in the Ancient World*. Cambridge: Cambridge University Press, 1978.

Glotz, G. *The Greek City and Its Institutions*. London: Routledge and Kegan Paul, 1950.

Goldwert, Marvin. *Democracy, Militarism, and Nationalism in Argentina, 1930–1966*. Austin: University of Texas Press, 1972.

Gouldner, Alvin W. *Enter Plato*. New York: Basic Books, 1965.

Gruen, Erich S. *The Last Generation of the Roman Republic*. Berkeley: University of California Press, 1974.

Hammond, N. G. L. *A History of Greece to 322 B.C.* Oxford: Oxford University Press, 1967.

Hands, A. R. *Charities and Social Aid in Greece and Rome*. Ithaca: Cornell University Press, 1968.

Hansen, Mogens Herman. *Eisangelia: The Sovereignty of the People's Court in Athens in the Fourth Century B.C. and the Impeachment of Generals and Politicians*. Odense (Denmark): Odense University Press, 1975.

———. *The Athenian Assembly in the Age of Demosthenes*. New York: Basil Blackwell, 1987.

———. "Was Athens a Democracy?" *Historisk-filosofiske Meddelelser*, 59. Copenhagen: The Royal Danish Academy of Sciences and Letters, 1989.

Havelock, Eric. *The Liberal Temper in Greek Politics*. New Haven: Yale University Press, 1957.

Heilbroner, Robert. *The Worldly Philosophers*, 6th edition. New York: Simon and Schuster, 1986.

Henry, Jules. *Jungle People*. Richmond: J. J. Augustin, 1941.

Hignett, C. *A History of the Athenian Constitution to the End of the Fifth Century B.C.* London: Oxford University Press, 1952.

Hobbes, Thomas. *Leviathan.* New York: Macmillan, 1986.

Hofstader, Richard. "The Paranoid Style in American Politics." In *The Paranoid Style in American Politics and Other Essays.* New York: Alfred A. Knopf, 1966.

Homer. *The Iliad.* Translated by Richard Lattimore. Chicago: University of Chicago Press, 1951.

Hornblower, Simon. *The Greek World 479–323 B.C.* New York: Methuen and Co., 1982.

Horney, Karen. "The Dread of Women." *International Journal of Psychoanalysis* 13 (1932): 348–60.

Humphreys, S. C. *Anthropology and the Greeks.* Boston: Routledge and Kegan Paul, 1978.

Jones, A. H. M. "The Athenian Democracy and its Critics." *The Cambridge Historical Journal,* XI, 1 (1953): 1–26.

―――. *Athenian Democracy.* Baltimore: Johns Hopkins University Press, 1986.

―――. *The Later Roman Empire, 284–602.* Baltimore: Johns Hopkins University Press, 1986.

Jones, J. Walter. *The Law and Legal Theory of the Greeks.* Oxford: Oxford University Press, 1956.

Kagan, Donald. *The Fall of the Athenian Empire.* Ithaca: Cornell University Press, 1987.

Krentz, Peter. *The Thirty at Athens.* Ithaca: Cornell University Press, 1982.

Larsen, J. A. O. "Freedom and its Obstacles in Ancient Greece." *Classical Philology,* 57 (1962): 430–4.

Lasch, Christopher. *The Culture of Narcissism.* New York: W. W. Norton, 1979.

Lattimore, Richard, trans. *Greek Lyrics.* Chicago: University of Chicago Press, 1960.

Linforth, Ivan M. *Solon the Athenian.* Berkeley: University of California Press, 1919.

Lintott, Andrew. *Civil Strife and Revolution in the Classical City, 750–330 B.C.* London: Croom Helm, 1982.

Lowenthal, Leo, and Norbert Guterman. *Prophets of Deceit.* Reprinted in Lowenthal, Leo, *False Prophets: Studies on Authoritarianism.* New Brunswick: Transaction Books, 1987.

McCoy, William James. "Theramenes, Thrasybulus and the Athenian Moderates." Ph.D. diss. Yale University, 1970.

Machiavelli, Niccolò. *The Prince and the Discourses.* Translated by Luigi Ricci. New York: The Modern Library, 1950.

Macpherson, C. B. *The Political Theory of Possessive Individualism.* New York: Oxford University Press, 1988.

Martines, Lauro. *Power and Imagination.* New York: Alfred A. Knopf, 1979.

Michels, Robert. *Political Parties.* Translated by Eden and Cedar Paul. Gloucester, Mass.: Peter Smith, 1978. (First English Publication, 1915.)

Mommsen, Theodor. *The History of Rome.* Translated by William Dickson. New York: Charles Scribner's Sons, 1900.

Moore, J. M. *Aristotle and Xenophon on Democracy and Oligarchy. Translations with Introductions and Commentary.* Berkeley: University of California Press, 1975.

Mossé, Claude. *Athens in Decline.* Translated by Jean Steward. London and Boston: Routledge and Kegan Paul, 1973.

Murdock, George P. *Our Primitive Contemporaries.* New York: Macmillan, 1934.

Cornelius Nepos. Translated by John Selby Watson. In *Justin, Cornelius Nepos, and Eutropius.* London: George Bell and Sons, 1876.

Nietzsche, Friedrich. "Homer's Contest." In *The Portable Nietzsche.* Edited and translated by Walter Kaufman. New York: Viking Press, 1954.

Nussbaum, Martha C. *The Fragility of Goodness.* Cambridge: Cambridge University Press, 1986.

Ober, Josiah. *Mass and Elite in Democratic Athens.* Princeton: Princeton University Press, 1989.

Ostwald, Martin. *From Popular Sovereignty to the Sovereignty of Law.* Berkeley: University of California Press, 1986.

Parke, H. W. *Greek Mercenary Soldiers.* Oxford: Oxford University Press, 1933.

Parsons, Talcott. *The Evolution of Societies.* Englewood Cliffs, N.J.: Prentice-Hall, 1977.

Pitkin, Hannah Fenichel. *Fortune Is a Woman.* Berkeley: University of California Press, 1984.

Pocock, J. G. A. *The Machiavellian Moment.* Princeton: Princeton University Press, 1975.

Pomeroy, Sarah B. *Goddesses, Whores, Wives, and Slaves.* New York: Shocken Books, 1975.

Pritchett, W. Kendrick. *The Greek State at War*, Vols. I and II. Berkeley: University of California Press, 1974.

Raaflaub, Kurt A., ed. *Social Struggles in Archaic Rome.* Berkeley: University of California Press, 1986.

Rhodes, P. J. *The Athenian Boule.* Oxford: Oxford University Press, 1985.

———. *The Athenian Empire.* Oxford: The Clarendon Press, 1985.

Rieff, Philip, ed. *Sigmund Freud: Therapy and Technique.* New York: Collier Books, 1963.

Roberts, Jennifer Tolbert. *Accountability in Athenian Government.* Madison: University of Wisconsin Press, 1982.

Rudé, George. *Europe in the Eighteenth Century.* Cambridge: Harvard University Press, 1972.

Sagan, Eli. *Cannibalism: Human Aggression and Cultural Form.* New York: Harper & Row, 1974.

———. *The Lust to Annihilate.* New York: Psychohistory Press, 1979.

———. *At the Dawn of Tyranny.* New York: Alfred A. Knopf, 1985.

———. *Freud, Women, and Morality.* New York: Basic Books, 1988.

Schumpeter, Joseph. *Capitalism, Socialism, and Democracy.* New York: Harper and Bros., 1947.

Sealey, Raphael. *A History of the Greek City States, ca. 700–338 B.C.* Berkeley: University of California Press, 1976.

———. *The Athenian Republic.* University Park: Pennsylvania State University Press, 1987.

Shapiro, David. *Neurotic Styles.* New York: Basic Books, 1965.

Smith, Lacey Baldwin. *Treason in Tudor England.* Princeton: Princeton University Press, 1986.

Starr, Chester G. *The Economic and Social Growth of Early Greece, 800–500 B.C.* New York: Oxford University Press, 1977.

———. *Individual and Community.* New York: Oxford University Press, 1986.

Stavely, E. S. *Greek and Roman Voting and Elections.* Ithaca: Cornell University Press, 1972.

Stone, Lawrence. *The Family, Sex and Marriage in England 1500–1800.* New York: Harper & Row, 1977.

Struve, Walter. *Elites Against Democracy.* Princeton: Princeton University Press, 1973.

Syme, Ronald. *The Roman Revolution.* Oxford: Oxford University Press, 1960.

Tucker, Robert C., ed. *The Marx-Engels Reader*, 2d edition. New York: W. W. Norton, 1978.

Von Laue, Theodore H. *The World Revolution of Westernization.* New York: Oxford University Press, 1987.

Wade-Gery, H. T. *Essays in Greek History.* Oxford: Basil Blackwell, 1958.

Waley, Daniel. *The Italian City-Republics.* New York: McGraw-Hill Book Co., 1969.

Weber, Max. *The Protestant Ethic and the Spirit of Capitalism.* Translated by Talcott Parsons. New York: Charles Scribner's Sons, 1958.

Whitehead, David. *The Demes of Attica, 508/7–Ca. 250 B.C.* Princeton: Princeton University Press, 1986.

Wirszubski, Ch. *Libertas as a Political Idea at Rome.* Cambridge: Cambridge University Press, 1968.

Woodhouse, W. J. *Solon the Liberator.* New York: Octagon Books, 1965.

Index

415